Trading Derivatives: The Theoretical Minimum

Trading Vanilla, Exotic and Corporate Derivatives

Mika Kastenholz

MIKA KASTENHOLZ

List of Figures

List of Tables

Contents

1. Preface

1.1 Introduction

As a consequence of the 2008/09 financial crisis the global (OTC) derivatives gross market value has significantly decreased [1]. This decrease is commonly regarded as a sign of deleveraging if one takes the position that measuring the exposure based on outstanding (gross) notional overstates potential risks significantly. Be it as it may, it is undoubtedly true that regulatory efforts have pushed for more control, oversight and capital requirements in the derivatives industry. As an indirect consequence, the volume in exchange-traded and cleared derivatives has also increased. However, as recently demonstrated for a rather small default event, central counterparty clearing (CCP) does not necessarily guarantee complete loss protection for its members [1]. Moreover, even if banks are better capitalized and operate on less short-term funding, significant leverage has shifted to the private sector [2] and non-bank financial intermediaries ((NBFIs)) [3]. Similarly, leveraged loans packaged in collateralized loan obligations (CLO) [4] have seen a surge over the past ten years [2]. Predicting the exact future outcome of these developments also in light of substantial central bank market activity is likely to be a futile effort. However, it is reasonable to assume that the role of derivatives, their usage and exposure will be a crucial determinant in the amplitude of any future financial crisis. This link arises because derivatives typically allow for leveraging exposure and thereby aim to maximize the return to the capital employed. In an ultra-low interest rate and quantitative easing environment, investors searching for substantial yield pick-ups are therefore often forced to employ derivatives.

It is possible to trade derivatives (even exotics) without much theoretical background. Just like driving a car does not require to understand how the engine works, it is possible to trade along with the numbers coming out of the risk management system. Moreover, if success or failure in trading is simply defined by profit or loss alone, then this approach will be successful for some operators. However, problems arise when the 'engine' numbers are suddenly different, strange or even wrong. This is because risk systems do not report figures with an attribute indicating whether they should

---

[1]https://www.bis.org/publ/otc_hy1810.htm
[2]https://www.bloomberg.com/graphics/2018-lehman-anniversary

be trusted. It is then the skill of a good trader or risk manager to realize that something is wrong. This recognition and further diagnosis is much easier with a solid understanding of the underlying math, models and products traversing the engine room. Moreover, any subsequent interaction with the engineering or quant department will be much more fruitful if the trader can express the problem in the language of financial engineering.

The required level of understanding quantitative modeling for a trader is not as high as that of a quant. To the trader, it is not essential to know the exact derivation of pricing and valuation models but rather to understand their limitations and assumptions. It will also be required to understand which models are valid to trade which kind of instruments in a respective asset class. This book aims to identify the required theoretical minimum when trading derivatives.

Derivatives are traded in various contexts. Asset managers or hedge funds use them to apply leverage or to invest in particular asset classes while employing as little capital as possible. Institutional clients such as pension funds or industrial corporations use derivatives to hedge out exposure such as foreign exchange or interest rate risk resulting from cash flows. Derivative trading desks at banks, on the other hand, manufacture financial products aimed to generate bespoke payouts, which often include derivative components. What is familiar to all these market players is that they should ideally understand the instruments they are dealing with in detail. This is amplified by the fact that derivatives are by design not only leveraged market instruments but may as well exhibit nonlinear price dynamics. If a contract is additionally traded over the counter (OTC) or characterized by inferior trading liquidity, the exposure might be hard to reduce quickly. The latter can then result in conflict concerning risk limits.

One key deliverable of this book is to illustrate the importance of various sub-topics in trading. This begins with the general pricing theory and respective models, their application and associated model risk. Throughout this book, the position is taken that finance, economics and derivative pricing is not characterized by fundamental laws similar to physics. In this sense, all presented models should be treated as sophisticated toy models even if they can be derived from quantum mechanics [5] or gauge symmetry [6]. Hence, mathematical connections are not necessarily a consequence of fundamental laws. Note that the term toy model is not meant to be derogatory. It should instead reflect the fact that these models will exhibit limitations and restrictions which may severely impair their applicability and validity if considered infallible.

Closely linked to pricing is the payout replication irrespective of whether one is operating within a risk-neutral measure or not. Very often, pricing a payout is much easier than deriving a proper replication or hedging strategy. This dilemma is amplified by the abundance of cheap computational power allowing to effectively *price* any payout via sampling methods such as Monte Carlo in no time. However, especially for complicated payouts, a proper replication of the derivative does not immediately follow from merely looking at the output of the associated (Monte Carlo) greeks at inception. Furthermore, in conjunction with the replication framework, successful traders need to go beyond models or math and develop an understanding of the markets. This includes a perspective on the general flow, potential market impact events as well as a view for the economic development at least at the domain level. Following the last financial crisis, the impact of a large derivative transaction on the capital and balance sheet of a financial institution is assessed up front and throughout the trade lifetime. This analysis holds irrespective of whether dealing with a vanilla interest rate swap or a complex multi-collateral derivative-backed loan transaction. Hence, at least some basic understanding of the corresponding valuation adjustments is required for front office trading personnel as well.

1.2 **Structure and Concept**

The structure of this book is designed to provide a hopefully clear and sensible path to understanding theoretical aspects, pricing problems, and risk of common derivative instruments. Since it is impossible to summarize both asset class as well as product-specific knowledge in all details in this limited space, the leading concept is to introduce general and relevant derivative knowledge which can then be translated into a particular domain. In other words, more in-depth topical knowledge is often required additionally and beyond the scope here. Nevertheless, there are still many repeating elements within derivative pricing and trading such as the construction of the forward, definition of the stochastic process as well as resulting risk-management considerations. Understanding this framework is the foundation upon which more domain-specific knowledge can be built on.

Following an introduction to the fundamental nature of risk neutral pricing, related elements and vanilla options (Chapter 2), the journey continues with exotic derivatives (Chapter 3), variance derivatives (Chapter 4) and finally multi-factor options (Chapter 5). The discussion in these first chapter will be steered from an equities trading perspective. Given the importance of interest rates as a basic component for pricing derivatives and discounting cash flows, Chapter 6 provides both an introduction to interest rates in general as well as an overview of some of the key products. The remaining large asset classes of Foreign Exchange and Commodities and discussed in Chapters 7 and 8, respectively.

Since Structured Products have played a key role in growing the derivative industry as a whole, Chapter 9 describes some of the key structures as well as typical market dynamics coupled to Structured Products issuance activity. Convertible Bonds (Chapter 10) are exciting financial products on their own since they implicitly contain hybrid (equity and interest rate) characteristics. Chapter 11 deals with Corporate Derivatives (CD), which are a key revenue contributor to banks. CDs entail specific challenges given the typically significant notional and resulting hedging problems due to potential liquidity shortages. Credit Risk (Chapter 12) is a universal trading desk exposure in that the counterparty default risk can be detrimental to the overall profitability of a transaction independently. Following the completion of the discussion on derivatives and their respective asset classes, Chapter13 summarizes various trading strategies including position sizing. Running a trading book incorporates risk, and Chapter 14 details derivative risk in general and its assessment within the Value at Risk (VaR) benchmark framework, expected shortfall and scenario analysis. Finally, as a reaction to the 2008/09 financial crisis, various valuation adjustments and charges are discussed (XVA), which derivative desks and traders need to be aware of today when pricing trades (Chapter 15).

As stated before, the attempt to condense all relevant knowledge about a vast topic such as cross-asset derivatives trading without information loss is bound for failure. Instead, the goal is to establish an accurate and solid foundation upon which the reader can build on. Luckily, even if the derivatives domain is large, there are general principles that hold irrespective of the asset or product class. If these principles are understood and thereafter recognized in a different context, the conclusions are often transferable as well. Hence, the primary aim is to provide solid transfer knowledge so that readers can confidently engage in a deeper discovery exercise within a particular subdomain later.

2. Vanilla Options

The derivatives genie is now well out of the bottle, and these instruments will almost certainly multiply in variety and number until some event makes their toxicity clear. Central banks and governments have so far found no effective way to control, or even monitor, the risks posed by these contracts. In my view, derivatives are financial weapons of mass destruction, carrying dangers that, while now latent, are potentially lethal [1](Berkshire Hathaway, Chairman's letter, 2002).

2.1 Context

Many things in life only make sense in the right context, and derivatives are no different. Hence, while some derivatives possess potentially toxic ingredients for clients and dealers alike, it makes sense first to understand how vanilla options relate contextually and quantitatively to their underlying, *i.e.* the financial instruments they are *derived* from. The following pages show that vanilla options are simply ways to purchase or sell the underlying asset employing *less* capital or *more* leverage.

The seminal work solving this puzzle via risk-neutral valuation dates back to F. Black, M. Scholes and R. Merton [7, 8] who themselves based their analysis on similar solutions to the same problem [9, 10, 11]. To appreciate their contribution to the quantitative finance canon, a simple stylized example will be presented.

2.1.1 Risk-neutral measure

Consider a simple two-state process for two stocks A and B as shown in Figure 2.1. One year from now, both assets will either be trading higher or lower with equal probability. These probabilities are real-world probabilities that have somehow been estimated. While this might appear like an unrealistic and contrived example, research analysts or asset managers consider scenarios like this all the time when they need to decide whether to *e.g.* buy Microsoft or Apple. Hence, which asset does one buy under this assumption? It should be relatively clear that for the same investment of

---

[1]http://www.berkshirehathaway.com/letters/2002.pdf

	today	1 year	probability
	A_0	A_1	
		200	$p_A=0.5$
Stock A	100		
		50	$q_A=0.5$
	B_0	B_1	
		300	$p_B=0.5$
Stock B	100		
		80	$q_B=0.5$

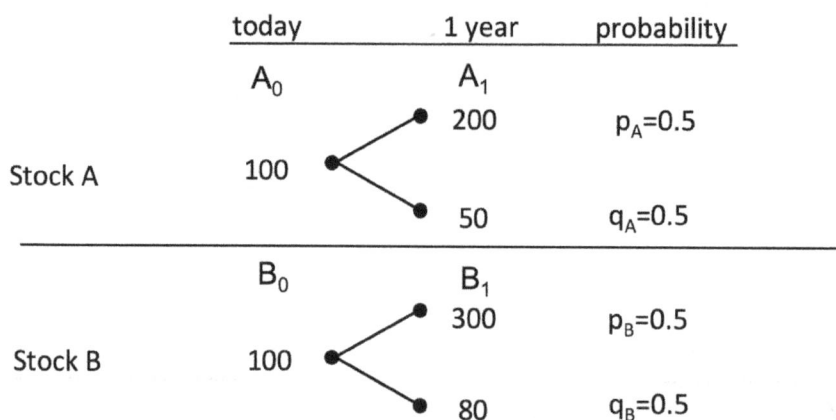

Figure 2.1: Illustration of a deterministic two-state process for two stocks A and B along with the respective real probabilities.

100, Stock B offers a higher upside (300 vs. 200) with less downside (80 vs. 50) in the scenarios, respectively. Hence, assuming the outcomes and probabilities are estimated correctly, it is completely rational to buy Stock B.

Next, a derivative comes in the picture, namely a *vanilla call option*. A vanilla call is a financial contract giving the owner the right but not the obligation to purchase an asset in the future at a price set today. Mathematically, the payout of such a contract V is given by

$$V_T = \max[S_T - K, 0] , \tag{2.1}$$

whereby S_T denotes the price of the stock at a pre-defined future time T and K the ultimate purchase price (also known as the strike price). The formula then effectively pays out the maximum of the (potentially positive) difference and zero. In the case above, the question is now which call option for the two stocks A and B is more expensive for the same strike $K=100$, *i.e.*

$$\max[A_T - 100, 0] \text{ or } \max[B_T - 100, 0] ? \tag{2.2}$$

Counterintuitively, in this case, call option A is **more** expensive even if stock B is still the better stock to own outright. If the reader is now confused, he is in good company. Many brilliant minds in mathematical finance did get this wrong in the past.

To develop an understanding of what is happening here, another example (see Figure 2.2) is presented to derive the conceptual framework of the Black-Scholes-Merton replication argument [7, 8]. The task at hand is to determine todays value of the following call option payout

$$\max[S_T - 110, 0], \tag{2.3}$$

i.e. the 110 strike call for a two-state process for an asset value of 100 with terminal spot values of 130 or 80 given probabilities of 0.7 and 0.3, respectively. There are two seemingly intuitive ways of approaching this question via a probabilistic analysis. Either,

(*i*) calculate the expectation value of the stocks, plug it in the call payout formula for S_T and discount with the interest rate to derive the present value today, *i.e.* $\max[(0.7 \cdot 130 + 0.3 \cdot 80) - 110, 0] =$

today   1 year   probability

● 130   p=0.7

                                              Interest Rates = 5%
100 ●

● 80   q=0.3

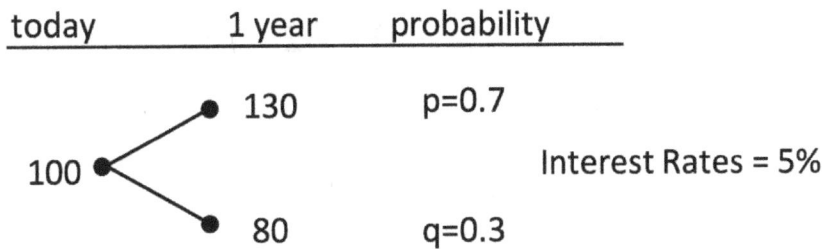

Figure 2.2: Illustration of a probabilistic process for a stock with two outcomes.

$\max[115 - 110, 0] = 5$, which after discounting yields $5/1.05 = 4.76$.

or

(ii) calculate the expectation value of the two possible payouts and discount, i.e. $0.7 \cdot \max[130 - 110, 0] + 0.3 \cdot \max[80 - 110, 0] = 0.7 \cdot 20 + 0 = 14$, which after discounting yields $14/1.05 = 13.33$.

Unfortunately, both ways of calculating the call option price are wrong here. It is rather easy to see why method (i) is incorrect: by playing with the probabilities, e.g. setting the up-and-down probabilities to p=0.1 and q=0.9, one derives an expectation value for the stock price of $S_T = 85$ below the strike. This input to the call formula then results in a call option value of zero. However, there is still a small but finite probability (10%) that the call option pays out more than zero if the asset ends up at 130. Hence, the call value cannot be worth zero as there is no free lunch, especially in finance.

The historic insight to approach the problem systematically was to wonder whether it is possible to create a portfolio composed of cash and stock such that the payout of the call option is replicated in both states. In other words, one demands that

$$(D \cdot S_T^+ - C^+) = (D \cdot S_T^- - C^-) \tag{2.4}$$

where S_T^+, S_T^-, C^+, C^- are the respective values of the stock and call in the up-state and down-state whereby D denotes the fraction of stock required to hold so that both outcomes are equal. Solving for D yields

$$D = (C^+ - C^-)/(S_T^- - S_T^+) = (20 - 0)/(130 - 80) = 0.4 . \tag{2.5}$$

Hence, to replicate the payout in both states, a trader needs to buy 0.4 units of the asset. Interestingly enough, the calculation above did not make use of any real-world probabilities. So indeed, they are not affecting the option price nor do any risk preferences. Note also that the strike price of the call option is not considered.

To recap, it is now possible to put all of this together. First, one purchases 0.4 units of the stock at 100, which costs $0.4 \cdot 100 = 40$. Assuming that one does not have the cash at hand, the trader needs to borrow the money whereby the financing cost is depending on the interest rate as $40 \cdot 0.05 = 2$. In other words, the so-called 'cost-of-carrying' the position is 42. The verification of the replication setup above is given by the incurred profit and loss (P/L) statement for each of the states in Figure 2.3. The future value of the investment is either +10 or -10, i.e. in discounted

0.4 x 130 = 52 → Profit = 10

40

0.4 x 80 = 32 → Loss = 10

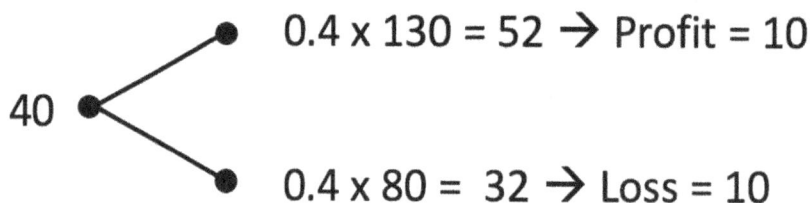

Figure 2.3: Profit and Loss outcome for holding a fractional stock purchased at a cost of 40.

present value terms $PV(10) = 10/10.5 = 9.52$. This coincides with the present value of the 110 strike call since the outcomes are either $\max[130 - 110, 0] = 20$ or $\max[80 - 110, 0] = 0$ in the so-called *risk-neutral* world. In this risk-neutral world, the associated risk-neutral probability equals $p^* = 0.5$. Moreover, the risk-neutral expectation value of the asset is simply its forward value, *i.e.* $F = 130 \cdot p^* + 80 \cdot p^* = 130 \cdot 0.5 + 80 \cdot 0.5 = 65 + 40 = 105$. But what does the expression *risk-neutral* actually mean? It means an indifference to the actual outcome of the process, *i.e.* indifference to the risk associated with the two states in the example. So how is it possible to determine the risk-neutral probability for a given distribution of outcomes? One simply demands that the respective *average* is equal to the forward F. In the two-state example, one then solves the forward equation

$$F = p^* \cdot S_T^+ + p^* \cdot S_T^- \tag{2.6}$$

for p^*, *i.e.*

$$p^* = (F - S_T^-)/(S_T^+ - S_T^-) = (105 - 80)/(130 - 80) = 25/50 = 0.5. \tag{2.7}$$

This general expression allows to solve for any call value, *e.g.* the 100 strike call is just given by $0.5 \cdot 30 + (1 - 0.5) \cdot 0 = 15$ or after discounting 15 / 1.05 = 14.29. In conclusion, the key to pricing options is finding the risk-neutral probability by determining the forward. Real world probabilities and/or expectations do not matter as they are typically not correct to construct the replicating portfolio.

The importance of the forward in pricing derivatives is not to be underestimated. It effectively represents the foundation upon which all pricing models build on. Mistakes in calculating the forward may lead to severe mispricing even if using very sophisticated ways of modeling the payout otherwise. As a consequence, it should now also be clear that long-dated payouts impose challenges in modeling the forward given increased parameter uncertainty in regard to the forward input variables (*e.g.* interest rates, dividends...).

It is now time to revisit the first example in Figure 2.1. Recall the claim that a call written on stock A is more expensive as shown in Figure 2.4 even if stock B is the better stock to buy. Following the replication argument, this is because it is simply cheaper to replicate the option written on stock B.

	today	1 year

A_0 A_1

Stock A   100

200

50

$$p^* = (F - S^-) / (S^+ - S^-)$$
$$= (100 - 50) / (200 - 50)$$
$$= 50 / 150 = 1/3$$

B_0 B_1

Stock B   100

300

80

$$p^* = (F - S^-) / (S^+ - S^-)$$
$$= (100 - 80) / (300 - 80)$$
$$= 20 / 220 = 1/11$$

$Option_A$: 1/3 x max(0, 200-100) + (1-1/3) x max(0, 50-100) = 1/3 x 100 + 1/3 x 0 = 33.33

$Option_B$: 1/11 x max(0, 300-100) + (1-1/11) x max(0,80-100) = 1/11 x 200 + 1/11 x 0 = 18.18

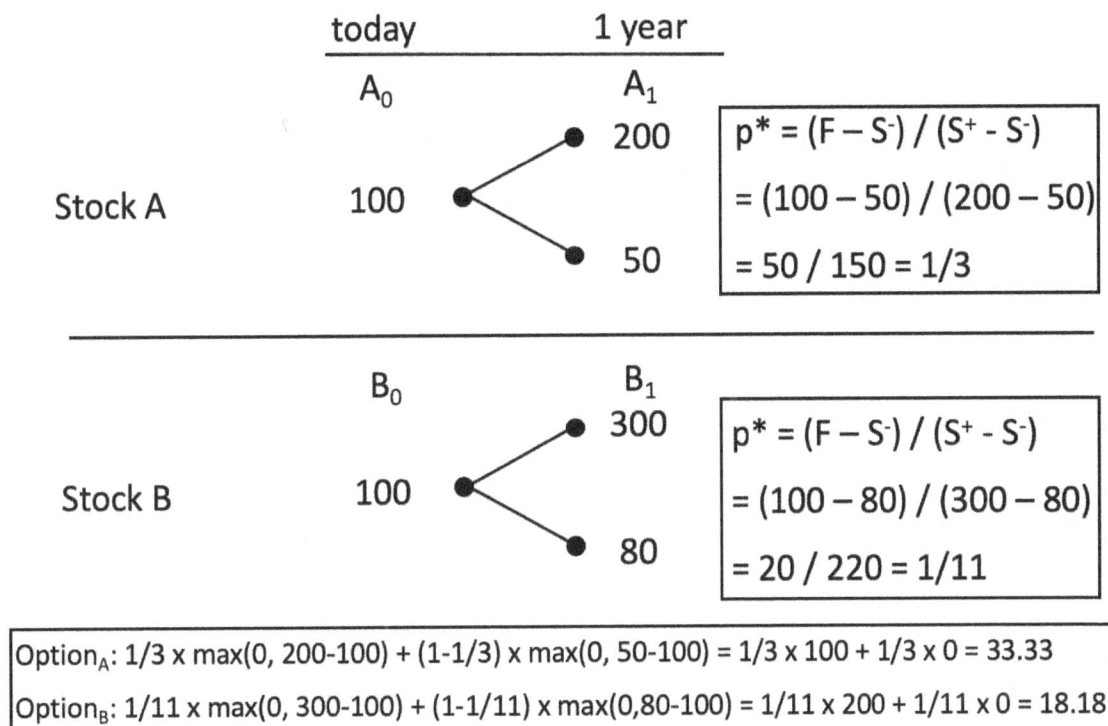

Figure 2.4: Profit and Loss outcome for holding a fractional stock purchased at the cost of 40.

It all boils down to the risk-neutral probabilities, which are lower for stock A. It is normal to be confused if not irritated about this. As stated before, despite earlier work on the topic resulting in similar mathematical expressions [9, 10, 11], it was not until the seminal work of Black, Scholes, and Merton when the replication argument [7, 8] provided the setting upon which derivative pricing is to be understood.

Ever since the introduction of the risk-neutral measure, attempts have been made to transform risk-neutral (pseudo-)probabilities derived from the options market into real-world probabilities [12]. What is typically required for the transformation is to estimate both state prices [13] as well as the pricing kernel [14]. For the level of discussion in this book, the state price is defined as the amount an investor would pay for a security paying out one dollar if a particular pre-defined state occurs in the future, and otherwise zero. The pricing kernel is related to the marginal utility of such an investor [13], which is also explicitly what the risk-neutral measure avoids specifying. In a recent development [15], it was shown that under strong assumptions, it is possible to derive both the pricing kernel and physical probabilities by only using state prices from the market itself. While the analysis is mathematically correct [16], the empirical tests so far have been mixed [17, 18]. Hence, for the time being it is still advised to remain skeptical about claims regarding market-invariant recovery of real-world probabilities in a model-free approach.

Finally, one needs to clarify that the setting of pricing derivatives under the risk-neutral measure is not the only possible approach. Admittedly, risk-neutral pricing provides the advantage that there is no need to estimate the expected return of assets. Compared to other measures (e.g. based on real-world probabilities) risk-neutral pricing thereby offers an approach that appears to be objective or rational by design. However, it is essential to recognize that for many of the parameter inputs used in practice, historical estimates or proxies are used, which in turn means that one is somehow blending risk-neutral pricing with physical measures. Moreover, in other disciplines of finance (*e.g.* insurance) option premia or contracts are often valued using a purely statistical approach. Hence, risk-neutral pricing is a chosen pricing measure and not a fundamental law upon which any type of financial calculation must necessarily obey. However, if a perfect replication approach is possible such as in the examples above, then the risk-neutral measure is the way to go forward.

2.1.2 Cash equity vs vanilla option

Since the option price derives from an underlying asset, it is worth to explore how these objects relate beyond mathematics. Returning to the stylized two-state process and plotting the expected returns for a cash equity investment vs. the vanilla option strategy in Figure 2.5 provides the following conclusion:

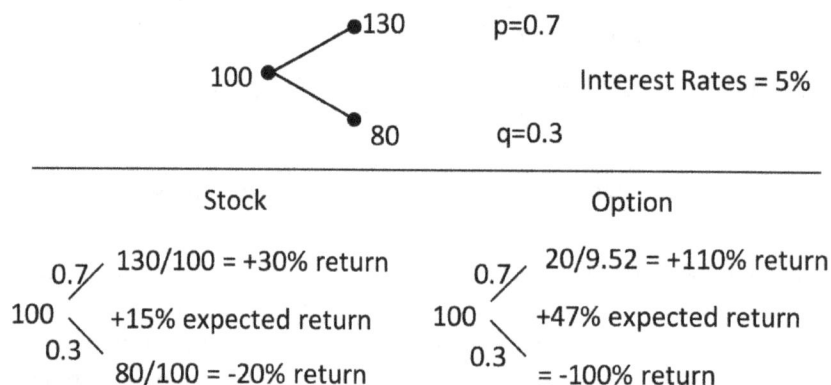

Figure 2.5: Expected return of cash equity investments vs the 110 strike vanilla call.

- The excess return over the (risk-free) interest rate of 5% is 10% for the cash equity and 42% for the option
- The option offers a factor of 4.2 more expected return, but also 4.2 times more risk
- The option is effectively a leveraged investment in the underlying stock
- In terms of risk vs return (*e.g.* Sharp ratio [19]) both are equivalent

In other words, on the (risk-free) tangential capital market line [20, 21] which relates both instruments in terms of return and volatility / risk, the option lies above the cash equity investment(see Figure 2.6).

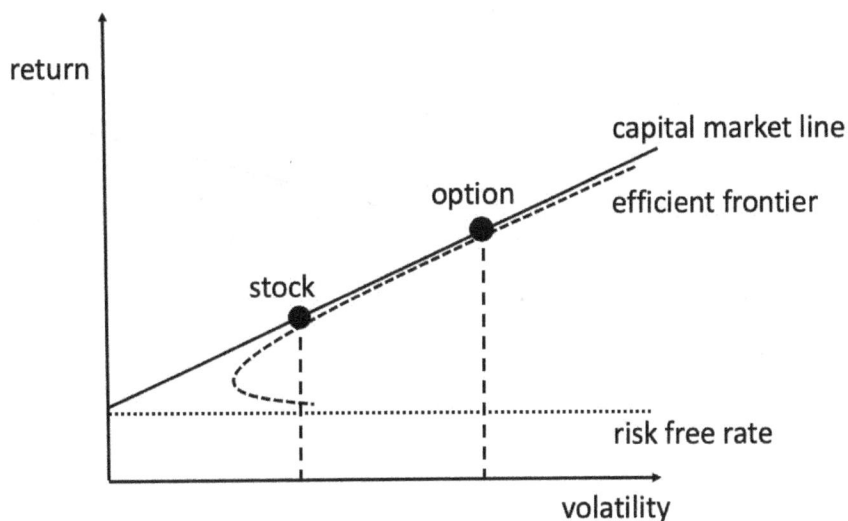

Figure 2.6: Expected return and risk (expressed in volatility) of a cash equity investment vs. the 110 strike vanilla call. The respective capital market line (solid), risk free rate (dotted) and efficient frontier (dashed line) are displayed schematically.

2.1.3 Asset returns

The foundation of financial and derivative mathematics is based on asset returns. The two main return definitions are the discrete and the continuous return (also known as log return). The discrete return is given by

$$R_t = \frac{(S_t - S_{t-1})}{S_{t-1}} = \frac{S_t}{S_{t-1}} - 1 \, , \tag{2.8}$$

while the continuous return is calculated by taking the natural logarithm

$$r_t = \ln\left(\frac{S_t}{S_{t-1}}\right) = \ln(R_t + 1) \, . \tag{2.9}$$

While most practitioners are familiar with those definitions, it is sometimes forgotten that they are not equivalent. As shown in Figure 2.7, r_t lower than R_t for large moves, which can introduce a bias. Moreover, the continuous return will tend to overestimate the return of an asset since the interest is always reinvested (also known as compound interest). The main advantage for the continuous return is that it is additive through time and, therefore, more convenient to calculate with.

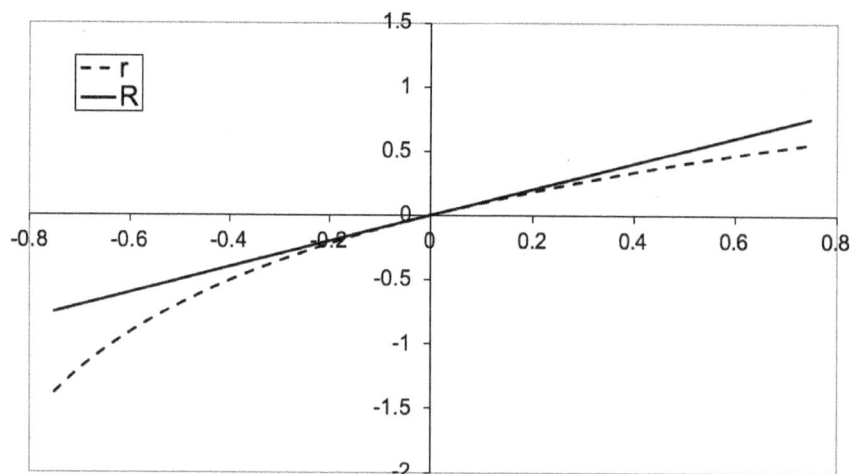

Figure 2.7: Discrete (solid line) versus continuous (dashed line) returns.

In the context of derivatives, the difference between discrete and continuous returns is important when discussing moment swaps later (see 4.1.2).

2.1.4 The Forward

One of the key takeaways from the last section was that derivatives are in general priced using the forward and that the pricing under the risk-neutral measure does **not** take into account real-life probabilities. An intuitive explanation for the necessity of taking into account the forward value of the underlying is that an option is typically a contract written on an event in the *future*. Since one deals with the future, the price is a function of the forward and thereby sensitive to parameters used to construct the latter.

The parameters used in the construction of a forward asset value are to some extend asset class specific. For example, equities do pay dividends, which affect the forward value, whereas interest rates or commodities do not. However, the general principle of compounding and discounting between the spot and the forward price remains the same. In the equities world, the forward F_t at time t is given by [22]

$$F(t,T) = S_t \cdot \exp[(r-d-bc)(T-t)] , \qquad (2.10)$$

where r is the interest rate, d the dividend yield, bc the borrow cost and T - t the time to maturity with $T > t$. Borrow cost refers to a topic in trading called shorting. Shorting an asset means to sell assets that you currently do not own. To not create energy out of nothing, the shorted asset is *borrowed* from an owner in a process that is governed by market exchange providers. The owner then receives a cash deposit from the shorter and pays the market interest rate on the cash. If the interest received is less than the market interest rate, there is a *borrow cost* to be paid. Higher borrow cost is an incentive to sell short because the forward is perceived to remain low. However, there is the danger of a so-called short squeeze, resulting from an unexpected increase in the asset price which at some stage forces short sellers to cover their shorts, *i.e.* buy back the assets in a rising market. This process is sometimes even triggered by the exchange in what is called a *forced buy-in* . The price may then shoot up excessively because there are not enough shares to cover the outstanding shorts quickly enough. In other words, the market faces a supply/demand imbalance.

The modeling of forwards in the commodity market is somewhat more involved [23, 24] and will be discussed in more detail later (see chapter 8). Nonetheless, one distinguishes in general between storable (Oil, Natural Gas) and non-storable commodities (Electricity). The generic spot-forward relationship for storable commodities is given by

$$F(t,T) = S(t) \cdot [1 + \underbrace{r(T-t)}_{Financing\ cost} + \underbrace{c(T-t)}_{Storage\ cost} + \underbrace{d(T-t)}_{implied\ dividend\ cost}] \,. \tag{2.11}$$

Here $F(t, T)$, $T > t$ is the forward curve prevailing at date t for a given commodity in a given location for all traded maturity dates $T = 1,2,...N$. It also reflects the seasonality in the case of seasonal commodities such as natural gas or agricultural goods. The relationship above is also known as the cost-of-carry equation given by

$$F(t,T) = S(t) \exp[r(t) + c(t) - y(t)](T-t) \,, \tag{2.12}$$

where $r(t)$ is the riskless interest rate on the date t, $c(t)$ is the storage cost (per unit of time and per dollar worth of commodity), and $y(t)$ the convenience yield, all continuously compounded. The convenience yield is defined as the premium received by the owner of the physical commodity and not accruing to the holder of a futures contract written on it. Given the storage costs for physical commodities, one should otherwise expect that the forward curve is always upwards sloping (contango). Since this is not always the case, in reality, the convenience yield was introduced to model this effect. Often, the convenience yield is defined net of storage costs, i.e. $\hat{y}(t) = y(t) - c(t)$. This then simplifies the equation above to

$$F(t,T) = S(t) \exp[r(t) + \hat{y}(t)](T-t) \,. \tag{2.13}$$

It is essential that no forward curve violates the cost-of-carry arbitrage, i.e. buying the commodity at spot level S, selling it at a future maturity T and paying the cost of storage and financing as long as the net cash flow is strictly positive. The cost-of-carry is here introduced in the context of commodities because there is a real physical cost in owning and storing the respective goods. In the derivative domain, this physical cost is typically zero, but there are other fees relating to margining, capital usage, funding or hedging costs. Hence, in the context of derivatives, cost-of-carry typically relates to the blended intrinsic cost running the business instead of paying for warehouses to store a physical commodity.

Forwards are traded in the market as Forward contracts, i.e. two parties agree to buy (long position) and sell (short position) an asset on a future date for a pre-defined price. Forward contracts are over-the-counter (OTC) instruments, i.e. they contain counterparty credit risk. Exchange-traded forwards exist as so-called Futures Instruments (*Futures*) with standardized contract specifications (expiry, reference asset, contract size etc.). However, Futures and Forwards are not equivalent unless interest rates are certain, i.e. only then does a rollover position in futures produce the same cash flow as the respective forward contract [25]. In the case of futures, the credit risk component compared to the forward contract is structurally mitigated since Futures are margined and cleared by central clearing houses. The settlement of both forward or future can be physical or in cash.

2.1.5 Stochastic Processes

The analysis so far, was conducted via stylized two-state processes. However, this is not realistic with how financial markets work in general. The most straightforward extension of a two-state model is to introduce more states. Increasing the state space is indeed how some option pricing models work, *i.e.* by valuing multiple discrete states in a tree-like network [26]. The generalization of this is a continuous time representation of the underlying stochastic process of the financial instrument. In finance, the workhorse of stochastic processes is geometric Brownian motion (GBM).

The stochastic differential equation (SDE) describing the GBM process is mathematically given by

$$dS_t = \mu_t S_t dt + \sigma_t S_t dW_t \,, \tag{2.14}$$

where dS_t is the infinitesimal asset price increment over the time interval *[t-1, t]*, μ_t a drift term, S_t the asset price at time t, σ_t the standard deviation (aka volatility) term and dW_t the Wiener process increment. The geometric property follows from the fact that μ_t and dW_t are proportional to S_t. The process has the following properties [27]:

- $E[\mu_t S_t dt + \sigma_t S_t dW_t] = \mu_t S_t dt$
- $VAR[\mu_t S_t dt + \sigma_t S_t dW_t] = \sigma_t^2 S_t^2 dt$

In other words, the expectation value of the process is equal to the deterministic (non-random) component while the variance is just the square of the standard deviation (also referred to as *volatility*) and asset price over a given time increment.

The SDE above (2.14) references a real-world stochastic process. In order to utilize the BSM framework, this equation and its corresponding solutions need to be moved to the risk-neutral measure. Luckily, this transition under the assumption of complete and frictionless markets with no arbitrage opportunities is trivial such that the SDE becomes

$$dS_t = r_t S_t dt + \sigma_t S_t dW_t \,, \tag{2.15}$$

whereby r_t is the risk-free rate which has replaced the expected return μ_t. Hence, instead of having to estimate the asset risk premium, one just requires the risk-free rate and volatility estimate, both of which are typically readily available from market data.

The stochastic driver for GBM is the Wiener process W_t. W_t is a random variable, so that ΔW is equal to $\varepsilon \cdot \sqrt{\Delta t}$ where ε is a standard normal distribution with zero mean and unit variance. Moreover, ΔW has the following main properties [27]:

- finiteness: the process remains finite since its variance scales with the time step
- continuous: the paths have properties of a fractal, but stay continuous
- Markovian: the conditional distributions depend only on the presence, *i.e.* the process has no memory such that ΔW in any two intervals Δt are independent
- Martingale: the conditional expectation of the future is the present
- Quadratic variation: if time is partitioned from 0 to t in $N+1$ points as $t_i = (i \cdot t)/n$ then the quadratic variation converges to: $\sum_{t=1}^{N}(W_{t_j} - W_{t_j-1})^2 \Rightarrow t$
- normal: over finite time increments the stochastic driver is normally distributed with zero mean and variance $t_i - t_{i-1}$. In other words: *E[dW]=0* and $E[dW^2] = dt$

The analytic solution to the GBM process above is given by

$$S_t = S_0 \exp\left[\left(r - \frac{\sigma^2}{2}\right)t + \sigma W_t\right]. \tag{2.16}$$

Considering the relative complex dynamics the equation generates, it is effectively so simple to be able to put in a spreadsheet. Figure 2.8 shows how GBM can be discretized in time to generate the typical dynamics. Note that all model parameters are constant even for the stochastic driver generating the dynamics.

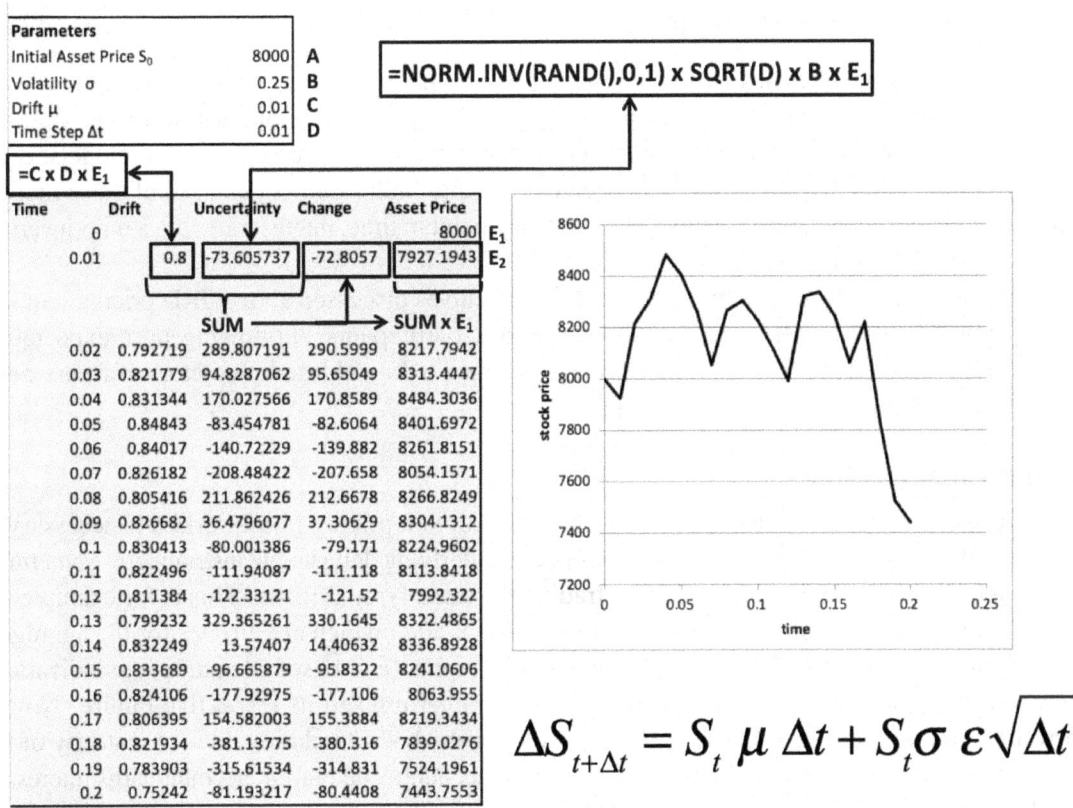

Figure 2.8: Illustration of the GBM process discretized in a spreadsheet.

The dynamics above are characteristic for a stochastic price process in the equities world. In the world of interest rates (IR) and interest rates derivatives (IRD), the stochastic process to model is the so-called instantaneous *spot rate* (also known as short rate) [28], but this rate is not observable in the market. It follows that if I_t is the price of an interest-rate dependent contract, then the instantaneous spot rate r_t at time t in a one-factor model is given by

$$dr_t - f(r_t,t)dt + g(r_t,t)dZ(t) , \tag{2.17}$$

with drift $f(r_t,t)$, diffusion process $g^2(r_t,t)$ and $Z(t)$ a Wiener process with unit variance. I_t is then a function of r_t and t and follows a similar stochastic process

$$dI_t = a(r_t,t)dt + b(r_t,t)dZ(t) . \tag{2.18}$$

A particular form for the stochastic rate in equation 2.17 is given by the CIR model [29]. In the CIR model the drift and variance have the following specification

$$f(r_t,t) = a \cdot (b - r_t) \text{ , with } a,b > 0 \qquad g(r_t,t) = \sigma \sqrt{r_t} \text{ with } \sigma > 0 . \tag{2.19}$$

Here the drift is modeled as a mean-reverting process to the average b while the diffusion is proportional to r_t following empirical evidence that volatility is increasing with the interest rate level. Hence, substituting the expression yields

$$dr_t = a \cdot (b - r_t)dt + \sigma \sqrt{r_t} dZ(t) . \tag{2.20}$$

The reason for choosing a mean-version model as a base model lies in the observation that IR are typically pulled back to some long-term average over time. This is not necessarily the case for equities. There are many extensions and modifications for single-factor short rate models, most notably Hull-White [30], which has also been extended to multi-factors [22]. All of these models typically imply an affine term structure [31], *i.e.* at any point in time, interest rates are a time-invariant *linear* function of a small set of common factors.

Contrary to the risk-neutral pricing of equity derivatives discussed above, IRD pricing requires assumptions about the risk preference of the market participants. Following pure expectation theory [32, 33, 34, 35] current forward rates are assumed to be unbiased predictors of future rates, which leads to the prediction of zero risk premia [36].

2.1.6 Forward versus Futures

Before discussing the classical Black-Scholes-Merton option pricing framework, it is necessary to take a small detour to highlight some subtleties of the underlying delta hedge instruments. Sometimes the delta hedge cannot be implemented by trading the underlying directly. This is for example the case of equity indices (*e.g.* the S&P500 [2] or Euro Stoxx 50 [3]) which are proxies for the aggregate performance of a set of stocks subject to individual weights (*e.g.* based on market capitalization). However, the index cannot be traded directly and is rather tracked its respective Future. Now, a forward is not the same as a future [22]. While the forward is settled only once at maturity of the contract, the future is settled daily including a margin account. The margin account earns interest or is subject to funding costs as a function of the position in the futures contract (long versus short). The daily margining renders the future path-dependent and entails a component which is a function of the stochastic rate impact as well as the correlation between this rate and the spot price. Consider a simple coupled equity-interest rate hybrid process given by

$$dS_t = \mu_t S_t dt + \sigma_t S_t dW_S(t) , \tag{2.21}$$

$$dr_t = -\kappa r_t dt + b dW_r(t) , \tag{2.22}$$

with

$$\mathbf{E}[dW_S dW_r] = \rho dt . \tag{2.23}$$

The first equation is the familiar stochastic process introduced in the previous section, the second equation is a short-rate type of model with κ denoting the mean reversion speed and ρ the correlation between the two processes. Following the derivation in [22], one obtains the relation between the future (Fut) and the forward (Fwd) as

$$Fut = c_T \cdot Fwd , \tag{2.24}$$

---

[2]https://us.spindices.com/indices/equity/sp-500
[3]https://www.stoxx.com/index-details?symbol=SX5E

with

$$c_T = \exp\left[\rho\sigma\alpha\frac{T}{\kappa}\left(1 - \frac{1 - \exp(-\kappa T)}{\kappa T}\right)\right], \tag{2.25}$$

and

$$\alpha = \sigma_r(t)\frac{\kappa}{1 - \exp(-\kappa T)}, \tag{2.26}$$

where T denotes the forward maturity. From the dependence of the relations on the maturity T, it is transparent that the so-called *convexity correction* c_T increases with longer expires. Moreover, in the case of positive correlation between forward and interest rate, a long position in the future will result in a benefit in the margin account due to either lower funding costs or higher interest irrespective of the market move. The opposite is true in the case of negative correlation between forward and interest rate. In terms of hedge ratio (*i.e.* delta), this correction needs to be taken into account, *i.e.* if one is short the forward the futures delta should be adjusted by $1/c_T$. This is especially important in the case of interest rate derivatives because the correlation between the interest rate future and the underlying interest rate is very high by construction. This topic will be revisited in later sections (see 6.2 for example).

2.1.7 Black-Scholes-Merton equation

Black, Scholes [7] and Merton [8] were able to derive the solution to a partial differential equation (PDE) allowing the valuation of option contracts following a GBM process with various assumptions. The equation can be obtained in many ways. At this point, the exact derivation is left to others [22, 37], and the focus is on analyzing the components. The BSM equation is given by

$$\underbrace{\frac{\partial V}{\partial t}}_{\Theta} + \frac{1}{2}\sigma^2 S^2 \underbrace{\frac{\partial^2 V}{\partial S^2}}_{\Gamma} + rS\underbrace{\frac{\partial V}{\partial S}}_{\Delta} - rV = 0 \tag{2.27}$$

The three terms in the PDE denote important partial derivatives by which option contracts are risk managed:

- $\Delta = \frac{\partial V}{\partial S}$ Delta: change of the option price for a move in the price of the underlying
- $\Gamma = \frac{\partial^2 V}{\partial S^2}$ Gamma: change of Delta as a function of the spot price
- $\Theta = \frac{\partial V}{\partial t}$ Theta: change of the option price over time

These so-called option 'greeks' are especially important for practitioners as they describe how the derivative value changes with market data and time to expiry. The following sections provide a full overview of these components in detail. The BSM PDE belongs to the family of convection-diffusion equations, which represent many physical phenomena as well. The volatility parameter thereby represents diffusion and the interest rate (drift) convection.

The most important variation of the BSM model is the Black-76 model [38, 39] (sometimes also referred to as the Black model or Black formula). The Black-76 model was primarily derived to price options on futures, which explains the original literature reference on commodity options since those are typically written on the future and not the spot price. In comparison to the original BSM formula, the spot price (S) is replaced by the discounted value of future price ($F_t \cdot \exp[-rt]$) whereby the underlying stochastic differential equation is given by

$$\frac{dF_t}{F_t} = \sigma dW_t. \tag{2.28}$$

As a market model, BSM retains the property of *market completeness* [40]. Market completeness refers to markets in which every contingent claim (such as a derivative) is replicable [41]. Even more so, every future state in this market can be constructed with market assets. Despite fulfilling this desirable property, the original BSM model and its subsequent modifications make several other assumptions, which are often criticized. However, which assumptions are manageable, and which are a problem? The following list provides a recap of the assumptions [42]:

(*i*) risk free rate is a constant
(*ii*) no dividends
(*iii*) no arbitrage possible
(*iv*) volatility is constant
(*v*) markets are normal, *i.e.* the rates of returns follow a normal distribution [43]
(*vi*) no transaction costs (bid / ask spread for trading the underlying equals zero)
(*vii*) unlimited liquidity whereby short selling always allowed
(*viii*) trading (*i.e.* buying/selling of underlying asset) is continuous
(*ix*) the process of the underlying asset is a diffusion, *i.e.* there are no jumps

The last three assumptions remain arguably the most problematic in practice and are not only limited to the BSM model. The argument here is that model deficiencies regarding unrealistic return distribution assumptions are sometimes overemphasized versus far more problematic assumptions regarding unlimited market liquidity. It is effectively always possible to use more sophisticated models or stress tests to assess the model risk given by the assumption (*i-v*) [44]. However, getting out of a bad trade, which was possibly even priced correctly at inception, is not possible in case a position cannot be liquidated. Another way to look at this is to realize that risk is not only quantifiable by the nature of a particular stochastic process and the resulting differences in realized variance. If one cannot *trade* what one tries to *model*, the potential model risk is secondary. The simplicity of the BSM model and its assumptions are also related to another virtue: robustness. In other words, while more sophisticated models are often more sensitive to input parameter errors or noise, it is quite hard to break the BSM model. Having said that it is important to note that if there are jumps, the canonical BSM replication strategy fails. In practice, markets are often diffusive but jumps certainly do occur from time to time. However, this potential impact is assessable via stress tests.

Finally, most financial models assume that the operators act like rational agents, *i.e.* all models assume users take the same decision given the same information. However, rationality must not always be the case and whether a wrong decision automatically results in a windfall profit for the other counterparty is uncertain, too. One must also stress that financial models are typically created without the purpose of providing explanatory meaning to the model subject. Hence, one is not dealing with theories or models which are fundamentally equivalent to how theoretical models are derived in physics even if the underlying mathematics is identical.

2.1.8 Implied Volatility

Implied Volatility is the standard deviation parameter which reprices an option market quote when inserted in the BSM equation [4] [45]. The inverse task of backing out implied volatility from option market quotes is a frequent undertaking of trading or risk management systems. Given that there is no closed-form inverse solution [46] this procedure is not exactly as trivial as it sounds even if the

---

[4]This requires the other parameters to be known or estimated as well.

other parameter space is fixed. What is essentially done in practice is to iterate based on an initial estimate until a sufficient level of repricing accuracy for a given option quote has been reached [47].

The result of a successful inversion procedure yields a set of implied volatilities $\sum \sigma(K,T)$ in strike and maturity space for a given asset. In a second step, it is then desirable to construct a continuous implied volatility *surface*. The latter enables the pricing of options which are not quoted in exact strike and maturity as well as enable to run more elaborate risk or scenarios on the portfolio. For the construction of such a generic surface, it is required to propose a mathematical function, which allows being fitted or parameterized to the extracted implied volatilities. One classically used parameterization for implied volatility is a parabolic function in log space applied on the forward price as

$$\sigma(K) = \sigma(F) + \beta \cdot \log \frac{K}{F} + \gamma \log^2 \frac{K}{F} \,, \tag{2.29}$$

where the parameter β represents the skew and γ the curvature of the surface. Figure 2.9 shows a representative example of fitting this parabola to a set of option implied volatilities. It is apparent that the fit is relatively good around regions close to the forward but increases too rapidly for lower strikes. As a remedy, it is possible to use a cutoff to truncate the tail of the curve. Otherwise, options in this region might be priced as too expensive. The advantage of the parabola (or other functions) is that the derivatives are typically analytically accessible. This topic is revisited in the context of more advanced volatility models such as *local volatility* in Section 3.1.4. A more advanced parameterization model called SVI was introduced by Gatheral [48] and is given by the function form

$$\sigma^2(y) = a + b \left[\rho(y - m) + \sqrt{(y - m)^2 + \sigma^2} \right] \,, \tag{2.30}$$

where $y = \ln \frac{K}{F}$ denotes the log-moneyness. All parameters a, b, ρ, σ, m are a function of expiry. The SVI model has an advantage in that it tends to avoid common induced arbitrage problems while still remaining very flexible. In addition, the OTM (wing) regions are fitted more naturally. Note that the fitting will be problematic for volatility surfaces which are not convex.

As mentioned earlier, the extraction of implied volatilities and the curve fitting is not a trivial task for any asset class [49]. Often sparse data or incorrect quotes require data cleaning and extrapolation. Moreover, the problem increases with the size of the instrument universe. An essential property for a fitted implied volatility surface is that it must be free from arbitrage. The expression arbitrage means that it must not be possible to construct a risk-free trading strategy exploiting inconsistencies in the underlying implied volatility surface and the derived option quotes. However, arbitrage in source data is almost impossible to avoid since the market trades bid and offer prices, but systems will often only store the mid value. This difference can introduce arbitrage even if the market prices are consistent on their own. Many necessary conditions for a surface to be arbitrage free are found in the literature [50] and range from implied volatility bounds for large strikes as well as bounds for the slope of the fitted curve. The most important non-arbitrage conditions to be aware of are

- Call spread arbitrage ($-\exp[-rT] \leq \frac{\partial C}{\partial K} \leq 0$): a call with higher strike must be less valuable than a lower strike call of the same maturity
- Butterfly arbitrage ($\frac{\partial^2 C}{\partial^2 K} \geq 0$): a butterfly (see 2.2.16 at strike K must have a positive value
- Calendar spread arbitrage ($\frac{\partial C}{\partial K} \geq 0$): a call with longer maturity must be more valuable than the same strike call of shorter maturity

- Variance ($\frac{\sigma^2 T}{T} \geq 0$): the total variance must increase with time

Sometimes different trading desks might also deliberately want to mark a particular position at a different volatility level depending on how they want to run the hedge ratio against a particular position. Another typical conflict of this sort may arise when exotics desks derive volatility marks for more sophisticated volatility models (*e.g.* Local Volatility) from an implied surface. Exotic derivatives are often sensitive to volatility marks in regions of the surface for which the marks need to be carefully adjusted to avoid spurious profit/loss (P/L) and hedge ratios when remarking the books. Hence, building a robust remarking process satisfying both vanilla and exotic desks is challenging.

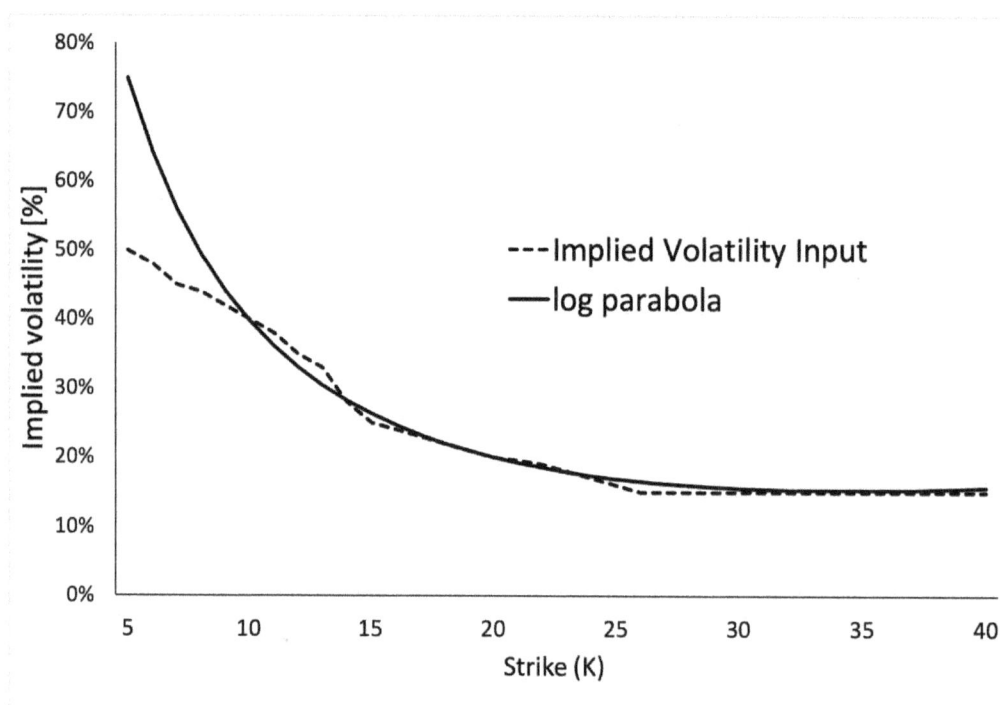

Figure 2.9: Illustration of a fitted parabola (F = 20, $\beta = -0.4$, $\gamma = 0.85$) to a stylized set of implied volatilities in strike space for a fixed maturity.

2.2 Option Greeks: basics

Understanding the basic option greeks [51, 52] corresponds to the primary school education of a derivative trader. Moreover, especially the relation between theta and gamma governs what might be called the P/L master equation in derivative trading. In the following pages, the profile of the basic greeks for an unhedged 100 strike long call position with a two-year maturity is examined to illustrate the typical behavior.

2.2.1 Delta

The discussion begins with the option spot delta (Δ), *i.e.* the change in option value as a function of the underlying asset price. As shown in Figure 2.10, the Δ profile starts as a relatively smooth sigmoidally shaped function and then approaches a step function at expiry centered around the strike. The step function indicates a binary or digital outcome, and it is in general advisable to not be on the wrong side of it. This is because the option is either worth something or nothing depending on which side the asset price hovers around the strike level. For someone owning the call unhedged (also referred to as a *naked* position) this is effectively a lottery ticket. However, for the counterparty who has sold the call and tries to replicate the payout, these situations are typically hairy because the delta may change from zero to one. This topic is discussed later in more detail, also in the context of digital and barrier options.

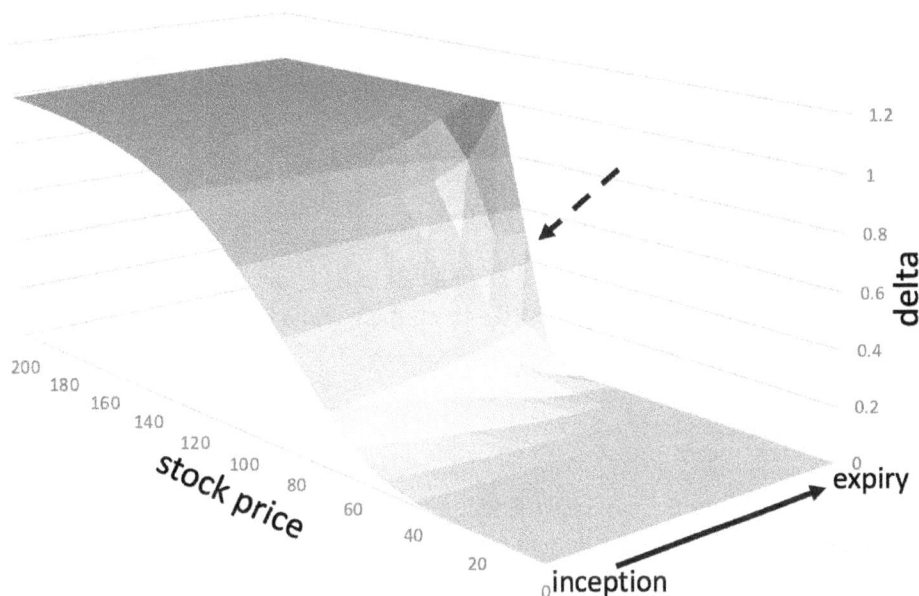

Figure 2.10: Profile of option delta for a 100 strike call in terms of stock price level and time to expiry. At expiry (dashed arrow), the option effectively becomes a digital payout at the strike level.

In general, the option delta is bound between 0 and 1 since it is governed by the cumulative distribution function, which is part of the solution to the BSM equation. Only in exceptional cases (*e.g.* substantial cost-of-carry or negative interest rates), the delta for vanilla options can indeed exceed 1 [53].

The delta can be calculated analytically in the case of a closed form solution to the underlying partial differential equation of the derivative. Otherwise, one needs to resort to the numerical finite difference approximation given by

$$\Delta_{\mathrm{num}} \approx \frac{V(S+\delta S)-V(S-\delta S)}{2\delta S} , \tag{2.31}$$

where δS is the shift in the spot value.

There are several reasons why the option delta is a central risk figure. Most importantly, it is the critical ingredient of the Merton replication argument as it provides the link to the underlying. Also, assuming sufficient underlying liquidity and market access, the hedge ratio can be adjusted quickly to smooth first order P/L variance efficiently.

2.2.2 Gamma

Closely related to the digital property of the delta at expiry is the gamma (Γ) profile given that it is the second derivative.

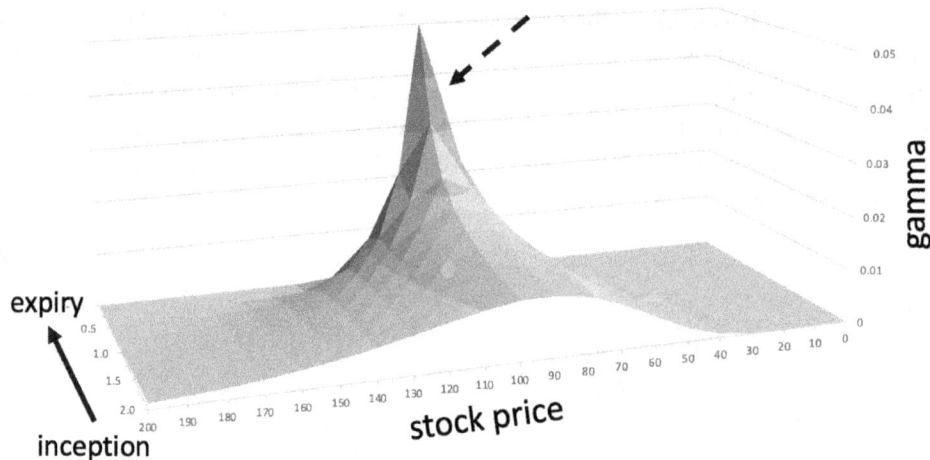

Figure 2.11: Profile of option gamma for a 100 strike call in terms of the asset price level and time to expiry. At expiry (dashed arrow) and at the strike level, the gamma profile is effectively a Dirac delta function.

As can be seen in Figure 2.11, the Γ profile also starts as a smooth and broad Gaussian-shaped function and then approaches the pointy Dirac delta function at expiry around the strike. This large gamma at expiry causes the option value and corresponding delta to fluctuate heavily. The latter is why practitioners pay close attention as to how to manage the option gamma in these situations. However, high gamma also provides trading opportunities for a long option position if it is delta hedged. This topic is later discussed in more detail when examining how delta hedging works in terms of P/L.

The numerical gamma is given by the following finite difference approximation

$$\Gamma_{\text{num}} \approx \frac{V(S+\delta S) - 2V(S) + V(S-\delta S)}{\delta S^2} . \tag{2.32}$$

2.2.3 Theta

The exact terminal value of an option is typically unknown at inception or strike setting. Hence, colloquially speaking, there is much optionality left. As the expiry date approaches, most of the optionality has decayed away, *i.e.* as the option matures, it naturally loses value every day. This process is measured by Θ, *i.e.* the (daily) decay of the options' future value over time.

Figure 2.12 shows the theta profile as the option approaches expiry. The picture resembles an inversion of the Γ profile shown in Figure 2.11. Hence, for a scenario close to expiry whereby the asset price is trading around the strike level, the option time value is largest as this is the point in time when it is decided as to whether it the expiry worthless or not. This so-called *theta-gamma relation* is arguably the most important metric to understand the P/L profile of any derivative book. This topic is also discussed later in detail (see 2.2.6).

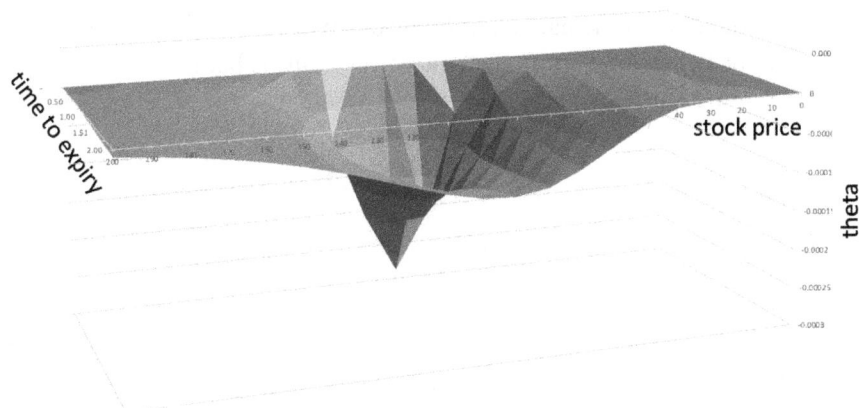

Figure 2.12: Profile of option theta for a 100 strike call in terms of stock price level and time to expiry. At expiry (arrow) and at the strike level, the theta profile is effectively a Dirac delta function.

2.2.4 Vega

The last of the basic greeks is not even a greek if one strictly defines them as partial derivatives of the option value with respect to variables and not constants. This last fundamental greek is called *vega*. Vega expresses the change of the option value for a change in the estimate of the volatility input. This input parameter is a critical determinant of the option value, which can lead to significant P/L swings or mark-to-market variance. As shown in Figure 2.13, the sensitivity to a change in this input parameter is largest at inception and smoothly decreases as the option approaches expiry. An increase in vega will always increase the value of a vanilla option since the upside and downside payoff is asymmetric. In other words, while the upside is in theory uncapped, one cannot lose more than the premium paid.

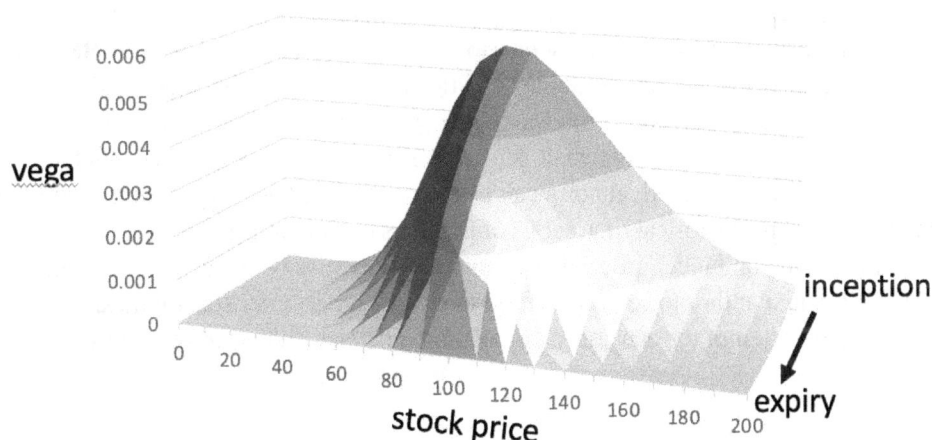

Figure 2.13: Profile of option vega for a 100 strike call in terms of stock price level and time to expiry.

In this context, it is already now useful to take a short detour to a more advanced topic in the context of more complex derivatives. The fact that one is varying a constant parameter can lead to problems when understanding the actual volatility exposure of more exotic derivatives (see also the discussion on volgamma below 2.2.5.3). In the case of vega, this is because the vega term couples to the gamma term (see equation 2.27) via

$$\frac{1}{2}\sigma^2 S^2 \Gamma.$$ (2.33)

Hence, for (exotic) options for which the gamma term changes *sign* for a particular value of the asset, an increase in vega might lead to the conclusion that the derivative is vega neutral even if this is not the case [54]. In other words, merely bumping the volatility at different spot levels to assess its impact on the option value is not an appropriate way of determining the worst-case value of some exotic options. One way of dealing with this is to use an uncertain volatility model [55], which couples the volatility measure to the sign of the gamma.

2.2.5   Higher order Greeks

Higher order greeks (*e.g.* Dvega/Dvol also known as volgamma or vomma) and cross-greeks (*e.g.* Dvega/Dspot also known as vanna) often display essential and critical information on the dynamics of a trade or whole derivative book [56]. For a complex and large portfolio, it is necessary to track these risk figures to avoid bad surprises such as systematic wrong way risk. Some of the cross-greeks may also be interpreted as scenario risks. In the case of a vanilla BSM derivative portfolio, most high order greeks are available analytically. However, since modern risk management systems often use more advanced option models (*e.g.* concerning the treatment of dividends or time variance of the volatility parameter), it is often necessary to calculate these high order greeks numerically. Unfortunately, numerical noise can be substantial for these higher order terms, so that it is recommended to keep a historical time series of previous calculations to identify statistical outliers. An extensive discussion on higher order greeks beyond the treatise below is given by Taleb [56] who is also arguably the first author to stress the importance of higher-order sensitivities. The discussion below is a subjective attempt to focus only on the most relevant higher-order greeks.

2.2.5.1   Vanna

Vanna is the change in vega as a function of spot (*i.e.* Dvega/Dspot). It is arguably the most important cross-greek. Mathematically, vanna is identical to Ddelta/Dvol, *i.e.* the change of delta with respect to changes in the implied volatility. For an option or portfolio with high vanna, it is therefore essential to understand that the volatility used to determine the delta is very important.

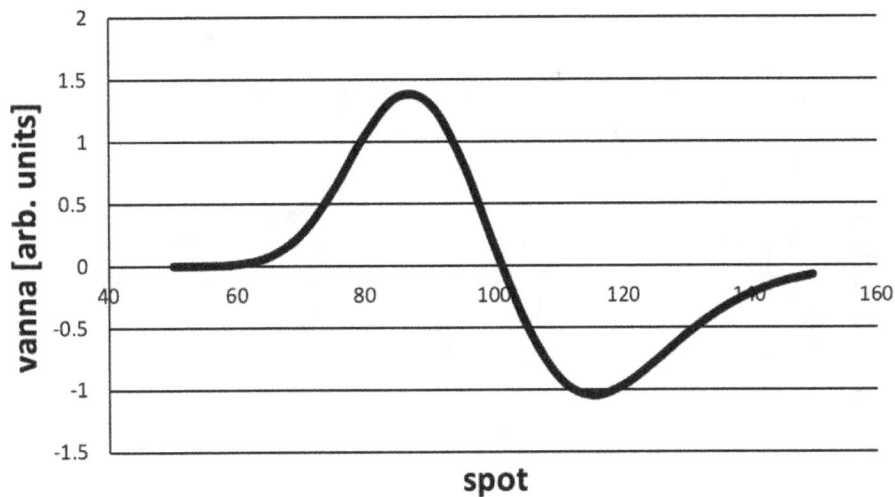

Figure 2.14: Profile of a vanilla option vanna profile for strike = 100, implied volatility = 20%, maturity = 0.5 years, borrow cost = 0, interest rate = 0.

Figure 2.14 depicts the vanna profile of a vanilla option. It is clear that there is a sign change around the strike. Note again that the vanna term has also a direct impact on the option delta. Since the option value is a function of spot S and implied volatility σ, the derivative with respect to spot taking into account the chain rule is given by

$$\frac{dV}{dS} = \frac{\partial V}{\partial S} + \frac{\partial V}{\partial \sigma}\frac{\partial \sigma}{\partial S}. \tag{2.34}$$

In this sense vanna also determines the dynamics of the forward volatility in relation to the spot. It is usually not possible to derive the dynamics from the underlying market data directly. As a consequence, traders need to be aware of the implicit dynamic assumptions a particular model takes in order to understand how this impact the delta. This topic will be discussed later in the context of skew dynamics (see 3.1.5).

2.2.5.2 Zomma

Zomma (Dgamma/Dvol) is the change in gamma as a function of volatility. Especially for stress scenarios, it is vital to understand the zomma behavior, given that it can significantly modify the underlying hedge ratio.

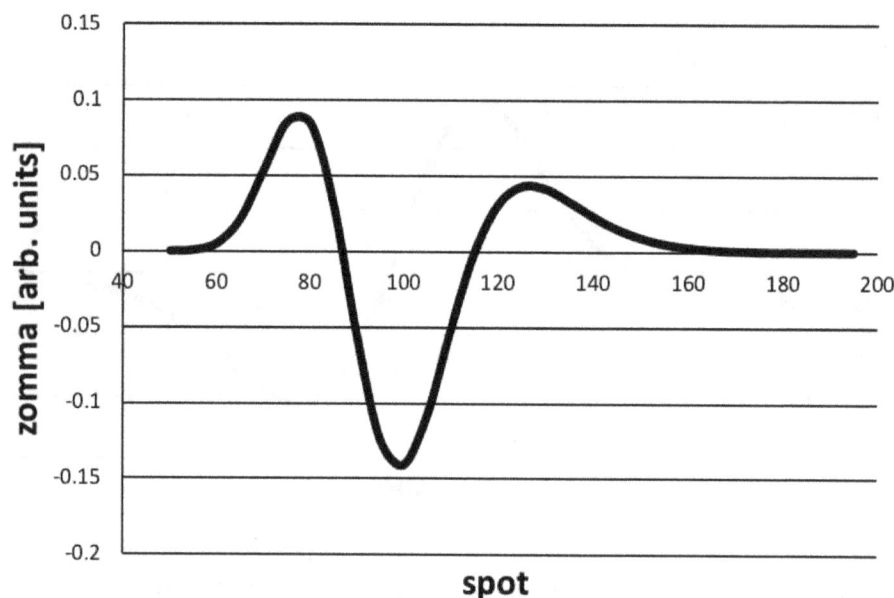

Figure 2.15: Profile of a vanilla option zomma profile for strike = 100, implied volatility = 20%, maturity = 0.5 years, borrow cost = 0, interest rate = 0.

Figure 2.15 depicts the zomma profile of a vanilla option. Zomma is negative in the ATM and slightly ITM/OTM region, but positive for far OTM options. Hence, implied volatility increases lead to a reduction in gamma for ATM options.

2.2.5.3 Volgamma

Volgamma (volga) or vomma is the change in vega as a function of a change in absolute volatility (*i.e.* Dvega/Dvol). It is arguably the most important higher order greek and especially relevant for more exotic derivatives. The expression volgamma follows from its similarity to the gamma term in the canonical BSM partial differential equation (2.27). Volgamma exposure whereby a position loses/gains vega upon an increase/decrease in the volatility parameter mark is a typical sign of wrong-way risk. In other words, the trader is forced to re-hedge the vega in market conditions opposed to the exposure of the book.

It is possible to write down the generic volgamma formula by taking the respective derivative of the price with respect to volatility

$$dV = \frac{\partial V}{\partial \sigma} \delta \sigma + \underbrace{\frac{1}{2} \frac{\partial^2 V}{\partial \sigma^2} \delta \sigma^2}_{volgamma} + O(\delta \sigma^2) \; . \tag{2.35}$$

The partial derivative expression is then as follows

$$d\Gamma_\sigma = \frac{1}{2} \left(\frac{\partial^2 V}{\partial \sigma_t^2} \right)_t d\sigma_t^2 \tag{2.36}$$

To get an idea for the associated cost for the hedging activity, one can take the integral from inception until expiry given by

$$\Gamma_\sigma = \int_0^T d\Gamma_\sigma(t)dt .$$
(2.37)

Pricing models that model the variance process stochastically do typically capture this effect implicitly. To quickly assess the volgamma charge at inception for a fixed maturity derivative it is possible to use the finite difference approximation and do a parallel bump (*e.g.* $\delta\sigma = 1\%$) of the implied volatility surface via

$$\Gamma_\sigma^0 \approx \frac{1}{2}(\frac{V_0(\sigma + \delta\sigma) - 2V_0(\sigma) + V_0(\sigma + \delta\sigma)}{(\delta\sigma)^2})\sigma_0 V_0^2 .$$
(2.38)

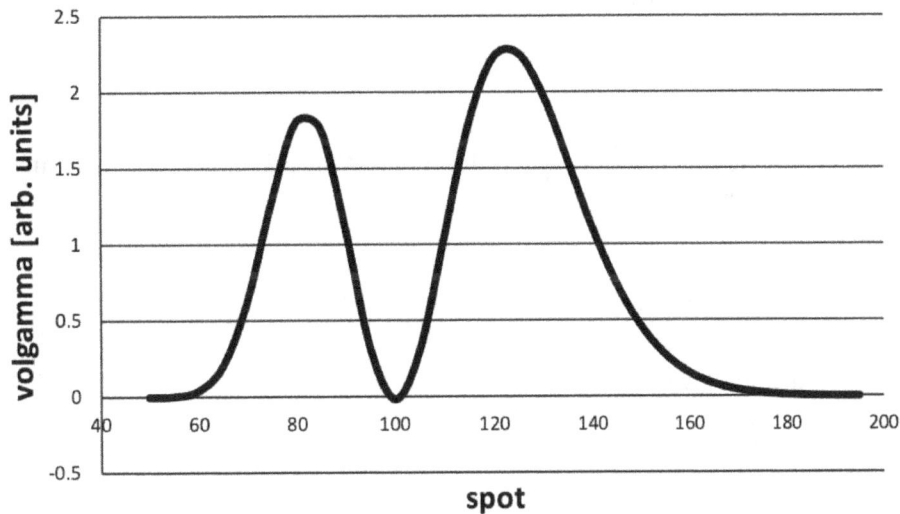

Figure 2.16: Profile of a vanilla option volgamma profile for strike = 100, implied volatility = 20%, maturity = 0.5 years, borrow cost = 0, interest rate = 0.

Figure 2.16 depicts the volgamma profile of a vanilla option. In the case of vanilla options, volgamma is highest for out-of-the-money (OTM) vanilla options, *i.e.* options are worthless in case they expired now. Positive volgamma means that for a long vega position, any (percentage point) increase in volatility generates more profit. Negative volgamma for a short vega position means that for a volatility increase, you lose less. Volgamma or volatility convexity is in particular important for more exotic options. As discussed above, a volgamma profile that reduces the vega of a position in case volatility levels increase forces traders to re-hedge the exposure at a time where implied volatility is expensive. The same is true in case implied volatility decreases: the position gains vega and incurs an additional mark-to-market loss since volatility is falling. The cost of such an adverse volgamma position can be substantial and needs to be estimated upfront as best as possible. In this case, the success or failure of a replication strategy is often determined by a correct or incorrect volgamma (scenario) analysis.

2.2.6 Units

Sound engineering demands to cross-check measurement unit consistency before concluding from it. For traders, this means to know the units in which the risk management system reports the risk figures.

For large portfolios, it is convenient to measure P/L in **units of money for returns in %**. To then make life easier, traders like to express greeks typically in cash terms. The transformation of the greeks above in cash terms goes as follows. The cash-delta or dollar-delta (*i.e.* $\Delta^\$$) is given by

$$\Delta^\$ = \Delta \cdot S_t = \frac{\partial V}{\partial S} \cdot S_t. \tag{2.39}$$

As a consequence, the delta P/L resulting from an x% move on the underlying is

$$P/L = \Delta^\$ \cdot x\%. \tag{2.40}$$

For cash-gamma, the relation is given by

$$\Gamma^\$ = \Gamma \cdot S_t^2 = \frac{\partial^2 V}{\partial S^2} \cdot S_t^2. \tag{2.41}$$

For a move of 1% this results in $\Gamma^{\$,\%} = \frac{\Gamma^\$}{100}$. It follows that the P/L impact due to gamma for an x% move in the underlying is

$$P/L = 50 \cdot \Gamma^{\$,\%} \cdot (x\%)^2. \tag{2.42}$$

2.2.7 Theta-Gamma relation

Recall the BSM equation given by

$$\underbrace{\frac{\partial V}{\partial t}}_{\Theta} + \frac{1}{2}\sigma^2 S^2 \underbrace{\frac{\partial^2 V}{\partial S^2}}_{\Gamma} + rS \underbrace{\frac{\partial V}{\partial S}}_{\Delta} - rV = 0. \tag{2.43}$$

If interest rate contribution is assumed to be effectively zero (which is realistic for a day-to-day change), then the Δ and $-rV$ term drop out of the equation. Hence, what remains is

$$\underbrace{\frac{\partial V}{\partial t}}_{\Theta} = -\frac{1}{2}\sigma^2 \underbrace{S^2 \frac{\partial^2 V}{\partial S^2}}_{\Gamma^\$}, \tag{2.44}$$

or explicitly

$$\Theta = -\frac{1}{2}\sigma^2 \Gamma^\$. \tag{2.45}$$

The expression above is the before mentioned theta-gamma relation, which expresses how much $\Gamma^\$$ one should expect for a given value of Θ assuming a specific input for the volatility parameter σ. This relationship is a crucial metric to determine whether the observed carry of a derivative portfolio is in line with expectation and should be used as a consistency check whenever the dynamics of a trading book appears to be off.

2.2.8 P/L Equation

The formulae above provide the foundation to derive the essential driftless P/L equation governing the dynamics of an option book. Consider a position in an option with a value of $V(S,t)$. Utilizing a standard second-order Taylor expansion, it is possible to express the P/L of the position as a function of the stock price S and time t as

$$
\begin{aligned}
P/L = \delta V(S,t) &= V(S+\Delta S, t+\Delta t) - V(S,t) \\
&\approx \frac{\partial V}{\partial t}\Delta t + \frac{\partial V}{\partial S}(\Delta S) + \frac{1}{2}\frac{\partial^2 V}{\partial S^2}(\Delta S^2) + ... \\
&\approx \Theta \cdot (\Delta t) + \Delta \cdot (\Delta S) + \frac{1}{2}\Gamma(\Delta S)^2,
\end{aligned}
\tag{2.46}
$$

where $\Delta S = S_{t-1} - S_t$ and $\Delta t = 1/252$ (reflecting one trading day for approximately 252 business days in a year). If the option is delta-hedged, then $\Delta = 0$ and the P/L equation simplifies to

$$
P/L = \Theta \cdot (\Delta t) + \frac{1}{2}\Gamma(\Delta S)^2.
\tag{2.47}
$$

Now recall the theta-gamma relationship from above, *i.e.* $\Theta = -\frac{1}{2}S^2\Gamma\sigma^2$. Substituting this expression for Θ in the P/L equation above yields

$$
P/L \approx \frac{1}{2}\Gamma \cdot \left[(\Delta S)^2 - \sigma^2 S^2 \cdot (\Delta t) \right],
\tag{2.48}
$$

where $(\Delta S)^2 = S^2 \cdot (\frac{\Delta S}{S})^2$. This leads to

$$
\begin{aligned}
P/L &\approx \frac{1}{2}\Gamma[(\frac{\Delta S}{S})^2 - \sigma^2 \cdot (\Delta t)] \\
&\approx \frac{1}{2}\Gamma^\$ \left[\underbrace{\left(\frac{\Delta S}{S}\right)^2}_{\text{daily realized variance}} - \underbrace{\sigma^2 \cdot (\Delta t)}_{\text{implied variance}} \right]
\end{aligned}
\tag{2.49}
$$

What does this mean in words? The daily P/L on a delta-hedged option or option portfolio is the cash-gamma weighted difference between the daily market moves (realized variance) and the expectation of this market move as given by the volatility mark of the book. Therefore, the option trader can try to minimize the adverse impact from these driving forces by smoothing the gamma (*e.g.* by booking the option differently; to be discussed later) or improving the realized variance estimate. Another way to look at this is to cast this into the essential question for the fair option value. Indeed, the fair value of the option is given by the implied volatility estimate σ for which the gamma weighted difference between realized and implied variance is zero over the whole lifetime, *i.e.*

$$
P/L = \frac{1}{2}\Gamma^\$ \left[\underbrace{\left(\frac{\Delta S}{S}\right)^2}_{\text{daily realized variance}} - \underbrace{\sigma^2 \cdot (\Delta t)}_{\text{implied variance}} \right] = 0
\tag{2.50}
$$

Expressed in variance terms, this means

$$
\sigma^2 = \frac{\int_0^T \Gamma^\$ (\frac{dS^2}{S})}{\int_0^T \Gamma^\$ dt}.
\tag{2.51}
$$

The above is valid if the averaging kernel $\Gamma^{\$}$ is always well defined, *i.e.* there are no spurious sign changes at different spots and time. While this is true for path-independent vanilla options, exotic options are a different story.

Finally, without a formal proof, the P/L of a delta-hedge option under a GBM process entails in principle three types of risks [57]:

- **variance risk**: the risk that the realized variance exceeds to implied variance over the path
- **vega risk**: the risk resulting from hedging the option at the *wrong* implied volatility resulting in an incorrect hedge ratio
- **model risk**: the risk resulting from using a model which does not account for the possible high path-dependency of the derivative

Therefore, derivative traders are not only exposed to variance risk. Note that the analysis ignore risks related to other forward components such as dividends or stochastic rates.

2.2.9 Trading Rules

Recall again the theta-gamma relation given by

$$\Theta = -\frac{1}{2}\Gamma^{\$}\sigma^2 \qquad (2.52)$$

and define $\Theta_{\text{per day}} = \Theta/365$. This yields the expression

$$365 \cdot \Theta_{\text{per day}} = -\frac{1}{2}\sigma^2\Gamma^{\$,\%} \cdot 100$$

$$-\underbrace{\frac{365 \cdot 2}{100}}_{=7.3} \cdot \frac{\Theta_{\text{per day}}}{\Gamma^{\$,\%}} = \sigma^2 \qquad (2.53)$$

It is then possible to derive the breakeven volatility, *i.e.* the average daily move or return required to offset the cost incurred by the Θ of the option. The breakeven volatility is given by

$$\sigma^2_{\text{breakeven}} = -2\frac{\Theta}{\Gamma^{\$}} \ . \qquad (2.54)$$

For example, consider a long vanilla option position with USD 500'000 $\Gamma^{\$}$ paid for by USD 5'000 Θ per day. To offset the theta cost, the break-even daily (close-to-close) move x on the asset in either direction has to be at least

$$-\Theta = 50 \cdot \Gamma^{\$,\%} \cdot (x\%)^2$$

$$x\% = \sqrt[2]{\frac{-\Theta}{50 \cdot \Gamma^{\$,\%}}} = \sqrt[2]{\frac{-(-5000)}{50 \cdot 500'000}} \approx 1.4\% \ . \qquad (2.55)$$

This result can now be translated into an annual volatility measure $\sigma = \sqrt[2]{252} \cdot 1.4\% \approx 22.6\%$ by scaling with the square root of time. Hence, the fair value position should, in theory, be marked at this level currently unless there is a valid reason not to do so. In other words, to pay for the daily theta, a delta-hedge position needs to move at least 1.4% a day in any direction from the current spot level.

As a recap, theta and gamma are proportional but with opposite signs. To benefit from the convexity (*i.e.* being long gamma), one needs to pay theta. Being short gamma means exposure to tail risk and negative convexity. Therefore, the position receives compensation in terms of theta as the optionality decays away over time.

2.2.10 Delta-hedging and trading the gamma

Consider the long position in the vanilla call again before. The delta of the option is *positive*, *i.e.* if the asset price goes up, the value of the option goes up, too. To make the option value locally invariant to the spot move, it is necessary to *sell* the underlying asset in the correct hedge ratio. This fraction of assets to sell at this local point is exactly the local delta value of the option. Hence, for a long call option position, the traders shorts the underlying asset at the exact fractional amount equal to the option delta at this point. This is illustrated in Figure 2.17 by the two straight lines (solid: option delta, dotted: short stock). However, recall that the option value is also driven by the second derivative with respect to spot, *i.e.* gamma. The gamma impacts the value of the delta as the spot moves. The functional profile of gamma is convex (dotted black squares), and this plays in favor of the holder of the call: irrespective of whether the stock moves up or down, the difference between the option value (increasing or decreasing) and profit/loss on the short stock position (loss or profit) is *always positive*. This explains how it is possible to make money by *actively* delta-hedging an

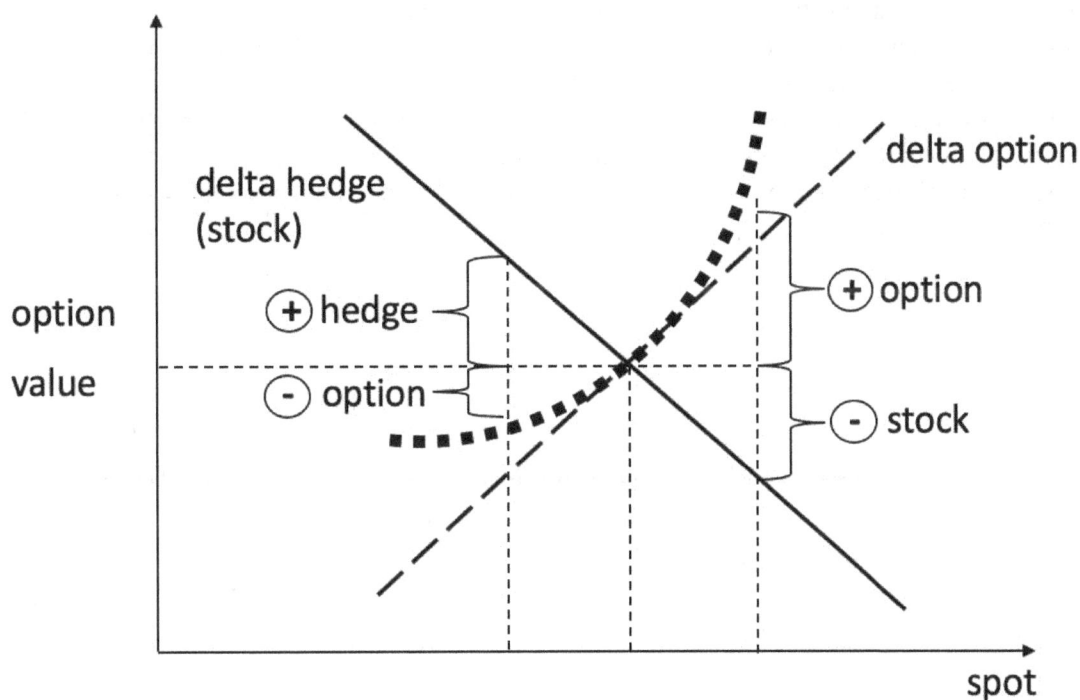

Figure 2.17: Option value versus underlying spot price, including the gamma profile. The option delta (dotted diagonal line) and the delta of the hedge (solid diagonal line) offset each other locally for small spot moves. Large moves in spot either way results in an *excess* P/L gain via the hedge or option value since the gamma of the option steers the option value in a nonlinear fashion.

option (intraday). By adjusting the delta through buying or selling the underlying such that it is again locally offsetting, it is possible to realize the mark-to-market profit and thereby offset the loss incurred on the theta. In other words, trading the gamma of the option means capturing or locking in the variance of the underlying. Does this mean it is always possible to fully capture the implied variance used to price the option? The answer is no because the gamma of the option is not constant for every spot level of the underlying (recall Figure 2.11). In other words, it depends at which spot level in comparison to the option strike the underlying realizes the variance. If this happens in a region far away from the strike where the gamma value is low (see path A in the stylized example in Figure 2.18), the position incurs a loss even if the realized variance exceeds the implied *on average*. On the other hand, if the variance is high close to the strike and expiry (path B in Figure 2.18), it is very likely that the high gamma also provides high P/L volatility. Hence, there is a clear path-dependency to the P/L of a gamma position in the case of vanilla option as it matters that the realized variance needs to exceed the implied variance at the right time. When to rebalance the delta intraday is a matter of skill unless one defines tight bands which are automatically exercised via the trade execution system. The (historical or implied) break-even volatility is one indicator as to when it makes sense to re-adjust the delta hedge. For a short gamma position, it is obvious that the spot should ideally not move at all so that the earned theta is conserved.

When comparing the gamma profile (Figure 2.11 with the one for vega (Figure 2.13 it is clear that they exhibit an opposite behavior towards expiry, *i.e.* vega decays whereas gamma grows with time to maturity ($\Gamma_{call,put} \sim \frac{1}{\sqrt{T}}$ vs $\Gamma_{call,put} \sim \sqrt{T}$. As an intuitive explanation for this behavior one should recall that gamma trading means capturing intraday or close-to-close variance. If an option is *short dated*, then a large intraday asset price move can alter the (final) option value significantly. Hence, the sensitivity to spot moves will increase. If an option is longer dated, then a significant intraday asset price move does not alter its (final) value as much because over the remaining lifetime a lot may still happen. Conversely, a vega move for a longer-dated option impacts the probability of expiring ITM much more versus a shorter dated derivative for which one captures the effect via gamma.

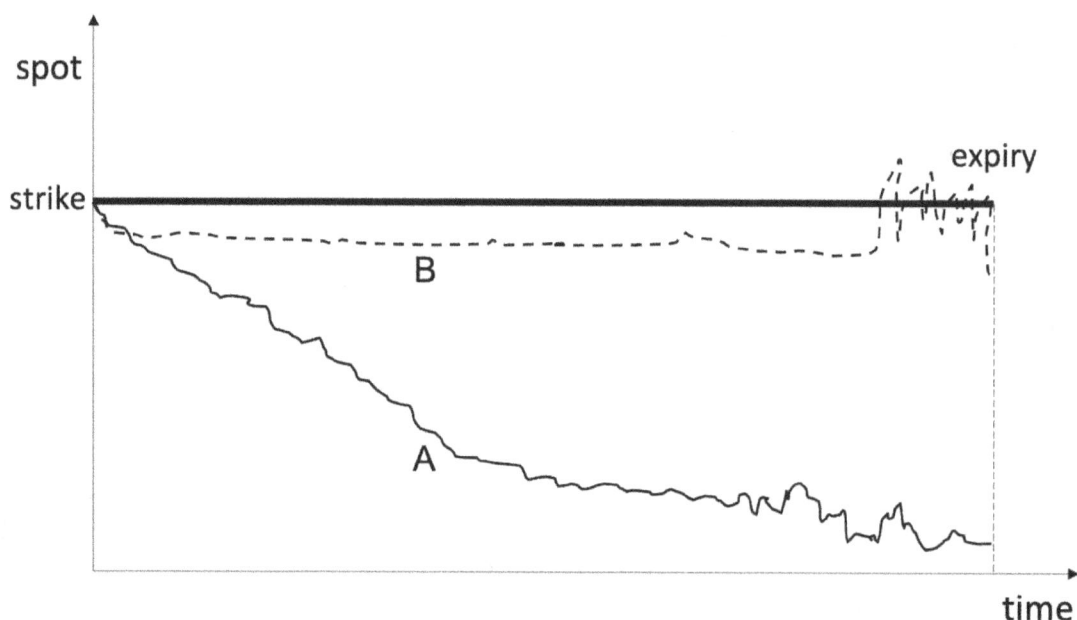

Figure 2.18: Path-dependence of the realized spot variance versus the option strike price for two hypothetical price paths A and B. Even if A and B have the same overall variance along the path, the P/L of the delta-hedged option will be very different.

When delta-hedging an option, the trading of the underlying will at some point impact its price in the market. It is intuitive that the impact must be a function of the sequential volume traded. While market microstructure [58, 59] modeling and execution algorithms are beyond the scope of this book, it is useful to know the widely accepted impact model. Many studies across several asset classes have demonstrated that the price change induced by the sequential execution of a total volume Q follows approximately the so-called $\sqrt{Q}$ law [60]. This means that the market impact I is proportional to $I \sim \sigma \sqrt{\frac{Q}{V}}$ where σ denotes the daily volatility of the asset and V the daily traded volume. The price difference between the average price over the total order and the price of the first execution is called *slippage* . Hence, minimizing slippage is a key requirement of a good execution algorithm or broker. In the case of derivatives with discontinuities (see Chapter 3.1.9), good execution is crucial given the nonlinearity of the payoff.

2.2.11 Vanilla Options: Terminology and Strategies

It is now required to introduce some essential terminology, which characterizes common derivative attributes. For starters, vanilla options come in two main types: Those who must only be exercised at maturity (European) and those which can be exercised any day during the lifetime (American). Finally, options that are only exercisable at certain points in time are called Bermudan options. Vanilla options can be issued or written by market participants such as banks, broker-dealers, or market makers and then be traded OTC or on exchanges as listed instruments. In addition, the underlying company itself may issue so-called exchange-traded *warrants*, which normally share the same principle characteristics as options. However, upon exercise, the company will issue new shares to settle the contract. Moreover, the maturity of warrants is often longer compared to regular options, which often makes them a source for longer-dated volatility (this is similar to Convertible Bonds, see 10). Note that the term (derivative) warrants is sometimes also used to denote light-exotic Structured Products (see chapter 9) whereby the underlying call or put is often leveraged further. Over its lifetime, the value of an option can be decomposed into its intrinsic value and its time value (see Figure 2.19). At expiry, the option will be determined by its intrinsic value, *i.e.* it is either worth something (referred to as 'in-the-money', **ITM**) or not (referred to as 'out-of-the money', **OTM**). The time value reflects the probability of the option to expire ITM and will in general by highest when there is most time to expiry. This is true even if the option is OTM at the time.

The strike of an option also impacts the payout significantly. In general, three different strike levels are distinguished (see Figure 2.20):

- **ATM (spot/forward)**: "At The Money spot/forward"
  → Strike equal to current spot or forward level
- **OTM (spot/forward)**: "Out of The Money spot/forward"
  → Strike at a spot or forward level for which the intrinsic option value is zero
- **ITM (spot/forward)**: "In The Money spot/forward"
  → Strike at a spot or forward level for which the option already has intrinsic value

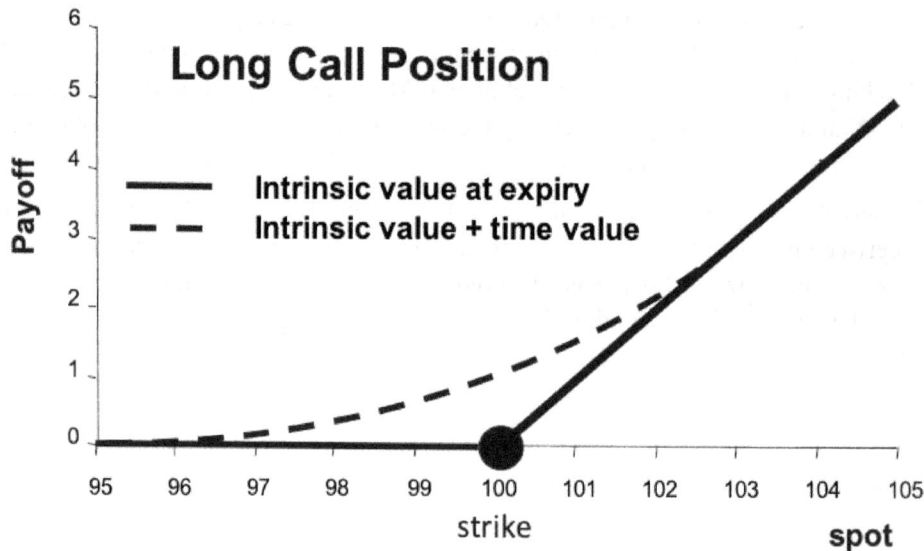

Figure 2.19: Illustration of the intrinsic value and time value of a long position in a vanilla call option.

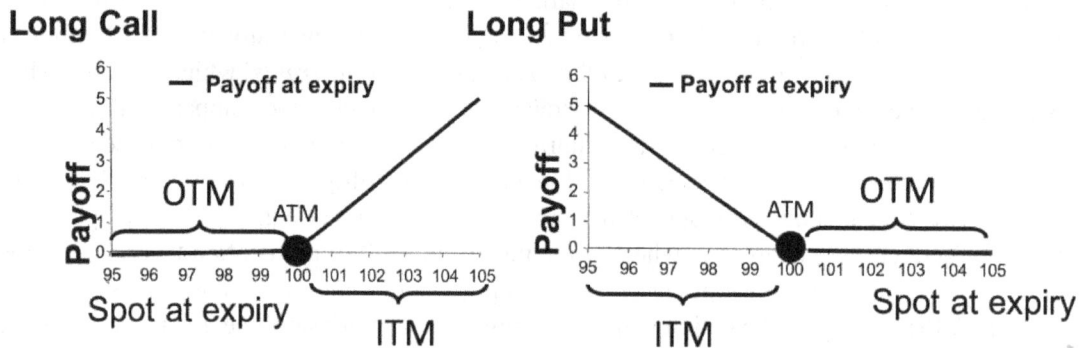

Figure 2.20: Illustration of the intrinsic value and time value for a long vanilla call and put position.

The combination of a set of vanilla options can provide more elaborate trading strategies both in strike and time (term structure) [61] space. The most basic strike space strategies are spread trades such as call- and put spreads (see Figure 2.21). In these strategies, two options of the same type but different strike and positional direction are traded. For example, a long 100 / 110 strike call spread position is composed of a long 100 strike call and a short 110 call position of an identical maturity. At expiry, the maximum payout on the option position (ignoring the respective premia paid / received) is the strike difference, *i.e.* 110-100 = 10. In other words, a call- or put spread caps the possible payout at the strike of the second option leg. Call- and put spreads are important option leg combinations implicitly or directly embedded in more exotic option payouts. Moreover, they are important elements when analyzing the time dynamics of the shape of the implied volatility surface. The volatility surface dynamics is examined more explicitly in Section 3.1.5.

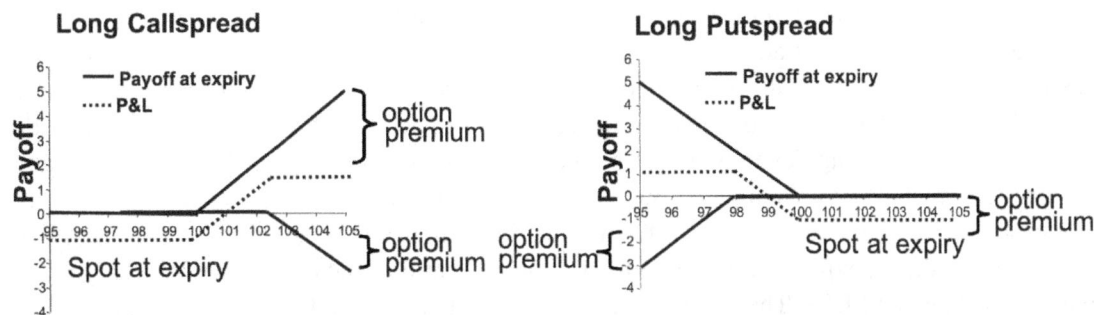

Figure 2.21: Illustration of a call- and put spread payoff.

2.2.12 Vanilla Options: Put-Call Parity

European vanilla call and put options of same strike and maturity are related via the so-called Put-Call parity condition. This relation is model independent. Violation of Put-Call parity is an arbitrage opportunity and therefore a consistency check (among others) for any volatility surface.

Put-Call parity is expressed as

$$C_t^E(K,T) - P_t^E(K,T) + div_t = S_t - K \exp[-r(T-t)] , \tag{2.56}$$

whereby $C_t^E(K,T)$ and $P_t^E(K,T)$ denote the call and put option values for the same asset for the same strike K and maturity T including the expected dividend div_t at time t.

For example, for a stock trading at 100 and a European call option expiring in 9 months struck at 110 valued at 9, with interest rates as 5% p.a., the corresponding put must be worth

$$P = C - S + K = 9 - 100 + 110 \cdot \exp[-0.05 \cdot 3/4] = 14.95 . \tag{2.57}$$

The derivation is straightforward based on the fact that C-P is equivalent to being long the stock S. Hence, selling the stock against C-P creates a fully delta-hedged position. At expiry, if the stock is above the strike, the payout on the call is S-K, the put is zero and the stock -S. The sum of these components is S-K-S=-K. The identical result, -K, is obtained if the stock is below the strike. Hence, the portfolio always guarantees to be worth at least -K, so that one can discount it back to the present. In other words, a position of long 1 stock + long 1 put (premium = -10) is equivalent to going long 1 call (premium = -10). Hence, in a way, a put is a call, and a call is a put.

Put-Call parity does not hold for American options. This is because the short position (*i.e.* either the put or call) might be early exercised, which creates an unhedged exposure compared to the stock price. In other words, it is then impossible to know today how much the portfolio is worth in the future. However, in the absence of dividends, it is possible to show that it is never optimal to *early exercise* an American call. The American put, on the other hand, needs to be exercised below a certain spot level as a function of the strike. The early exercise of American options in the presence of dividends will be revisited later.

2.2.13 Vanilla Options: Listed vs. OTC

Financial products such as vanilla options are either exchange-traded (*i.e.* listed) or traded between two counterparties directly. The latter is a so-called over-the-counter (OTC) transaction. When dealing with a listed contract, it is crucial to consider the contract multiplier (*i.e.* contract size) of the instrument. Whereas OTC trades typically have a multiplier of 1 by default, a listed contract unit (as known as 'lot') is often equivalent to 100 or more individual options. The final fixing for stock options is typically the official exchange closing price (*e.g.* at 17.30 for Swiss stocks). For index options, the official fixing depends: It can be the exchange closing price or the EDSP (Exchange Delivery Settlement Price). An intraday auction effectively determines the EDSP before the close of the exchange (*e.g.* from 10.20 until 11.00). Hence, for index options, the fixing terms need to be known. Index futures expire every 3 months starting in March of the respective year whereby the final price is then the EDSP. The months of the year carry letters from F to Z (Jan = F, Feb = G,..., and Dec = Z). Hence, the 4 future contracts of this year are H1, M1, U1 and Z1. Listed options will sometimes also be labeled this way.

2.2.14 Vanilla Options: implied volatility surface

The term *volatility* is associated with various meanings. In the financial or trading context, volatility is defined as the standard deviation of some variance. Then, it has typically these two primary meanings:

(*i*) **historical volatility**: realized volatility of price returns over a certain time and measure, *e.g.* the annualized standard deviation of daily stock returns:

$$
\sigma_{realized} = \sqrt{\frac{252}{n-1}\sum_{i=1}^{n}(r_i - r')^2} \,, \tag{2.58}
$$

where $r_i = \ln(\frac{S_t}{S_{t-1}})$ and $r' = \frac{1}{n}\sum_{i=1}^{n} r_i$. The expression above for the daily volatility can then be multiplied by a factor $\sqrt{A}$ whereby A is the respective return frequency. This allows the (daily) measure to be translated to other time averages. For example, in order to obtain the annualized volatility, assuming 252 trading days, the calculation is $\sigma_{realized,252} = \sqrt{252} \cdot \sigma_{realized}$.

(*ii*) **implied volatility**: the volatility implied by option or derivative market price quotes for a specific underlying, maturity and strike as backed out from an option pricing model (*e.g.* BSM).

Before discussing implied volatility further, it is worth pointing out some details on the calculation of realized volatility. First, equation 2.58 is only the most basic way of measuring the close-to-close realized volatility over n days. This measure cannot represent any drift or potential overnight jumps, which could for example occur following earnings announcements after trading hours. Moreover, the convergence of the measure is often not good for smaller sample sizes. One advanced calculation method which can handle drift, overnight jumps and is efficient for small sample sizes is the Yang-Zhang measure [62]. The calculation takes into account not only close prices, but also the opening and intraday high and low. While the formula is somewhat more complicated, it is still trivial to implement.

In colloquial terms, implied volatility is a metric for the expectation of the market for the future realized volatility of an asset. Unless specified otherwise, going forward, the term volatility means implied volatility in the context of option pricing models. In an ideal world, the realized and implied volatility turns out the same. However, this is typically not the case and thereby also a source for trading opportunities.

BSM assumes a flat implied volatility surface in strike and expiry (as known as *term structure*), but this was never really in line with the market [61]. Already Black &Scholes [7] and later

Macbeth & Merville [63] observed that options of different strikes and maturities trade at different implied volatility levels. Nevertheless, after the 1987 crash, the volatility skew became more pronounced [64, 65, 66, 67].

For a given maturity T, how do vanilla options with different strikes then trade at different volatilities? Figure 2.22 illustrates the four common implied volatility shapes in the strike space for a fixed option expiry. In the stock market one typically see volatility surfaces with a 'skew'

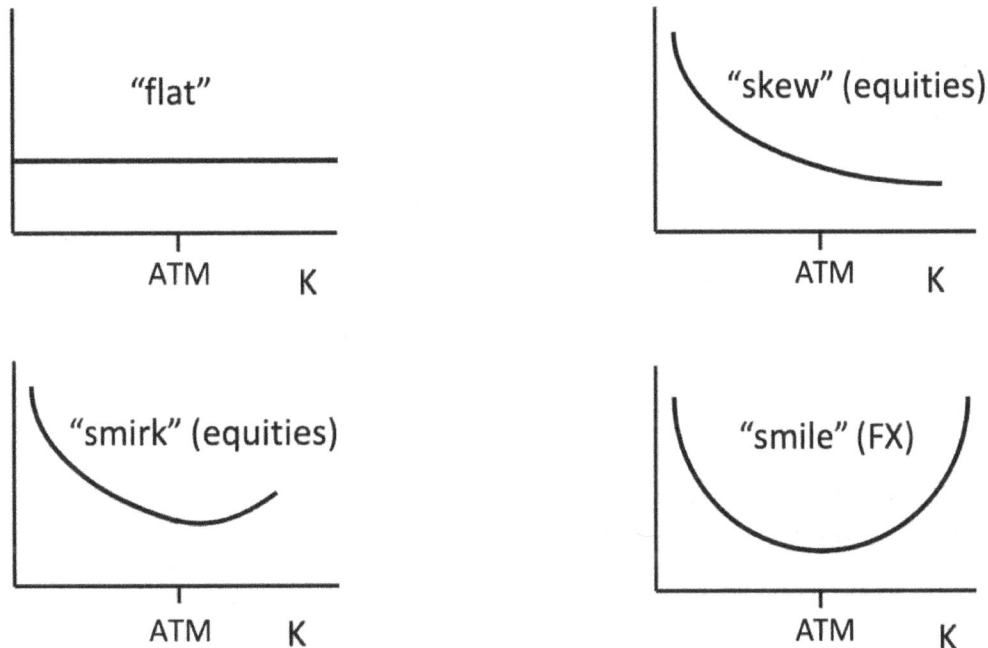

Figure 2.22: Illustration of the four common volatility surface shapes for a fixed maturity in strike space.

shape reflecting the fact that downward moves such as sell-offs typically happen much faster than rallies to the upside. This observation is often referred to as the *implied leverage effect* whereby a large (adverse) market price move has direct impact on the leverage within the company's capital structure [68, 69]. Moreover, this surface is dynamic, *i.e.* it can change somewhat from day to day. Typical transformations are illustrated in Figure 2.23. As a side note, it appears that the market is often overreacting in skew relating price changes especially for longer dated derivatives [70].

These movements may generate significant P/L variance in a derivative portfolio. Parallel shift sensitivity as already been identified as 'vega' (see 2.2.4). Given that the vega calculation entails only a parallel shift of the whole curve, the quantification is relatively straightforward. Contrary to this, skew and kurtosis exposure is non-trivial to quantify consistently given that the curve perturbation is more complex by definition.

Measuring absolute implied volatility historically is relatively simple. However, it is important to consider a consistent reference (*e.g.* strike), *i.e.* normalize it somehow with respect to the current market level / regime. Trading absolute volatility via vanilla options is often employed via straddles (long/short call strike K plus long/short put strike K) or strangles (long/short call strike $(K+X)$ plus long/short put strike $(K-X)$) in order to eliminate at least locally the P/L effect of other greeks such

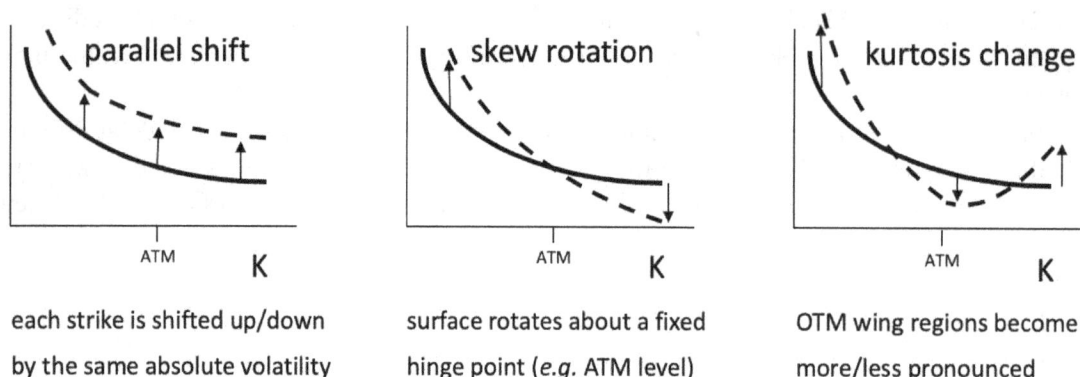

each strike is shifted up/down   surface rotates about a fixed   OTM wing regions become

by the same absolute volatility   hinge point (*e.g.* ATM level)   more/less pronounced

Figure 2.23: Illustration of common volatility surface transformations.

as delta given the opposite sign of the respective greeks in a call and put (see Figure 2.24).

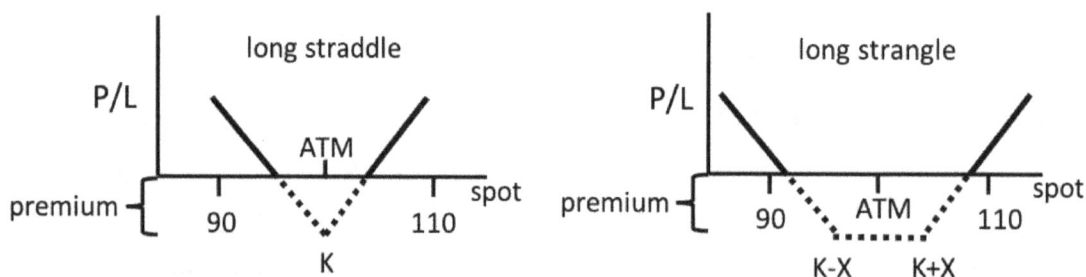

Figure 2.24: Illustration of a long straddle and long strangle position.

Traders mostly assume a diffusive Brownian framework to convert (daily) volatility to different time frames quickly

$$\sigma_t = \sigma_{\text{daily}} \cdot \sqrt{\text{days}} \ . \tag{2.59}$$

For example, as already shown in the break-even volatility derivation, the annualized volatility (assuming 256 trading days) given a daily standard deviation of 2% is: $2\% \cdot \sqrt{256} = 32\%$ [5]. The frequently heard statement "volatility scales with the square root of time" is formally not correct; rather, volatility is the standard deviation scaled by the square root of time *in the case* of a Brownian process. It is wrong to assume that the latter is always true in all markets or market conditions.

Within the framework of a risk management system, it is essential to know whether volatility is expressed in business or calendar days. Some systems define volatility based on business days instead of calendar days. Converting calendar-day referenced volatility into business day volatility requires scaling by

$$\sqrt{\frac{\text{business days to expiry}/\text{business days per year}}{\text{calendar days to expiry}/365}} \ . \tag{2.60}$$

---

[5]The general scaling relation can be expressed using a Levy exponent as $\sigma_t = \sigma_{\text{daily}} \cdot t^{1/\alpha}$. For $\alpha = 2$ one recovers the Brownian scaling law.

Finally, it is important to define the term *forward volatility* in a quantitative manner. Whereas spot volatility refers to implied volatility starting today and ending at some point in the future, forward volatility refers to a volatility period already starting the future. Many volatility trading instruments (see Chapter 4) or forward starting derivatives are explicit bets on this quantity. Because variance is additive, volatility between two dates is explicitly linked given by

$$\sigma_{t_{n-m},t_n} = \sqrt{\frac{\sigma_{t_0,t_n}^2(t_n - t_0) - \sigma_{t_0,t_{n-m}}^2(t_{n-m} - t_0)}{(t_n - t_{n-m})}} \, , \tag{2.61}$$

whereby σ_{t_0,t_n}^2 is the spot volatility in the period $t_0 < t_n$ and $\sigma_{t_0,t_{n-m}}^2$ the spot volatility in the period $t_0 < t_{n-m}$. Table 2.1 shows a stylized example for the calculation. Note that this assumes that the skew is constant (see below).

t_n	$t_{n-m} - t_n$	σ_{t_0,t_n}	σ_{t_0,t_n}^2	σ_{t_{n-m},t_n}^2	σ_{t_{n-m},t_n}
30	0-30	31.00%	9.61%	9.61%	31.00%
60	30-60	28.00%	7.84%	6.07%	24.64%
90	60-90	26.50%	7.02%	5.39%	23.21%
120	90-120	26.25%	6.89%	6.50%	25.49%
150	120-150	26.00%	6.76%	6.24%	24.97%
180	150-180	26.00%	6.76%	6.76%	26.00%
360	180-360	25.90%	6.71%	6.66%	25.80%
720	360-720	25.50%	6.50%	6.30%	25.09%
1080	720-1080	25.00%	6.25%	5.75%	23.97%

Table 2.1: Example of the forward volatility calculation (last column) based on implied spot volatilities for different maturities.

2.2.15 Vanilla Options: Trading skew

The mathematical definition of skew [67, 71] is the first derivative of the implied volatility surface with respect to the strike, *i.e.*

$$\text{skew} = \frac{\partial \sigma(K,T)}{\partial K} \, . \tag{2.62}$$

Alternatively, in the context of the return distribution, skew refers to the 3rd moment, *i.e.* skewness $= E[(\frac{r-\mu}{\sigma})^3]$. If the skew is quantified consistently, then it is possible to determine when it is (historically) rich or cheap. Several simple measures exist to quantify skew (changes) based on an implied volatility surface. These include for example the 90% - 110% volatility spread with relation to the ATM volatility levels

$$\text{skew} = \sigma(90\%ATMK,T) - \sigma(110\%ATMK,T) \, , \tag{2.63}$$

or, alternatively, the volatility difference between the 25% and 50% option delta

$$\text{skew} = \sigma(25\%\Delta\text{Call},T) - \sigma(50\%\Delta\text{Call},T) \, . \tag{2.64}$$

It turns out that it is non-trivial to derive a measure that is entirely independent of spot and the absolute volatility level. Intuitively, it makes sense to normalize a skew measure to make it more invariant to changes in other parameters. One measure which practitioners use often and which exhibits these properties is

$$\text{skew} = \frac{\sigma(25\%\Delta \text{Put}, T) - \sigma(25\%\Delta \text{Call}, T)}{\sigma(50\%\Delta Call, T)} \ . \tag{2.65}$$

In this context, it is a reasonable question why practitioners sometimes work in the delta and not in the strike space when quantifying skew or other curve properties? Note that the delta is not only the hedge ratio of the option, but also a proxy for the risk-neutral probability of reaching the strike [6]. A low delta (*e.g.* 10%) is therefore equivalent to a low strike and a high delta (*e.g.* 100%) to a high strike option. The ATM delta is typically around 50%. Hence, one is somewhat eliminating the spot and absolute volatility dependence by using this metric.

Trading skew with vanillas typically involves trading strike spreads for the same maturity. For example, trading delta hedged, vega neutral call or put spreads (PS), *e.g.* go long the ATM / 90% ATM PS. Other strategies include so-called risk reversals (long/short OTM Put plus short/long OTM Call) or the 25 delta risk reversal (short/long 25 delta put plus long/short 25 delta call). Figure 2.25 shows the respective P/L impact given a change in the skew shape.

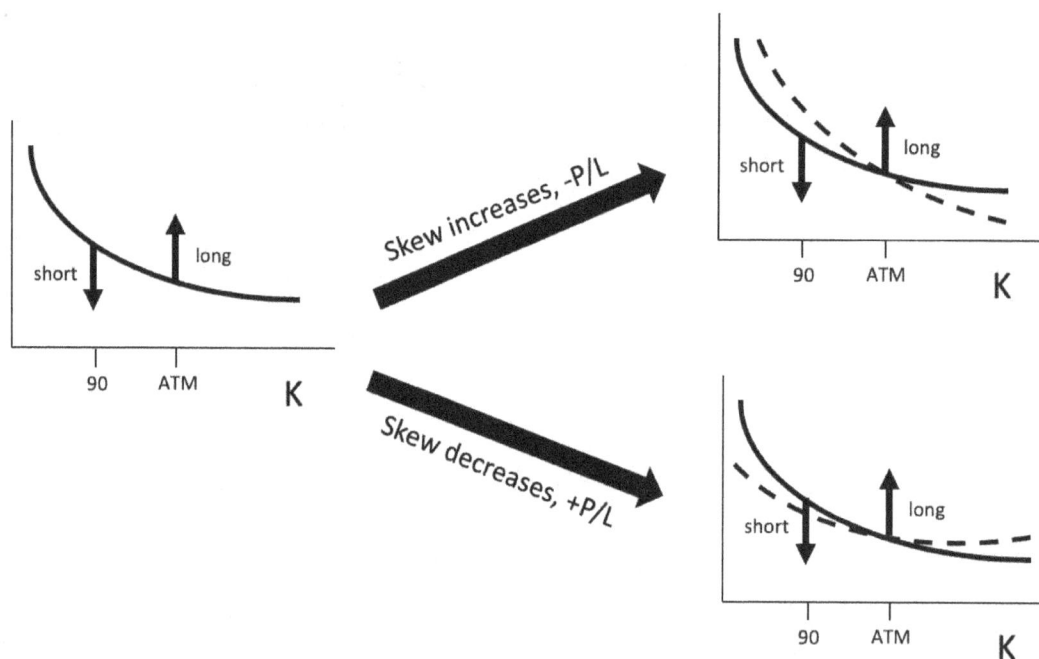

Figure 2.25: Illustration of the P/L resulting in a typical call- or put spread skew trade given a steeping or flattening of the curve.

---

[6]This is formally not correct, but increasingly accurate with decreasing time to expiry

2.2.16 Vanilla Options: Trading kurtosis

The mathematical definition of kurtosis [67, 71] is the second derivative of the implied volatility surface with respect to the strike, *i.e.*

$$\text{skew} = \frac{\partial^2 \sigma(K,T)}{\partial K^2} \ . \tag{2.66}$$

Alternatively, in the context of the return distribution, kurtosis is defined as the 4th moment, *i.e.* kurtosis $= E[(\frac{r-\mu}{\sigma})^4]$. If it was already tricky to measure skew consistently, kurtosis is even more difficult. This is also because when calculating the curvature or fourth moment of the distribution, noise in the data has even more impact. Typically, the finite difference approximation can be used directly (centered on a particular strike region of the curve), *i.e.*

$$\text{kurtosis} = \frac{[\sigma(90\%K,T) + \sigma(110\%K,T) - 2 \cdot \sigma(100\%K,T)]}{10\%} \ . \tag{2.67}$$

Practitioners refer to kurtosis trades also as exposure in implied volatility *convexity* (see also 2.2.5.3). Some typical vanilla kurtosis trades include butterfly (spreads) or in general selling/buying ATM and far OTM options vs. buying/selling closer OTM options. The butterfly spread is a more advanced combination of vanillas, *e.g.* long ATM call butterfly = short 2 times ATM call, long 1 ITM call, long 1 OTM call (see Figure 2.26. Here, a rise in the volatility in the wings gives positive P/L. Note that there exist many more 'wing' spreads combinations (*e.g.* condor, irons etc.).

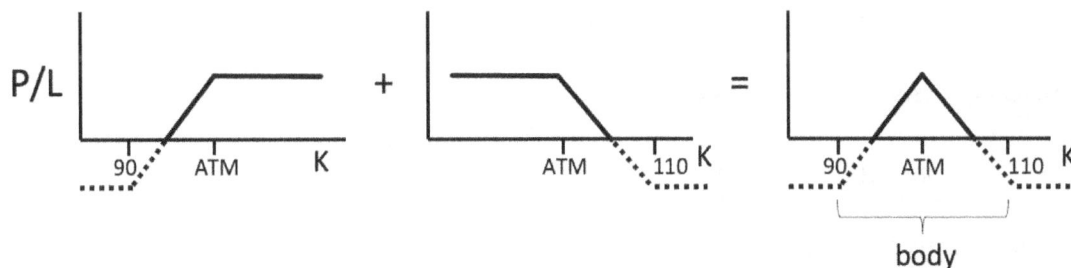

Figure 2.26: Illustration of the construction of a long butterfly spread via vanilla options.

It is often difficult to fully insulate skew and kurtosis exposure in a vanilla trade. Skew trades are typically simpler and therefore also easier to monitor/realize. Sometimes skew and kurtosis sensitivity is linked to parameters in stochastic volatility models (*e.g.* Heston, see Section 3.1.7). In such a setting, to obtain large skew, the volatility-of-volatility (VoV) parameter needs to be high, and the spot-volatility correlation parameter negative. The balance between these variables compared to a historical analysis may deliver (model-dependent) trading opportunities. The spot-volatility dynamics (*i.e.* how does implied volatility change with spot?) in a given market regime is also an important factor determining the success of a skew or kurtosis trade. Given its importance in general, spot-volatility dynamics is discussed in detail later (see section 3.1.5).

2.2.17 Vanilla Options: Exercise Risks

If the underlying for an option trades near its strike close to expiry, the trader who is short the contract often suffers from the large short gamma position. In addition, at expiry the derivative may get *pinned* on the strike (pin risk) [72] . The term 'pin' formally refers to the option expiring exactly at the strike. In practice, the definition is more lose, meaning that depending on the clearing exchange, options do only get auto-exercised if the closing price is above a specific interval with respect to the strike (*e.g.* \$0.01 on the OCC [7]). Otherwise, the exchange requires an exercise notice from the option holder.

For example, imagine a position of long the 100% strike put, short the 100% strike call and long the underlying. The aggregate position looks perfectly hedged, but now the market closes exactly at 100%. Should the trader exercise or not? The problem is that one can exercise the put, deliver the underlying and *hope* that the calls are not exercised. If one decides not to exercise the put, the hope is that the calls get exercised so that one can deliver the underlying. Hence, the trader is in both scenarios unsure about the delta position following the option expiry.

These issues are further complicated by the fact that the clearing process does not coincide with the exchange close precisely. Hence, if important news hit the market after the close, it might be beneficial to exercise an OTM option to receive or get rid of the underlying delta. Typically, pinning occurs because traders try to monetize sizeable long gamma positions before expiry. Since the theta of the option increases as well, it is often necessary to trade the gamma of the option by trading the underlying (buy low / sell high) in increasingly smaller amounts to break-even overall.

Some remedies for the situation, which are not only applicable in a pinning scenario, are to either take a view or close out (*i.e.* buy back or sell depending on the position) the contract before it expires. This interest can be observed if the *open interest* on a particular strike is high and the stock has been hovering around the strike price for some time already . The open interest is a quantity reported by the exchange for listed option contracts. A high open interest indicates that there may be a desire to trade/close the option for a particular strike and expiry.

2.2.18 Vanilla Options: Corporate Actions

In particular, in the context of equity underlyings and related (vanilla or exotic) derivatives so-called Corporate Actions (CA) may significantly impact the stock price, its dynamics and related instruments. CAs are extraordinary events, which may occur during the lifetime of a company and typically alter the stock price. CAs include:

- dividend payments or rights (regular & extraordinary)
- (reverse) stock splits
- company spin-offs
- mergers & acquisitions (takeover)
- rights issues
- share buybacks

Sometimes CAs is a combination of the above. Because CAs affect the stock price and therefore typically the *moneyness* of associated derivatives, the contract terms must be adjusted to render the contract invariant to these in principle *a priori* unpredictable changes. Missing a CA or failing to readjust a position may be very costly and introduce spurious P/L.

2.2.19 Corporate Actions: Dividend payments

Dividend payments (DP) are the most common CA and are effectively priced in when creating the forward based on announced dividends or estimates. Hence, uncertainty in dividends is a market risk participants factor in when pricing the forward of the derivative contract, *i.e.* it is not something the

---

[7]https://www.theocc.com/

contract can be adjusted for after the fact. For example, in case a company starts or ceases dividend payments, the terms of derivative contracts are typically not adjusted. Figure 2.27 illustrates the mechanics of dividend payments. Following the approval of the suggested dividend amount by the company's General Assembly (GA), the stock price drops on the so-called dividend *ex-date* by the amount of the dividend declared. The actual payment of the dividend to the shareholder then happens (several weeks) later, but the trading book accrues the dividend already to offset the drop in the stock price on the $ex-date$. Some stocks pay periodic dividends as a cash distribution (from its earnings) to investors. In Europe and Asia, this is typically done annually, in the US quarterly. Recall that a high dividend (yield) lowers the forward and thereby directly affects the expectation value of an option written on the asset.

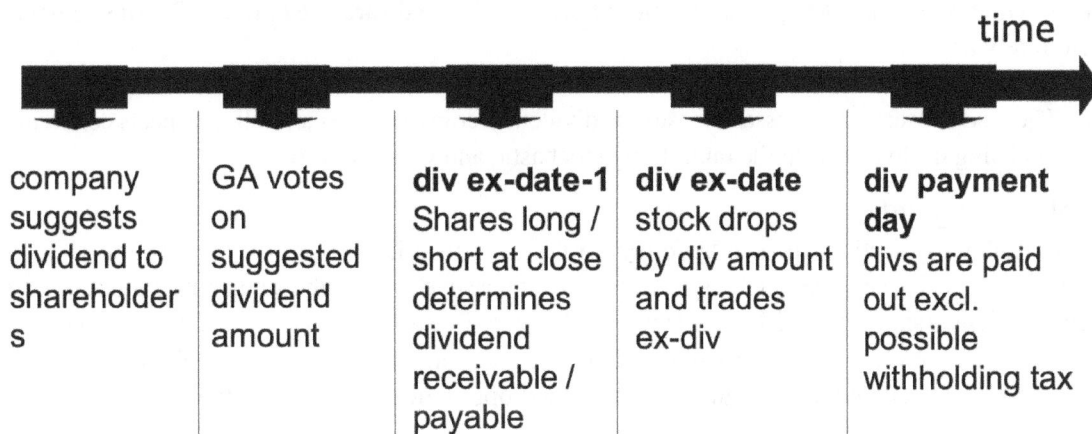

time

| company suggests dividend to shareholders | GA votes on suggested dividend amount | **div ex-date-1** Shares long / short at close determines dividend receivable / payable | **div ex-date** stock drops by div amount and trades ex-div | **div payment day** divs are paid out excl. possible withholding tax |

Figure 2.27: Illustration of a typical dividend payment process.

One exception to the non-adjustment of dividends are special dividends, *i.e.* especially declared extraordinary dividends (EOD). Here, the effect of the EOD (drop in spot price) on the ex-date is sometimes offset by a stock split. Otherwise, the terms of affected derivative contracts need adjustment to mitigate spurious gains or losses.

2.2.20 Dividend trading

Equity trading books typically exhibit exposure to the difference between implied dividends (*i.e.* the future dividends at which the positions are marked today) and realized dividends. This exposure can be determined by merely bumping the implied marks by a fixed percentage number (*e.g.* +10%) and observing the resulting P/L effect. Hence, similar to vega, one calculates the *dividend delta* $\frac{\partial V}{partial\text{div}}$ which quantifies how much the book is to gain or lose in value upon an increase (decrease) of the dividend marks. Given that there is a natural positive correlation between the performance of stocks and their corresponding dividend payouts, the resulting exposure can be seen as an indirect spot delta exposure. In other words, dividends offer an alternative to direct equity spot exposure. Finally, it follows that at some point, the dividend exposure needs to be limited since it may exceed agreed upon risk limits.

There are three main and three less common instruments for trading dividends listed in this order below:

(*i*) **Synthetic forward**: long/short European call at strike K + short/long European put at strike K +

short/long respective delta of the underlying

(*ii*) **Dividend swap**: formally a *contract for difference* (CFD). The fixed dividend payer and the floating dividend payer agree on a dividend strike (*e.g.* EUR 2,-) for the next or several dividend payments on a respective asset. At expiry of the contract, the difference between the actual dividend and the previously agreed strike is settled in cash. Dividend swap realized dividends are typically defined on *gross* dividends, *i.e.* excluding tax deductions.

(*iii*) **Dividend futures**: Forwards on dividends, *i.e.* $FV_t(\text{div future}_{t,T}) = PV_t(div_{t,T}) \cdot (1 + r_{t,T})^{T-t}$

(*iv*) **Dividend option**: Just like calls and puts may be written on stock prices, the same can be done for dividends.

(*v*) **Dividend swaption**: Option to enter a dividend swap in the future at a specified pre-defined strike. This instrument is rarely traded.

(*vi*) **Dividend variance swap**: instrument to trade the dividend variance (strike). This instrument is also rarely traded.

The next subsection discusses the various dividend trading vehicles as well as aspects concerning the modeling of dividends in the underlying stochastic and volatility process.

2.2.20.1   Synthetic Forward

In the following section, the synthetic forward is examined in more detail to illustrate dividend trading further. If one were to sell dividends, it is not possible to short the stock outright because this results in a net (short) delta risk also. However, it is possible to go long/short the stock synthetically via European options and sell/buy physical delta against it. Consider the example in Figure 2.28. The strategy is delta neutral because the combined option delta originating from the call and put

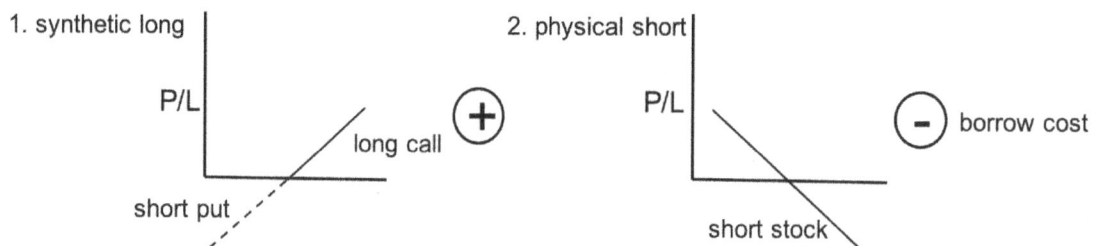

Figure 2.28: Illustration of a synthetic forward position.

offsets the stock delta exactly. Note that the expiry of the options needs to be *after* the respective dividend ex-date(s) one is targeting. Keep in mind that the combined P/L on the ex-date is zero if the actual dividend is equal to the (expectation) mark of the trading book. However, in case of dividends increase/decrease before there is additional P/L as a result of changing the mark. Longer-dated synthetic forwards are affected by more dividend periods. Note that in case of selling dividends via a synthetic forward, the borrowing cost paid on the short physical delta is a secondary risk embedded in the strategy.

Following the introduction of the first dividend trading vehicle, there are also some tax aspects to consider. Dividends which are distributed to the shareholders are, even if at risk, sources of income. The full untaxed dividend amount is called the *gross* yield and the taxed amount the *net* yield. The taxes are typically subtracted at source meaning the investor receives only the net amount in cash. However, the exact withholding tax amount varies between different countries and consequently the tax domicile of the investor. This has sometimes led to *dividend washing* or *dividend stripping* schemes whereby equity holdings would be transferred to jurisdictions of lower taxation just prior to the ex-date and thereafter move back to the original domicile location. This practice is a form of tax arbitrage and *illegal*. For example, investors domiciled in Switzerland can claim back the full (or partial) withholding tax amount on Swiss shares from the tax authorities. Therefore, a simple trade consists of acquiring foreign Swiss shares physically before the ex-date through a synthetic forward (through the inverse of Figure 2.28) and then exercise the forward after the ex-date to send the shares back. If the traders involved in the forward transaction between the two countries cooperate on the respective benefit both can make a riskless profit. More complicated schemes involve network of holding companies passing dividends between them before and after the ex-date, but the underlying principle is the same. As mentioned before all of these operations are essentially tax evasion schemes and therefore illegal. The interested reader may explore one of the latest episodes in Europe on his/her own [73] [8].

2.2.20.2 Dividend Swap

The dividend swap is a CFD purely on the gross dividend amount. Hence, there is no need to trade physical stock delta on top. Note that generally, only ordinary dividends qualify for the payout, excluding special dividends and returns of capital. The present value of a dividend swap is simply the sum of the expected dividends discounted back to today. At expiry, only the difference between the strike and the actual dividend is settled in cash so that the P/L is given by

$$P/L = N \cdot (\text{realized dividend} - \text{implied dividend}) , \tag{2.68}$$

where N is the swap notional which is either in units of the actual number of shares or in so-called basket notional sizes for indices (*e.g.* 1 index point of dividend equals 1 USD). The realized dividend is calculated as the total amount of all qualifying dividends going ex by the underlying equity or index, between the start (exclusive) and end (inclusive) dates.

Apart from tax differentials (gross versus net), the difference between the dividend swap and the synthetic forward comes down to the borrowing cost. As a lesson from the 2008/09 financial crisis, long dividend exposure (or a dividend swap for that matter) should be considered as a long stock and short put position. Because even if a given stock did not go bankrupt or reach zero in price during the crisis, its future dividend was often cut to zero. Hence, the dividend yields displayed rather large discontinuities contrary to what investors had assumed before. Put differently, similar to volatility, dividends exhibit skew. This skew tends to be higher than the implied volatility skew since dividends are typically cut to zero before the respective share price collapses completely. As a consequence, dividend volatility is higher, too.

2.2.20.3 Dividend Future

Dividend futures are contracts based upon the future settlement of the realized dividends going ex-in the respective calendar year. They are a relatively new financial instrument, which started trading after 2008 only. Similar to dividend swaps, the primary driver can be sell-side derivatives desks seeking channels to reduce their (long) dividend exposure. Hence, structurally these desks are short dividend futures by the nature of the primary flow business, which is a short forward exposure. This structural flow, in turn, may lead to a disconnection in the dividend future term structure versus the option market or general economic analyses [74, 75, 76]. The critical difference between divided futures and dividend swap lies in counterparty risk, which is manifested in different margining

---

[8]https://cumex-files.com/en/

requirements. Contrary to dividend swap it is not possible to claw back missing dividends after expiry, which may for example result from canceled dividends due to bankruptcy.

In principle, the fair value FV_t of a dividend future at time t on the underlying during a time interval $[t,T]$ can be derived from put-call parity (assuming a deterministic dividend yield) as

$$FV_t(\text{div future}_{t,T}) = PV_t(div_{t,T}) \cdot (1+r_{t,T})^{T-t} \,, \tag{2.69}$$

where $PV_t(div_{t,T})$ is the present value of the dividends paid on the asset in the time interval and r the respective risk-free rate.

2.2.20.4 Dividend Options

Dividend options on indices are by now listed instruments. The pricing is typically done via an extension of BSM [38], whereby the underlying is a respective dividend future. The implied volatility is then based on the implied volatility of the underlying dividend future. Similar to regular derivatives written on the corresponding equity index, the dividend implied volatility also shows skew and term structure. The payoff of a vanilla dividend call/put within a specified time period T is given by

$$\max[0, I \cdot (\sum_i^n div_i - K, 0)] \,, \tag{2.70}$$

where $I \pm 1$ indicates a call or put, respectively. Hence, the final payout is the difference between the sum of all dividends within the time period T and the strike. Note that as the dividends are declared and paid out within the observation period, the final payout becomes increasingly determined. This is analogous to Asian options (see 3.1.3) and means that the volatility of the dividend underlying decreases as the option approaches maturity. The main dividend hedging instrument are dividend futures which exist for stock indices as well as for stocks [77].

2.2.20.5 Dividend trading: early exercise

Recall that the American call or put on a dividend paying stock might need to be exercised early before the stock goes ex-div. Because of the early exercise feature, the American options are in general more valuable than their European counterparts, *i.e.*

$$C_t^A(K,T) \geq C_t^E(K,T) \text{and} P_t^A(K,T) \geq P_t^E(K,T) \,. \tag{2.71}$$

Put-call "parity" for American options with dividends derives from the put-call parity relation for European options applying the relation above as

$$S_t - d \cdot \exp[-rT] - K \leq C_t^A(K,T) - P_t^A(K,T) \leq S_t - K\exp[-rT] \,. \tag{2.72}$$

The unambiguous way to determine whether an American option should be early exercised before the ex-div date is to check whether the alive option value is smaller than its intrinsic value (plus some tolerance), *i.e.*

$$\text{Value}_{call,put} < \text{Value}_{call,put}^{intrinsic} \rightarrow \text{exercise} \,. \tag{2.73}$$

Some risk management systems do this automatically and flag for exercise. Also, there exist several early exercise approximations or rules of thumb. These approximations are typically correct when the case is clear but may result in a wrong assessment in tight situations. Note that all approximations base themselves on traditional BSM model assumptions, put-call parity, no skew and no term structure; this will typically not be identical to what a modern risk management system does (internally). Hence, it is advisable to be careful. The **typical** approximation is derived as follows for American calls. It starts with a comparison of the expected payout of two portfolios:

(*i*) long position in stock S

(*ii*) long position in a European call $C(K,T)$ written on S, plus a long deposit equal to $(div + K)\exp(-rT)$

At expiry, portfolio (*i*) will be worth $S_T + div$, while portfolio (*ii*) is worth $S_T - K + div + K = S_T + div$ if it redeems ITM or $div + K$ if the call expires OTM. Hence, the payout on (*i*) is equal or lower than (*ii*) at all times. This means (*i*) must be cheaper. Expressed mathematically,

$$C^E(K,T) + (div + K)\exp[-rT] \geq S_0 . \tag{2.74}$$

Because the American call is always more expensive, it follows that

$$C_t^A(K,T) \geq S_t - (div + K)\exp[-r(T - t)] . \tag{2.75}$$

It is then required to *exercise* if at any time the value of the call is less than the current payout $(S_t - K)$, *i.e.*

$$\begin{aligned}
S_t - K &> C_t^A(K,T) \\
S_t - K &> S_t - (div + K)\exp[-r(T - t)] \\
div &> K\exp[1 - \exp[-r(T - t)]] \approx K \cdot r(T - t)
\end{aligned} \tag{2.76}$$

Intuitively, what is done here is to compare the dividend yield to the interest rate expense resulting from buying/holding the shares until expiry. The approximation gets better if the value of the corresponding American put is also added. This should be done for cases that are not clear because one is implicitly selling a put by exercising the call (recall that short put is equal to selling the call and receiving shares). Note that the value of this put is a function of the volatility as well.

The rule of thumb for exercising the American put early follows the same reasoning. Here one would exercise if the interest rate earned on a cash deposit equal to the strike K is larger than the dividend payment. More accurately, one can check whether the interest on the strike is larger than the corresponding American call, which will implicitly also take the dividend into account. In general, it is a sensible exercise to check how the exercise boundary from the approximations compares to the "exact" one from the risk management system. It is common to find that the approximations undervalue holding the option because they base themselves on the simplest model.

2.2.20.6 Dividend modeling

Dividend modeling is tricky, among other things, because it requires calibration in conjunction with the volatility model [78]. Here the focus is not on the fact that for dividend payments, there is an inherent uncertainty in the exact magnitude and the timing of the ex-div date. Nevertheless, in the case of a delta-hedged (replicating) portfolio, the error in the forecast P/L is also a function of the difference in the expected and realized dividend impacting the option delta.

The out-of-the-box BSM model only deals with dividend yields, *i.e.* a continuous payment over time. However, dividend yields are not in line with the discrete cash payments observed in practice. The more often a dividend is paid, the better this approximation gets (*e.g.* for index options/products).

One can take three main approaches to improve the original dividend yield-based models

(*i*) model the dividends as absolute cash payments, *i.e.* on the ex-div date the stock drops exactly by the dividend amount
(*ii*) model the dividends as a yield proportional to the stock price level
(*iii*) do a mixture of (*i*) and (*ii*)

Approach (*i*), while intuitively the most realistic approach, leads to a model that cannot be cast back into the analytically solvable BSM framework. Moreover, in the case of *spot-invariant* large periodic absolute dividend payments, the probability for reaching a future spot price of zero increases significantly. In this case, the terminal spot distribution is not in line with a lognormal diffusive process [79]. At the same time, it is also unrealistic to assume that a company continues to pay the same absolute dividend amount in the case its stock price drops by a large amount. Hence, as a general rule, absolute dividends are a more realistic representation for short-dated trades, while proportional dividends are better for longer-dated trades. As a consequence, especially when trying to model a full dividend curve, one is forced to apply a calibrated mixture between absolute and proportional dividends [80], *i.e.* method (*iii*) above. Note that the mixing ratio between absolute and proportional dividends will impact the pricing in particular for more exotic derivatives (*e.g.* digital or barriers options). Therefore, it is recommended to price new payouts independently with absolute and proportional dividends to assess the mixing impact in particular with respect to particular spot levels. Cash and proportional dividends can be joined in a linear fashion [81] as

$$d_i = (1 - w_i)d_i^{exp} + \cdot w_i \frac{d_i^{exp}}{F_{t,t_i^-}} S_t \, , \tag{2.77}$$

whereby $w_i \in 0, ..., 1$ denotes the mixing weight between the expected absolute and proportional dividends d_i^{exp} on dividend date t_i, and F_{t,t^-} is the forward prior to an ex-date. Hence, a series of expected absolute dividends including mixing weights will determine the schedule in the stochastic process.

There are typically three main approaches for inserting cash (absolute) dividends into the BSM framework.

- Escrow(ed) dividend model: Assumes that the asset price minus the present value of all dividends to be paid before the maturity of the option follows a geometric Brownian motion

$$d\hat{S}_t = r\hat{S}_t dt + \hat{\sigma}\hat{S}_t dW_t$$
$$\text{with } S_t = \hat{S}_t + D_t(T) \text{ and } D_t(T) = \sum_{t < t_i < T} d_i \exp\left[-r(t_i - t)\right] \tag{2.78}$$

- Forward dividend model: Assumes that the asset price plus the forward value of all past dividends follows a geometric Brownian motion

$$d\hat{S}_t = r\hat{S}_t dt + \hat{\sigma}\hat{S}_t dW_t$$
$$\text{with } S_t = \hat{S}_t + D_t(T) \text{ and } D_t(T) = \sum_{0 < t_i < T} d_i \exp\left[-r(t_i - t)\right] \tag{2.79}$$

- Piecewise lognormal model (also known as diffuse and drop): Assumes that the asset price jumps downward at each dividend date and follows a geometric Brownian motion between those dates

The first two models provide an analytical solution but are not satisfactory because even for two options A and B with two different maturities $T_A < T_B$, the price dynamics for time $t < TA$ is different because dividends between $T_A and T_B$ is taken into account in one case but not the other. Hence, the diffuse and drop model is clearly preferred in theory and practice [82, 83, 84, 85, 86].

In a nutshell, it is important to analyze how dividend models affect the terminal stock price distribution given the forward curve. For the escrowed model and the diffuse and drop model, both distributions have the same mean, but the standard deviation of the escrowed model is lower compared to the diffuse and drop model. This difference in variance results because the diffuse and drop model cannot predict the future dividend, which results in a hard shift of the terminal price distribution. Therefore, the implied volatility in the escrowed (and similar) model needs to be adjusted (up), which requires joint calibrating with the volatility surface already. One way to spot potential issues with absolute dividend models is to price a strip of options with increasing expiry and look for potential price jumps/drops between ex-div days. There are some simple consistency checks, which all models need to obey. For example, consider a 100 strike European call with an absolute dividend at 10, expiring exactly on the dividend ex-date. In this case, the premium has to be equal to the 90 strike call, expiring one day after, *i.e.*

$$EC(K = 100, T = ex - date) = EC(K = 100 - 10, T = ex - date + 1) . \tag{2.80}$$

If this equality does not hold, one can trade the shorter maturity call against the longer maturity call for an almost riskless profit. There are some dividend models, which do not calibrate the volatility correctly in the transition between the ex-dates leading to a discontinuity (see Figure 2.29). This is because in order to match the two calls above, the volatility of the 90 call needs to increase. Effectively, it is necessary to make sure that the pricing follows a piecewise (lognormal) model, *i.e.* the stock price jumps down after the ex-date and follows a GBM process between dividend payments with a respective volatility adjustment. Note that experienced (vanilla) option traders will independently examine the option price behavior carefully across dividend dates when pricing a contract close to this transition. Finally, note that it is worth paying attention to dividend modeling also for instruments or clauses which aim to eliminate the dividend impact by design. For example, corporate trades (see chapter 11) as well as convertible bonds (see chapter 10) often include dividend protection clauses to remove the P/L impact of changes in the dividend amounts. However, as shown in [87], standard methods such as adjusting strikes by the dividend amount (as known as *path-dependent re-striking*) [8] or simply pricing the derivatives as if the dividends were zero, does not guarantee P/L invariance along the path in case of delta-hedging.

2.2.21 Corporate Actions: Stock Splits

In the case of a stock split, the number of outstanding shares changes. For example, after a 3:1 stock split there are three times as many outstanding shares, but each share is trading by a factor of three less than the price before the split to not create share capital out of nothing. The motivation for a stock split lies in increased availability of outstanding shares at a 'lower' price, which can lead to an increase of the shareholder pool.

In the case of a reverse stock split, the amount of outstanding shares changes, too. In this case, the amount of shares is decreased, *e.g.* in a 1:3 reverse stock split the investor receives one new share for three old shares, which thereby reduces the availability of outstanding shares. Investors holding less than the minimum old exchangeable shares are settled in cash.

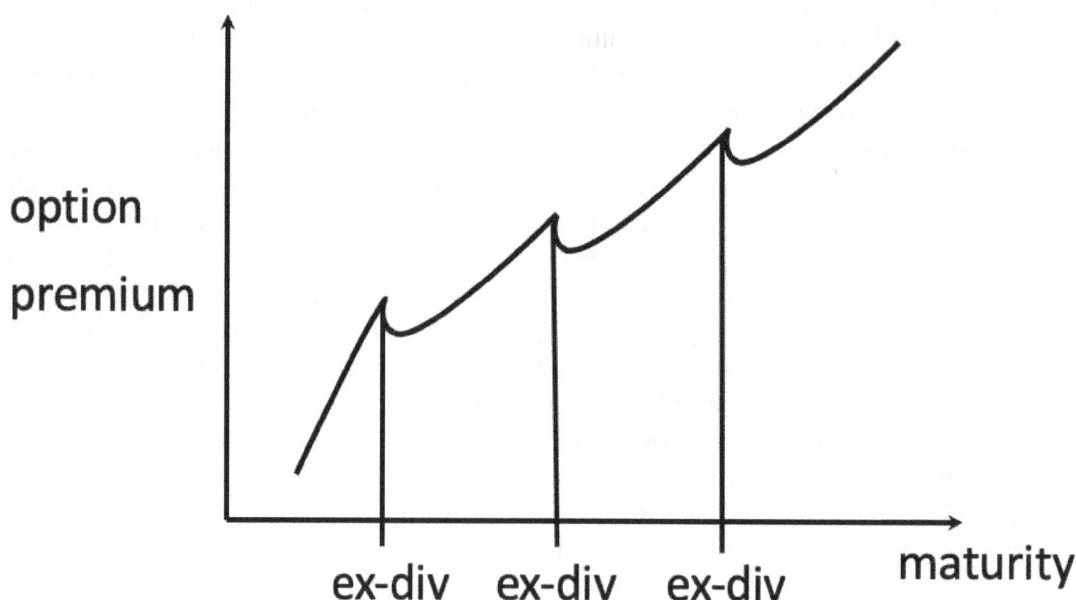

Figure 2.29: Illustration of option price discontinuities across ex-div dates.

2.2.22 Corporate Actions: Spin Off

In the case of a spin-off, a parent company aims to take part of its operations into a separate entity. This CA might go in hand with a listing for the latter. For example, company X spins off part of its operations into new company Y and subsequently becomes company X'. Hence, $X = X' + Y$. Existing derivative positions written on X will now become a derivative on the basket asset (also known as the 'combo') $X' + Y$. The exact ratio will be set accordingly with the shareholder receipts, $e.g.$ the shareholder of X might receive 0.75 X', 0.1 Y and some cash Z. The combo basket market data (volatility, dividends etc.) will also need to be updated.

2.2.23 Corporate Actions: Mergers & Acquisitions

In the case of a takeover or acquisition, one company is incorporated into another firm and cease to exist, $e.g.$ $X + Y \rightarrow X$. Shareholders of the takeover company are either paid in stock of the acquiring entity ($e.g.$ 1 X for 3 Y) or cash.

In case of a merger, two companies form a new entity, $e.g.$ $X + Y \rightarrow Z$. Derivative contracts written on either X or Y now contain a new or altered underlying. The exact replacement is part of the terms and conditions, but typically in the case a company ceases to exist, it is replaced by an entity in its peer group. The replacement is often at the discretion of the valuation agent in case of securitized notes. Note that a replacement can potentially result in differences concerning market data ($e.g.$ the replacement company might be less liquid and more volatile). Moreover, for the event of a takeover/merger in a multi-underlying derivative contract containing both affected entities may lead to significant P/L impact if the terms are not covering this event, $e.g.$ a worst-of n stock basket becomes a worst-of $n-1$ stock basket.

2.2.24 Corporate Actions: Rights Issues

In the case of a rights issue (RI), a company issues the right for a stock purchase at a *reduced* price to existing shareholders. Shareholders may exercise or sell the rights in the market. The number of outstanding shares in the market changes in a similar way like a stock split.

RI are the most common way to increase ordinary capital for a company without increasing its debt. Instead, shareholders invest more in the firm's equity. The advantages of a RI are its fast implementation and the ability to potentially raise a substantial amount of capital quickly. However, the announcement of a RI often also acts as a negative catalyst for the share price since analysts typically do not interpret the need for a capital raise as a good sign. It is therefore paramount to obtain a solid backing from the largest existing shareholders to arrange for a favorable capital raise.

The adjusted price (AP) after the RI is given by

$$AP = \frac{N_0 \cdot S_c + N_N \cdot (S_{Sub}) + D}{(N_0 + N_N)}, \tag{2.81}$$

where S_c is the closing price before the effective date of the RI, N_0 the number of shares before the RI, N_N the number of shares after the RI, S_{Sub} the subscription price and D the dividend. Note that rights issues can be combined with embedded options. For example, in order to make the capital raise more attractive, the stock may be puttable back to the company by the investors. These type of features are often part of preferred shares issuance programs.

2.2.25 Corporate Actions: R-Factor

Following the overview of various corporate actions above, the next section illustrates how derivative contracts are potentially adjusted.

As discussed above, derivative contracts are typically adjusted after a CA to avoid unfair price jumps. In practice, for every CA, the respective exchange publishes a so-called *R-factor* (also known as the adjustment factor). The R-factor is then used to adjust the strikes of the affected derivatives.

In the case of the RI before, the R-factor is given by

$$R_f = \frac{N_0 \cdot S_c + N_N \cdot (S_{Sub}) + D}{(N_0 + N_N) \cdot S_c}. \tag{2.82}$$

Typically, the corporate action is announced by giving the ratio of old to new shares, *e.g.* a 3 for 9 rights issue for which the old share is worth 30, the subscription price 14 and dividends zero one gets

$$R_f = \frac{9 \cdot 30 + 3 \cdot (14 + 0)}{(9 + 3) \cdot 30} = 0.866. \tag{2.83}$$

The strike of an option is then adjusted by multiplying the old strike and dividing the original number of options by the R-factor to neutralize the effect.

2.2.26 Corporate Actions: Special Dividends

When special dividends (SP) are paid out, it is advisable to be very careful. There exist two main adjustment methods for derivative contracts in the case of SP (recall that regular dividends are typically not adjusted for because they are commonly known in advance or predictable by market participants):

(*i*) **absolute adjustment**: the adjusted strike is the old strike minus the special dividend, whereby the contract size remains unchanged (typically done in the United States)

(*ii*) **proportional adjustment**: the adjusted strike is determined using the R- factor taking into account the cum-dividend share price in proportion to the special dividend (typically done in Europe) as

$$R_f = \frac{S_{cum-div} - D_{special}}{S_{cum-div}} . \tag{2.84}$$

The idea of both adjustments is to leave the option market participants invariant to the special dividend payment. Unfortunately, none of these methods is theoretically 'correct' (except when the SP does not affect the stock volatility; in this case proportional adjustment is correct) [88]. The proportional adjustment can lead to huge windfall wins or losses, especially if asset managers need or want to optimize potential tax impacts and start trading shares extensively before and after the ex-date. Therefore, it is advisable to simulate the adjustment scenario before.

In some special situations, incorrect handling of corporate actions may result in large P/L losses. For example, in 2007, the German chemical producer Altana AG sold its pharmaceutical business and decided to pay out the proceeds to its shareholders via a large special dividend. In total, Altana, trading itself at the time around EUR 50, paid out: EUR 1.3 (regular dividend) + EUR 0.5 (Bonus) + EUR 33 (special dividend) = EUR 34.80. Hence, more than half of its share price. What complicated matter was that shareholders were to be taxed at 85% or more depending on whether the dividend would need to be declared as income. Hence, there was an interest among various participants to reduce their long share position to optimize taxes. As a result, the stock dropped from approximately EUR 51 to EUR 46.56 in the closing auction alone before the ex-day. Therefore, the stock should open at EUR 46.56 – EUR 34.80 = EUR 11.76, whereby the adjustment was to be done using a proportional R-Factor. The corresponding R-Factor was determined as $R_f = (45.56 - 1.3 - (33 + 0.5))/(45.56 - 1.3) = 0.25983$. This adjustment meant that for example, all outstanding EUR 54 strike calls turned into EUR 14.03 calls with the number of contracts increased by $1/R_f = 3.8486$. As market participants rushed to cover their shorts, the stock surged over the next four days to as high as EUR 20.90. Combined with limited liquidity, short call writers were in trouble and rushed to cover the short delta positions. Hence, the market dynamics were amplified by the way the options were adjusted for. What had happened as well is that some market participants had shorted the stock into the auction and covered the delta by buying OTM calls. These OTM calls suddenly became ITM due to the resulting short squeeze. The combined loss for some market-making desks was estimated to be around EUR 700m. Hence, it is advisable to conduct a detailed scenario analysis in advance when dealing with unusual or potentially large corporate actions.

Practical Tips 2.2.1 Questions to ask your quants and risk system support:

- theta: which contributions does it contain (only pure gamma or dividends as well etc.)?
- volatility: does the system use business or calendar day units?
- volatility: for (American) options, does the system use a volatility skew and/or term structure?
- volatility: how is volatility inter- and extrapolated in strike and maturity space?
- dividend modeling: absolute dividends, dividend yield, proportional dividends or a mixture?

- dividend modeling: how is dividend protection modeled?
- dividends/volatility: is volatility calibrated in line with the dividend model?
- pricing: how are forward starting vanilla options priced exactly?
- greeks: how is the delta/gamma calculated/represented on expiry day? does the system support intraday time?
- in general: how is trading time discretized and how is a trading day represented (*e.g.* day, hour, minute)?
- interest rates: how is the yield curve constructed, which instruments are used
- cash balance: what is the cash balance of the book for different currencies?
- capital and refinancing costs: what capital and refinancing costs do the position incur currently?

3. Exotic Options

3.1 Introduction

Exotic derivatives lie beyond the scope of vanilla options and combinations thereof. As the name implies, exotic options are less common versus their vanilla counterparts. A more precise definition is that the terminal exotic option payout is typically highly path-dependent, *i.e.* events during the lifetime of the option may lead to significant changes in the terminal payoff. As a consequence, model risk, higher order greeks as well as hedging strategies become both more critical and challenging.

The following list is a comprehensive summary of exotic option properties:

- exhibit reduced market liquidity, *i.e.* are not exchange-traded
- valuation becomes increasingly model dependent
- payout replication solely via trading of underlying asset practically impossible
- increased nonlinear behavior for second-order and cross-greeks
- increased sensitivity to volatility surface dynamics (skew or kurtosis) and higher order greeks (*e.g.* vanna, volga)
- complex valuation dynamics
- increased P/L variance
- often (highly) path-dependent payout

Recall that vanilla option payoffs are *not* path-dependent. The void of path-dependency is because the payout is fully determined by the conditional probability of spot at strike versus spot at expiry. Even if the BSM assumption of a constant implied volatility surface is not a reflection of reality, it is possible back out the terminal conditional probability from the market quotes. However, for exotics and other path-dependent options, the terminal payout typically depends on intermediate spot levels as well. Hence, the payoff becomes a product of all conditional probabilities and effectively the forward shape of the implied volatility surface between *t-1* and *t*. This forward shape is not a liquid observable market parameter and therefore fitting the vanilla surface does not guarantee to price an exotic option correctly. In other words, only one constraint (vanilla repricing), does not guarantee to get the correct path probability right. Given an infinite solution space, it is therefore important to not severely misprice a payout versus getting the 'correct' solution. Note that the *P/L* of a delta-hedged vanilla option *is* actually path-dependent due to the implicit gamma weighting (see 2.2.8). Exotic options on the contrary exhibit path dependency for both P/L and terminal payout.

In general, derivative desks are split into groups covering vanilla options, flow / light exotics and medium / heavy exotics. Exotic look-a-likes are vanilla option combinations, which appear to have exotic characteristics, but can be replicated via vanilla options alone (*e.g.* the chooser or lookback options). Light / flow exotics are derivatives with less complex dynamics / path dependency, *e.g.* Asian options, basket options, worst-of / best-of options, simple barrier options, variance / volatility swaps. Heavy exotics are options with complex dynamics and higher order risk sensitivity, *e.g.* cliquet options, bespoke dispersion trades or options on variance.

3.1.1 Exotic Options: Valuation instruments

Whenever possible, it is desirable to value payouts analytically for reasons of speed, computational expense, accuracy and numerical stability. The BSM option-pricing framework is such an analytical framework since it offers closed-form solutions. However, many sophisticated pricing models or payoffs required for the valuation of exotic options are not accessible analytically.

The second best alternative to a closed-form solution is the use of finite difference methods to numerically price the derivative [89]. The approach works by discretizing the respective partial differential equation in time and iteratively solving it subject to the payoff boundary conditions. This is also the reason why this approach is commonly referred to as partial differential equation solvers (PDE solver). However, a key requirement is that the option value can indeed be expressed as a PDE. If this is not possible it is required to resort to Monte Carlo simulation [90]. Indeed, the generic solution to any non-analytically available pricing or optimization problem is a numerical method called Monte Carlo [91] (MC). Despite its nuclear/particle physics origins [90], MC simulation also became the workhorse of computational finance due to the vast range of applicability and increasingly cheaper access to computational power. Also, it is effectively trivial to parallelize if the simulated paths are independent (see below). However, it is precisely for the same reasons that MC can be dangerous because it may encourage to think less about the payout replication given that the valuation is relatively easy. Hence, even if MC solves pricing problems, it does not offer any help to address replication issues.

MC works by creating simulated returns for the asset path(s) using random numbers drawn from a specified underlying distribution. The final option price is then determined by repeatedly *averaging* over the resulting option payoff for each path. Due to the law of large numbers, the convergence to the right price is eventually guaranteed. For example, in the case of a vanilla call this would mean

$$\mathbf{E}[\max[0, S_T - K]] \approx \frac{1}{N} \sum_{i=1}^{N} [0, S_T - K] \, , \qquad (3.1)$$

where N is the number of simulated asset paths.

While MC is very versatile and powerful, obtaining convergence can strain the computational expense significantly for certain payouts. As a rule of thumb, the MC variance / error is of the order $O(1/\sqrt{N})$, *i.e.* increasing the precision by a factor 2 requires 4 times more additional paths. Various techniques have therefore been developed to overcome this problem such as trivial parallelization, generation of more uniform random numbers (low discrepancy sequences) or antithetic sampling (*i.e.* path-mirroring) [91]. The calculation of greeks via MC is possible, but (*i*) increases the computational expense and (*ii*) is prone to numerical instability for higher order derivatives (*e.g.* gamma, volgamma etc.). MC greeks are typically implemented as parameter bumps, *e.g.* for delta calculate value of option at spot S_0 and $S_0 \to S_0 + \delta S_0$. For example; the numerical delta is then obtained as the finite difference of the derivative value at two different spot level given by

$$\Delta = \frac{\partial V}{\partial S} \approx \frac{V(S_0 + \delta S_0) - V_0}{\delta S_0} , \tag{3.2}$$

where δS_0 denotes the shift in spot (*e.g.* 1% of the current spot).

3.1.2 Exotic look-a-likes

Exotic look-a-likes appear to be exotic options but are just a combination or slight modification of several vanilla derivatives. Recognizing seemingly exotic payouts as a combination of vanillas before resorting to numerical methods is an indication of an experienced trader.

3.1.2.1 Chooser option

The vanilla European call / put chooser option [92] allows the holder to choose at a pre-defined date whether the option for the terminal payout is a call or put (see Figure 3.1). This feature sounds exotic and path-dependent but can be replicated entirely using vanillas. The key to pricing it lies in the determination of the asset forward price between the chose date and the expiry.

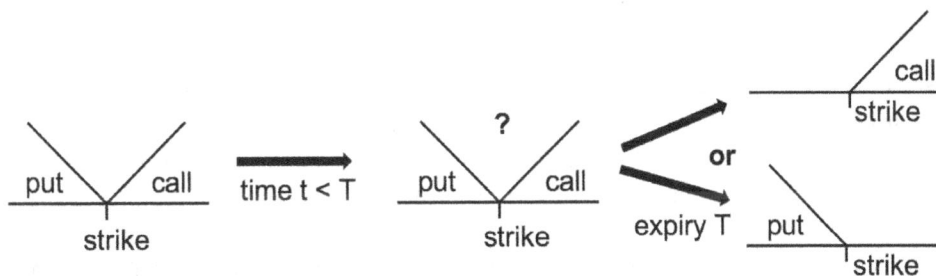

Figure 3.1: Illustration of the chooser option.

For example, consider a 20 strike chooser option written on an asset, expiring in 1 year with the obligation to choose after 2 months. To hedge the payout, it is necessary to determine the current forward on the underlying at 2 months, and between 2 month and 1 year (expiry). Assume that the 2 month - 1-year asset forward is 20, while the 2 month forward is at 19 (*e.g.* due to a dividend payment during the lifetime). In this case, the option can be hedged by buying a 1 year 20 strike EC and a 2 month 19 strike EP. There are two cases to consider:

(*i*) After 2 months, the underlying trades above 19 and the put expires worthless. A rational investor will then choose the EC because the forward for the remaining lifetime is higher than 20. In other words, the call is worth more than the put and should be selected.

(*ii*) After 2 months, the underlying trades below 19 and the put expires ITM. The hedger then exercises the put and sell the physical stock delta at the strike. The combined position is then long delta on the vanilla call and short delta on the physical shares, which is a synthetic put position. Because the 10 month forward is below 20, the investor will now choose the 20 strike put. The analysis is illustrated in Figure 3.2. As a general recipe, the price of the vanilla chooser is given by

$$V_{\text{chooser}} = EC(K_C, T_1) + EP(S_F, T_2) , \tag{3.3}$$

with K_C as the fixed strike, T_2 the option expiry date, T_2 the chose date, stock level S_F such that forward at T_2 for expiry T_1 equals K_c, *i.e.* choose S_f so that forward value $F(S_f, T_1 - T_2) = K_C$. The

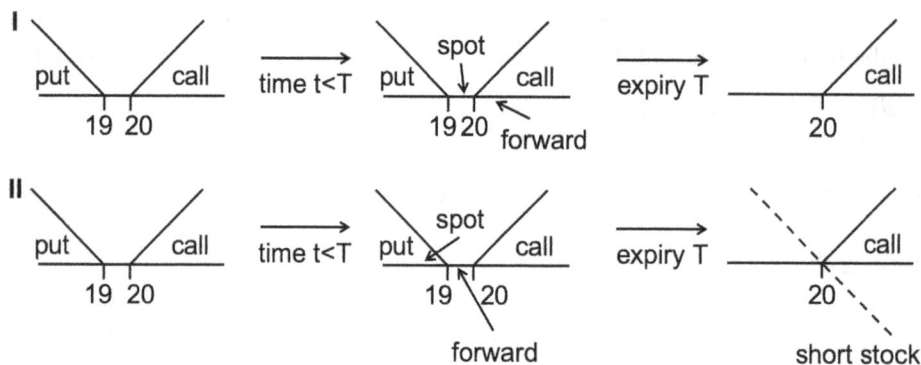

Figure 3.2: Illustration of the chooser option replication.

motivation of trading a chooser over a straddle lies in the assumption that the asset price moves sharply in one direction following a day before the choose date (*e.g.* earnings announcement). In other words, it is more suitable to implement as a directional bet.

3.1.2.2 Forward starting options

In the case of forward starting options, the absolute strike is not set on the day of the trade (*e.g.* today's open or close price), but at some pre-defined date in the future. It is then common to contractually agree that the future or forward starting strike is a certain percentage of the asset price, *e.g.* 100% of the closing price in three months. Note that also the greeks are forward starting and typically show value.

There is no definite recipe for pricing forward starting options. If the period between the trade date and the strike date is close, the price of the spot and forward start are very similar. The most reliable method is to do a Monte Carlo simulation for the spot between trade date and strike date to estimate the impact. The spot dynamics of the volatility skew has a large impact on the pricing of the forward start option. Volatility spot dynamics denotes how the ATM volatility reacts to moves of the asset spot level. For example, if ATM volatility rises/falls as the spot decreases/increases, the dynamics are called sticky strike (see discussion on skew dynamics later 3.1.5). Hence, if the forward starting option is valued at the current ATM spot volatility and the skew dynamics were sticky strike, then the position loses / gain in case of a short/long vega exposure in case the spot moves down / up. This risk can be hedged out by running a shadow delta against the skew risk. Hence, in case of the typically increasing downside skew, short/long vega positions are implicitly long/short the physical asset and delta needs to be sold/bought to eliminate the effect. Hence, potential loss/gain from the vega upon a spot move is (partially) offset by delta P/L.

In addition to spot skew, the skew term structure (also known as the forward implied volatility skew) is essential to consider. Skew term structure denotes the shape of the skew in the future: does it flatten out or stay at the current level? Typically, the skew decreases along with the term structure (see Figure 3.3). However, this is not always realistic. Effectively, the best guess for the (forward) skew around the ATM point in *e.g.* 1 year is the current spot skew. Hence, trades that are sensitive to the forward skew need to be priced with care. Forward skew is discussed in more detail for the case of cliquet or strike resetting options later (see Figure 3.25). Note that even American vanilla options can exhibit model-dependent valuation differences relating to whether the valuation model takes into account the volatility term structure. This includes both option value as well as overall vega.

Therefore, it is advisable to examine the valuation models for American options in detail.

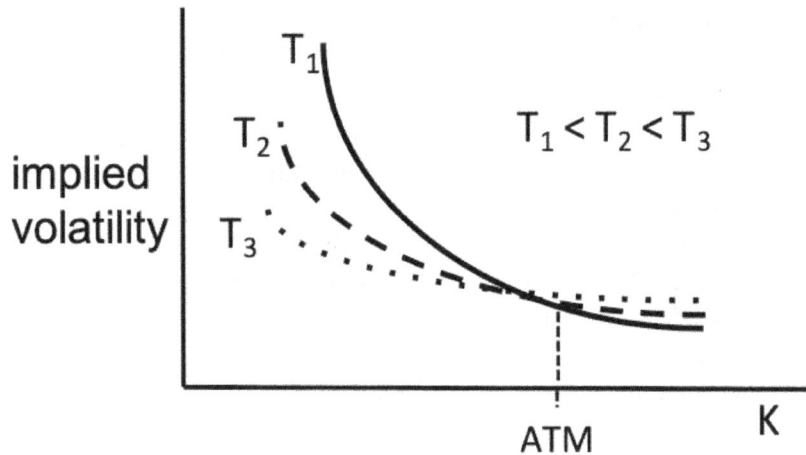

Figure 3.3: Illustration of the typical implied volatility term structure for three different maturities $(T_1 < T_2 < T_3)$.

In general, the underlying greeks for forward starting options are smaller in value compared to the spot starting variant unless the strike setting is very close. The exception here is vega, which typically shows similar levels. Finally, note that the value of the forward volatility is typically the key parameter determining the value of the forward starting option. Sometimes this quantity cannot be implied from market data, *i.e.* one may consider to calculate the forward volatility based on the additivity of variance principle (see 2.2.14). However, this method may result in absurdly high or low forward implied volatility depending on the shape of spot term structure. In other words, since the strike of the forward starting option is coupled to the forward itself, this way of determing the forward volatility will not work. Therefore, it is critical to understand how the pricing model determines the forward volatility.

3.1.3 Asian options

The economic motivation for Asian options lies in making the option price cheaper by reducing the 'optionality' somehow. In general, this is accomplished by averaging out or fixing parts of the payoff during the lifetime before expiry. Three main Asian option variants can be distinguished:

(*i*) In the **Asian (out) option**, the final fixing level is not determined on one single day, but as an average over several days
(*ii*) In the **Asian (in) option**, the initial fixing level is determined over several days
(*iii*) In the **Asian strike (in) option**, the strike level is determined over several days

Averaging may be the geometric and arithmetic, *i.e.* for an Asian out call the variants are

$$Call^{\text{geometric}} = \max\left[0, \prod_{i=1}^{N} S_i^{1/N} - K\right] \text{ vs.} \tag{3.4}$$

versus

$$Call^{\text{arithmetic}} = \max\left[0, \sum_{i=1}^{N} S_i - K\right],$$ (3.5)

where N denotes the number of averaging days.

The primary rationale for having averaging days is that it is thereby possible to partially lock-in the strike or payout. As a consequence, the Asian (out) option is cheaper compared to its vanilla counterpart because the averaging decreases the overall volatility.

The Asian out option with geometric averaging is simple to price because the geometric average of a lognormal random variable underlies a lognormal distribution as well. Therefore, it is possible to express the variance of the product of the geometric average as a simple arithmetic average of the individual variances (assuming an inter-variance correlation of zero). This analysis then effectively results in an adjusted volatility and return measure, *i.e.*

$$\sigma_{\text{geometric}} = \sqrt{\frac{1}{N^2} \sum_{i=1}^{N} \sigma_i^2}$$

$$r_{\text{geometric}} = \frac{1}{N} \sum_{i=1}^{N} r_i$$ (3.6)

From the equation above, it is clear that the volatility of the Asian option is *smaller* than the volatility of an option of an identical maturity. All other parameters being equal, lower volatility or lower uncertainty also means lower option price.

The Asian out option with arithmetic averaging turns out to be more challenging to model. The difficulty arises because the arithmetic average of a lognormal random variable does not follow a lognormal distribution. However, in practice, the arithmetic average is often just approximated by the geometric average above. Cutting corners here is justified by recognizing that the geometric average is the lower bound for the arithmetic average due to Jensen's inequality

$$\sqrt[N]{\prod_{i=1}^{N}(S_i)^{w_i}} \leq \frac{1}{N} \sum_{i=1}^{N} w_i S_i \text{, with } \sum_{j=1}^{N} w_j = 1.$$ (3.7)

In case one is unsure about the implementation of the arithmetic average, it is advised to compare the pricing with a Monte Carlo simulation. As a modeling takeaway, pricing geometric averages are always more straightforward also for other exotics and therefore the preferred choice when structuring new payouts.

3.1.3.1 Asian options: Greeks

In the Asian out option, every averaging day partially determines the final payout. Therefore, it should not surprise that this affects the greeks as well.

Consider a short position in a 1 year, 20 strike call with 6 monthly average out dates before expiry. Assume that the stock trades at 30 before the first average out date. The delta on the option is higher than the delta on the equivalent vanilla call because 1/6 of the payout is **locked in** already. However, since 1/6 of the payout is determined, there is also 1/6 excess delta compared to a delta of 100 in case of an ITM expiry. Hence, it is necessary to sell 1/6 of the full ITM delta. Assume now that the asset trades at 10 on the second setting date. Again, 1/6 of the Asian weight in the final payout is locked in. In this case, the payout component is zero, and the overall delta is purely against other future settings. In summary, it is required to sell excess delta in case the option has an ITM Asian setting and otherwise do nothing. Because part of the payout is being locked in, the Asian option is often compared to a vanilla option with shorter duration. Given the way gamma and vega relate in time, this consequently means that an Asian option has *more* gamma and *less* vega than its equivalent vanilla counterpart. Therefore, to hedge gamma and vega of an Asian out option, a vanilla option of shorter maturity can be traded as a proxy hedge.

Given that the Asian feature allows for a reduction of the greeks at expiry, it is sometimes also used to smooth out potential payoff discontinuities. The latter can also be a problem for large vanilla option positions in the context of corporate derivatives (see section 11), *i.e.* payoff/greeks smoothing can independently be a very valuable tool there as well.

3.1.4 Local Volatility

In the BSM model, implied volatility is considered to be constant. Market practitioners immediately realized that this does not make a lot of sense and started to define implied volatility $\sigma(K,T)$ as a function of strike K and expiry T (see Section 2.1.8). Moreover, some simple formulas have been derived to further adjust volatility for skew and kurtosis [93]. This is effectively also how vanilla options are still priced today in terms of the variance component. Given that the vanilla option payout is path-invariant, this approach is justifiable.

How does this picture change for exotics, which are characterized by strong payoff path dependency? If one is working with a spot- and time to expiry invariant variance function, then the mark-to-market valuation of the option during its lifetime is likely incorrect in many scenarios. Through the seminal work of Dupire [94, 95] it became possible to translate a constant volatility grid in strike and expiry into a volatility surface in spot and time to expiry, *i.e.* $\sigma(K,T) \rightarrow \sigma(S_t,t)$. The asset diffusion equation then becomes

$$dS_t = \mu_t S_t dt + \sigma_t(S_t,t) S_t dw_t \ . \tag{3.8}$$

Note that $\sigma(K,T) \neq \sigma(S_t,t)$ and that this transformation is not as trivial as it might seem. The function $\sigma(S_t,t)$ is called *local volatility* (LV) as it provides a deterministic local (in spot and time) estimate for the variance. Indeed, if properly calibrated, LV reprices all option market quotes accurately, *i.e.* it encompasses the vanilla market quotes. If Monte Carlo is the computational workhouse in financial engineering, then LV is effectively its theoretical counterpart when pricing exotic derivatives. Nevertheless, LV is arguably also the most criticized model in theory yet remains the most used in practice.

The derivation of the LV surface is mathematically relatively straightforward and ultimately involves taking partial derivatives in the strike and expiry dimension across the implied volatility surface $\sigma(K,T)$. Instead of deriving the model completely, the focus here is on discussing its properties. Dupire [94], Derman and Kani [96, 97] derived the formula to calculate local volatilities from market implied volatility quotes, expressed below as the local variance

$$\sigma_{K,T}^2(S_t,t) = 2 \frac{\frac{\partial C_t(K,T)}{\partial T} + rK \frac{\partial C_t(K,T)}{\partial K}}{K^2 \frac{\partial^2 C_t(K,T)}{\partial K^2}} \tag{3.9}$$

The three partial derivatives can be replicated with the following vanilla trading strategy

$$\sigma^2_{K,T}(S_t,t) = 2\frac{\left[\frac{\text{Calendar Spread}}{\Delta T}\right] + rK\left[\frac{\text{Vertical Spread}}{\Delta K}\right]}{K^2\left[\frac{\text{Butterfly Spread}}{\Delta K^2}\right]}, \tag{3.10}$$

i.e. spreads along the term structure (calendar spread), strike (vertical spread) and curvature (butterfly spread). The calendar spread consists of two options with the same strike K but different maturities T and $T - \Delta T$ weighted by $2/\Delta T$. The vertical spread consists of two options with identical maturity $T - \Delta T$ but strikes $K^+ = K + \Delta K$ and $K^- = K - \Delta K$ weighted by $2rK/\Delta K$, respectively. Finally, the butterfly calls have identical maturity $T - \Delta T$ with a long position each at K^+ and K^- as well as two short calls at K. The butterfly is weighted by $K^2/\Delta K^2$.

Unfortunately, given incomplete and potentially noisy input data regularization methods are typically required to end up with a smooth output function (*e.g.* fitting a smooth function to the input data first before applying the formula). Such as parametric function can again be a parabola, as suggested in Section 2.1.8. To use such a function, it is required to rewrite the equation above such that the implied volatilities are used as input instead of option prices. This can be done by rewriting the BSM equation for a call option C in terms of the log-strike y (moneyness) whereby $y = log(K/F)$, yielding the expression [37]

$$\sigma^2_{LV}(K,\delta t) = \frac{\sigma^2_{imp} + 2\delta t\sigma_{imp}\frac{\partial\sigma_{imp}}{\partial\delta t} + 2(r-d)Kt\sigma_{imp}\frac{\partial\sigma_{imp}}{\partial K}}{\left(1 + Kd_1\sqrt{\delta t}\frac{\partial\sigma_{imp}}{\partial K}\right)^2 + K^2\delta t\sigma_{imp}\left(\frac{\partial^2\sigma_{imp}}{\partial K^2} - d_1\sqrt{\delta t}\left(\frac{\partial\sigma_{imp}}{\partial K}\right)^2\right)}, \tag{3.11}$$

where $\sigma_{imp} = \sigma(K,t)$ with $\delta t = T - t$ such that t is the market date on which the volatility smile is observed and S_0 the asset price on that date. The parameter d_1 is given by

$$d_1 = \frac{-\ln(S_0/K) + ((r-d) + 1/2\sigma^2)\delta t}{\sigma_{imp}\sqrt{\delta t}}, \tag{3.12}$$

whereby t and S_0 are the time and the asset price on which the volatility surface is observed.

An example of this transformation between an implied volatility surface and local volatility is shown in Figure 3.4. It is immediately visible that the slope / skew in the LVM is in general much steeper for a fixed maturity compared to the source implied volatility surface. This means that options which mainly depend on the downside volatility will be priced higher compared to a generic implied volatility pricer. There are cases where this local volatility benefit is justified. However, especially for very low strikes, the LVM skew tends to be very steep and it is often impossible to realize the variance benefit in real trading.

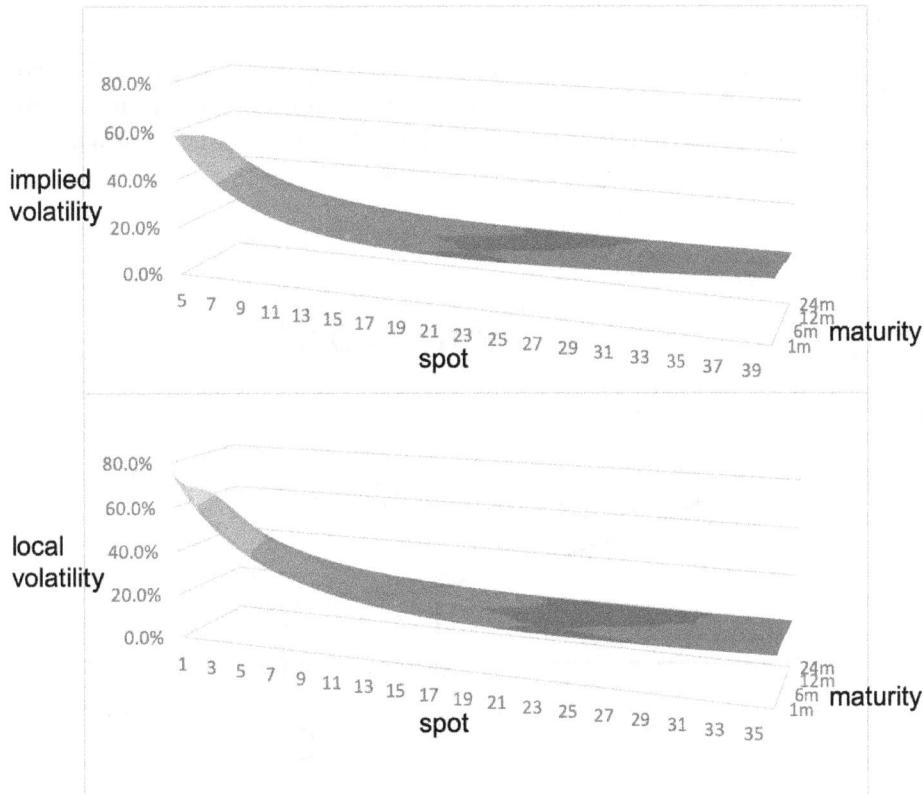

Figure 3.4: Illustration of the Dupire transformation between implied volatility (top) and local volatility (bottom).

As a summary, key properties of LV [98] are as follows

- LV reprices vanillas correctly when calibrated properly
- The spot dynamics fully explain LV instantaneous volatility moves
- LV assumes that the LV surface at a future spot and time remains constant, *i.e.* a calibration of the LV surface tomorrow should result in no change compared to today
- LV skew rises approximately twice as fast compared to the implied market, *i.e.* far out downside volatility tends to be (too) 'rich' in skew
- LV skew flattens out quickly over time which is a problem for forward skew sensitive options
- BSM volatility is approximately the average LV over the most likely path from current spot to strike [99, 48]
- Monte Carlo greeks (delta, gamma) can be unstable subject to how LV is implemented
- Because all volatility risk in LV is correlated with a spot move of the underlying, LV is market complete [41]

One main disadvantage lies in the fact that LV needs to be recalibrated frequently to be in line with the market. This will, in turn, result in adjusted hedge ratios and potential P/L variance. Note that this criticism is not reserved for LV alone as other models need to be recalibrated as well.

3.1.5   Skew Dynamics

As discussed in previous sections, implied volatility typically varies in the strike and maturity dimension. To calibrate and use a volatility model in trading, it is therefore vital to know how this surface evolves within the model when the spot moves. In other words, what happens to ATM volatility as a function of spot (see Figure3.5)?

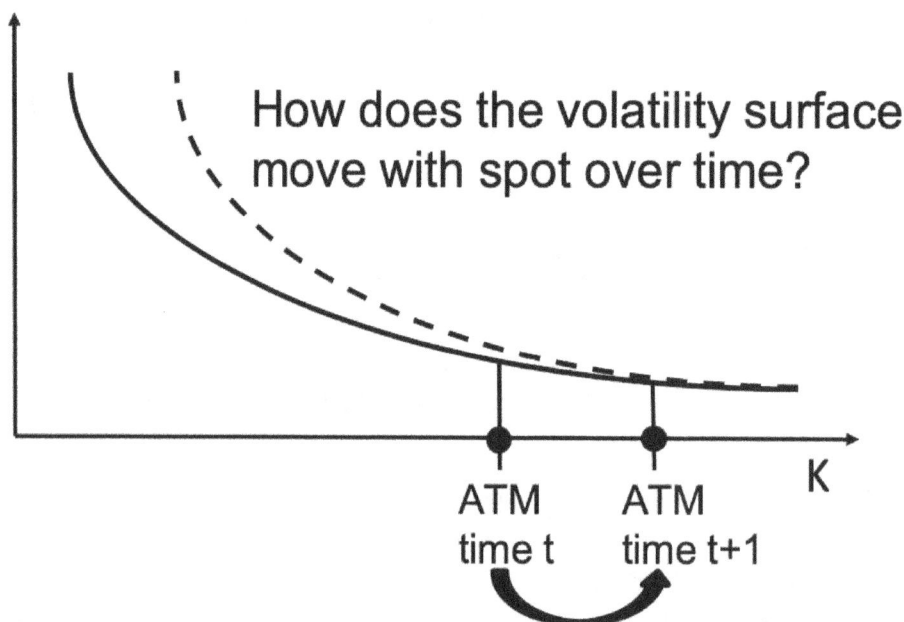

Figure 3.5: Illustration of the volatility surface dynamics in time.

Practitioners have devised three main models / regimes for volatility surface dynamics [100, 101]:

- **Sticky (or fixed) strike dynamics**: the implied volatility at a respective absolute strike stays constant

  $\rightarrow$ ATM volatility increases if the underlying spot decreases
- **Sticky moneyness (or floating strike or sticky delta) dynamics**: the implied volatility at a fixed delta or moneyness strike stays constant

  $\rightarrow$ ATM volatility decreases if the underlying spot decreases
- **Sticky implied tree (or sticky local volatility or super sticky strike) dynamics**: the implied volatility at a fixed strike moves in the opposite direction to the underlying, *e.g.* decreases as spot increases

  $\rightarrow$ ATM volatility rises approximately two times faster than sticky strike volatility

Figure 3.6 illustrates the respective dynamics further.

Sticky (or fixed) strike dynamics are typically observed in stable market regimes and the dynamics are in line with the BSM model. Hence, models following these dynamics typically fare well in fast rallies or slow sell-offs. Sticky moneyness (or floating strike) dynamics are often seen in trending market regimes, *e.g.* in a slow rally. The delta implied by the model is larger than the BSM delta. Sticky implied tree (or sticky local volatility or super sticky strike) dynamics are often observed in jumpy market regimes. The delta implied by the model is smaller than the BSM delta. Hence, models like this fare well in fast sell-offs and slow rallies.

I. Sticky (or fixed) strike dynamics

spot moves down (up)

ATM vol increases (decreases)

ATM ← ATM   K

II. Sticky moneyness (or floating strike) dynamics

spot moves down (up)

ATM vol stays constant

ATM ← ATM   K

III. Sticky implied tree (or sticky local vol or super sticky strike) dynamics

spot moves down (up)

ATM vol rises twice as fast as spot

ATM ← ATM   K

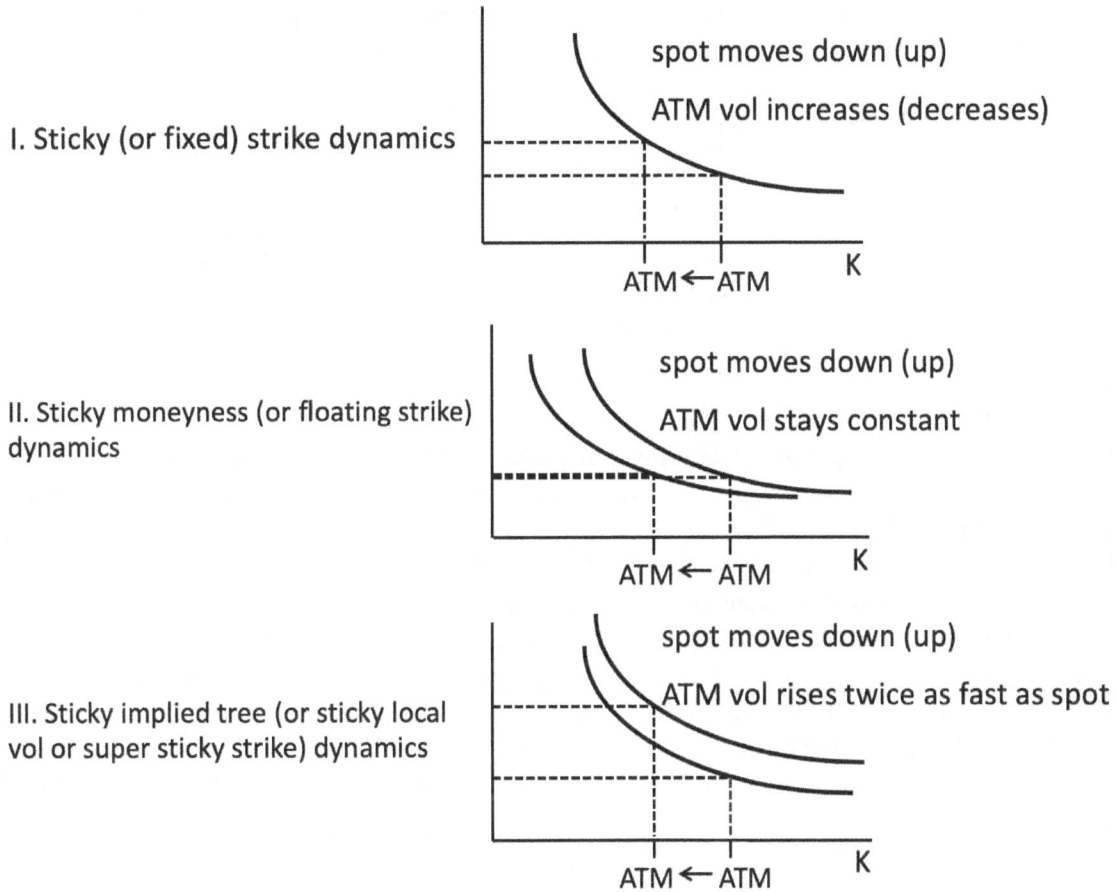

Figure 3.6: Illustration of the three main volatility surface skew dynamics: I. Sticky strike, II. Sticky moneyness and III. Sticky implied tree.

While this may sound all a bit academic, there are at least three reasons why market dynamics and their connection to a volatility model is essential. First, if one understands how volatility moves in a particular market regime and how the model represents it, it is possible to adapt the trading /hedging strategy to it. Second, the P/L attribution from derivative positions is different depending on the model used to value them. Finally, because of the former, the risk limit can be different as well since delta and vega P/L may be represented differently.

Given the frequent use of LV in valuing derivative positions, it is worth pointing out some of the crucial properties in more detail. Practitioners tend to like LV, among other things, because part of the skew and the volatility surface dynamics transfers into the delta [102]. The advantage is that the delta / underlying is a typically liquid asset, which can be traded quickly. The LV dynamics are in line with universal properties of markets (jumpy, fast sell-offs, slow rallies). For a short vega position, the local volatility delta is larger, *i.e.* to be delta flat, it is necessary to sell more physical delta. Mathematically, the relation can be seen as follows

$$\Delta_{total} = \Delta_{BSM} + vega\left(\frac{\partial \sigma}{\partial S} \cdot I\right), \tag{3.13}$$

whereby the indicator function I is zero for the baseline BSM delta, -1 for sticky moneyness and +1 for sticky local volatility. Finally, Table 3.1 illustrates the implied delta provided by the respective models following a particular spot/volatility scheme.

Delta	Sticky Delta		Sticky Strike		Sticky LV
Call Delta	Δ_C	>	Δ_C	>	Δ_C
Put Delta	Δ_P	>	Δ_P	>	Δ_P
abs(Put Delta)	$|\Delta_P|$	<	$|\Delta_P|$	<	$|\Delta_P|$

Table 3.1: Recap of the model implied delta for the three spot / volatility scenarios.

3.1.6 Quanto and Composite options

Quanto and Composite options are derivatives that allow the final payout to be in a different currency than the underlying currency. As a consequence, these options are also dependent on the respective foreign exchange (FX) rate. Even without formal proof, it seems intuitive that the *correlation* between the FX rate and the underlying asset must be a parameter in the pricing of these options.

Quanto and composite options serve a different purpose concerning their payout connection to FX rates. Whereas the Quanto option is designed to insulate the holder from exchange rate fluctuations, the composite option payoff explicitly depends on it. This is illustrated in Figure 3.7. The P/L of the Quanto call is just a function of the asset terminal spot value whereby the composite call P/L also depends on the final fixing of the FX rate. The latter can be beneficial or detrimental to the final payoff, *i.e.* for the same asset, a favorable FX rate move can increase the terminal value of the option significantly.

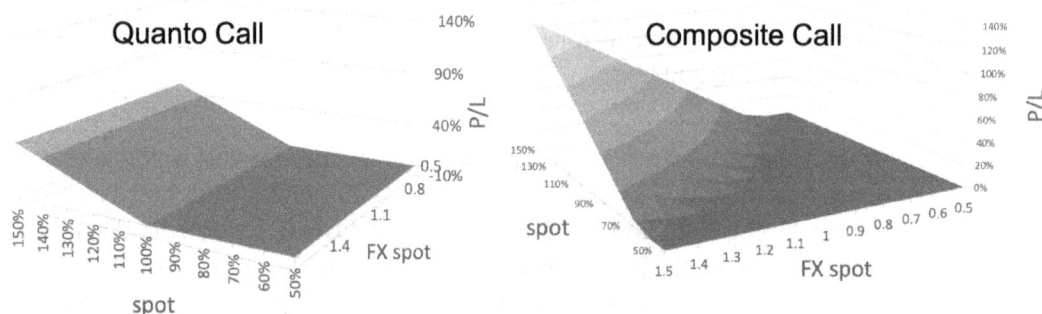

Figure 3.7: Illustration of the Quanto and composite call P/L for a strike at 100 and the initial FX set at 1.00.

FX is arguably a somewhat less complicated asset class compared to *e.g.* Fixed Income or Equities. There are typically no corporate actions, bespoke lifecycle events, the liquidity is high, and the market effectively operates 24/7. However, confusion can arise if the definition for the direction of the FX Pair concerning the quote is not clear. In the following discussion, the exchange rate FX_t at time t is defined as exchanging the derivative payout currency into 1 unit of underlying currency [1].

---

[1] In general, FX rates are quoted as ccy1/ccy2, *i.e.* number of units CCY2 per unit CCY1; this is the FOR-DOM *i.e.* FOReign-DOMestic FX convention

A similar dilemma arises when discussing the correlation between an asset and the FX rate. Therefore, the correlation between an asset (*e.g.* equity) and the FX rate ρ_{EQFX} is defined such that if it is positive/negative, it means that as the currency rate goes up, the underlying increases/decreases.

The formula for a vanilla Quanto option expressed in the payout currency is given by

$$\max\left[0, FX_0 \cdot I\left(\frac{S_T}{S_0} - K\right)\right], \tag{3.14}$$

with $I=1$ (call) and $I=-1$ (put). The FX exposure of the option is fully hedged since FX_0 is fixed at trade inception. Hence, the payout depends only on the final fixing of the underlying in the payout currency. As a consequence, the option holder is guaranteed to receive any payout in absolute terms of his reference currency.

Contrary to this, the composite option payout is given by

$$\max\left[0, I\left(\frac{FX_T \cdot S_T}{FX_0 \cdot S_0} - K\right)\right]. \tag{3.15}$$

Here the payout clearly depends on the underlying *and* FX rate evolution at expiry.

Figure 3.8 shows an example of the respective payout differences for a Quanto and composite call written on the Nikkei (traded in YEN) with USD as its payout currency for different equity and FX performance scenarios [2]

---

[2] The final call payout is obviously floored at zero, *i.e.* the investor never has a negative payout. Therefore, the negative percentage shown in the Figure does only concern performance.

10' 000 NKY
100 USDJPY
→ NKY($) 100

t=0   T

Branch 1

12' 000 NKY, 80 USDJPY — NKY($) = 12000/80 = 150 (+50%)
$Quanto = +20%, no FX benefit
$Composite = +50%, benefit from strong YEN

12' 000 NKY, 100 USDJPY — NKY($) = 12000/100 = 120 (+20%)
$Quanto = +20%
$Composite = +20%

12' 000 NKY, 130 USDJPY — NKY($) = 12000/130 = 92 (-7.7%)
$Quanto = +20%, no FX effect
$Composite = -7.7%, weak YEN effect

Branch 2

10' 000 NKY, 80 USDJPY — NKY($) = 10000/80 = 125 (+25%)
$Quanto = 0%, no FX benefit
$Composite = +25%, benefit from strong YEN

10' 000 NKY, 100 USDJPY — NKY($) = 10000/100 = 100 (+/-0%)
$Quanto = 0%
$Composite = 0%

10' 000 NKY, 130 USDJPY — NKY($) = 10000/130 = 77 (-23%)
$Quanto = 0%, no FX effect
$Composite = -23%, weak YEN effect

Branch 3

9' 000 NKY, 80 USDJPY — NKY($) = 9000/80 = 112 (+12%)
$Quanto = 0%, no FX benefit
$Composite = +12%, benefit from strong YEN

9' 000 NKY, 100 USDJPY — NKY($) = 9000/100 = 90 (-10%)
$Quanto = 0%
$Composite = -10%

9' 000 NKY, 130 USDJPY — NKY($) = 9000/130 = 69 (-31%)
$Quanto = 0%, no FX effect
$Composite = -31%, weak YEN effect

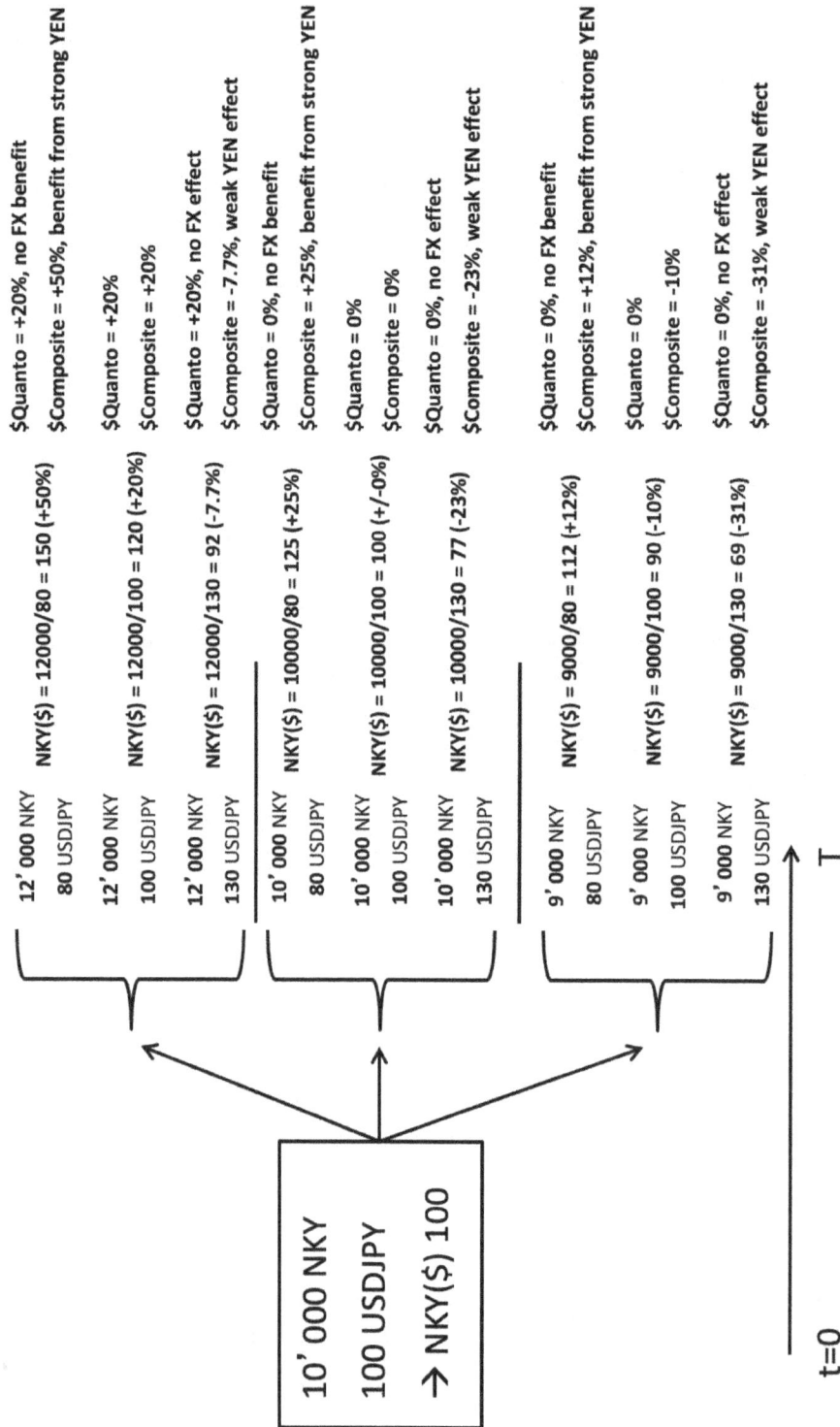

Figure 3.8: Illustration of a Quanto and composite cash flow example for a series of permutations between the underlying asset spot price and the FX rate.

3.1.6.1 Quanto forward adjustment

The traditional way of pricing a Quanto option (Q) follows from a simple adjustment to the vanilla forward (F) as

$$Q = F \cdot \exp[-\rho_{FX-AS} \cdot \sigma_{AS} \cdot \sigma_{FX}] \,, \tag{3.16}$$

where ρ_{FX-AS} is the FX to asset correlation (in the number of Quanto units per underlying currency unit), σ_{AS} the asset implied volatility and σ_{FX} the FX currency pair implied volatility. The FX equity correlation is now again said to be positive if underlying and underlying currency move in the same direction. Hence, for an *increasing* correlation the Quanto forward will *decrease*.

Note that the simple formula above is cutting several corners. Therefore, more elaborate adjustment methods are discussed later (see 3.1.6.5).

3.1.6.2 Quanto option dynamics

Given that investors often want to express their view on the underlying asset alone hedging out potential FX exposure is a frequent requirement. Therefore, Quanto options are encountered more frequently compared to composite options. Despite their seemingly simple nature, it is essential to understand the hedging behavior resulting from a Quanto option portfolio from the traders' point of view.

Consider selling a NKY Quanto USD forward to an investor, *i.e.* the trading book is *short* a liability in USD. The daily P/L is given by

$$P/L_t = -\$(\text{US Notional}) \cdot (NKY_t - \text{Quanto strike}) \,. \tag{3.17}$$

At inception, the trading book is *short* the NKY in USD, *i.e.* to hedge the equity one buys the NKY in YEN (*e.g.* via futures) and thereby goes *long* USD against YEN. This is because of the need to deliver the **USD performance of the NKY**. The exposure and risk are summarized in Figure 3.9.

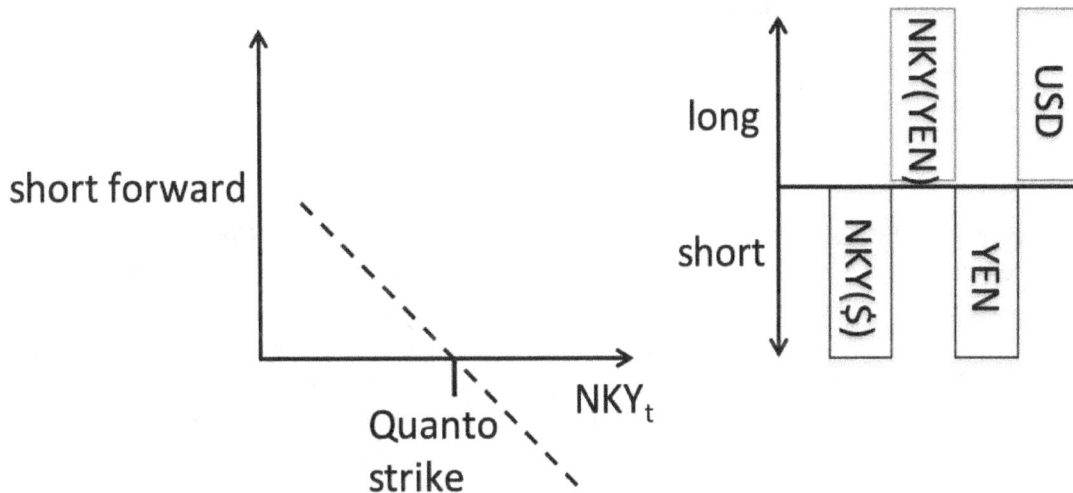

Figure 3.9: Illustration of a Nikkei Quanto USD forward exposure and risk.

The important question is now how the exposure is changing when the asset price or the FX rate moves. Figure 3.10 illustrates the behavior in case the FX rate moves. It is obvious that a move in the FX rate triggers a move in the equity delta because one either needs to deliver more or less of the NKY performance in the Quanto currency. Moreover, if the correlation is positive, one will sell/buy the NKY high/low. On the contrary, if the correlation is negative, one sells/buys the NKY low/high. Clearly, a positive correlation is more beneficial for the trader who is short the forward.

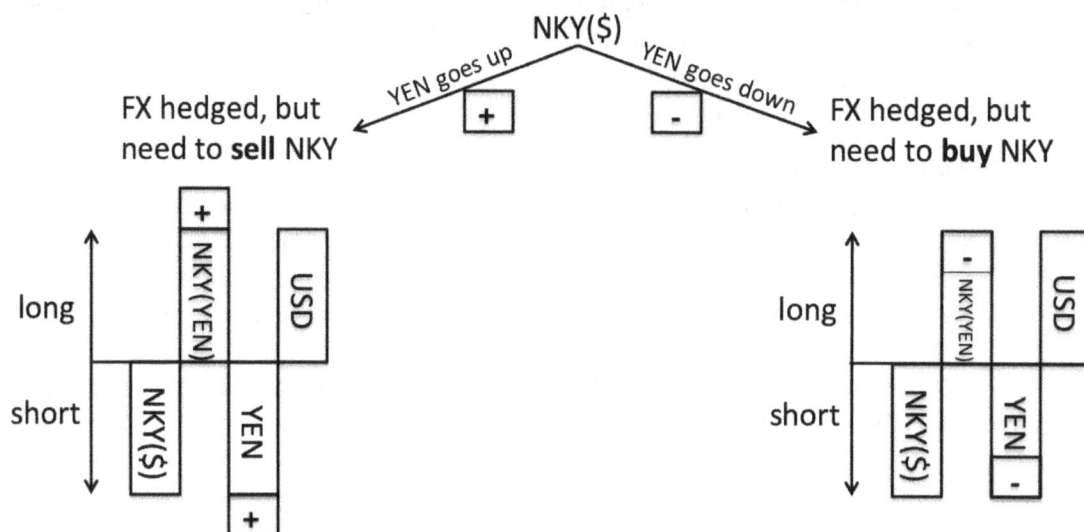

Figure 3.10: Illustration of a Nikkei Quanto USD forward scenario in case the FX rate moves. If the equity-FX correlation is positive, one will sell / buy the NKY high / low. If equity-FX correlation is negative, one will sell / buy the NKY low / high.

Figure 3.11 illustrates the behavior in case of equity price changes. Contrary to before, one now needs to adjust the FX hedge running against the position. Similar to before, if the correlation positive, one buys/sells the USD low/high. If the correlation negative, one buys/sells the USD high/low. Hence, in the case of a short Quanto forward position, the trader benefits from a positive correlation. In other words, the Quanto forward is then lower than the regular forward. The key question is obviously whether the correlation on the forward (possibly at inception) is always positive over the trade lifetime.

In 2008, the derivative market in Europe was exposed to large NKY Quanto EUR (short forward) positions via various exotic instruments. During the sell-off in the fall of 2008, the EURJPY FX correlation did turn negative, *i.e.* the YEN rallied while the equity market was selling off. This meant that operators were forced to sell the NKY at lower levels additionally. Hence, in this case, the Quanto forward exposure even contributed to the sell-off.

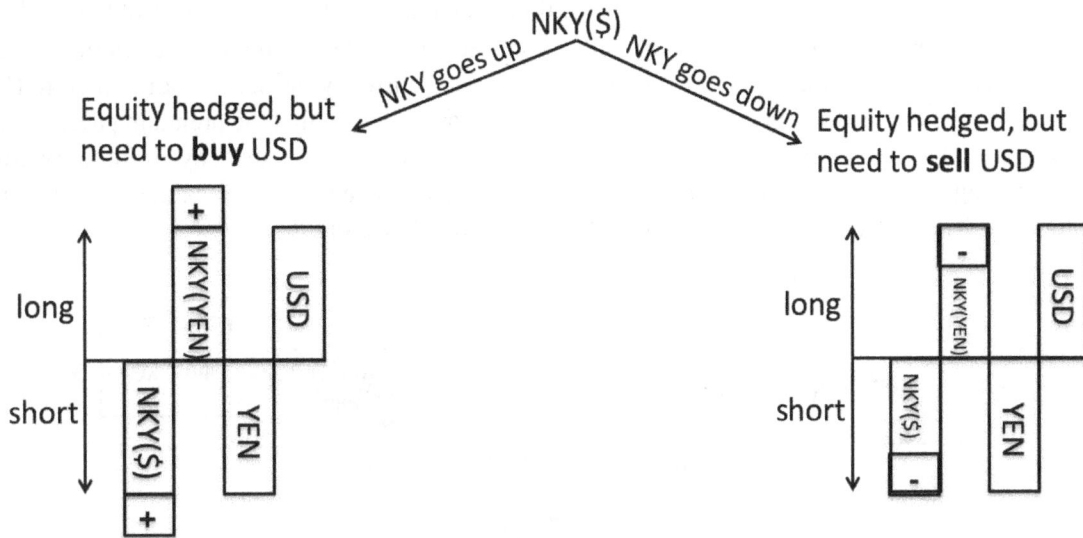

Figure 3.11: Illustration of a Nikkei Quanto USD forward scenario in case the equity performance changes. If equity-FX correlation positive, one will buy/sell the USD low/high. If equity-FX correlation negative, one will buy/sell the USD high/low.

3.1.6.3 Composite Option

As mentioned before, composite options are less frequently traded (especially for retail investors). However, they are instrumental for investors who want to protect the value of a foreign currency asset holding in their home/reference currency. The respective call/put composite formula for the FX expressed in payout currency is given by

$$\max\left[0, I\left(\frac{FX_T \cdot S_T}{FX_0 \cdot S_0} - K\right)\right], \tag{3.18}$$

with $I = +/- 1$ for a call or put option, respectively. The motivation for preferring the payout above is as follows. Consider a US investor holding 10'000 foreign shares currently trading at CHF 50. The USDCHF exchange rate is currently 2:1, *i.e.* 2 USD equals 1 CHF. Therefore, his holding today is worth $10'000 \cdot CHF50 = CHF500k$ or $USD1$m. To protect the investment, the investor buys a 1 year ATM composite put, *i.e.* the strike is USD 100 (note that the strike is now in the investors' reference currency). In one year, the shares are still trading at CHF 50, but the exchange rate has weakened to 1:1. Hence, there is a USD 500k loss on the shares due to the FX move alone. However, the put is now ITM and pays $10'000x\max(0,100\text{-}50) = USD500k$. Therefore, the loss is offset by the put the USD reference currency.

3.1.6.4 Composite Forward adjustment

For composite options, the traditional BSM adjustment is not on the drift but the volatility term as given by

$$\frac{dF}{F} = r_{comp} \cdot dt + \sqrt{\sigma_{EQ}^2 + 2 \cdot \rho_{EQFX} \cdot \sigma_{FX}\sigma_{EQ} + \sigma_{FX}^2}dW_t, \tag{3.19}$$

whereby the FX rate is defined as the composite currency per 1 unit of the underlying currency. All things being equal, it is evident that the forward for the composite option is typically higher, given that it includes two volatility components. This consequently makes the option more expensive.

For composite options, the FX hedge at inception is somewhat different. It is helpful to visualize the cash flows at inception for the example above in a schematic representation (see Figure 3.12). In essence, because the option is financed in the *composite* currency the seller not required to FX hedge the *premium* received in exchange for the option. However, note that the premium payer needs to hedge the FX on the premium to ensure financing in the composite currency. In other words, when paying for the premium in composite currency, one first needs to sell local currency to buy composite. The hedge itself works then the other way around (see Figure 3.13).

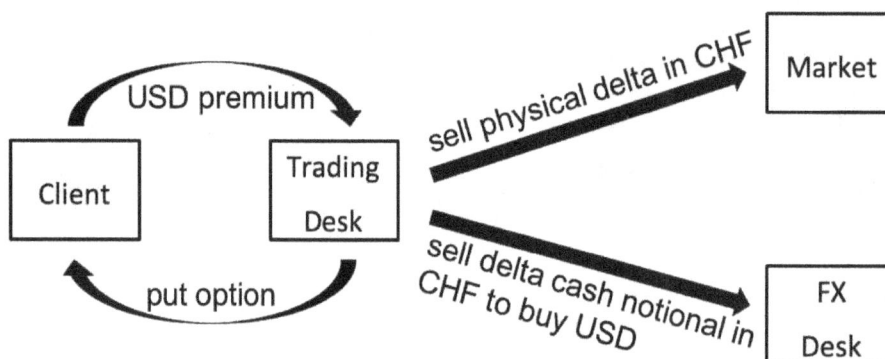

Figure 3.12: Illustration of a composite FX hedge at inception in case the trading desk receives the option premium.

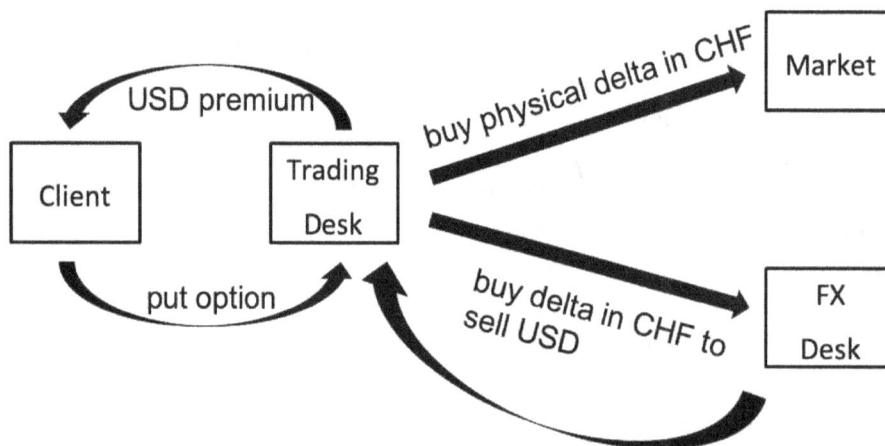

Figure 3.13: Illustration of a composite FX hedge at inception in case the trading desk pays the option premium.

In summary, for composite options, one needs to evaluate whether to buy / sell delta *and* pay / receive premium. The relation is summarized in Table 3.2.

Mechanism	Direction	Direction
Delta hedge	buy asset (local currency)	sell asset (local currency)
Resulting FX	buy local, sell composite	sell local, buy composite
Premium	pay	receive
Resulting FX	buy local, sell composite	do nothing

Table 3.2: Recap of composite option FX hedges.

Note that if the delta on the option changes, the FX needs to be adjusted accordingly, *i.e.* the relation is dynamic. In other words, the delta notional and the FX notional need to be in line to be fully hedged. Finally, at the expiry of the trade, the FX hedge needs to be unwound as well.

3.1.6.5 Quanto and Composite forward adjustment problems

While the Quanto and composite option hedging dynamics described above are model independent and true, the common question about the accuracy of the model-implied hedge ratios remain. In this sense, the approaches described above leading to the traditional Quanto and composite option pricing via an adjusted BSM formula remain standard but are not without problems. For example, in the formulas for both the Quanto and composite forward adjustment, it was not discussed which equity and FX volatility to use (ATM, OTM or a blend?). This is not at all obvious, and the respective pricing approximations are somewhat simplistic [103]. Moreover, the standard BSM Quanto methodology of adjusting the forward by the Quanto drift [103] can lead to wrong prices and risk as the joint moves in volatilities and spots over the lifetime are not fully captured. The FX skew risk is also missing. In other words, especially for large trading books, the adverse impact of the standard approaches can be quite significant. One remedy is to express both equity and FX dynamics in a local volatility model to obtain spot and FX level dependencies in time for both volatilities [104, 105, 106]. Regarding the Equity-FX correlation, it is crucial to recognize that this can indeed be unstable, including sign switches. In this sense, it is also critical to realize that the vega for Quanto / composite call/put options differs as a function of the correlation, *i.e.* Quanto / composite calls and puts have different vega unless the correlation is zero compared to vanillas. Due to the FX/spot dynamics especially Quanto options have an impact on the crash scenario risk of the trading book, *i.e.* stressing a large Quanto book must take FX moves into account as well. To improve crash risk, it is certainly advantageous to have a net position for which the book gets longer reserve currencies (*e.g.* USD, YEN) in a market downturn.

3.1.7 Stochastic volatility models: Heston

Even if the volatility in the LV model varies as a function of the spot, it is not a stochastic volatility model. In other words, once calibrated, the LV function $\sigma(S,t)$ is fully deterministic and does not contain any stochastic driver. One may argue that given the need for a frequent recalibration the actual process then becomes stochastic in volatility as well, but this does not mean that a calibrated LV model at time t is inherently stochastic. To approach this problem, an additional stochastic driver on top of the diffusive process is required. This class of models is called stochastic volatility models (SVM) [107].

Arguably the most well-known SVM and somewhat of a benchmark model such as BSM is the Heston model [108, 109]. It offers fast computation of European option prices and a reasonably good fit to market data in different regimes. However, to be market complete, it requires the use of a single option (in addition to stock delta). This is because delta-hedging can only remove variance risk which is correlated to the moves of the underlying. Hence, in case this correlation breaks down (as can be the case), an additional option hedge is required. The volatility in the Heston process is independent of the stock price level and represented as an Ornstein-Uhlenbeck-type [110] mean reversion process. For increasing spot levels, the volatility of a fixed strike and constant maturity increases as well. The mathematical representation of the model is given by

$$\frac{dS_i}{S} = (r-d) \cdot dt + \sqrt{v_t} dW_t^A , \tag{3.20}$$

with

$$dv = \kappa(\theta - v_t)dt + \eta\sqrt{v_t}dW_t^B . \tag{3.21}$$

The two stochastic drivers dW_t^S and dW_t^V are Brownians for the asset and the volatility process with a correlation ρ between -1 and +1 such that $dW_t^S dW_t^V = \rho dt$. v_t is the instantaneous variance, κ a mean reversion parameter, θ the long term variance and η the volatility of volatility (vol-of-vol) [3].

The correlation and the vol-of-vol parameter generate the volatility skew in the model (see Figure 3.14). More specifically, the vol-of-vol controls the magnitude and the correlation the tilt in the resulting surface. Unfortunately, the parameters are not as independent as one might wish, *i.e.* interdependency must be understood and carefully examined when fitting the model.

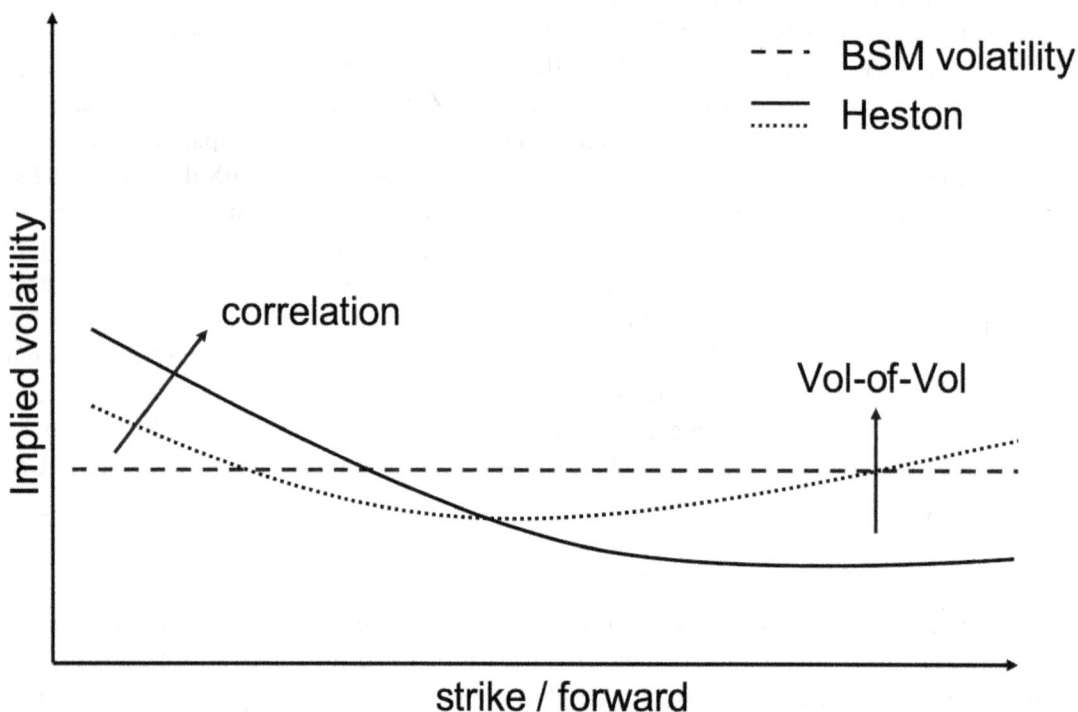

Figure 3.14: Illustration of implied volatility skew and curvature adjustment in the Heston model.

The parameter interdependence is a general issue with almost all SVM. This problem has partly to do with the fact that it is non-trivial to intuitively link market implied volatility with instantaneous

---

[3]Note that the Heston model uses the same stochastic process as the CIR model for the case of the interest short rate (see equation 2.20).

variance expressed via some potentially strongly varying and arbitrary parameters. This problem is not purely academic. By introducing more parameters, the parameter calibration procedure may introduce model risk on its own. Taking the example of the Heston model, two different calibration procedures may lead to different prices for exotic options despite fitting the vanilla market prices equally well [111, 112]. Hence, introducing more parameters or a theoretically superior model may well lead to pricing inconsistencies or calibration risk despite a perfect calibration.

A problem specific to Heston is that the process for the instantaneous variance may reach zero with nonzero probability. Even if this made sense, it causes numerical issues. In order to ensure this does not happen the so-called Feller condition is typically enforced, i.e. $2\kappa\theta \geq \eta^2$. Unfortunately, when calibrating to market data, this condition is often violated. Another drawback is that the Heston model implies an undesirable joint-dynamic between short-term skew and volatility as the short-term skew is *inversely* proportional to short-term ATM volatility $\frac{d\sigma(K,T)}{dK} \approx \frac{\rho\eta}{4\sigma_{\text{ATM}}}$ [113]. Unfortunately, there is no empirical evidence for this behavior.

3.1.8 Local Stochastic volatility models

In practice, tier-1 banks do not use an out-of-the-box Heston model to price or value products sensitive to stochastic volatility. Rather, the preferred model of choice today is a mixed LV-SV model, i.e. a so-called Local Stochastic Volatility (LSV) Model [114, 115, 116, 117, 118]. The LSV is calibrated to the implied volatility surface while retaining the ability to model the volatility process stochastically. The resulting model is effectively LV with an additional noise factor following a particular probability distribution.

Even if not necessarily advisable given the discussion above, it is possible to derive a SVM whereby the stochastic part of the volatility follows the Heston model as

$$dS_t = (r-d)S_t dt + \sqrt{v_t} f(S,t) S_t dW_t^S . \tag{3.22}$$

While all other parameters are identical to the Heston model, the function $f(S,t)$ must satisfy

$$\sigma^2(S,t) = f^2(S,t) \, \mathbf{E}[V_t | S_t = S] , \tag{3.23}$$

i.e. the local volatility function $\sigma(S,t)$ is calibrated to the respective market quotes. The major difficulty lies in the calibration procedure and also in which order the parameter calibration is conducted [119]. Nonetheless, in an ideal setting, one ends up with a LSV model that reprices vanillas and accounts for volatility convexity as well. It is in any case advisable to assess the latter component by repricing very convex derivatives such as variance options to be able to assess the residual volatility stochasticity.

3.1.9 Barrier Options

Barrier options are arguably the most commonly traded exotics and come in several variations (e.g. knock-in / knock-out options and digital / binary options) [120, 121, 122, 123]. The term barrier typically refers to a pre-defined price observed with respect to the asset spot level over the lifetime. Once the barrier is touched, some features of the payout either becomes alive (knock-in option) or get removed (knock-out option). Apart from contract-specific terms, barrier options tend to share the following characteristics:

- (high) path-dependency
- option value and greeks change significantly upon barrier event

- the payout is typically (partially) discontinuous
- increased sensitivity to volatility surface dynamics (*e.g.* skew/kurtosis changes)
- increases the difficulty to replicate the payout
- increased mark-to-market P/L variance

3.1.9.1 Barrier Options: Digital

Digital options are fundamental components of many exotic payouts irrespective of the asset class. Due to their binary nature, digitals can both be dangerous but may also offer large P/L opportunities. Sometimes digital risk can be hidden in opaque payouts or at least not be immediately visible at inception. Therefore, it is advisable to analyze payouts for these types of discontinuous scenarios carefully. Luckily, there are some general principles and hedging techniques one can employ across all asset classes to mitigate dangerous situations before they occur.

A typical (European) digital option pays out a pre-defined value in case the underlying closes above (or under) a particular level at expiry. This is effectively a binary bet (see Figure 3.15). For example, a 1 year 10% ATM digital option on the S&P 500 pays out 10% times the notional if the S&P 500 closes above the current ATM strike in one year. In other words, at expiry, the option is worth either zero or 10% times the notional. If one sells this option for a notional of USD 100m, the trader is potentially facing a USD 10m bet at expiry.

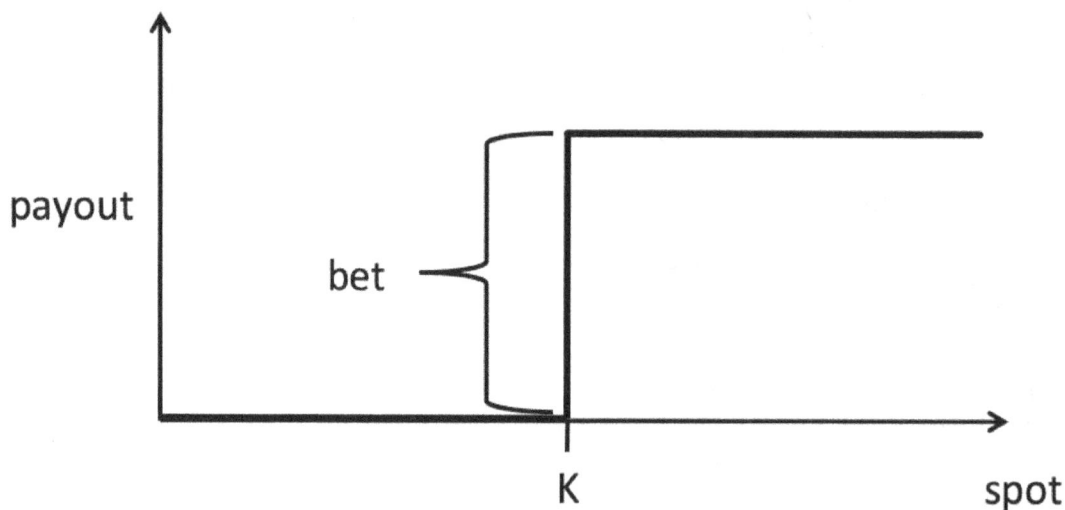

Figure 3.15: Illustration of digital option payoff / bet centered at a strike K.

Using the BSM replication argument, trading the underlying generates the payout if the asset spot passes through the barrier, *i.e.* the trader aims to buy enough of the asset at a lower price to later sell for a profit above the barrier. Depending on the bet size and the liquidity of the underlying, the risk can be very tricky to manage. The conventional approach is to consider the digital as the limit of an infinitely tight call spread given by

$$\text{digital}(K) = \lim_{\varepsilon \to 0} \frac{1}{2\varepsilon} \left[C(K - \varepsilon) - C(K + \varepsilon) \right] = -\frac{\partial C(K)}{\partial K} \tag{3.24}$$

whereby ε determines the width of the call spread (see Figure 3.16).

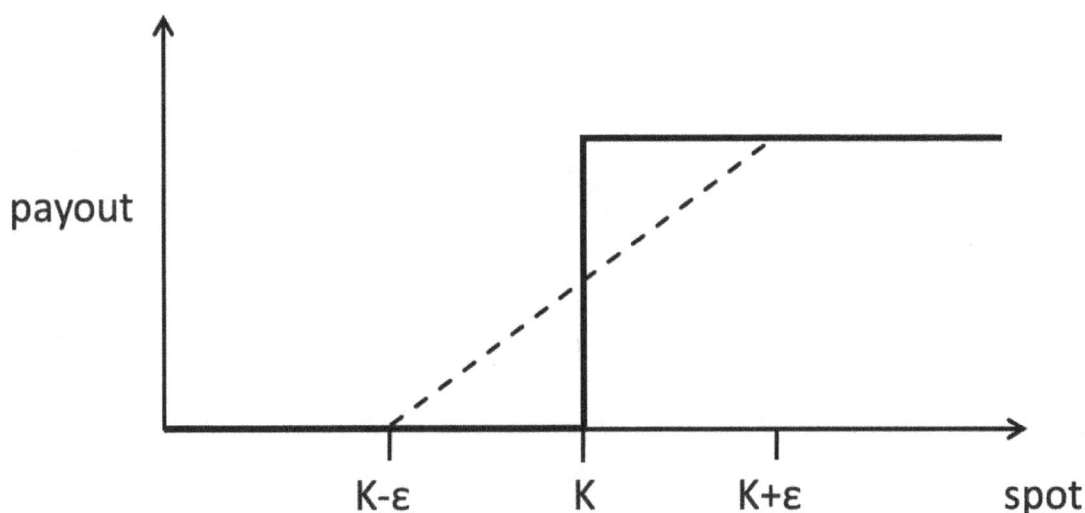

Figure 3.16: Illustration of hedging a digital option payoff (solid line) using a call spread (dashed line).

In other words, $1/\varepsilon$ call spreads of width 2ε are required to replicate the digital. In principle, there are at least two ways to manage the trade. Indeed, it might be possible to buy and sell the required amount of vanilla options below and above the strike (barrier) to generate the digital payoff. However, for large bets, this might be impossible and too expensive, depending on available strikes and liquidity. Alternatively, one can actively manage the risk of the trade such that the performance is solely generated by trading the underlying alone. To do the latter, practitioners typically represent the call spread by shifting the barrier away from the original barrier strike, to take the liquidity of the underlying into account (*i.e.* the maximum delta tradable, see Figure 3.17). This practice is a so-called **overhedge**, *i.e.* a recipe for creating a hedge ratio *in excess* compared to the one implied/required by the model. In the example above for the S&P 500, one might assume a maximum tradable underlying delta of CHF 250m (via futures), so that the *barrier shift* equates to: $0.5 \cdot 10\% \cdot 100m/250m = 2\%$. What the barrier-shift does in practice is to allow for building up the delta position earlier. The technique of using barrier shifts is common risk management or an overhedge technique traders apply when dealing with discontinuous payoffs [120, 121]. This approach is also known as *barrier bending* implying the aim to smooth out the discontinuity. It is also possible to use a more elaborate mathematical function for the barrier-shift which further smoothens the delta build up by using *e.g.* a sigmoidal profile compared to a straight line. Whether to manage the risk of a particular trade close to the barrier using the shift or not is a matter of practical experience and taste. Some traders prefer to trade at the model-implied delta and thereby monetize the barrier-shift before expiry as a windfall profit. Besides, the proceeds can be used to buy gamma using other options, and in general cover potential losses in case the digital expires ITM.

barrier shift

$$\text{barrier shift} = \frac{1}{2} \frac{dig \times N}{\text{delta max}}$$

payout

90   100   spot

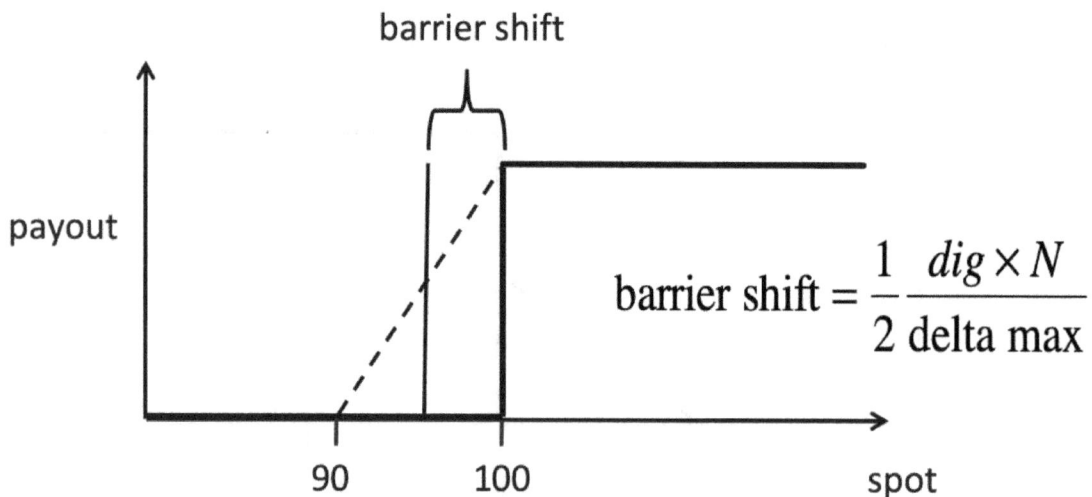

Figure 3.17: Illustration of hedging a digital option payoff using a barrier shift.

3.1.9.2 Barrier Options: Digital Greeks

In terms of risks or greek sensitivities associated with digital options three stand out: vega, skew and gamma. On the vega side of things, the sign (long/short) of the vega exposure depends on the forward. If the forward is lower than the current spot, then the holder is long volatility because an increase in volatility elevates the probability of reaching the barrier. The opposite is valid for a forward price higher than the current spot. However, note that the exposure may change as a function of time to maturity as well.

In terms of skew, given that the digital can be considered as the limit of an infinitely tight call spread, it is clear that it must be sensitive to skew (around the strike). The seller of the option is short the call spread and therefore short skew. Pricing the digital with a volatility model that does *not* take skew into account typically leads to a misprice in terms of vega/skew risk. The greeks exposure above is mainly essential for pricing the option at inception. More relevant is arguably the evolution of gamma and vega close to the barrier and in case the spot moves through it. As shown in the case of barrier options below, gamma, vega, and less importantly, theta exposure reverses sign as the spot passes through the barrier. The sign change leads to situations whereby the position exhibits *mixed* convexity in case the payout transitions between OTM and ITM. In the case of a short digital, the trader is then short gamma when OTM and long gamma when ITM. In the worst-case scenario, the spot exhibits significant realized variance as it passes through the barrier, resulting in delta losses, whereby it then stops moving such that the position incurs further losses on the long gamma / short theta beyond the barrier. In case re-hedging becomes necessary by selling gamma to cover the theta, it is then possible to get trapped on both sides of the barrier. This scenario is later revisited for interest rate (spread) range accrual notes for which trading desks incurred substantial losses in 2008.

3.1.9.3 Barrier Options: Types

Barrier options are typically less expensive compared to their vanilla counterparts and exist in four main flavors: Down-and-Out (knock-out family), Up-and-Out (knock-out family), Down-and-In (knock-in family) and Up-and-in (knock-in family). Here the first attribute refers to the activation direction (*e.g.* 'down' means that activation occurs following a downside barrier hit) whereas the other attributes refer to the event following an activation (*e.g.* 'in' means that the option converts to a vanilla option). Out of the 8 possible (put / call, in / out) barrier option combinations only 4 trade frequently (see Figure 3.18.

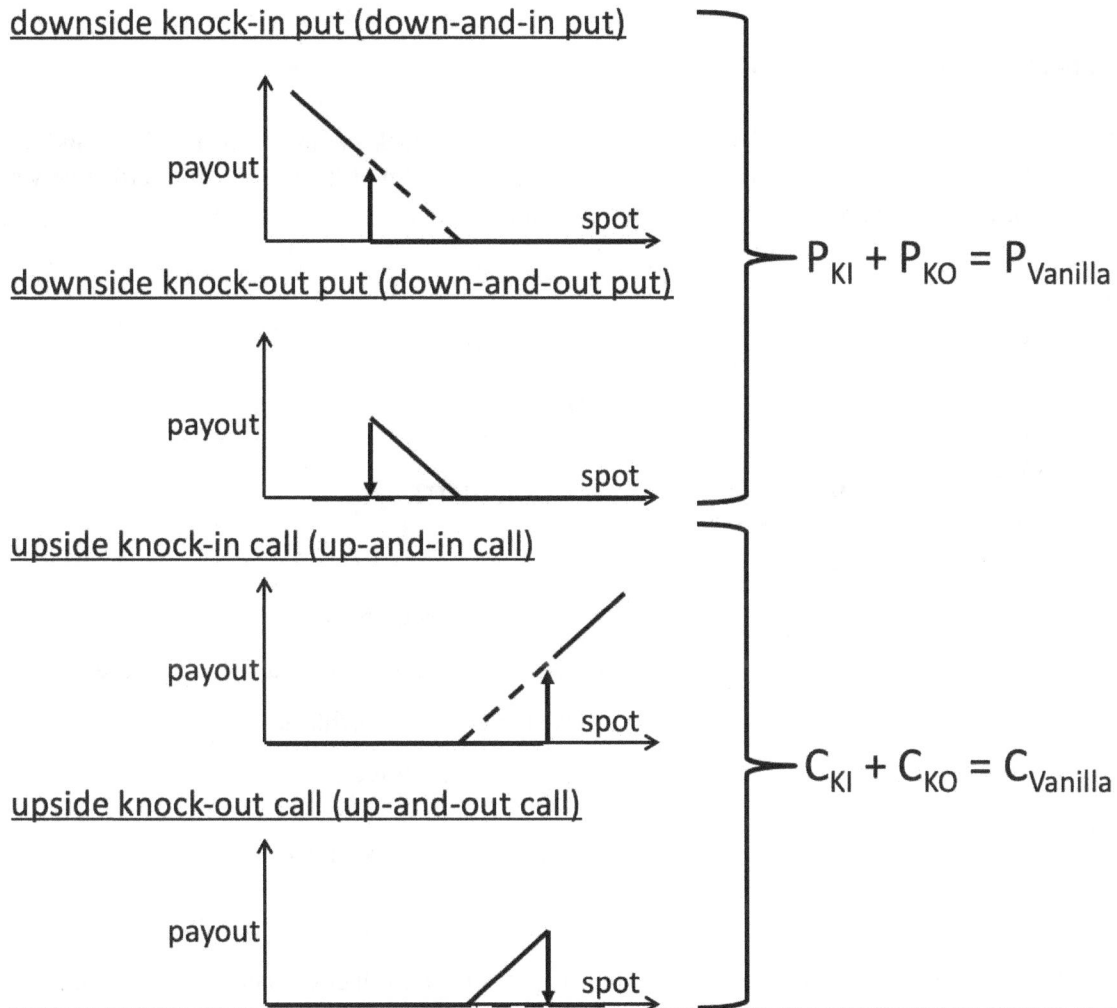

<u>downside knock-in put (down-and-in put)</u>

<u>downside knock-out put (down-and-out put)</u>

$$P_{KI} + P_{KO} = P_{Vanilla}$$

<u>upside knock-in call (up-and-in call)</u>

<u>upside knock-out call (up-and-out call)</u>

$$C_{KI} + C_{KO} = C_{Vanilla}$$

Figure 3.18: Illustration of the most common (in/out) barrier option types. Note that the combination of two in and out barrier options reproduces the canonical vanilla option.

The downside knock-in put (down-and-in put) is thereby clearly the most common overall as it is a frequent component in retail Structured Products. Note that the vanilla option counterpart of a barrier option payoff can be synthetically created by combining the respective knock-in and knock-out option, *i.e.* Vanilla = knock-in + knock-out. The strike, as well as the barrier, can be OTM, ATM and ITM concerning the fixing. Moreover, the barrier monitoring can be discrete, continuous or within in a pre-defined window. The latter property has significant risk-management consequences and is addressed later.

Knock-out options are sometimes traded with a rebate to compensate for the knock-out (*e.g.* in case of a rebate knock-out, the option holder receives a payment/rebate of X% times the trade notional). Double barriers rarely trade in the equity market but are relatively commonly seen in FX.

Note that double barriers (*e.g.* double no-touch also known as range binary, a common instrument in the FX market; see discussion below 3.1.9.6) are often very convex in terms of dvega/dvol and typically require a stochastic volatility model. In general, barrier options are priced using the LVM model for equities and some form of LVS model in the FX space.

3.1.9.4 Barrier Options: European knock-in put

The European (*i.e.* meaning barrier observed at expiry only) knock-in (also known as down-and-in) put can be statically hedged using vanilla put spreads. The width of the put spread is effectively a barrier shift and is chosen as a function of bet size and liquidity.

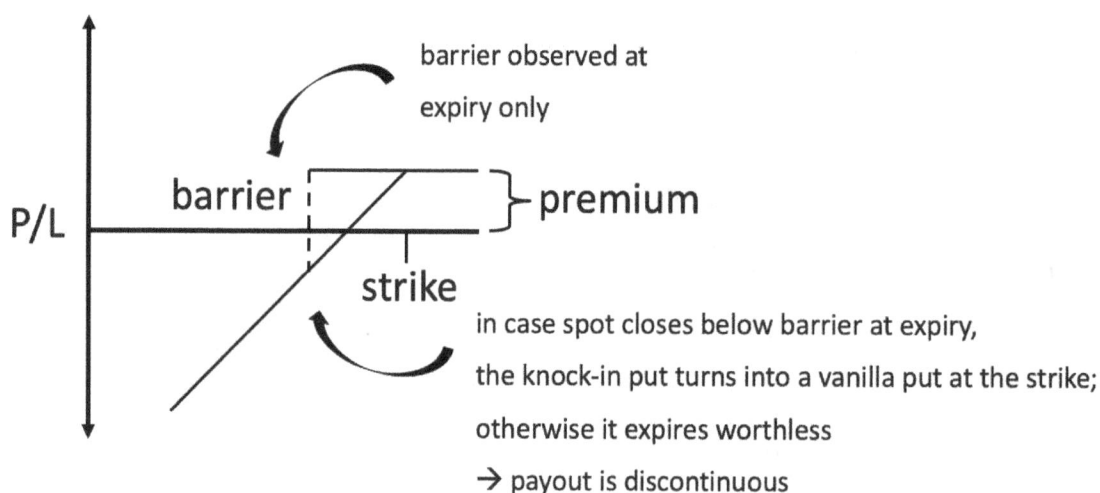

Figure 3.19: Illustration of European knock-in put.

Consider a 100% strike, 60% barrier ki-put expiring in 1 year. If it closes below/at 60% it finishes ITM with a value of at least 40%. In other words, the bet is 40% times the notional at maturity. This bet can be hedged with a leveraged vanilla put spread of width X. The maximum amount of leverage one can obtain in terms of liquidity in the market determines the width, *i.e.* this is the same analysis as before with the digital option.

Assume one needs to trade the puts with a width of 5% due to liquidity constraints. The replication portfolio is:

- long 1 times the 60% strike 1Y put
- long 40/5 = 8 times the 60% strike 1Y put
- short 40/5 = 8 times the 55% strike 1Y put

The replicating portfolio is illustrated in Figure 3.20.

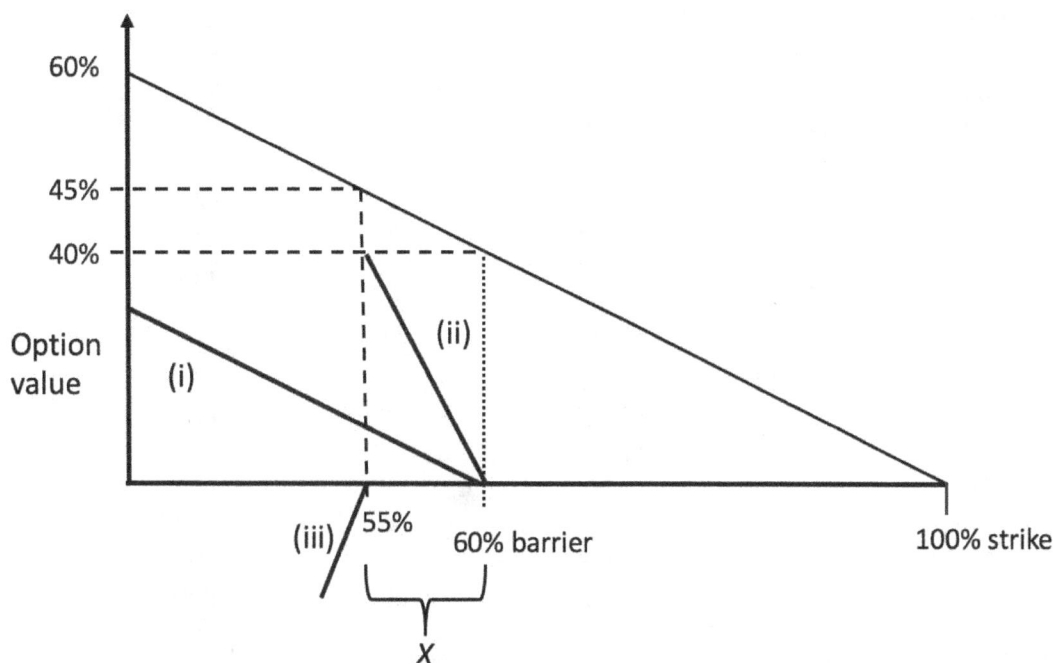

Figure 3.20: Illustration of European knock-in put hedge for a barrier at 60% (dotted line) using a putspread width of $X=5\%$: (*i*) long 1 times the 60% strike 1Y put, (*ii*) long 40/5 = 8 times the 60% strike 1Y put and (*iii*) short 40/5 = 8 times the 55% strike 1Y put. The solid black lines (*i*,(*ii*),(*iii*)) denote the respective option payouts schematically.

The pricing with a put spread of width X is equivalent to applying a barrier shift. In other words, the price is more conservative/cheaper before the barrier, which can be seen when comparing the payouts in absolute terms (see Table 3.3). Hence, the replication is done via an overhedge, *i.e.* the hedge is worth more than the actual source trade. Note that these type of (barrier shift) overhedge techniques are independent of the asset class, *i.e.* they can be applied to equity, foreign exchange, commodity and interest rate derivatives.

final fixing spot	EP ki 100/60	long 1 x 60 EP	long 8 x 60EP	short 8 x 55EP	SUM repl. portfolio
60.00%	40.00%	0.00%	0.00%	0.00%	0.00%
59.00%	41.00%	1.00%	8.00%	0.00%	9.00%
58.00%	42.00%	2.00%	16.00%	0.00%	18.00%
57.00%	43.00%	3.00%	24.00%	0.00%	27.00%
56.00%	44.00%	4.00%	32.00%	0.00%	36.00%
55.00%	45.00%	5.00%	40.00%	0.00%	45.00%
54.00%	46.00%	6.00%	48.00%	-8.00%	46.00%
53.00%	47.00%	7.00%	56.00%	-16.00%	47.00%
52.00%	48.00%	8.00%	64.00%	-24.00%	48.00%
51.00%	49.00%	9.00%	72.00%	-32.00%	49.00%
50.00%	50.00%	10.00%	80.00%	-40.00%	50.00%
49.00%	51.00%	11.00%	88.00%	-48.00%	51.00%
48.00%	52.00%	12.00%	96.00%	-56.00%	52.00%
47.00%	53.00%	13.00%	104.00%	-64.00%	53.00%
46.00%	54.00%	14.00%	112.00%	-72.00%	54.00%
45.00%	55.00%	15.00%	120.00%	-80.00%	55.00%

Table 3.3: P/L of European knock-in out versus =components and sum of the replicating portfolio.

3.1.9.5 Barrier Options: American Knock-in Put

The American knock-in put is arguably the most common light exotic derivative component embedded in many Structured Products (see Chapter 9). Since it is possible to replicate the European knock-in using vanilla options fully, it is not a path-dependent derivative. The same is not valid for the American variant of the option for which the barrier can be breached typically at any time before expiry. If one knew the exact date of the barrier breach *ex-ante* the same replication strategy as for the European variant would work. However, this is not the case. As a consequence, the hedging strategy becomes dynamic. The seemingly small variation of turning a discrete barrier into a continuous one also has a significant impact on the risk management requirements. For starters, it is now required to monitor a potential knock-in event intraday, *i.e.* requiring both risk management system and trader to be alerted whenever the spot is approaching a respective barrier. Monitoring requirements sound like a small thing but depending on the size of the asset universe covered, including different time zones, it does increase the organizational complexity significantly. Moreover, as the following analysis shows missing a (delta-hedged) barrier can have large adverse P/L consequences.

The characteristic risk profile of long American knock-in of strike K and maturity T is as follows

- short delta
- long gamma (peak on the downside mostly)
- long vega (downside)
- long skew (at inception)
- short Dvega/Dspot & Dvega/Dvol
- long dividends
- short Ddiv/Dspot

Hence, to hedge first order risk, one needs to least buy the underlying and sell vega via vanillas (or exotics). Buying the underlying is trivial but selling vega is not given that the vega peak shifts as a function of the time to expiry of the option (see Figure 3.21). Hence, at inception one is faced with a vega profile centered around the strike, which could be covered by selling a vanilla (put) at the strike. However, the peak is then moving closer towards the barrier with a decreasing lifetime. Finally, if the option were to knock-in, the peak would again be centered at the strike since it converts to a vanilla European put. Please note as well that the vega profile is also decreasing as the spot moves closer to the barrier, *i.e.* dvega/dspot is potentially not in line with what one would desire in a distressed situation. Also, the dvega/dvol profile is also against the buyer of the option, *i.e.* as volatility increases, the vega exposure decreases.

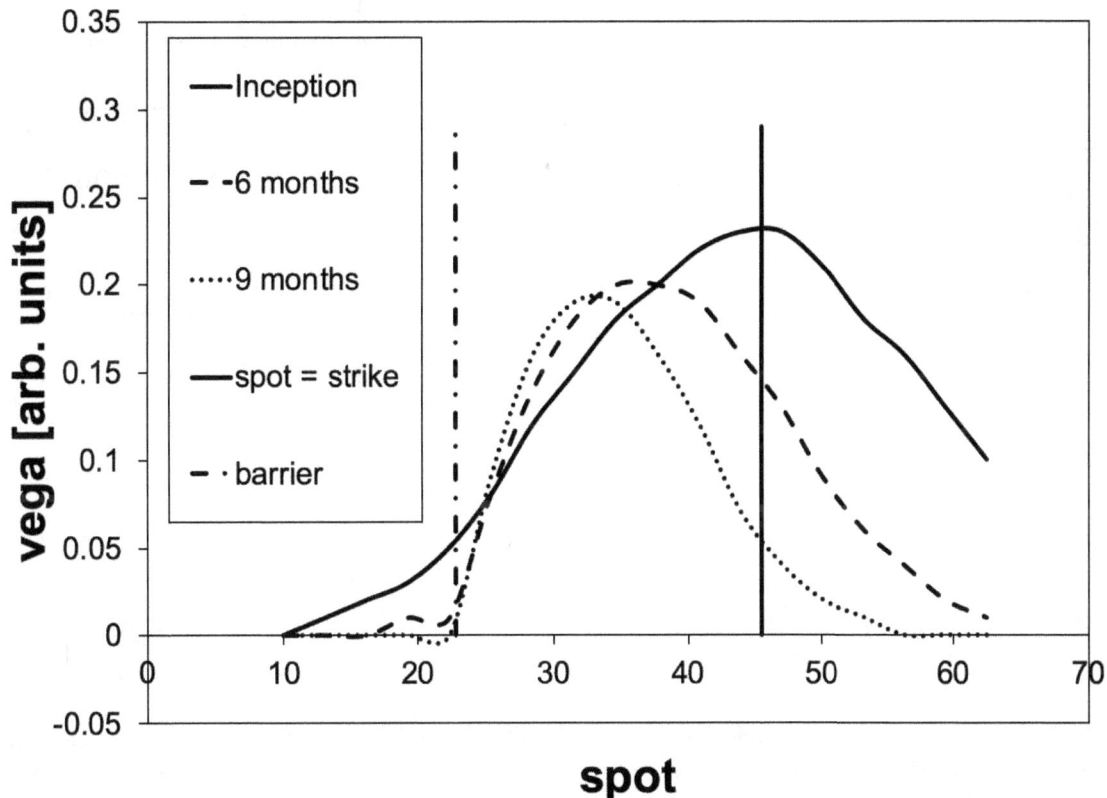

Figure 3.21: Illustration of the vega for an American knock-in put as a function of time to maturity.

The delta profile of the American knock-in is another key risk factor when the spot approaches the barrier. As shown in Figure 3.22, the delta close to the barrier near expiry can be significantly larger than 100%, *i.e..* the option buyer is increasingly buying more of the underlying asset to be delta flat. However, once the barrier is triggered, the delta resets to 100% in line with a deep ITM put, which means that the trader is forced to sell the excess delta into a falling market. If one is not able to liquidate the excess delta at the right level, the trade potentially incurs a large loss on the delta hedging activity. This particular risk is often called *gap risk* denoting the possibility of a sharp price drop whereby the asset 'gaps' such that losses cannot be mitigated by hedging [4]. This is also reflected in the gamma profile whereby the option holder is long gamma before the barrier and short as the asset spot passes crosses it. This type of risk profile is identical to a risk reversal (long call /

---

[4]The term gap risk is also used in the context of other financial product. For example, collateralized loans can experience a sudden drop in the collateral value (gap) resulting in a shortfall/credit event versus the loan.

short put) and in general not trivial to manage especially for large and/or illiquid positions of the underlying.

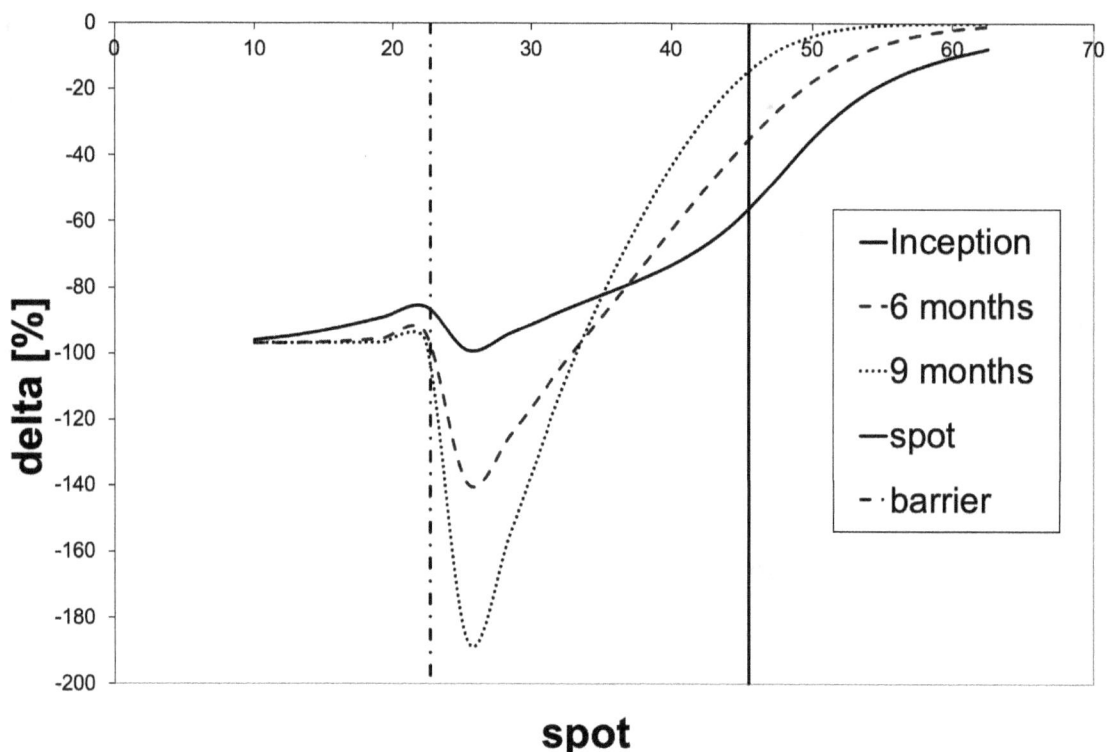

Figure 3.22: Delta spot scenario for the American knock-in put. Upon a barrier hit the excess delta of the underlying needs to be sold in a falling market.

The question now is how to hedge the American knock-in in practice. The answer depends on various factors such as liquidity of the underlying, maturity and barrier level of the option. Typically, practitioners sell a downside put against the barrier for trades with maturity shorter or equal to 1 year (*e.g.* selling a 90% strike put is often sufficient). For trades with maturity larger than 1 year, one needs to either sell a put with a lower strike, trade a downside ratio put spread or trade a risk reversal. As a consequence, the basis risk between position and hedge increases.

If possible, it is advisable to buy some vega/gamma below the barrier to help with the scenario of a barrier hit. Most often, the barrier-shift profit upon a release is used to unwind the hedge. The lower the barriers, the more difficult it is to hedge the exposure and volatility-of-volatility increases in importance. Selling index options against single stock barriers means running a dispersion book and the resulting correlation exposure needs to be carefully monitored. As a consequence, mark-to-market P/L variance increases as well. Selling credit (*e.g.* CDS, iTraxx) against the barrier introduces basis risk since credit and equity markets are sometimes dislocated (*e.g.* early 2010).

Another variation on the American barrier lies in the monitoring frequency of the barrier itself. While the barrier monitoring is typically intraday, it is sometimes contractually observed only on the close. The corresponding adjustment from a continuously priced barrier, to a barrier on the close, can be done by modifying the implied volatility used in the model. Since the probability of hitting a barrier on close *only* must be less compared to the continuous case, the volatility is effectively decreased. Alternatively, it is possible to adjust the barrier level to reflect the increased probability of a barrier hit in the continuous versus discrete case [124] as $V_c(B) = V_d(B \cdot \exp[+/- \beta \sigma \sqrt{T/m}]$. Here $V_c(B)$ and $V_d(B)$ are the values of the continuous and discrete versions of the same barrier option with barrier level B, monitoring events m and $\beta = -\zeta(1/2)/\sqrt{2\pi} \approx 0.5826$ (with ζ being the Riemann zeta function). The + applies if $B > S_0$ and - applies if $B < S_0$. Hence, in case of a knock-in put the barrier is shifted further away for a discretely monitored barrier. Note that all closed-form barrier pricing formulas and PDE pricers assume that barriers are continuously monitored. For Monte Carlo pricing, the simulated path for the continuous case is typically only with daily time increments, $i.e.$ this assumes a discretely monitored barrier. However, for the latter, it is not standard to adjust for the difference to a continuous barrier. The reason is that it is questionable whether the $increased$ path-dependency of a discrete barrier is fully captured by any (ad-hoc) adjustment in practice. For example, trading the required delta given a barrier hit in the closing auction can be very inconvenient and certainly more complicated than managing the barrier intraday.

Finally, it is worth to revisit the impact of dividend modeling. Recall that mixing absolute and proportional dividends may have an impact on the derivative price (see section 2.2.20.6). In the case of the downside barrier put (or structures embedding them), the trader is long dividends for a long put position. However, in case the dividends are modeled proportionally, the dividend delta at lower spot regions is less given that they move proportionally with the spot. As a consequence, the price with absolute dividends is more expensive. Hence, for longer dated trades, the mixing cutoff in time needs to be carefully assessed.

3.1.9.6 Barrier Options: Double-No-Touch (DNT)

As a rule of thumb, it is good practice to expect high vanna and volgamma sensitivity when encountering any barrier option. In particular, concerning volgamma, it should now be known from the earlier discussion that both BSM and LVM are not suitable to assess this impact alone. One barrier product which is very sensitive to volgamma despite its relatively simple payout is the so-called Double-No-Touch (DNT) option. The DNT is frequently traded in the FX market and is effectively a double barrier digital option. For the DNT, the holder receives a predetermined payout if, during the life of the trade, the underlying never crosses neither an upside nor a downside barrier with respect to the initial strike, $i.e.$

$$P/L = N \cdot H \,, \tag{3.25}$$

where $H = 1$ if the underlying asset always traded within the range and $H=0$ otherwise. Through intuition, the holder of this option is short vega since he wants the asset to move as little as possible, $i.e.$ volatility is not desired. However, how does this look like for the volgamma? It should not surprise that the shape depends on the placement and separation of the two barriers. For a narrow symmetrical DNT, the exposure is shown in Figure 3.23. Vega as well as volgamma take the shape of a Gaussian of opposite sign. Hence, for a long DNT, the holder is always short vega and long volgamma. Hence, in terms of volgamma, falling volatility benefits the holder proportionally more than the other way around since a decrease in volatility adds value to the option (recall that the holder is short vega).

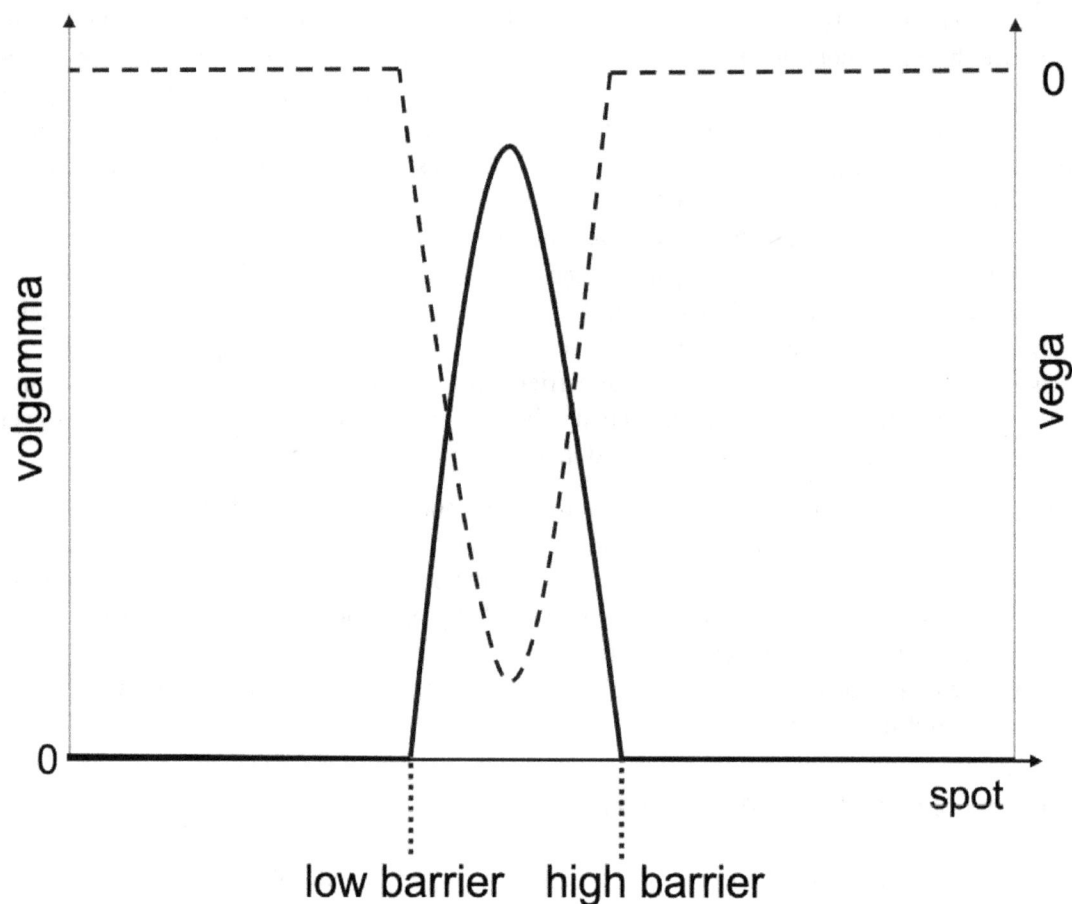

Figure 3.23: Illustration of a DNT vega (dashed line) and volgamma (solid line) exposure (six month maturity, barrier +/- 5% above/below strike.

When the barriers are farther apart, the picture is more complex (see Figure 3.24. The vega exposure for the holder is still negative, but in the central region, the impact of an increase in volatility to the option value is limited as the spot is relatively far away from the barrier. As the spot approaches the barriers, this effect changes, *i.e.* the option picks up more vega. Regarding volgamma, it is either positive, negative or neutral depending on the vicinity of the spot with respect to the barrier. Close to the barrier, a decrease in volatility has a larger impact on the option value versus the same shift in the opposite direction since the derivative is already worth practically nothing. The opposite is true in the central region for the same argument. The pricing of these contracts and its embedded volatility convexity calls for a stochastic volatility model since both BSM and LVM likely underprice the contract. How much stochastic volatility benefit a trader wants to grant is then a question of the risk appetite as well as the current market. As a final and curious remark, note that it is also possible for a *long* DNT position to exhibit a *long* vega profile. Similar to scenarios for which also vanilla derivatives may show unusual behavior in the greeks [53] this scenario can happen if the forward takes an extreme shape. In the particular example of a DNT [125], the forward curve is sharply upwards sloping so that an increase in volatility would effectively decrease the probability of hitting the respective barrier.

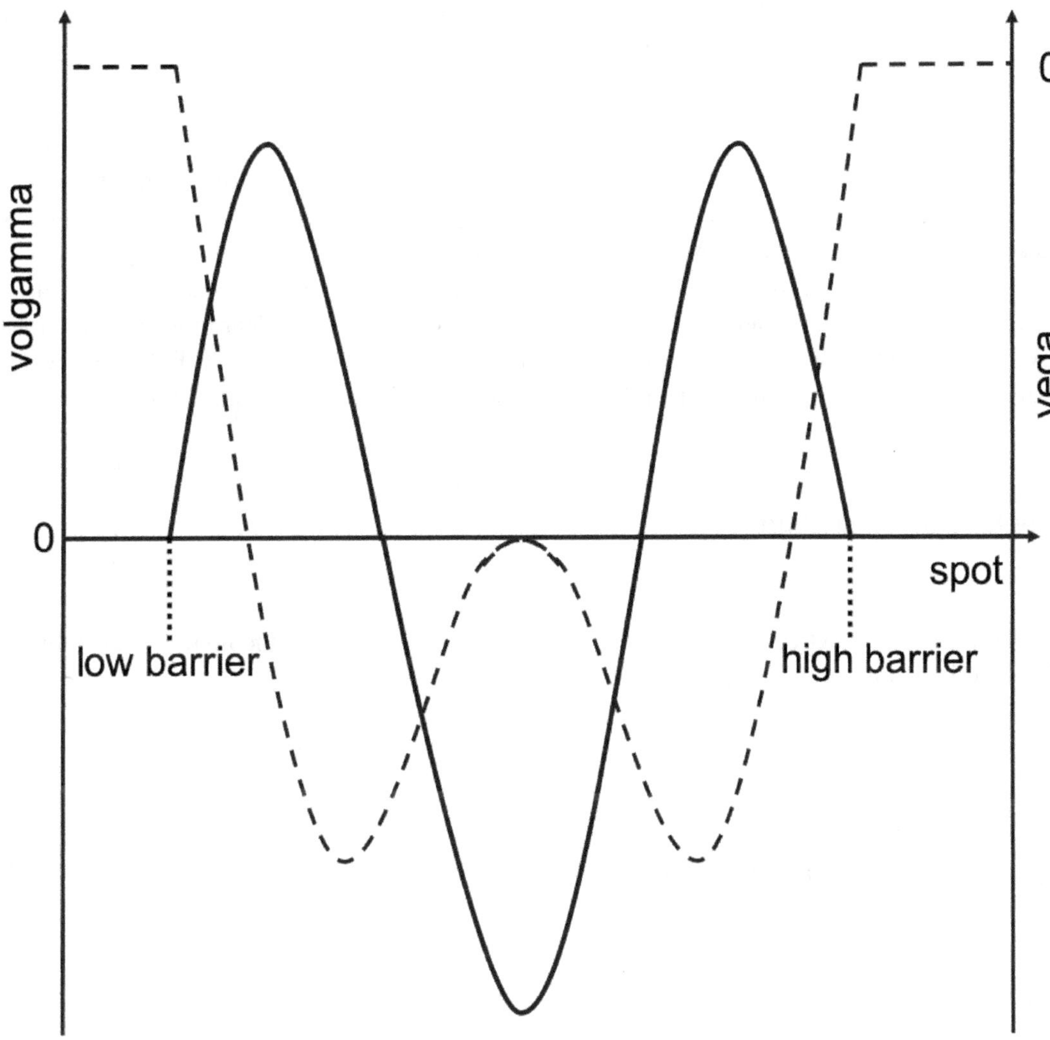

Figure 3.24: Illustration of a DNT vega (dashed line) and volgamma (solid line) exposure (six month maturity, barrier +/- 10% above/below strike.

3.1.10 Exotics: Cliquets

Cliquets options [126, 127] encompass a large group of exotics, which became very popular in early 2000 for the retail Structured Products market. Although the demand has decreased since then, it is worth understanding the properties and risks associated with cliquets to study *model risk*.

In a nutshell, cliquet options are derivatives for which the strike is resetting (periodically) at future times until expiry. Because the strike resetting feature does at first sight not appear to induce any complications, the resulting risk was often only discovered when trading books which were short the options started to bleed money. The Estimates about the mark-to-market losses on cliquet retail positions are around $1bn between 2000 and 2005 [128, 127]. There are three main issues when pricing cliquets:

- how is the forward skew modeled, *e.g.* what shape is the spot skew in 1 year forward?
- what is the trade sensitivity to volatility convexity (volgamma)?

- what is the trade sensitivity to the implied dynamics of the (stochastic) model process itself?

The feature of a strike 'reset' was already encountered when discussing forward starting options. The critical question here is again, which volatility to use for pricing the contract considering that market quotes are typically for contracts with a fixed strike and fixed maturity today. It follows then that these options must be priced off a *forward* implied volatility surface. Unfortunately, such a surface cannot be backed out of the vanilla option market. In particular, it is not clear in which direction of *today's* ATM point of the surface the option eventually strikes in the future (OTM, ITM, ATM?). Therefore, it is evident that this contract depends a lot on the forward skew modeling.

3.1.11 Cliquets: caps and floors

Consider a simple cliquet call option with a local floor and cap whereby the final payout is the sum of the N periodically capped and floored returns

$$\sum_{i=1}^{N} \max \left[floor, \min \left[cap, \frac{S_{t_i}}{S_{t_{i-1}}} - K \right] \right] . \tag{3.26}$$

Here, the cap and floor may be symmetric ($-cap = floor$). Effectively, this is a sum of locally capped and floored forward starting call options. In the case for which the floor is zero, this is a sum of forward starting call spreads. The dealer typically sells this option to the client, which in turn means being short the ATM forward starting leg and long the OTM forward cap. Hence, it is important to know how the respective volatility model is representing the forward skew, *i.e.* does it flatten out, stay constant or go up compared to the spot starting skew now? For example, if the forward skew is flat (*i.e.* the ATM vol is equal to OTM vol) the seller of the option pays too much for the OTM forward cap. The problem is illustrated in Figure 3.25. If the forward skew goes down or decays in the model, the trader sell/buy the ATM/cap too low/high. There exists a class of models that preserve the current spot skew by construction. These so-called Independent Increment Model (IIM) models [129] effectively keep the current spot skew conserved by construction, *e.g.* the 1 year forward starting skew is identical to the current spot skew. The idea is that a given period return is independent and that the process for the stock price is only the product of independent variables. This assumption is not completely realistic, but it provides a tool to assess forward skew sensitivity in an extreme scenario. Unfortunately, the drawback is that these models will typically not fit the options market for all maturities because the initial return distribution does not completely determine those prices.

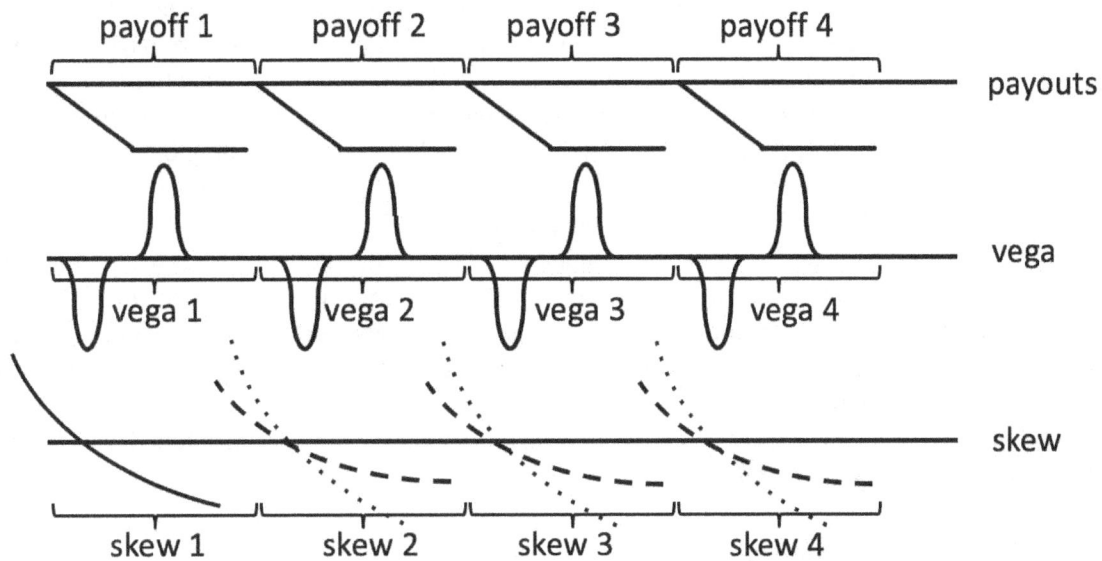

Figure 3.25: Illustration of cliquet skew with a decay along the sequential payouts (dashed line).

Many cliquet mispricings occurred because dealers were not aware of the exact forward skew dynamics implied by their pricing models at the time. The LV model exhibits forward skew dynamics that are not suited for pricing cliquets. This is because in LV the skew flattens out over time, *i.e.* ATM and OTM volatility *converge*. Why should the skew not flatten out? Because for all things being equal the best guess for the volatility ratio of *e.g.* a 100/110 call spread starting in 1 year is that it should be equal to the ratio of the same option spot starting today (ignoring term structure effects on the absolute volatility level). So why does LV flatten out over time? The flattening occurs because long-dated option market quotes typically exhibit flatter skew. Since LV is calibrated to this market, the result means a flattening skew (see Figure 3.26).

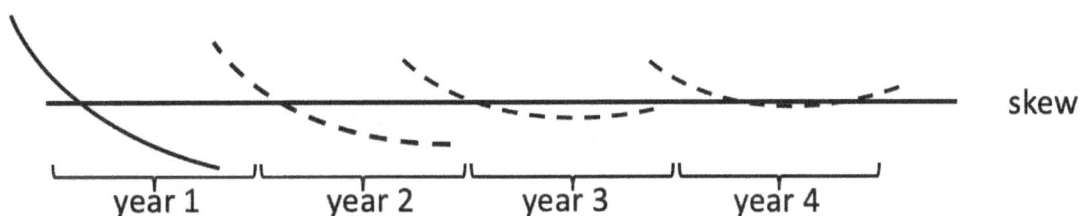

Figure 3.26: Illustration of the decay of the LV forward skew.

3.1.12 Cliquets: reverse put cliquet

The reverse put cliquet (and variants thereof) [127] were also prevalent among retail investors in early 2000. The payout is mathematically given by

$$\max\left[0, coupon + \sum_{i=1}^{N} \min\left[0, \frac{S_{t_i}}{S_{t_{i-1}}} - 1\right]\right].\tag{3.27}$$

Hence, the payout works by subtracting the worst periodic performance of the underlying from a fixed coupon. The coupon itself can be very large (*e.g.* 60%) and can deliver a large payout in case there are no or few substantial negative returns. Effectively, the client (long the cliquet) has sold a series of restriking ATM puts. Because of the ATM feature, (forward) skew is not such an issue here, but volgamma is. Note that there is a significant vega difference depending on the length of the periodic observation periods, *i.e.* since vega (in a Brownian diffusion) scales with the square root of time, 12 monthly options have $(12)^{1/2}$ larger vega than the corresponding 12 month option. The value of the reverse put cliquet increases in a low volatility environment and, as a consequence, the seller of this option will need to buy/sell vega in a high/low volatility environment. BSM, LV and IIM misprice this volatility convexity because they do not represent it in the model (at all). In order to assess the volgamma, a stochastic volatility model is required. However, sometimes even an out-of-the-box Heston model misprices the product to some degree. Even more so, the higher the reset frequency, the larger the problem due to the vega time scaling property mentioned above. The effect also becomes more pronounced when the cap & floors are asymmetric.

3.1.13 Cliquets: Napoleon cliquet

The Napoleon cliquet appears similar to the reverse put, but here one subtracts the worst return over the whole time period:

$$
\max\left[0, coupon + \overset{i=1,\ldots,N}{\min}\ \min\left[0, \frac{S_{t_i}}{S_{t_{i-1}}} - 1\right]\right]. \tag{3.28}
$$

The Napoleon structure is notorious for having caused severe losses due to mispricings in the past [127, 130, 131]. For the seller, the Napoleon option is long vega, short skew and short volgamma. Moreover, it depends significantly on how the **conditional distributions** in the pricing model change. In other words, the *pricing process* determines the value of this product to a large extent. For example, how likely is it in the process model to have two bad (*i.e.* negative) periods after each other? This is a function of how *conditional* spot and volatility distributions are treated in the process. In other words, the model-implied **serial return correlation** becomes important. For example, an IIM model has, by construction, no serial correlation at all, *i.e.* it misprices this product completely. On the other hand, LV does imply a serial correlation because each spot is linked to different local volatility (or the returns are locally lognormally distributed).

3.1.14 Gap Options and Jump Diffusion Models

It is clear that payouts, which are a function of jumps/gaps should be priced with models taking this into account. One such example is the gap option. Gap options make the parent option they are derived from cheaper. This is achieved by determining the strike over the lifetime of the trade, *i.e.* it is ultimately set at maturity. For example, a 1 year gap call will have a final strike K_F equal to $K_F = 100\% + $ leverage · number of gap. In other words, the strike is a function of the number of gaps (see Figure 3.27). The leverage is a pre-defined quantity (*e.g.* 50%) and the gap is the sum of all positive daily returns exceeding a barrier level (*e.g.* 5%). Hence, in a moderately bullish market in which the underlying does not rise each day excessively, the holder of this option receives the same payout as for a vanilla call, but for *less* premium paid upfront. Similarly, gap puts can be used to buy cheaper downside protection. The seller of these options is *long* volatility convexity and *benefits* from large moves of the underlying.

barrier breached

gap barrier   new gap barrier

initial strike   new strike

final fixing

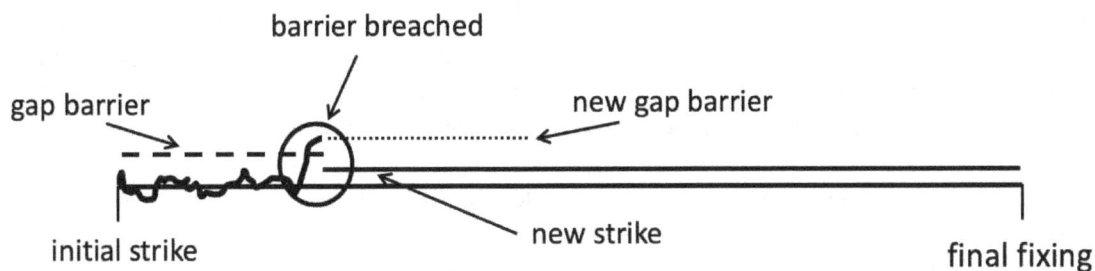

Figure 3.27: Illustration of the gap call mechanics whereby the final strike is determined by the number of gaps over the lifetime.

Another typical structure along those lines is the crash put . These options are typically quoted only on liquid underlyings. The payout is monitored daily and defined as

$$\max\left[0, \text{gap} - \frac{S_t}{S_{t-1}}\right].$$ (3.29)

For the gap value, it is common to use something between 90%-80%. The product terminates once the payout is ever positive. Hence, for a gap of 90%, the product knocks out if the underlying ever loses more than 10% on a single day. Long crash/gap options are added to trading books to offset severe (crash) risks from other trades. Therefore, they are not hedged also because a replication strategy does not exist in practice.

The pricing of this contract typically involves a jump-diffusion (JD) model. In a standard Jump diffusion (JD) model, the stochastic differential equation is given by

$$dS_t = \mu S_t dt + \sigma dW_t + dJ_t.$$ (3.30)

The dynamics only differ from a normal Brownian motion by the addition of the dJ_t term whereby $J_t = \sum^N_{ti=1} Y_i$ is a compounding Poisson process with independent jump sizes λ. The number of jumps N_t is identically distributed and obey a fixed jump intensity Y_i. Between the jumps, the process follows a standard Brownian motion. To make things even easier, one can consider a normal distribution for the jumps. In practice, it is often not easy to calibrate a JD model and fit the market implied volatility surface as well. However, it is possible to combine a local volatility model with JD so that the two worlds can be bridged somewhat. Note that analytical pricing models based on the BSM framework [132] are not good representations for these derivatives.

3.1.15 Long maturity trades and unusual features

Trades with a longer maturity (*e.g.* 5 years and beyond) whereby various parameters impact the valuation are challenging. This difficulty arises naturally because the stochastic element of the parameters themselves (*e.g.* interest rates, dividends, implied volatility, etc.) and their coupling (*e.g.* the correlation between equity and interest rates or the correlation between implied volatility and spot) is more difficult to predict at inception. For starters, the impact of switching from a deterministic LVM to SVM should be assessed. Since interest rate volatility is typically much lower than for example equity volatility, considering the yield curve as constant is typically acceptable for shorted dated trades. However, for longer-dated trades, stochastic rates may have a significant effect given equity-interest rate correlation and interest rate gamma [5]. Hence, assessing the impact of stochastic rates in a joint equity/interest rate model can be important for longer-dated trades. Moreover, the way dividends are modeled (*e.g.* absolute dividends versus a proportional model) has a much larger impact as well and it is advisable to assess the impact or at least be conservative.

Some trades may have unusual terms, *e.g.* very low barrier with respect to current spot (< 30%) or uncommon features (*e.g.* knock-out dividend swaps [133]). It is highly recommended to assess whether special terms render the commonly accepted valuation methodology problematic. For example, in the case of very low barriers, conditional probabilities become much more important, *e.g.* how does the volatility surface evolve conditional on a low spot level in the far future? Hence, the conditional process implied by the stochastic model process can be a critical risk component.

3.1.16 Model flowchart

Following the discussion on the seemingly infinite model zoo so far including their potential model risks, it should not surprise that there is not (yet) a generic silver bullet model suitable for all exotic payouts. Even if it were possible to calibrate a cross-asset stochastic-local-volatility-jump-diffusion model consistently, it is not guaranteed that the calibration is always in line with the market. In other words, parameter- and model-sensitive trades should ideally be assessed by comparing the option value in different models. On the exotics side, volatility convexity is *typically* the most severe problem. Therefore, the price difference between LV and SV is a sensible metric, *e.g.* via

$$I = \frac{\max(V_{LV}, V_{SV}) - \min(V_{LV}, V_{SV})}{\max(V_{LV}, V_{SV}) + \min(V_{LV}, V_{SV})} = \frac{|V_{SV} - V_{LV}|}{V_{SV} + V_{LV}} . \tag{3.31}$$

Any (significant) deviation away from zero for I is an indication of model sensitivity especially concerning volgamma.

Going one step further, Figure 3.28 depicts a simplified model decision tree. The flowchart provides a standard guideline to investigate model sensitivity to avoid severe mispricings. Do not forget that all errors due to model shortcuts (*e.g.* constant interest rates, constant dividends etc.) amplify with increasing trade lifetime. Hence, longer dated derivatives need to be priced with special care and possibly with enough valuation reserves over the lifetime.

---

[5]Interest rate gamma is only a topic if one is dealing with a derivative with explicit exposure to rates

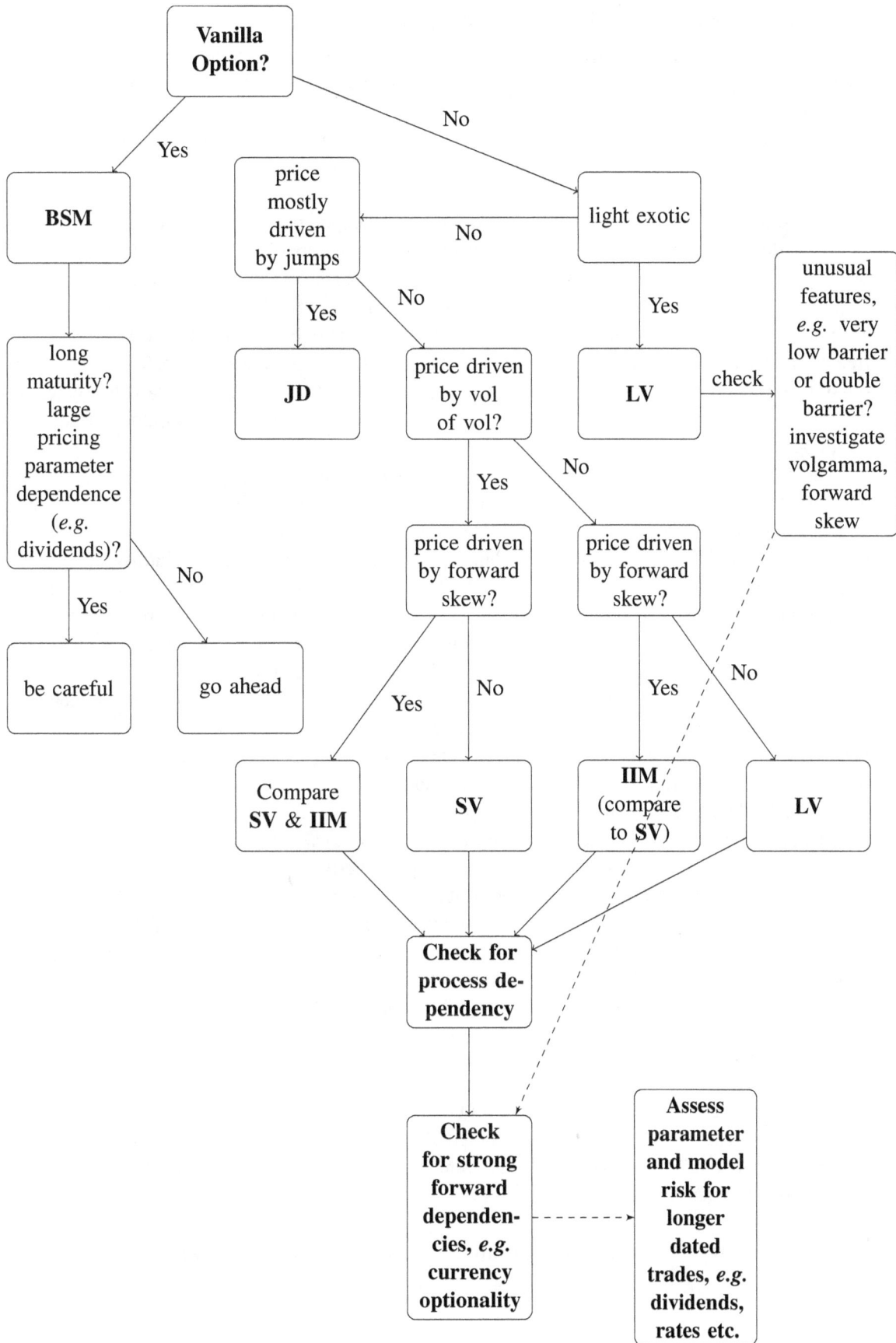

Figure 3.28: Model choice flow for pricing options.

3.1.17 Replicate, hedge, overhedge, underhedge or do nothing?

One fundamental question when dealing with derivative positions is whether one should try to replicate or hedge a position in the first place. This question might sound odd at first but is of critical importance as explained below.

In the case of trading an (insulated) outright bet (*e.g.* a directional trade), the answer is that hedging or de-risking should only come into play in case one intends to lock in a profit or loss. Hence, the critical risk mitigant at inception is arguably position sizing (see next section). The other reason why one might decide not to replicate or hedge specific trades is that the hedging cannot be done or only in a very model-dependent manner. An imperfect (or even wrong) replication or hedging strategy might then, in turn, lead to losses on *both* source trade as well as the hedge. Impossible or very model-dependent replication strategies are, for instance, bets on metrics that are not tradable directly. For example, trading a bet on the debt/equity ratio of a company, its free cash flow or earnings outperformance versus its peers cannot be traded directly. Even if it is possible to (econometrically) model all of these observables such that they somehow translate into the underlying performance and thereby derivative greeks for the asset, the assumptions for this link might be substantial.

The picture is more precise in the case of delta-hedging an underlying whereby one believes that the market is not correctly valuing the underlying implied volatility. As shown in the literature [134], delta hedging at the ratio given by the implied volatility leads to a smoother P/L path, but at the cost of higher uncertainty for the final value. Contrary to this, hedging at forecast volatility equal to the realized volatility provides certainty on the final P/L, but at the cost of a more volatile P/L path over the lifetime. This difference ultimately results from the intrinsic nature of the P/L path-dependency of a delta-hedged derivative and in this sense, different delta ratios will make a different impact.

Equally important are considerations on the influence of the volatility mark on the gamma value of a position. As the volatility mark decreases, the gamma of ATM calls and puts increases. Contrary, when volatility is marked higher, the gamma of both ITM and OTM calls and puts decreases. This is because a derivative marked at high implied volatility experiences less of a delta change given a movement of the underlying as the mark itself already implies this possibility. Hence, if one desires to delta hedge less frequently upon a market move, then the implied volatility mark needs to be high. Less frequent delta hedging makes sense in trending markets, *i.e.* traders want to let the delta *run*. In case markets are more volatile and frequently mean-reverting, hedging at a low volatility mark provides more gamma and thereby more frequent delta adjustments to monetize the path. In the case of short gamma positions, the situation is reversed to react more quickly. It is clear that in the context of a large trading book, these considerations can in practice be applied only for individual trades. However, for corporate derivatives (see Chapter 11), risk managing large positions via adjustments to the model parameters can be an important tool to reduce the P/L variance.

Practical Tips 3.1.1 Questions to ask your quants / risk system support:

- Implied volatility surface: which parameterization of the implied volatility surface is the system using and what are the parameters?
- Implied volatility surface: how is the term structure and skew extrapolated?
- Implied volatility surface: how does the implied forward volatility behave in the pricing models?
- LVM: How is the local volatility calibrated/treated in the wing regions?

- SVM: Which stochastic process are we using and how do we calibrate the model?
- How are the dividends treated in all volatility/valuation models?
- How are barrier shifts modeled/booked?
- Are there any unusual trades on the book (*e.g.* cliquets, low barriers, etc.)?
- Are there any model reserves booked against (very) convex or unusual trades?
- Are there any long-dated trades for which the forward sensitivity or the impact of stochastic rates needs to be assessed?
- What is your model delta for different options (vanilla, exotic) compared to BSM and a simple stochastic vol model (*e.g.* Heston)?
- Which spot/vol dynamics or correlation does the stochastic process/volatility model imply?
- How does the forward skew behave in the stochastic process/volatility model?
- What process model / serial return correlation does the stochastic process/volatility model imply?
- What is the model parameter interdependence (during calibration) and what is the model dependency on the calibration protocol itself?

4. Variance and Volatility trading

4.1 Introduction

Trading variance or volatility has become a separate asset class over the last thirty years [135], and as such promises to be an independent diversification vehicle in portfolio management [136]. Completely isolating pure volatility or variance exposure from other market components is non-trivial and requires dynamic hedging of the P/L contributors as the case of vanilla options has shown. For this reason, the financial industry has devised dedicated contracts to provide isolated volatility or variance exposure directly. This insulation is, on the one hand, desirable because it offers better vehicles to hedge specific exposure more directly. On the other hand, investors seeking to exploit volatility differences through relative value trading can do so without adding other exposure/risk implicitly.

4.1.1 Introduction to moment swaps: the log contract

Typically, four moment swaps (and variants thereof) are considered in trading:

- variance swap (order $= k = 2$)
- volatility swap (order $= k = \frac{1}{2}$)
- skew swap (order $= k = 3$)
- kurtosis swap (order $= k = 4$)

All moment swaps are based on the **log contract** [137]. The log (forward) contract is a financial instrument, which pays the continuous return of the underlying asset at expiry, *i.e.* the 'log-performance' as given by

$$\log_T = \ln \frac{S_T}{S_0} = \ln(S_T) - \ln(S_0) \,. \tag{4.1}$$

By construction, the log-contract is a forward contract, *i.e.* cash flows occur at expiry. As shown in Figure 4.1, the log contract is clearly a nonlinear / convex instrument in spot or forward. The nonlinearity also qualifies the log contract as an exotic payout in principle.

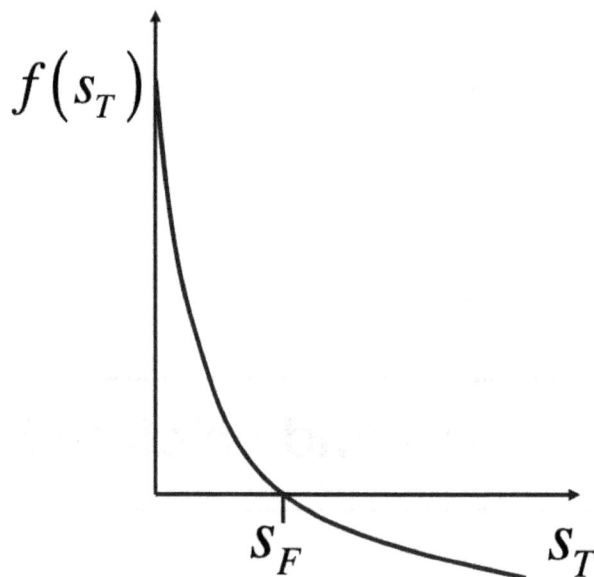

Figure 4.1: Illustration of the payout of a short log contract position.

The log (forward) replication formally given by

$$\log_T = \ln\frac{S_T}{S_F} = \frac{S_T - S_F}{S_F} - \int_0^{S_F} \frac{1}{K^2}\text{Put}(K,T)dK - \int_{S_F}^{\infty} \frac{1}{K^2}\text{Call}(K,T)dK \ . \tag{4.2}$$

The equation above contains three components for a long position:

- long forward position, opened at S_F (ATM Forward), paying $(S_T - S_F)$ at expiry. This is effectively the discrete return of the underlying with a long position of $1/S_F$ units.
- short position in a put portfolio with weightings $1/K^2$ and strikes running from zero to S_F at ideally infinitesimal distances.
- short position in a call portfolio with weightings $1/K^2$ and strikes running from S_F to infinity at ideally infinitesimal distances.

If the log contract is delta-hedged dynamically, there is a hedging error because it is not possible to hedge in continuous time. As a consequence, one is therefore effectively approximating the continuous by a discrete return. In the BSM (constant volatility) world, one can derive the dynamics for the log contract as

$$\log_t = \ln\frac{S_t}{S_0} - \frac{1}{2}\sigma^2(T-t) \tag{4.3}$$

Clearly, for t=T, the continuous return is recovered.

The greeks for the log contract are then given by

$$
\begin{aligned}
\Delta &= \frac{\partial \log_t}{\partial S_t} = \frac{1}{S_t} \\
\Gamma &= \frac{\partial^2 \log_t}{\partial S_t^2} = -\frac{1}{S_t^2} \\
\text{vega} &= \frac{\partial \log_t}{\partial \sigma} = \frac{1}{2}\sigma \cdot T \\
\Theta &= \frac{\partial \log_t}{\partial T} = -\frac{1}{2}\sigma^2
\end{aligned}
\tag{4.4}
$$

As a conclusion from the above, it is evident that the log contract exhibits constant cash gamma invariant of spot and time. It is useful to summarize some other elementary properties of the log contract. The long log contract position

- is short skew. This is because the weightings of the put options with low strikes grow exponentially.
- contains more put than call options in the replicating portfolio.
- is delta neutralized at the time of the return observation, *i.e.* typically at the daily closing. The intraday delta deviation to the close is the hedging error.
- is in theory model-independent because for the pricing all is required are prices for the options portfolio.
- is straightforward in terms of cash flow calculations due to the additivity of the logarithm.
- is typically only traded as an intrinsic component of a moment swap (*e.g.* variance swap see next section)

Finally, the log contract represents the sum of all underlying moments. The isolation of a particular moment (*e.g.* the second moment / variance) therefore works only via extracting it from the log contract. This procedure will be illustrated in the following sections.

4.1.2 Variance Swap

The Variance Swap (varswap) [138, 139] belongs to the product family of moment swaps and is effectively a contract for difference (CFD). The general expression for a moment swap [140] M^k on moment k expiring at time T and days to expiry n is given by

$$
M^k = N \cdot \left[\left(\sum_{i=1}^{n} [\ln(\frac{S_t}{S_{t-1}})]^k \right) - K \right] .
\tag{4.5}
$$

Note that the formula above is based on the continuous asset return (see 2.1.3), which is an approximation of the discrete return. The same principle holds if the log contract is discretely delta-hedged. Therefore, the difference between the discrete and continuous return contains all higher moments. When a moment swap is (daily) delta-hedged, then the hedging error of the log contract component is realized in the same interval, which is in turn part of the replication mechanism.

Compared to other moment swaps the varswap by far the most liquid and frequently traded. The payout is deceivingly simple. Buyer and seller agree on a variance strike and settle the difference between the realized variance and the strike at expiry such that

$$M^2 = N_{Var} \cdot \left[\left(\sum_{i=1}^{n} [\ln(\frac{S_t}{S_{t-1}})]^2 \right) - K \right],$$ (4.6)

whereby N_{Var} denotes the variance notional and n the days to expiry. The variance swap is typically expressed using continuous instead of discrete returns whereby the mean return is effectively set to zero. This modification is the reason why varswaps have convenient properties such as additivity in time, *i.e.* independence of trends in the time series. Hence, the varswap is defined via its root-mean-square variance and thereby compatible with the BSM model.

The variance swap notional is typically expressed as a vega notional (*e.g.* \$100k per vega/volatility point). Therefore,

$$N_{Var} = \frac{N_{vega}}{2 \cdot K}$$ (4.7)

whereby the vega notional is expressed as the leading order P/L change resulting from increasing the strike by 1, *i.e.*

$$N_{Var}(K+1)^2 = N_{Var}K^2 + \underbrace{2K \cdot N_{Var} \cdot 1}_{N_{vega}} + 1^2.$$ (4.8)

The P/L expression is given by

$$P/L = N_{Var} \cdot (\sigma^2 - K^2) = N_{vega} \cdot \left(\frac{\sigma^2 - K^2}{2K} \right).$$ (4.9)

Variance swaps are instruments, which are convex in volatility. The convexity means that a long varswap position profits more from a spike in volatility than it loses if volatility decreases. This feature is the primary reason why variance swap *strikes* trade typically above the respective ATM volatility level of the same maturity. The difference is known as the *convexity premium*.

One of the crucial questions is now how to replicate the variance swap. To identify the required components, a Taylor expansion of the continuous return equivalent for a generic (long) position of a moment swap yields

$$M^k = \left[\ln\left(\frac{S_{t_i}}{S_{t_{i-1}}}\right) \right]^k = k! \left[\underbrace{\left(\frac{\Delta S_{t_i}}{S_{t_{i-1}}}\right)}_{\text{long underlying}} - \underbrace{\ln\left(\frac{S_{t_i}}{S_{t_{i-1}}}\right)}_{\text{short log contract}} - \underbrace{\sum_{j=2}^{k-1} \frac{1}{j!} \left[\ln\left(\frac{S_{t_i}}{S_{t_{i-1}}}\right) \right]^j}_{\text{short moment swap series}} + \underbrace{O\left[\ln\left(\frac{S_{t_i}}{S_{t_{i-1}}}\right) \right]^{k+1}}_{\text{higher order terms}} \right].$$

(4.10)

In the case of the variance swap ($k = 2$), the expression simplifies to

$$M^2 = \left[\ln\left(\frac{S_{t_i}}{S_{t_{i-1}}}\right) \right]^2 = 2 \left[\underbrace{\left(\frac{\Delta S_{t_i}}{S_{t_{i-1}}}\right)}_{\text{long underlying}} - \underbrace{\ln\left(\frac{S_{t_i}}{S_{t_{i-1}}}\right)}_{\text{short log contract}} + \underbrace{O\left[\ln\left(\frac{S_{t_i}}{S_{t_{i-1}}}\right) \right]^3}_{\text{higher order terms}} \right].$$ (4.11)

In practice, the higher moments are ignored, *i.e.* a replication error does exist. Ultimately, the varswap is effectively extracting the second moment of the log contract. Hence, what remains is a replication strategy consisting of the underlying and the log contract. When recalling the replication of the log contract, the replicating portfolio consists of the put and call options [141] before. Therefore, the fair varswap rate at time t depends only on the value of the replicating option portfolio. The corresponding expectation value for the future variance is thereby model independent, *i.e.* one can sum the weighted put and call options for the given maturity to calculate the varswap rate. The assumption is a liquid and broad range of quoted option prices, which is however often not the case. As a workaround, one can then either use a model to extrapolate into strike regions which are not quoted or use a strike cutoff, *i.e.* ignore strikes below / above a certain threshold.

Due to the property of the embedded log-contract, the variance swap exhibits constant dollar gamma (*i.e.* $\Gamma^{\$} = \Gamma \cdot S^2$) irrespective of the spot level and the remaining time to maturity. Recall that vanilla options show a non-constant (dollar) gamma profile. However, an inverse to the square-strike-weighted continuum of vanillas (as present in the log-contract) generates a constant dollar gamma profile.

4.1.2.1 Variance swap greeks

In the case of a BSM constant volatility surface, the delta of the variance swap must be zero. The reason is that the variance payout is not a function of the spot. However, *intraday*, the variance swap accumulates cash delta in line with the product of cash-gamma and the current percentage spot move. In other words, the position gets longer / shorter delta as the underlying goes up / down. Moreover, because the payout measures close-to-close variance, it is beneficial if the move is in one direction only. Finally, at the end of the trading day, the measured close-to-close variance is added to the realized variance, and, as a consequence, the accumulated cash delta resets to zero at the fixing of the closing price (see Figure 4.2). Hence, in case the varswap was delta hedged *intraday*, the respective net amount needs to be offset at the closing in the case to be neutral again for the next day. This activity can often be observed in the closing auction for certain assets such as large stock indices.

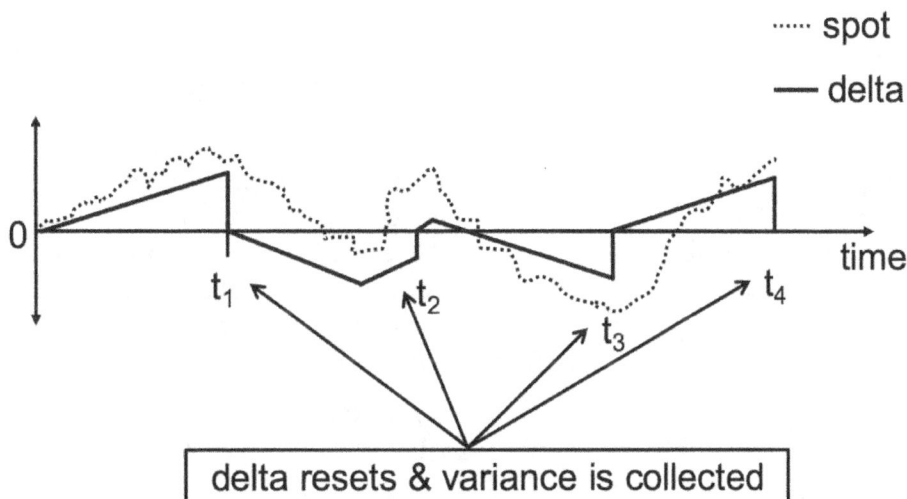

Figure 4.2: Illustration of the daily variance swap delta reset.

As mentioned earlier, a constant BSM volatility (in strike) is typically not observed in reality, *i.e.* there is skew or some other curvature in the surface. Because of skew, the variance swap does, in fact, show a delta already at inception. This so-called *skew* delta or varswap shadow delta is positive for a short variance position, *i.e.* to hedge one needs to sell delta in the underlying [142]. The skew delta emerges because the low strike options have a higher weight in the replication portfolio and typically also trade at higher volatility. With negative skew, the skew delta for a long varswap position is negative, *i.e.* the holder benefits from a down move more. Note that the skew delta effect can be significant depending on how steep the downside skew is.

4.1.2.2 Forward starting Variance Swap

Variance swaps can be traded spot starting (*i.e.* variance accrues from today until expiry) or forward starting. Since variance is additive, the calculation of the forward variance is trivial. Building on the previous relations the following equation is obtained

$$F^2(t,T) = \frac{T}{T-t}K_T^2 - \frac{t}{T-t}K_t^2 \,, \tag{4.12}$$

with K_x being the variance swap strike of maturity x and $F(t,T)$ the forward variance swap strike between $t < T$. For example, consider a 3-month varswap struck at 15 and a 1-year varswap struck at 20. The 9-month varswap starting in 3 months ending in 1 year is then given by $1/4 \cdot 15^2 - 20^2 = 3/4 \cdot F^2$. Therefore, $F = 21.4$.

Hence, it is possible to construct a forward variance swap via two spot starting variance swaps, *i.e.* for a long position in the t,T forward varswap, one buys $T/(T-t)$ spot variance of maturity T and sells $t/(T-t)$ spot variance of maturity t. However, it is important to see that one *cannot* uses the same notional on the two spot varswaps. Consider the previous example again. Imagine one wants to trade USD 100'000 on the 3M,12M varswap. Just like for a spot varswap this represents a notional of $\$100'000/(2 \cdot 21.4) = \$2'336$. Therefore, it is required to sell $3/9 \cdot \$2'336 = \$778'000$ notional on the 3M spot varswap and $12/9 \cdot \$2'336 = \$3'115$ on the 12M spot varswap. In terms of vega notional this equates to $\$778'000 \cdot 2 \cdot 15 = \$24'000$ and $\$3'115 \cdot 2 \cdot 20 = \$125'000$. Note that the combined notional of the two spot starting varswaps *exceeds* the vega notional of the forward variance. Besides, more notional on the leg with the longer maturity is necessary. Both factors can lead to higher costs for the forward variance because of the need to cross two bid/offer spreads in the market. Moreover, the spread on the long maturity varswap might be larger.

4.1.2.3 Variance Swap Caps

Variance swaps trade for several assets such as stock indices and single stocks, whereby the liquidity is much better on the former. If a single stock variance swap is quoted at all [1], it typically entails an additional cap. The cap refers to a ceiling that the realized variance cannot exceed. The cap is normally expressed as a multiplier of the initial strike, *e.g.* $m = 2.5$. The reason for caps is that the risk of an idiosyncratic large price movement is far larger for single stocks versus stock indices.

The introduction of the cap yields the following P/L expression

$$P/L = N_{var} \cdot ((\min[\sigma, m \cdot K])^2 - K^2) = N_{vega} \cdot \left(\frac{(\min[\sigma, m \cdot K])^2}{2K} - K^2 \right) . \tag{4.13}$$

It should not surprise that many varswap caps were hit during the 2008/09 financial crisis. What followed was the discovery that some market participants had mispriced the cap. The reason was that the cap is equivalent to an option on variance. This is best seen by decomposing the payoff as shown in Figure 4.3.

---

[1] Typically single stock variance swaps are also dividend protected, *i.e.* the dividend amount on the ex-date is added to the spot to make the return dividend invariant.

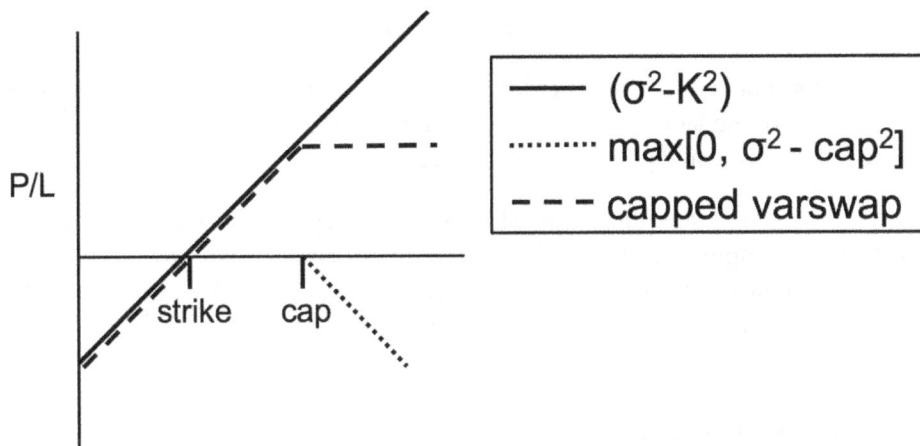

Figure 4.3: Illustration of the variance cap components: a long position in a variance swap (solid line) minus a capped option on variance (dashed line) results in a capped variance swap (dotted line).

What is deceiving is that the cap option can indeed have value at some point. For example, consider a short position in a 12 month single stock varswap for USD 200k notional at a strike of 35. The cap is initially set to $2.5 \cdot 35 = 87.5$. After the first 3 months, the market is calm, and volatility realizes at 20%. To lock in the profit, the trader decides to buy a 9 month varswap struck at 35, cap at 87.5, for a notional of $200k - 3/12 \cdot 200k = 150k$. After that, the market experiences a crash and realizes at 110% for the remaining 9 months. One might assume to be flat risk, but then this is what happens:

- realized variance 12M: $(1/4 \cdot 20 \cdot 20 + 3/4 \cdot 110 \cdot 110)^{1/2} = 96 =$ cap reached
- short variance 12M: $(35 \cdot 35 - 87.5 \cdot 87.5)/2/35 \cdot 200k = -21.8m$
- long variance 9M: $(35 \cdot 35 - 87.5 \cdot 87.5)/2/35 \cdot 150k = +16.4m$

The sum is a net loss of USD 5.4m because the variance cap optionality was not taken into account correctly.

4.1.2.4 Corridor Variance Swap

The corridor variance swap [143] represents the class of conditional variance swaps [138]. Here the accrual of the daily variance is restricted to a spot price range of the underlying asset. Hence, it only includes variance if the underlying trades in a pre-defined corridor. It is intuitive that the corridor variance should be cheaper compared to the general variance swap since it is restricted, *i.e.* conditional to the range. Variants of the corridor varswap include downside varswaps (down-variance: corridor set for a price range from a barrier down to zero) and upside varswaps (up-variance: corridor set for a price range from a barrier up to infinity).

The generic variance accrual equation is now modified to

$$M^2 = N_{Var} \cdot \left[\left(\sum_{i=1}^{n} I_t \cdot [\ln(\frac{S_t}{S_{t-1}})]^2 \right) - K \right] , \tag{4.14}$$

where the indicator function I is given by

$$I_t = \begin{cases} 1 : & \text{if } A < S_{t-1} < B \\ 0 : & \text{otherwise} \end{cases} \tag{4.15}$$

The parameters A and B are the barriers, which can be zero or infinity, respectively.

Variance and corridor variance swaps can be hedged by a static portfolio of options of an identical maturity. In the case of the latter, the exposure is hedged using an options continuum weighted by the inverse of the strike squared within the specified range.

Conditional variance swaps allow expressing specific views on volatility contingent on a spot market level. For example, investors seeking distinct tail-risk / crash protection may purchase conditional down-variance, which only becomes activated in the event of a market sell-off. Hence, if the market stays above the down-barrier, the P/L is zero.

4.1.3 Volatility indices and futures

Volatility indices such as the VIX [2] aim to reflect the future return volatility of particular markets or rather specific market indices. The VIX itself is the market's risk-neutral expectation for the return volatility over the next 30 days of the S&P 500 Index. It is constructed as the square root of the fair value of the 30-day variance swap, *i.e.*

$$\sigma_{VIX}^2 = \frac{2\exp[rT]}{T}\left[\sum_{K_i<F_T}\frac{\Delta K}{K_i^2}\mathrm{Put}(K_i) + \sum_{K_i>F_T}\frac{\Delta K}{K_i^2}\mathrm{Call}(K_i)\right] - \frac{1}{T}\left(\frac{F_T}{K_0}-1\right)^2. \tag{4.16}$$

The VIX itself is then quoted as

$$VIX = 100\cdot\sqrt{\sigma_{VIX}^2}. \tag{4.17}$$

The VIX future is the liquidly tradable instrument of the VIX index which is traded in lot sizes of USD 1000 per contract. The settlement value of a VIX future is, by design, the 30-day variance swap level. Because it is a future, this future represents today's expectation of the square root of the 30-day *forward* variance.

It is critical to understand that the VIX future of maturity T delivers exposure to the 30 day volatility starting *at* T, *i.e.* not volatility ending at T. As shown in Figure 4.4 for a sample Sep2012 VIX expiry, the Sep2012 VIX future value is today's expectation of the VIX level on the Sep2012 expiry, as it is implied on that day by the Oct2012 S&P 500 index listed options market.

---

[2]http://www.cboe.com/vix

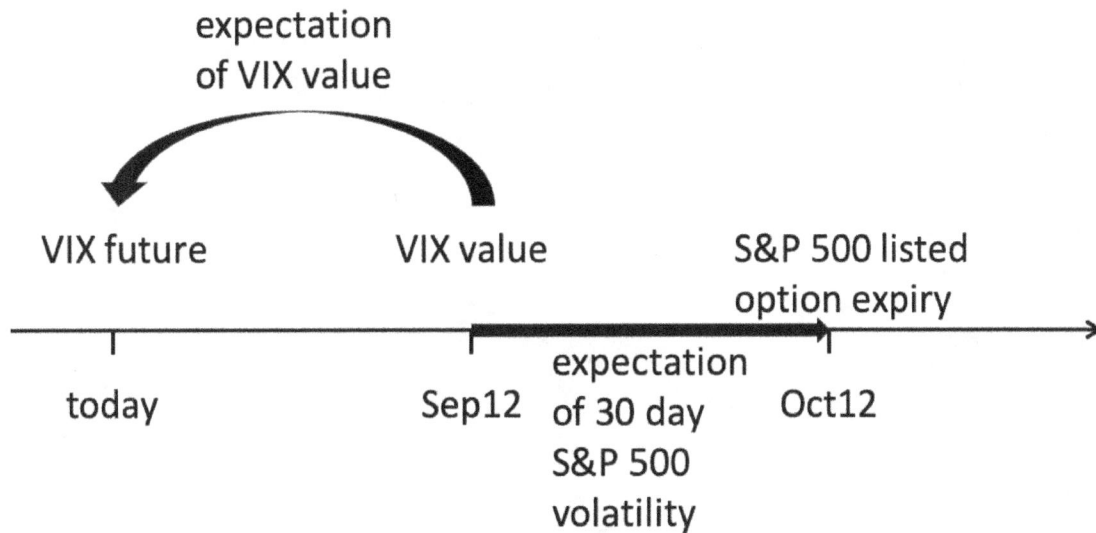

Figure 4.4: Illustration of VIX future exposure for the Sep12 VIX expiry.

VIX futures are cash settled unless the position is closed/rolled before expiry. Note also that neither the VIX nor its future is necessarily a good forecast of future volatility (in analogy to implied volatility derived from the vanilla option market).

4.1.3.1 VIX future vs. forward variance swap

From the discussion above, it should be clear that the forward variance swap and the VIX future are related. More explicitly, the fair value variance swap strike K at expiry is given by the VIX as

$$K = \text{VIX} \cdot \sqrt{\left(\frac{252}{bd} \cdot \frac{30}{365}\right)} \tag{4.18}$$

where bd is the number of business days in the corresponding period. It is also possible to relate the respective forward varswap vega notional to the number of VIX futures contracts as

$$\text{vega}_{\text{fwd varswap}} = N_{VIXFuture} \cdot 1000 \frac{1}{\sqrt{\left(\frac{252}{bd} \cdot \frac{30}{365}\right)}} \cdot \tag{4.19}$$

Recall that each VIX contract has a Vega of USD 1'000 and that the variance swap level moves by $\sqrt{\left(\frac{252}{\text{business days}} \cdot \frac{30}{365}\right)}$ points for each point the future moves.

Still, the two instruments are not exactly equivalent. The main difference is that of a linear (VIX future) and nonlinear (varswap) instrument, which becomes apparent in the P/L whenever encountering large realized variance. More precisely, the VIX future is missing the convexity of the forward varswap. This difference is illustrated in Figure 4.5.

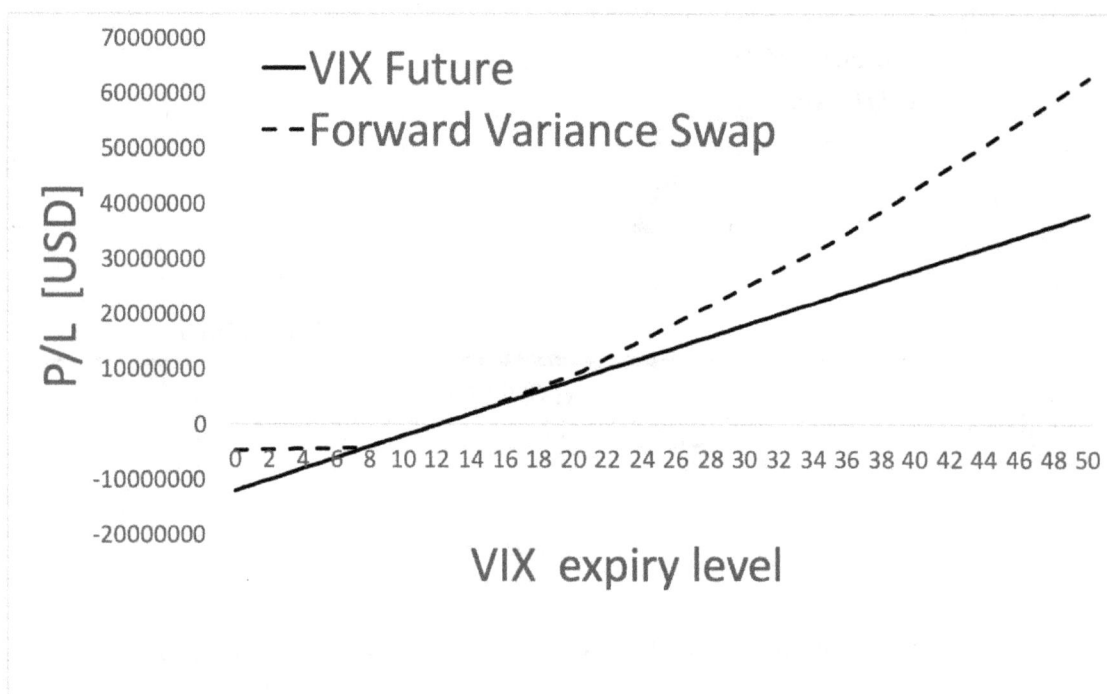

Figure 4.5: Illustration of convexity difference between the 3M VIX future and corresponding forward variance swap (strike = 12).

However, the missing part is recovered by adding a VIX option portfolio of the same maturity, *i.e.*

$$\text{VIX future} + \text{VIX option portfolio} = \text{forward starting variance swap} . \qquad (4.20)$$

Hence, the VIX future P/L at expiry is almost perfectly replicated via a combination of forward-starting variance swaps and VIX options. Unlike the combination of index options required in the replication of spot-starting variance swaps, this strip requires no dynamic hedging. The recipe to replicate the forward starting variance swap is as follows:

- Long N VIX futures contracts
- long VIX put and call options (put for strikes below the futures price, calls above the futures price) with a spacing of $N/F(t) \cdot \delta K \cdot 10$

The synthetic forward-starting variance position then has a variance notional of

$$N_{var} = \frac{N \cdot 1000}{F(t) \cdot 2(\frac{252}{\text{business days}} \cdot \frac{30}{365})} \qquad (4.21)$$

4.1.4 Volatility Swap

Naively, one could think that a volatility swap (volswap) [144, 145] offers even better properties because, after all, it is exchanging (realized) volatility. The payout is straightforward, *i.e.*

$$P/L = N_{volswap} \cdot (\sigma_R - K_{volswap}) . \qquad (4.22)$$

The realized annualized volatility is then calculated as usual via

$$\sigma_R = \sqrt{\frac{252}{N} \sum_{i=1}^{N} \left(\ln \frac{S_i}{S_{i-1}} \right)^2 } .$$ (4.23)

However, an immediate problem arises because volatility is not additive, *i.e.* a linear combination between realized and future volatility is *not* possible. For this reason, it is still often assumed that it is not possible to derive a highly *model-independent* static replication approach for the volatility swap [144]. However, as shown by P. Carr and R. Lee, a replicating vanilla portfolio consisting of straddles, calls and puts under the assumption of frictionless trading and no replication costs can be derived, which provides a decent replication [146, 147, 148, 149].

Nevertheless, before 2008, the volatility swap market was rather illiquid. However, since then, volswaps have become more popular because their behavior in extreme market conditions is more benign. This difference is because whereas varswap is convex in volatility, the volswap is linear.

In the case of zero correlation between the stochastic process of the underlying and the respective volatility, the volatility strike is approximately equal to the ATM implied volatility [148]

$$K_{volswap} \approx \sigma_{ATM} .$$ (4.24)

Another simple approximation [149], which is independent of the correlation assumption above to first order, finds that the volswap is approximately equal to the implied volatility of the vanilla option for which both vanna and volgamma is zero.

At inception, the volatility swap provides a linear payout concerning volatility changes. Because of the missing convexity, volatility swaps are cheaper than equivalent variance swaps. Moreover, due to Jensens inequality $\sqrt{K_{varswap}} \geq K_{volswap}$. This difference is called the convexity adjustment and grows with the volatility level (see Figure 4.6).

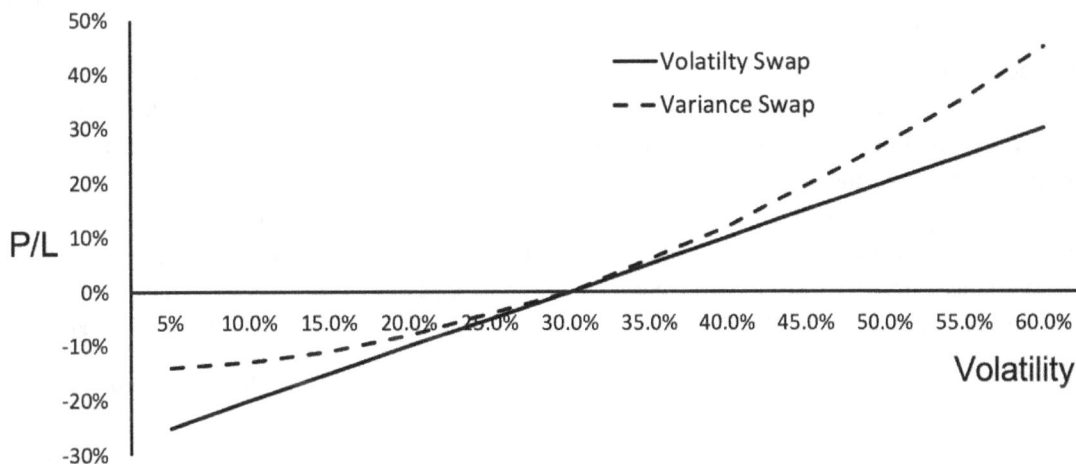

Figure 4.6: Illustration of convexity difference between the varswap and volswap for the same strike.

Over the lifetime of the volswap, it tends to behave in a linear fashion with respect to volatility changes. However, especially towards the maturity, volswaps may pick up some convexity due to joint effects between realized and future volatility.

4.1.5 Moment swap: Difficulties

Similar to vanilla options, the modeling of discrete cash dividends is tricky, *e.g.* the vega on a varswap with proportional vs. absolute dividends is quite different. Also, on index varswaps, the return calculation is typically not adjusted for dividend payments, *i.e.* different dividend models affect the pricing. Varswap payouts are fixed to the cash close, *i.e.* if hedged with futures, then there is basis risk. On long dated varswaps, the impact of stochastic rates can be significant. The realized variance may be computed as an arithmetic or geometric average, whereby the latter has some more benign properties in case of a short position. It is possible to value varswaps using the static replication approach, *i.e.* evaluating the two integrals over the put and call portfolio. Unfortunately, the convergence of the put integral can be difficult since the $1/K^2$ strike terms increases rapidly. To overcome this problem, strike cutoffs may be used beyond which option values are simply ignored. In addition to static replication, the models used by most tier-1 banks to price moment swaps is the Variance Curve Model (VCM) [150].

VCM represent a class of stochastic volatility models, which must satisfy a particular variance curve functional analogous to yield curve calibration models in fixed income. However, contrary to the yield curve, VCM are then calibrated to the variance-swap-market term structure. VCM take the whole term-structure of the fair variance swap strikes as an input and are in this regard similar to yield curve models. Given the previous discussion of the Heston stochastic volatility model, the following discussion is based on the VCM compatible 'Double Heston' model. Note that the standard Heston model does not satisfy the consistency condition imposed by the afore-mentioned variance curve functional [150]. The dynamics of the Double Heston model are given by

$$dS_t = \mu S_t dt + \alpha \sqrt{v_{1,t_t}^x} dW_t^S , \tag{4.25}$$

with

$$
\begin{aligned}
dv^1 &= \kappa_1 (v_t^2 - v_{1,t}) dt + \alpha_1 \sqrt{v_{1,t}} dW_t^1 \\
dv^2 &= \kappa_2 (\theta - v_{2,t}) dt + \alpha_2 \sqrt{v_{2,t}} dW_t^2 .
\end{aligned}
\tag{4.26}
$$

Here the standard Heston model has been extended by an additional mean reversion speed $\kappa_1 \gg \kappa_2$, which allows for a better calibration of both short and long term implied volatility to the variance curve. As a side note, the Double Heston is analogous to the double mean reverting factor models common in the fixed income world [151].

The model parameters are the mean reversion speed κ, μ_t the instantaneous volatility-of-volatility and $\rho_{S,x}$ the correlation between the spot and volatility. The advantage of calibrating a VCM model to the variance curve term structure is that it can then be used to consistently price the whole family of related payouts including highly convex options such as calls on realized variance [3]. Here the payoff is a function of the realized variance $\sigma_R^2 = \frac{252}{n} \sum_{i=1}^n \left(\log \frac{S_{t_i}}{S_{t_{i-1}}} \right)^2$ of the asset returns as

$$N \cdot \max[0, \sigma_R^2 - K^2] . \tag{4.27}$$

The delta hedge for such an option on realized variance is a variance swap itself. Variants of the above include puts as well as caps on the call, *i.e.* $N \cdot \max[0, \min[cap^2, \sigma_R^2] - K^2]$. Similarly, options on volatility indices such as the VIX, which are also traded as listed instruments, can be priced. Note that the Double Heston model is not necessarily the best model to calibrate to the variance swap market nor to price corresponding derivatives.

---

[3]Note that some variance options can also be simply priced using BSM whereby the forward is the expected future variance.

4.1.6 Power Options

Power or leverage options [152, 153, 154] are closely related to moment swaps in the sense that they can often be statically replicated. The term *power* typically refers to exponents on the underlying and/or strike within the payout. For example, the symmetric power option payout is given by

$$\max[[I \cdot (S_T - K)]^p, 0] \text{ with } I \pm 1 \text{ denoting call or put} \tag{4.28}$$

where p denotes the power exponent. Alternatively, the asymmetric power option retains the power only on the underlying

$$\max[I \cdot (S_T^p - K), 0] . \tag{4.29}$$

Often the respective payouts are also capped in order to restrict the enormous convexity faced by the short position holder. As a concrete example, consider the payout of an asymmetric power option with a strike at 100 and a power of 2. This is equivalent to a strike of 10 for the regular call. Figure 4.7 shows the respective payoff of 30 regular call options with the payoff of one power call. Up to a terminal spot of 20, the power call delivers less payout compared to the portfolio after which it then increases exponentially.

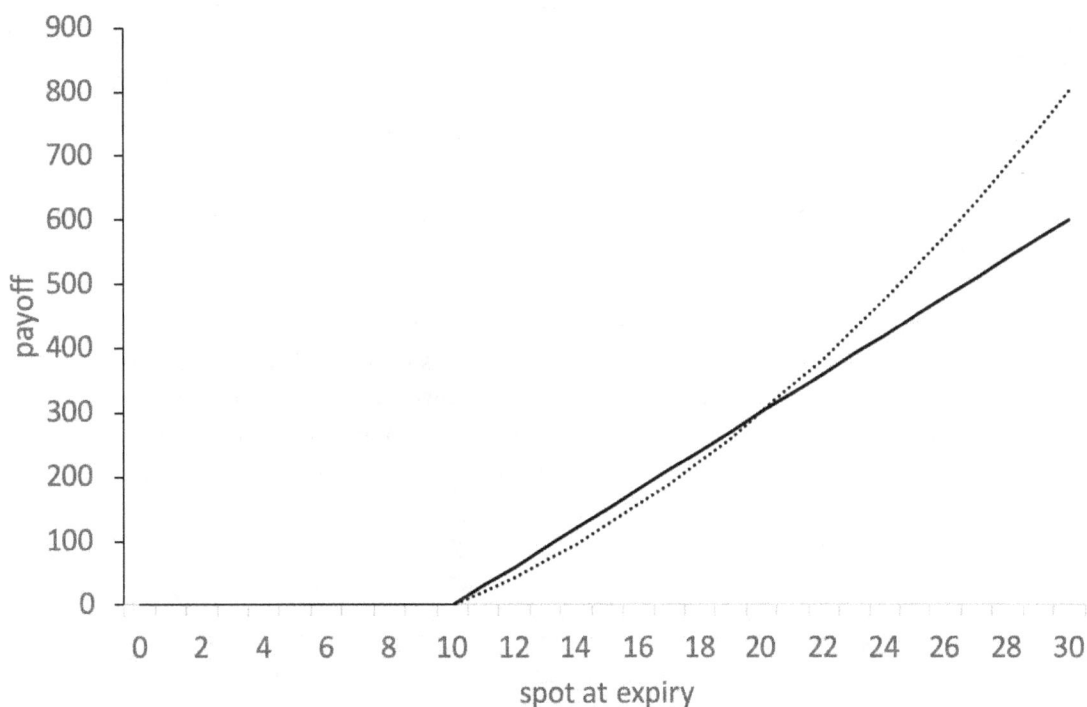

Figure 4.7: Comparison of the payoff for a portfolio of 30 regular call options of strike 10 (solid line) with one asymmetric power option call at strike 100 (dotted line).

As a general rule, derivative payouts with exponents must be approached with caution as they are designed to provide more leverage and lead to increasingly nonlinear (convex) payouts. More leverage will also mean that replication error or pricing mistakes are amplified as well. BSM-type models can be used to price power contracts, but the assumption of lognormal returns and constant volatility can be a severe mistake since higher moments are ignored by construction. The situation gets increasingly problematic as the exponents get larger. However, given that power options exhibit a non-discontinuous payout, it seems intuitive that a replication portfolio of vanilla options actually exists. For the example above, the replicating portfolio via a linear approximation is given by $21 \cdot C(K) + \sum 2C(K + \Delta K)$ (with $\Delta K = 1$) as shown in Table 4.1, the sum of the vanilla option portfolio payouts lines up with the power option payout perfectly.

spot	10	11	12	13	14	15	16	17	18	19	20	21	22	23	24	25	26	27	28	29	30
PO	0	21	44	69	96	125	156	189	224	261	300	341	384	429	476	525	576	629	684	741	800
21 O(K)	0	21	42	63	84	105	126	147	168	189	210	231	252	273	294	315	336	357	378	399	420
VO(K+1)	0	0	2	4	6	8	10	12	14	16	18	20	22	24	26	28	30	32	34	36	38
VO(K+2)	0	0	0	2	4	6	8	10	12	14	16	18	20	22	24	26	28	30	32	34	36
O(K+3)	0	0	0	0	2	4	6	8	10	12	14	16	18	20	22	24	26	28	30	32	34
O(K+4)	0	0	0	0	0	2	4	6	8	10	12	14	16	18	20	22	24	26	28	30	32
O(K+5)	0	0	0	0	0	0	2	4	6	8	10	12	14	16	18	20	22	24	26	28	30
O(K+6)	0	0	0	0	0	0	0	2	4	6	8	10	12	14	16	18	20	22	24	26	28
O(K+7)	0	0	0	0	0	0	0	0	2	4	6	8	10	12	14	16	18	20	22	24	26
O(K+8)	0	0	0	0	0	0	0	0	0	2	4	6	8	10	12	14	16	18	20	22	24
O(K+9)	0	0	0	0	0	0	0	0	0	0	2	4	6	8	10	12	14	16	18	20	22
O(K+10)	0	0	0	0	0	0	0	0	0	0	0	2	4	6	8	10	12	14	16	18	20
O(K+11)	0	0	0	0	0	0	0	0	0	0	0	0	2	4	6	8	10	12	14	16	18
O(K+12)	0	0	0	0	0	0	0	0	0	0	0	0	0	2	4	6	8	10	12	14	16
O(K+13)	0	0	0	0	0	0	0	0	0	0	0	0	0	0	2	4	6	8	10	12	14
O(K+14)	0	0	0	0	0	0	0	0	0	0	0	0	0	0	0	2	4	6	8	10	12
O(K+15)	0	0	0	0	0	0	0	0	0	0	0	0	0	0	0	0	2	4	6	8	10
O(K+16)	0	0	0	0	0	0	0	0	0	0	0	0	0	0	0	0	0	2	4	6	8
O(K+17)	0	0	0	0	0	0	0	0	0	0	0	0	0	0	0	0	0	0	2	4	6
O(K+18)	0	0	0	0	0	0	0	0	0	0	0	0	0	0	0	0	0	0	0	2	4
O(K+19)	0	0	0	0	0	0	0	0	0	0	0	0	0	0	0	0	0	0	0	0	2
SUM O	0	21	44	69	96	125	156	189	224	261	300	341	384	429	476	525	576	629	684	741	800

Table 4.1: Presentation of the asymmetric power option (PO) replication portfolio (O) for a power of 2. The sum of the vanilla options is equal to the PO payout.

Similar to the discussion with moment swaps, the replication portfolio is only perfect if all strikes can be traded at a sufficient level of liquidity. If this is the case, then the replication portfolio will over-replicate (also known as *superreplication*) the power derivative since one is not trading a continuum of strikes (see below). In other words, the replication portfolio will be more expensive.

Carr [57, 155] provides a general replication formula for any twice differentiable European payout $f(S_T)$ as

$$f(S_T) = \underbrace{f(S_*)}_{\text{zero coupon bond}} + \underbrace{f'(S_*)(S_T - S_*)}_{\text{forward}} + \underbrace{\int_0^{S_*} f''(K) \max[K - S_T, 0] dK}_{\text{put options}} + \underbrace{\int_{S_*}^{\infty} f''(K) \max[S_T - K, 0] dK}_{\text{call options}},$$

(4.30)

whereby S_* denotes the ATM forward price. The formula should remind the reader of the log contract replication and is effectively based on the same analysis. Numerical integration of the expression above for a respective power option payout will yield the price of the replication portfolio.

4.1.7 Vega risk analysis

When trading volatility directly or embedded in other derivatives, it is paramount to be able to display and analyze the resulting vega risk. In principle, there are two main approaches for determining vega risk sensitivity in a portfolio

(*i*) sensitivity analysis by doing point-wise spot bumps on the surface itself
(*ii*) sensitivity analysis by perturbing the parameters of the respective volatility surface mathematical function

Recall that in practice risk systems first fit a mathematical function to the implied volatility market data to create a smooth surface, which can then be inter- and extrapolated flexibly. This function will typically also be analytically differentiable so that *e.g.* a local volatility transformation is more easily accessible. In any case, the volatility function may quite possibly contain non-intuitive explanatory parameters describing the shape and form of the surface. The sensitivity of the option portfolio to a change in these parameters is called *parameter risk*. If the parameter risk analysis works consistently, it is not so important whether the parameters convey any information concerning typical surface modulations (*e.g.* steepness, skew, convexity). While the parameter risk approach is a sensible and natural idea, most risk systems work with a point bump analysis on the surface itself to be discussed next.

The example of a knock-in put has shown that exotic option vega dynamics in spot and time are complicated. As a consequence, hedging out exotic vega risk is non-trivial and often requires a dynamic adjustment of the hedge portfolio. What is effectively needed is a vega map in spot and maturity for the whole portfolio. The technique of obtaining a vega map in maturity is called *bucketing* [4]. Here one bumps the (local) volatility surface for each instrument in different time buckets by $X\%$ (typically 1%) and registers the P/L impact of the trading book. In order to avoid the creation of arbitrage (*e.g.* falling variance in time) the bumps are typically applied by employing two maturity shifted bumps (see Figure 4.8 whereby the parallel vega impact for a particular time point is obtained as the difference between two time points before and after.

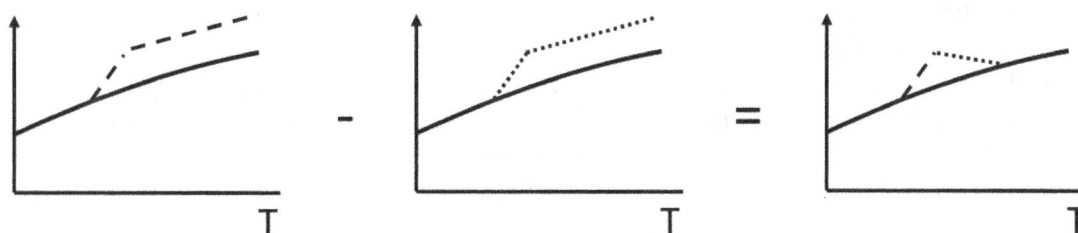

Figure 4.8: Illustration of a volatility surface bump along the term structure.

The vega bucketing allows obtaining the term structure exposure of the portfolio. This is useful but missing the dimension in spot space. One feasible approach is the following: calculate the vega buckets on the portfolio for different spot levels (*e.g.* -30%, -20%,...,+20%, +30%). The resulting analysis provides an idea of how the vega exposure varies with the spot level (see Table 4.2).

To go one step further, the same can also be done for a virtual portfolio of pre-defined vanilla or exotics options. The resulting vega exposure maps are then matched by changing the weights on the fictitious portfolio utilizing a least squares minimization. While this approach sounds sensible and indeed returns a natural mapping of exotic to vanilla vega, there several some problems:

---

[4]The same approach can be used for other risk figures such as interest rates as well.

Spot	T1	T2	T3	T4	T5	T6	T7	T8	T9	T10	T11	T12
85%	-146,852	410	-65,748	-38,268	-147,848	87,142	38,423	-74,513	78,705	-4,244	52,927	-73,838
90%	-134,165	4,115	-48,510	-12,588	-135,889	104,980	33,047	-105,358	77,814	-6,426	40,538	-85,887
95%	-135,835	8,243	-27,621	2,052	-115,713	112,859	30,369	-138,112	69,230	-8,578	28,693	-97,258
100%	-151,983	9,513	-4,151	22,960	-111,764	136,868	11,853	-174,756	60,331	-10,245	15,196	-107,788
105%	-193,041	11,525	12,147	45,992	-102,251	141,893	-12,276	-209,645	46,495	-11,345	1,780	-117,356
110%	-252,667	9,500	23,778	59,604	-84,216	141,140	-39,356	-245,496	32,967	-12,829	-11,879	-125,880
115%	-324,397	8,210	29,966	61,899	-68,169	139,239	-66,477	-276,495	19,194	-14,781	-23,663	-133,320

Table 4.2: Example of a portfolio vega exposure in spot and time.

- it is not clear whether this minimization leads to a local minimum only
- it is not clear whether one faces a frustrated system consisting of multiple solutions
- it is not clear how often the obtained portfolio needs rebalancing

Table 4.2 provides a view on the trading book vega in time whereby each time bucket carries equal weight. This view might not be an ideal representation of the risk since vega in the front months tends to be more volatile than vega in the backend of the term structure. Hence, in times of market stress, the front month volatility is typically much more affected than the back of the term structure. In other words, front-month vega reacts quicker while long-term volatility has more inertia. To obtain an idea of the exposure reflecting the maturity vega reactivity better, practitioners tend to weight their exposure as a function of time. What is required is to choose a vega pillar (e.g. 3 month) and weight the exposure in other months by a factor equal to $\sqrt{90/\text{days to expiry}}$. Hence, in this example, the vega expiring in 1 month would be weighted by $\sqrt{90/30} = 1.73$ and the vega expiring in 1 year vega by $\sqrt{90/365} = 0.5$.

Practical Tips 4.1.1 Questions to ask your quants / risk system support:

- How is the vega exposure risk bucketing calculated exactly?
- Are there any variance swaps with caps on the books?
- Are there any highly convex volatility derivatives on the book?
- How is the variance swap/volatility swap priced valued, e.g. static replication or variance curve model approach? In the case of the static replication approach, is there a (downside) strike cut-off applied to ensure that the $1/K^2$ term in the integral converges?
- How are dividends treated in the calculation of volatility derivatives (incl. the variance swap)?

---

5. Correlation and multi-factor options

5.1 Introduction

The coverage so far only involved uncorrelated financial products in the sense that correlation was not a parameter in the pricing. The absence of correlation does not mean that a portfolio of univariate financial products exhibits no correlation risk. The opposite is typically the case. However, while correlation is a key component in portfolio construction [20] it was so far not required when pricing the individual instrument.

5.2 Co-variance and correlation

In layman's terms, correlation tries to estimate how two or more things move or behave together. First, and foremost, correlation is not necessarily a measure of (in)dependence nor related to causality. Instead, it is a Gaussian and geometric concept and as such, often reduces complex dynamics to a very simple if not misleading quantitative measure. Similar to volatility, correlation can be defined as historical or implied. The following section first discusses how to estimate the realized correlation.

Arguably the most known realized correlation estimate is the Pearson correlation coefficient [156] given by

$$\rho_{i,j}^{\text{Pearson}} = \frac{\sum_{k=1}^{N}(x_k - \bar{x})(y_k - \bar{y})}{\sum_{k=1}^{N}\sqrt{(x_k - \bar{x})^2}\sqrt{\sum_{k=1}^{N}(y_k - \bar{y})^2}} \ . \tag{5.1}$$

The calculation/regression above is always done using time series returns and not directly on the point data itself to avoid obvious non-stationarity issues [1]. While beyond the scope here, it should at least be pointed out that additional measures might need to be taken to avoid non-stationarity and multicollinearity problems in financial time series data. However, even if these issues do not exist in the corresponding data, there are at least two other problems with the Pearson estimate: It

---

[1] Stationary processes exhibit constant mean and variance (weak stationarity) or constant moments (strong stationarity) over time. Hence, assets which grow over time on average will not be stationary since their mean is not constant.

is biased for finite sample sizes and not robust, *i.e.* sensitive to outliers. There exist more robust estimators such as Spearman [157] or Kendall's tau [158], but the problem of finite sample sizes and outliers does not necessarily vanish. Fortunately, due to the law of large numbers, Pearson's estimate converges to the true correlation definition with sufficient sample size, *i.e.* the asymptotic convergence is guaranteed.

$$\lim_{N \to \infty} \rho_{i,j}^{\text{Pearson}*} = \frac{\sum_{k=1}^{N}(x_k - \bar{x})(y_k - \bar{y})}{\sum_{k=1}^{N}\sqrt{(x_k - \bar{x})^2}\sqrt{\sum_{k=1}^{N}(y_k - \bar{y})^2}} = \frac{E[xy] - E[x]E[y]}{\sqrt{E[x^2] - E^2[x]}\sqrt{E[y] - E^2[y]}} \quad (5.2)$$

What is therefore done in practice is to take advantage of a central property in the diffusion process, namely that terminal distributions (variance, co-variance) can be sampled along the path. More concretely, it is possible to improve the statistics via creating a time trace for the average correlation via a time window (*e.g.* 1 week or 1 year) and then calculate the correlation by averaging the windows of the historical data. Figure 5.1 illustrates the method which is even easily implementable in a spreadsheet.

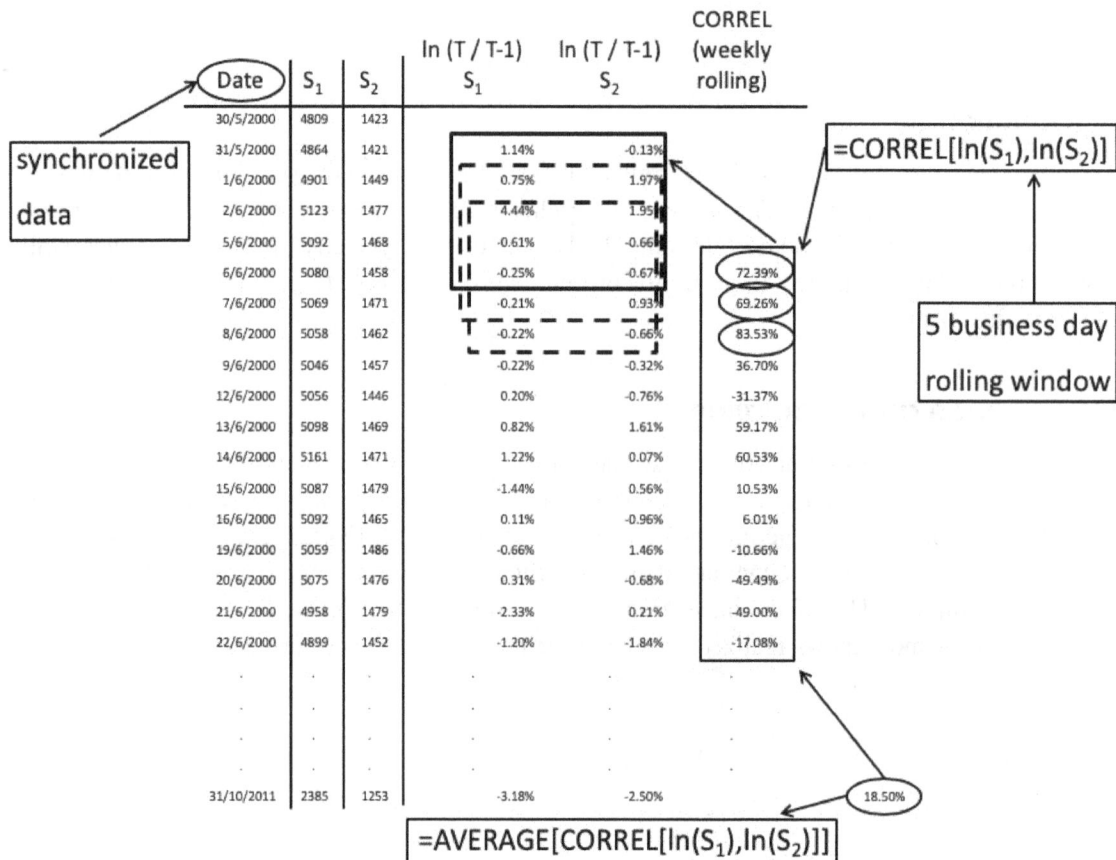

Date	S_1	S_2	ln (T / T-1) S_1	ln (T / T-1) S_2	CORREL (weekly rolling)
30/5/2000	4809	1423			
31/5/2000	4864	1421	1.14%	-0.13%	
1/6/2000	4901	1449	0.75%	1.97%	
2/6/2000	5123	1477	4.44%	1.95%	
5/6/2000	5092	1468	-0.61%	-0.66%	
6/6/2000	5080	1458	-0.25%	-0.67%	72.39%
7/6/2000	5069	1471	-0.21%	0.93%	69.26%
8/6/2000	5058	1462	-0.22%	-0.66%	83.53%
9/6/2000	5046	1457	-0.22%	-0.32%	36.70%
12/6/2000	5056	1446	0.20%	-0.76%	-31.37%
13/6/2000	5098	1469	0.82%	1.61%	59.17%
14/6/2000	5161	1471	1.22%	0.07%	60.53%
15/6/2000	5087	1479	-1.44%	0.56%	10.53%
16/6/2000	5092	1465	0.11%	-0.96%	6.01%
19/6/2000	5059	1486	-0.66%	1.46%	-10.66%
20/6/2000	5075	1476	0.31%	-0.68%	-49.49%
21/6/2000	4958	1479	-2.33%	0.21%	-49.00%
22/6/2000	4899	1452	-1.20%	-1.84%	-17.08%
⋮	⋮	⋮	⋮	⋮	⋮
31/10/2011	2385	1253	-3.18%	-2.50%	18.50%

synchronized data

=CORREL[ln(S_1),ln(S_2)]

5 business day rolling window

=AVERAGE[CORREL[ln(S_1),ln(S_2)]]

Figure 5.1: Illustration of calculating an average correlation estimate between two assets S_1 and S_2 via the rolling window method. Ultimately, the final correlation estimate is obtained by averaging over the windowed correlation estimates along the path.

While this method is an elegant way of generating a correlation time trace as well as a hopefully realistic average correlation measure, it remains an estimate. This problem increases with the number of assets in the correlation matrix since the length of the historical time series used in the calculation needs to be aligned, *i.e.* insufficient sample size decreased the statistical significance of the estimate. Hence, in the case of trading books with a large number of assets (> 100), it is recommended to apply regularization techniques to deal with potentially unreliable correlation estimates, which are ultimately not only used in pricing and valuation but also for risk management purposes. While the theory and exact way of using these techniques to clean up estimated correlation matrices are beyond the scope of this book, the reader is referred to a recent analysis of the most common methods [159].

5.2.1 Asynchronous data

Data science in finance has a significant advantage in that the sample size is typically large, *i.e.* new price data is often available every day at different frequencies. However, various (daily) time series are not always in sync in time due to time zone differences. For asynchronous time series, this typically underestimates the correlation if it is based on a naive calculation based on the respective daily closing prices [160]. However, because markets do influence each other, it can be expected that over a period of *e.g.* 3 or 5 days, the daily bias in the correlation estimate should average out. Hence, as a proxy, if faced with fully or partially asynchronous time series data, the correlation should be calculated between some average (closing) price. In practice, using a proxy of 5 days when calculating log returns before estimating the correlation is often acceptable to not severely underestimate the correlation. However, if possible, it is recommended to use a more advanced estimator such as Hayashi-Yoshida [161].

5.2.2 Instantaneous versus terminal Correlation

As a side note, it is useful to introduce the notion of instantaneous and terminal correlation. Instantaneous correlation is defined as the correlation observed in the simulation of a stochastic process given the input parameters. The terminal correlation, on the other hand, is the correlation measured as an average over the simulation. Ideally, they turn out to be the same. However, due to the use of a stochastic process, this is not guaranteed. Models that mix non-constant or time-dependent volatilities tend to produce a *decorrelation* effect along the simulated path. As shown in the literature [162], this effect increases with higher instantaneous correlation and more strongly varying (time-dependent) volatility. In the LVM the decorrelation effect is about 1% p.a. for an instantaneous correlation of 70%. In a SVM, the effect is typically even larger. Hence, if one wanted to make sure not to 'misprice' a multi-factor option due to the decorrelation effect of the stochastic model process, the instantaneous correlation has to be moved higher.

5.3 Multi-factor options and BSM

Multi-factor options are derivatives for which the price is a function of the individual asset risk factors and the *co-movement* of the assets over the lifetime. In other words, multi-factor options somehow couple the individual returns to synthesize the final payout. This coupling (constant) is called correlation or co-variance. The accurate estimation of the correlation constant is one of the key P/L drivers for multi-factor options. The critical risk quantity impacting correlation risk is the so-called cross-gamma, *i.e.* the change of the value of the option price with respect to the movement in two of the underlying assets.

The multivariate extension of the BSM equation is given by

$$\underbrace{\frac{\partial V}{\partial t}}_{\Theta} + \frac{1}{2}\sum_i\sum_j \rho_{ij}\sigma_i\sigma_j S_i S_j \underbrace{\frac{\partial^2 V}{\partial S_i \partial S_j}}_{\Gamma_{ij}} + \sum_i r S_i \underbrace{\frac{\partial V}{\partial S_i}}_{\Delta_i} - rV = 0 \,. \tag{5.3}$$

The gamma term Γ_{ij} is now effectively a symmetric matrix whereby the diagonal elements $i=j$ correspond to the univariate 'vanilla' gamma and the off-diagonal elements are referred to as the cross-gamma terms. The symbol ρ_{ij} represents the correlation matrix itself. If the interest rate r is set to zero while assuming a delta-hedged position, the equation can be rearranged to recognize the multivariate cash gamma

$$\underbrace{\frac{\partial V}{\partial t}}_{\Theta} = -\frac{1}{2}\sum_i\sum_j \rho_{ij}\sigma_i\sigma_j \underbrace{S_i S_j \frac{\partial^2 V}{\partial S_i \partial S_j}}_{\Gamma_{ij}^{\$}} \,. \tag{5.4}$$

The corresponding P/L over a spot move dS_i and time step dt is then given by

$$P/L = \frac{1}{2}\sum_i\sum_j \Gamma_{ij}^{\$}\left[\; \underbrace{\frac{dS_i}{S_j}\frac{dS_j}{S_j}}_{\text{realized co-variance P/L}} - \underbrace{\rho_{ij}\sigma_i\sigma_j dt}_{\substack{\text{implied co-variance,}\\ \textit{i.e. theta P/L}}}\;\right]\,. \tag{5.5}$$

The sell-side derivatives industry is typically long gamma and short cross-gamma via Structured Products issuance, *i.e.* the sign of the diagonal and off-diagonal elements is positive/negative, respectively. Because correlation in the equity world is typically positive, a short cross-gamma position has *positive* theta for this asset class.

During times of market stress (*e.g.* fall 2008) the realized co-variance can exceed the expected (implied) co-variance significantly, *i.e.*

$$\frac{\Delta S_i}{S_i}\frac{\Delta S_j}{S_j} \gg \rho_{ij}\sigma_i\sigma_j\Delta t \,. \tag{5.6}$$

Therefore, trading books with short correlation exposure suffer in the daily carry of the position. In order to stop potential P/L bleed and get the theta in line with realized co-variance P/L, the book correlation mark then needs to be adjusted higher. This correlation remark will, of course, have a net negative mark-to-market P/L impact on the book.

It is also possible to extend more complicated stochastic process models to the multi-factor setting. While this extension is rather straightforward in the case of LV, SV and SVM require additional correlation pairs to be estimated. This need arises because not only asset spot-spot correlation is required, but also a correlation between spot and volatility as well as volatility and volatility (see Figure 5.2. Hence, in a multi-factor setting, these models become even more parameter-rich since it is necessary to define at least three correlation matrices. Moreover, the estimation needs to guarantee that all resulting matrices are *positive semi-definite* (see discussion below).

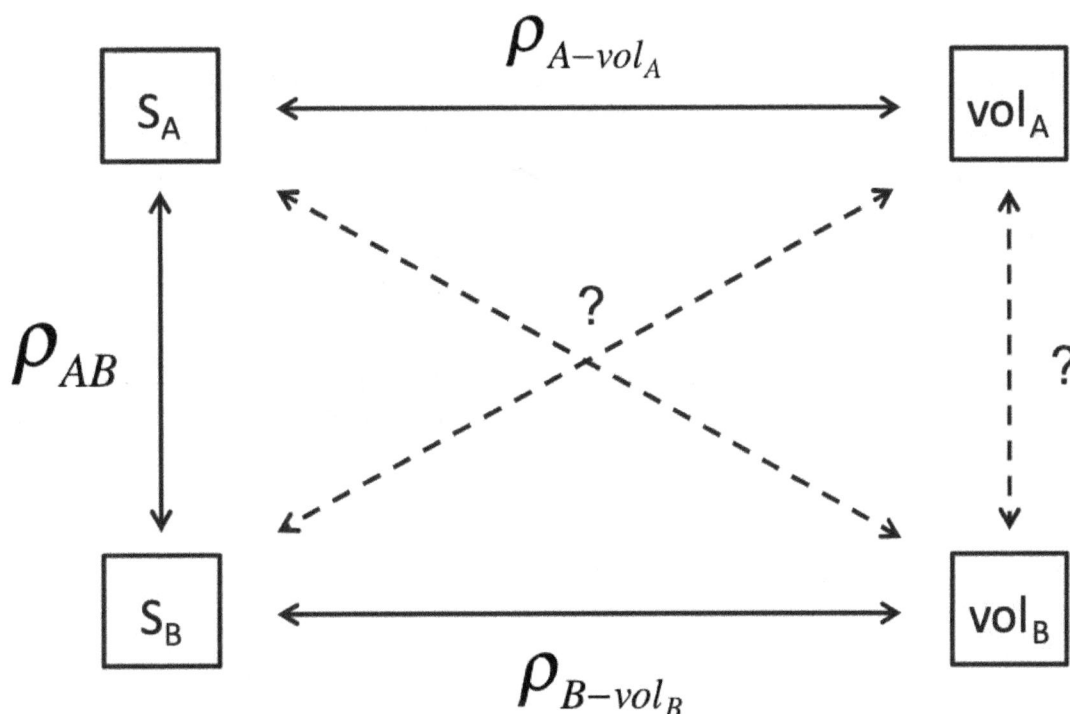

Figure 5.2: Illustration of the required correlation estimates for a multi-factor SV model: spot-spot, volatility-volatility and spot-volatility.

5.3.1 Generating correlated random variables

The standard way of generating correlated random variables is the so-called Cholesky decomposition [163]. However, one problem which often occurs is that the resulting correlation matrix is not symmetric and positive definite. Without going into details, it is trivial to see that *e.g.* for a three variable case, there must be some constraints between the pair-wise correlation numbers. For example, consider the random variables A, B and C. Correlation between AB = 0.8 and AC = 0.9. Now, can the pair BC take any arbitrary value between -1 and +1? The answer is found by investigating the variance for the portfolio $P = X - Y - Z$ assuming a standard deviation of 1 for each component given by

$$var[P] = \sigma_A^2 + \sigma_B^2 + \sigma_C^2 - 2\rho_{AB}\sigma_A\sigma_B - 2\rho_{AC}\sigma_A\sigma_C - 2\rho_{BC}\sigma_B\sigma_C = -0.4 - 2\rho_{BC} . \tag{5.7}$$

In order for the portfolio variance to be positive it is required that $\rho_{BC} \geq 0.2$. This condition is called *positive semi-definite*. Negative definite correlation matrices imply a portfolio with negative variance. While it has not yet been discussed how to generate correlations at all in detail, one method is obviously to somehow estimate it from the historical (realized) correlation. The problem there is that historical data often suffers from problems such as non-synchronicity, outliers or sparsity (*e.g.* for assets that have been trading for a short time only). Those issues may contribute to obtaining a correlation matrix which is not positive semi-definite.

5.3.2 Basket option

Consider a basket B of individual stock returns. The expected portfolio return is then simply the weighted sum of the individual returns given by

$$B_t = \sum_{i=1}^{N} w_i S_{i,t} \, , \tag{5.8}$$

with $\sum_{i=1}^{N} = 1$ and $E[R_B] = \sum_i w_i E[R_B]$. If the arithmetic average is approximated by the geometric average, then the variance of a basket of individual stock returns is given by the sum of the individual variances weighted by the correlation

$$\sigma_B^2 = VAR\left[\ln(\sum_{i=1}^{N} w_i S_i^t) \right] \approx VAR\left[\ln\left(\prod_{i=1}^{N} S_{i,t}^{w_i} \right) \right]$$

$$\sigma_B^2 = \sum_{i}^{N}\sum_{j}^{N} w_i w_j \sigma_i \sigma_j \rho_{ij} \text{ with} \rho_{ij} = 1 \text{ if } i = j \tag{5.9}$$

$$\sigma_B^2 = \sum_i w_i^2 \sigma_i^2 + 2\sum_{i>j} w_i w_j \sigma_i \sigma_j \rho_{ij} \, .$$

A correlation coefficient smaller than 1 thus reduces the overall variance of the portfolio. As a consequence, the basket option is *cheaper* than the sum of the individual options themselves.

The basket call option is a commonly traded payout given by

$$C_{\text{basket}} = \max\left[0, \sum_{i=1}^{N} w_i \frac{S_T}{S_0} - K \right] \, . \tag{5.10}$$

Because of the correlation effect (*i.e.* the reduced variance), this option is cheaper than the simple sum of the individual component options. The holder of the basket call is therefore long correlation since an increase in correlation increases the total variance. The holder of the basket call is also long volatility and long both diagonal and cross-gamma.

Figure 5.3 illustrates the relationship between the basket price and the correlation level. The so-called *correlation delta* is the change of the option price for a change in correlation and can be written down explicitly for a basket consisting of two stocks only given by

$$\underbrace{\frac{\partial V_B}{\partial \rho}}_{\text{correlation delta}} = \frac{\partial V_B}{\partial \sigma_B} \cdot \frac{\partial \sigma_B}{\partial \rho} = \frac{\partial V_B}{\partial \sigma_B} \cdot \left(\frac{w_i w_j \sigma_i \sigma_j}{2\sigma_B} \right) \, . \tag{5.11}$$

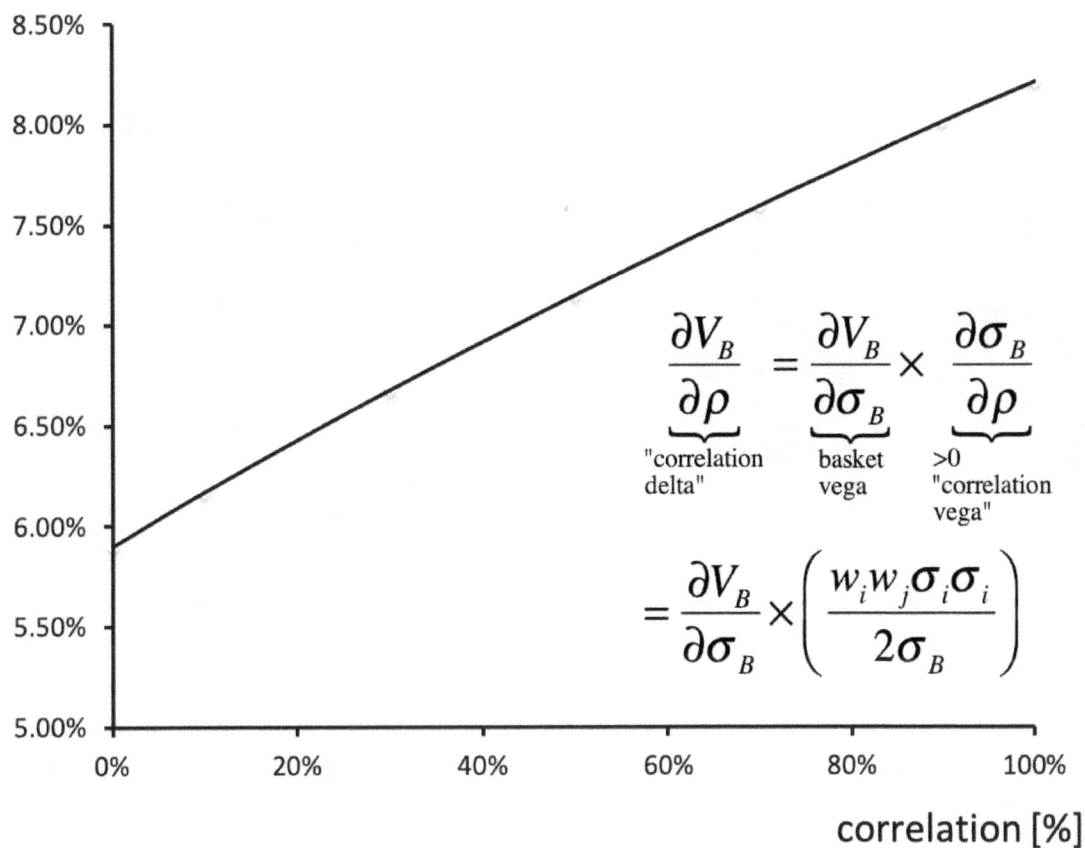

The figure contains the following equations:

$$\underbrace{\frac{\partial V_B}{\partial \rho}}_{\substack{\text{"correlation} \\ \text{delta"}}} = \underbrace{\frac{\partial V_B}{\partial \sigma_B}}_{\substack{\text{basket} \\ \text{vega}}} \times \underbrace{\frac{\partial \sigma_B}{\partial \rho}}_{\substack{>0 \\ \text{"correlation} \\ \text{vega"}}}$$

$$= \frac{\partial V_B}{\partial \sigma_B} \times \left(\frac{w_i w_j \sigma_i \sigma_i}{2\sigma_B} \right)$$

correlation [%]

Figure 5.3: Illustration of the basket price versus correlation for a 2 underlying basket, volatility = 20%, no skew, $r = bc = d = 0$ and 1 year expiry.

Increasing correlation reduces the overall diagonal and cross-gamma of the basket. On the contrary, increasing correlation increases the vega sensitivity of the basket option. It is important to note that the vega components of a basket shift as a function of the (co)-movement of the spots (see Figure 5.4). This switch can be unpleasant because it means that potential vanilla vega hedges need to be adjusted, too.

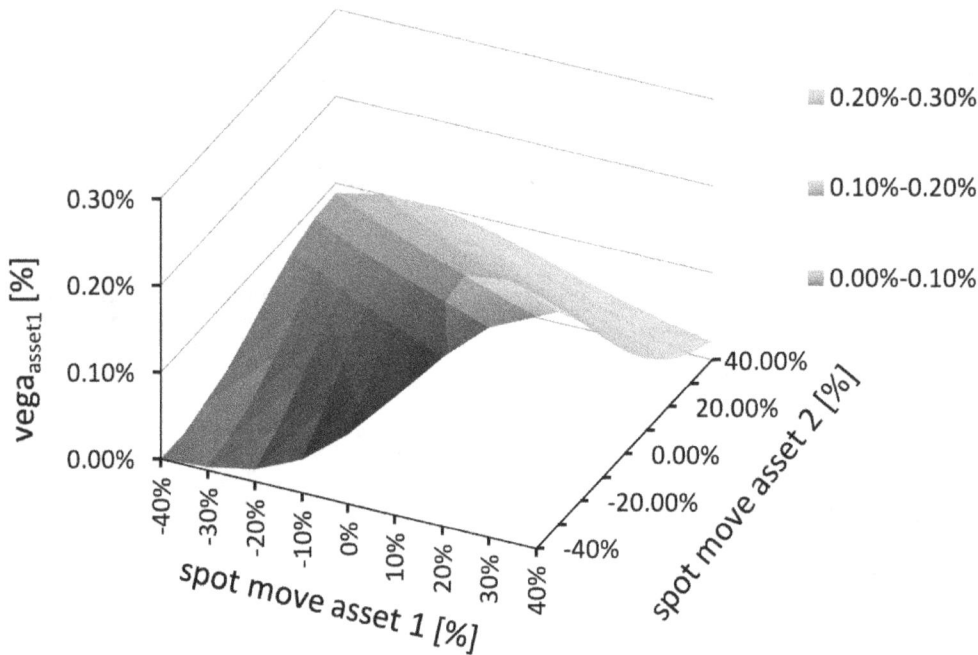

Figure 5.4: Illustration of a basket component vega change versus spot moves for a 2 underlying basket, volatility = 20%, no skew, $r = bc = d = 0$ and 1 year expiry.

5.3.2.1 Basket Option Pricing

In order to derive an analytical basket option pricing model, the question is whether it is possible to define the basket volatility consistent with the true basket dynamics. If this were the case, then a BSM approach is justified. The problem here is again that if the basket components are lognormal, then the (weighted) sum cannot be, *i.e.*

$$\sum \ln(S_i) = \ln \prod S_i \neq \ln \sum S_i . \tag{5.12}$$

In other words, recall that the earlier expression was indeed for the variance of the basket and not the variance of the log of the basket

$$\underbrace{VAR[B]}_{\neq VAR[\ln B]} = \sigma_B^2 = \sum_i w_i^2 \sigma_i^2 + 2 \sum_{i>j} w_i w_j \sigma_i \sigma_j \rho_{ij} . \tag{5.13}$$

In any case, this approximation is called the Gaussian approximation. The Gaussian approximation can be improved further by so-called moment matching [164]. The idea is to approximate the basket again using the dynamics of lognormal geometric Brownian motion. However, it is ensured that the first two (or more) moments of this approximate basket *match* the moments of the true basket on the N underlyings at a certain time T (*e.g.* for a European option this would be the maturity). The result is a still relatively simple analytical expression for the basket variance $\sigma_{B,MM}^2$, which can now be used in the BSM framework (shown below for matching the first two moments and no dividends):

$$\sigma_{B,MM}^2 = \frac{1}{T} \ln \left(\frac{\sum_{i,j} w_i w_j S_0^i S_0^j \exp[(\rho_{ij} \sigma_i \sigma_j) T]}{(\sum_{i=1}^N w_i S_0^i \exp[-T])} \right) . \tag{5.14}$$

Alternatively, one can evaluate the basket options using Monte Carlo. Typically, the Gaussian approximation is not accurate in case of

- a high volatility basket
- low correlation
- a combination of the above
- OTM basket options

To some extent, moment matching suffers from similar issues but becomes more accurate when indeed all first four moments are matched. To assess the accuracy of these approximations, it is advisable to always carry out a MC simulation also, especially in the cases above.

5.3.3 Cross-gamma P/L

Consider the toy example of a cash cross-gamma in percent $\Gamma_{AB}^{\$,\%} = $ -\$250k between a pair of assets (A & B), whereby there is no diagonal gamma at all. In this case, the position is short correlation, *i.e.* one would like the underlyings to disperse away from each other as much as possible. Now, recall that (as for diagonal gamma), the cross-gamma does not only produce P/L, but it changes the individual deltas of the components of the option, too. Figure 5.5 illustrates the expected P/L for the four possible spot price co-movements. Hence, in case of a move of $+1\%$ for asset A and -1% for asset B, the P/L amounts to $2 \cdot 0.5 \cdot 100 \cdot (-250k) \cdot +1\% \cdot -1\% = +\$2'500$. The delta change on asset 1 due to the asset 2 is then: $-250k \cdot 100 \cdot -1\% = +250k$, *i.e.* the position gets longer delta in line with the market for asset A. The delta change on asset 2 due to the asset 1 is: $-250k \cdot 100 \cdot +1\% = -250k$, *i.e.* the position gets shorter delta in line with the market for asset B.

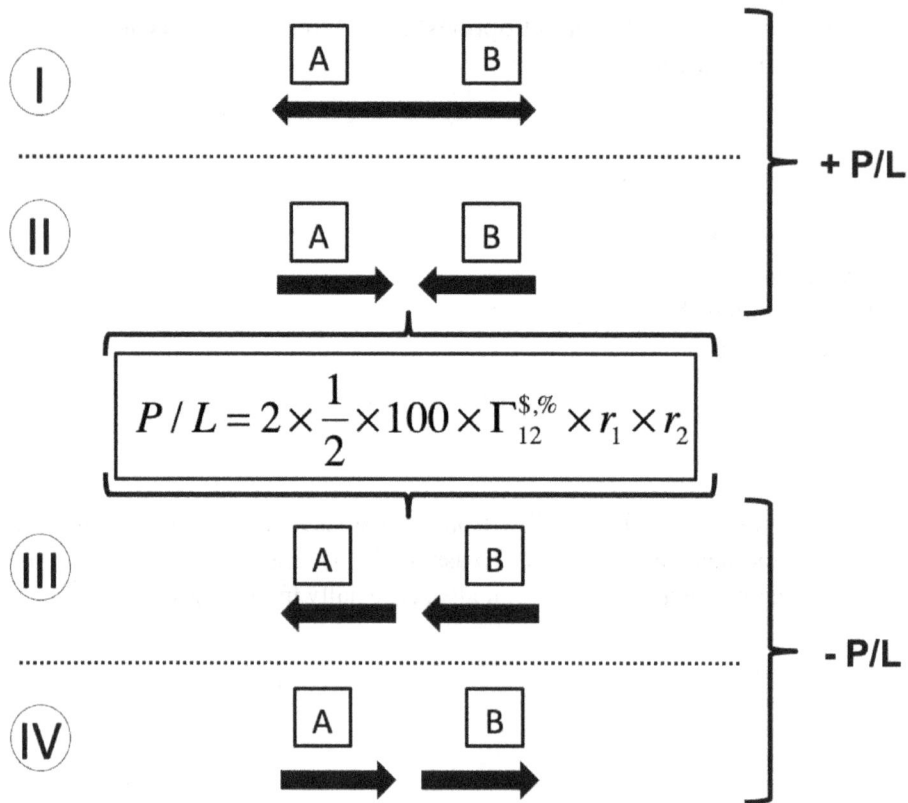

$$P/L = 2 \times \frac{1}{2} \times 100 \times \Gamma_{12}^{\$,\%} \times r_1 \times r_2$$

Figure 5.5: Expected cross-gamma P/L for a stylized two stock example with four potential spot co-movements.

A more concrete example is the ATM straddle dispersion trade, given by a short ATM straddle on an asset basket and long ATM straddles on each of the basket components. Hence, the overall exposure is flat diagonal and short cross-gamma, *i.e.* the position benefits from dispersion overall. The P/L scenario is visualized in Figure 5.6 for a two stock basket, where each component has a volatility of 20%, *r=bc=d=0* and 1 year expiry with a notional of USD 35m.

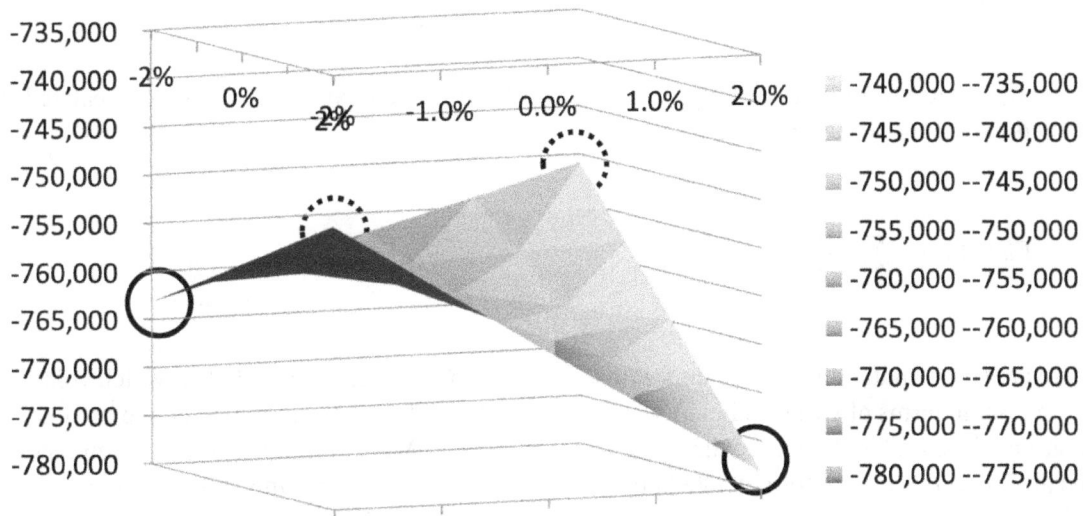

Figure 5.6: Expected cross-gamma P/L for a stylized two stock example with four potential spot co-movements.

5.3.4 Cross-gamma hedging

The perfect hedge for any position is to either offset it with the same or almost identical instrument in the opposite direction (ignoring potential counterparty credit risk). Unfortunately, this is rarely possible in reality. As a consequence, operators are often forced to proxy-hedge positions.

For the case of cross-gamma exposure, it is possible to proxy hedge long/short cross-gamma by a short/long diagonal gamma position. However, which ratio of gamma to cross-gamma should one run? While this is a non-trivial question to answer a back of the envelope calculation in the BSM framework allows obtaining the diagonal gamma position offsetting the cross-gamma P/L. Recall the full gamma P/L (expressed herein matrix-vector notation) for a delta-hedged portfolio given by

$$\Gamma_{PL} = \frac{1}{2}(\delta S_1 ... \delta S_N) \begin{pmatrix} \Gamma_{1,1} & \cdots & \Gamma_{1,N} \\ \vdots & \ddots & \vdots \\ \Gamma_{N,1} & \cdots & \Gamma_{N,N} \end{pmatrix} \begin{pmatrix} \delta S_1 \\ \vdots \\ \delta S_N \end{pmatrix} = \frac{1}{2} \sum_{i,j=1}^{N} \Gamma_{i,j} \cdot \delta S_1 \cdot \delta S_j. \tag{5.15}$$

The gamma matrix with zeros on all off-diagonal elements which provides the same P/L as above is then given by

$$\begin{pmatrix} \Gamma_{1,1}^* & 0 & 0 \\ 0 & \ddots & 0 \\ 0 & 0 & \Gamma_{N,N}^* \end{pmatrix}, \tag{5.16}$$

so that

$$\Gamma_{PL}(\delta S_1 ... \delta S_N) = \frac{1}{2} \delta S^T \cdot \Gamma \delta S \approx \frac{1}{2} \delta S^T \cdot \Gamma^* \cdot \delta S \,. \tag{5.17}$$

Using the relationship $dS_i dS_j = \rho_{ij} \sigma_i \sigma_j S_i S_j dt$ (*i.e.* re-arranged expectation value of realized vs implied co-variance) one finds[165]

$$\Gamma_{ii}^* = \Gamma_{ii} + \sum_{k=1, k\neq i}^{N} \frac{S_k \sigma_k}{S_i \sigma_i} \rho_{ik} \Gamma_{ik} \,. \tag{5.18}$$

There are some limitations or problems with this approach. For once, it is not clear which volatility to use both in terms of strike and maturity. A natural choice for maturity would be the correlation duration of the trading book, but the strike remains unclear. Moreover, it is somewhat impractical to calculate this measure for a whole book and implement a macro trading strategy. However, on a single large trade, it sensible to assess at the theoretical offsetting diagonal gamma as a guiding principle when deriving a proxy-hedge strategy.

Vanilla greeks can be hedged by other vanilla options. Depending on the liquidity, this hedge is in principle perfect. Concerning exotic options, it is apparent that it becomes more difficult to hedge the exotic exposure via vanillas because of differences in the greek profiles in spot/time/volatility, etc. The easiest proxy hedge for cross-gamma is to trade diagonal (vanilla) gamma. The ratio of long gamma to short cross-gamma needs to be adjusted in different market regimes (*e.g.* +1.5 / -1 during stress or +0.5 / -1 during calm periods). This ratio naturally drives the overall carry of the book (theta + delta / gamma / co-variance P/L). If the idea is to hedge out the co-variance risk fully, then this is only possible by trading a correlation dependent product against the book exposure. Unfortunately, the liquidity here is often not excellent and might not completely offset the correlation exposure of the book. As usual, this problem is worse for single assets compared to indices.

5.3.5 Worst-of forward

As one key component of the worst-of knock-in put, the worst-of forward is the most common exposure a standard structured product or exotics book carries (implicitly).

In the worst-of forward, the holder is long correlation and short vega by construction [2]. However, the vega sensitivity on the basket as a function of the spot is not constant. The short worst-of forward position has an undesirable dvega/dspot (vanna) exposure, *i.e.* it loses / gains vega for decreasing / increasing spot levels [3]. The dynamics is shown in Figure 5.7. The exposure is magnified in case a worst-of knock-in put is added (see Figure 5.8). The result is a vanna , which is effectively impossible to hedge (statically) via vanillas.

---

[2]Note that a forward on a *basket* is just the weighted sum of the single forward, *i.e.* a basket forward has **no** correlation exposure.

[3] The best of forward has the opposite risk sensitivity for obvious reasons.

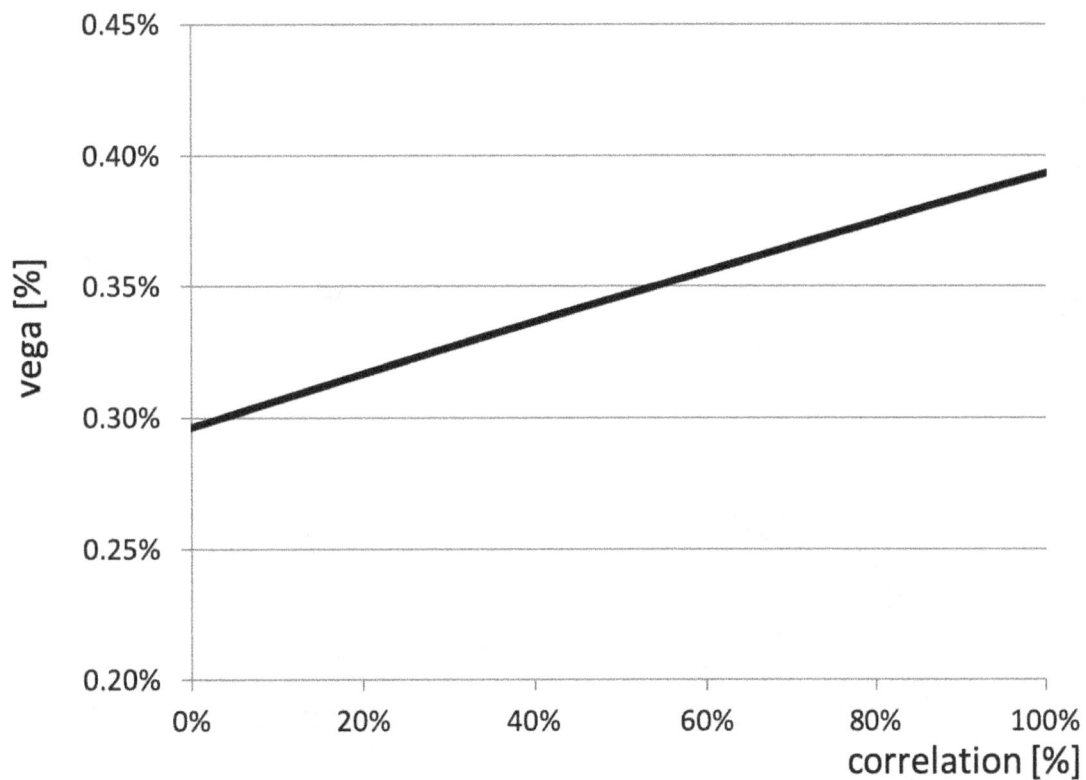

Figure 5.7: Vega versus basket spot price (assuming perfect correlation between all basket components) for a short worst-of-forward position (3 assets, 20% volatility, $r = bc = d = 0$, 3 years to expiry).

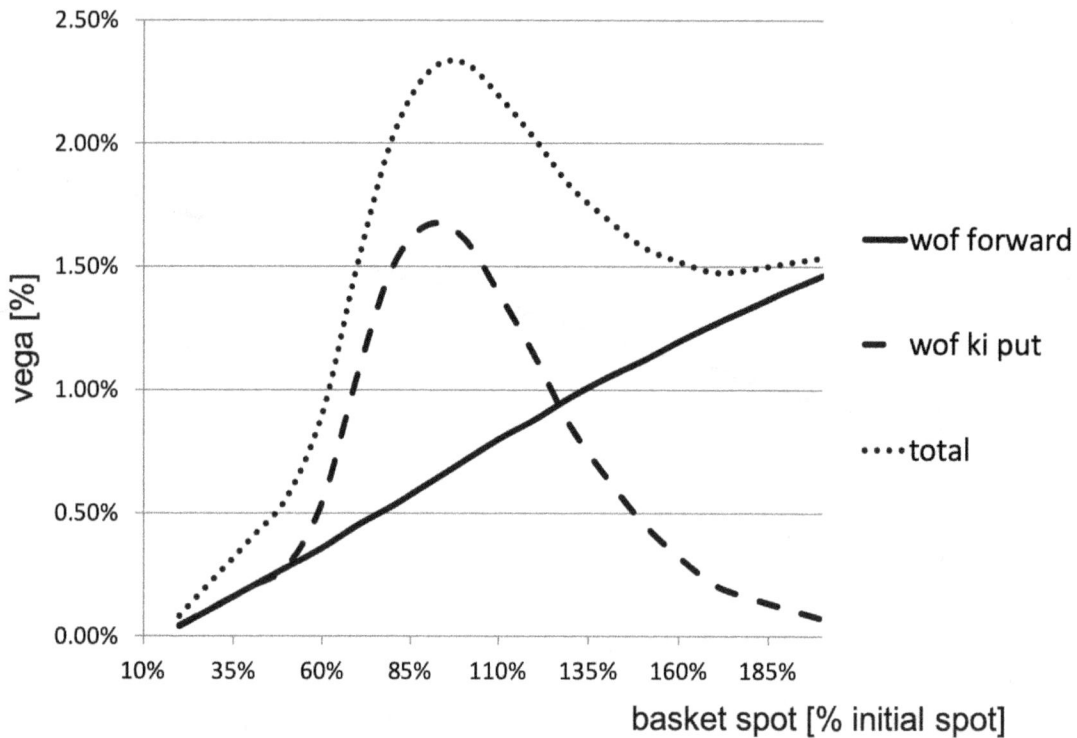

Figure 5.8: Vega versus basket spot price (perfect correlation) for a short worst-of-forward position (solid line), a long knock-in put position (3 assets, 20% volatility, $r = bc = d = 0$, barrier = 50%, 3 years to expiry; dashed line) and the aggregate exposure (dotted line).

worst-of and best of options are arguably the most commonly traded correlation instruments, whereby the former outnumber the latter significantly. Often the motivation for trading or investing in a worst-of structure is that they render the derivative overall cheaper. For example, buying a call on a basket is much more expensive than buying a worst-of call on the components. Alternatively, selling a put on a basket generates less premium than selling a worst-of put in the components. Therefore, the investor can obtain or sell more leverage for the same premium, assuming the correlation realizes in line with the estimate.

5.3.5.1 Worst-of knock-in put

The worst-of knock-in (ki) put is practically embedded in all retail Structured Products. Here, the client typically sells a worst-of ki-put to finance either a coupon or some upside participation (*e.g.* via calls), *i.e.*

$$P_{wof} = \max\left[0, K - \min\left(\frac{S_{i,T}}{S_{i,0}}, \frac{S_{j,T}}{S_{j,0}}, ..., \frac{S_{N,T}}{S_{N,0}}\right)\right]. \tag{5.19}$$

The dealer is typically long the structure and thereby short correlation, long diagonal and short cross-gamma. It is intuitive that the trader consequently benefits from a decorrelation because this will, in turn, increase the probability of a negative return (or a barrier hit in case of a knock-in option). Note that the short cross-gamma only reduces if one of the assets becomes a clear underperformer.

Worst-of structures can become painful if two (or more) stocks compete for the worst position close to a barrier or trigger for which the potential payout change is significant and discontinuous. In this case, the greeks will not only become unstable but often also flip between the competing basket components. Moreover, with an increasing amount of assets, it becomes increasingly difficult to carry out the individual hedges. For example, on a worst-of with 3 assets, all risks are somewhat evenly distributed at inception (unless the forwards are very different) and the hedge overlay is allocated on the 3 assets equally. Now, in the case of a 20 asset basket, the same risk is distributed over 20 assets, but it becomes increasingly impractical to micro-hedge each asset exposure. One might argue that with an increasing number of assets, the basket behaves increasingly like an index. While this is true in theory, it is not always possible to find a suitable index to proxy the basket behavior. The practice of running an index hedge against a basket of stocks is called dispersion trading. Note that it becomes then imperative to also track the implicit index correlation exposure size versus the basket correlation exposure.

5.3.5.2   Worst-of knock-out put

Some correlation structures change the sign of the cross-gamma as a function of the performances between the underlyings. The sign switch is dangerous since the correlation exposure becomes even less predictable. Alternatively, one can even demonstrate that there are regions for which the correlation risk is somewhat meaningless. Figure 5.9 shows such a situation for a worst-of basket with two assets. It is visible that there are regions in which the cross-gamma switches sign. Cross-gamma sign switches are very problematic from a pricing and risk management point of view alike. On the pricing side, a constant (bid or offer) correlation parameter input cannot capture the risk quantitatively. Therefore, the pricing impact needs to be assessed using a model which can switch between bid and offer correlation marks as a function of the cross-gamma sign (see 5.3.9.2). From a risk management point of view there will be regions where the correlation exposure is somewhat meaningless and can lead to large fluctuation in the respective parameter risk. Therefore, it is recommended to run an extensive scenario analysis in the respective region so as to avoid frequent re-hedging operations.

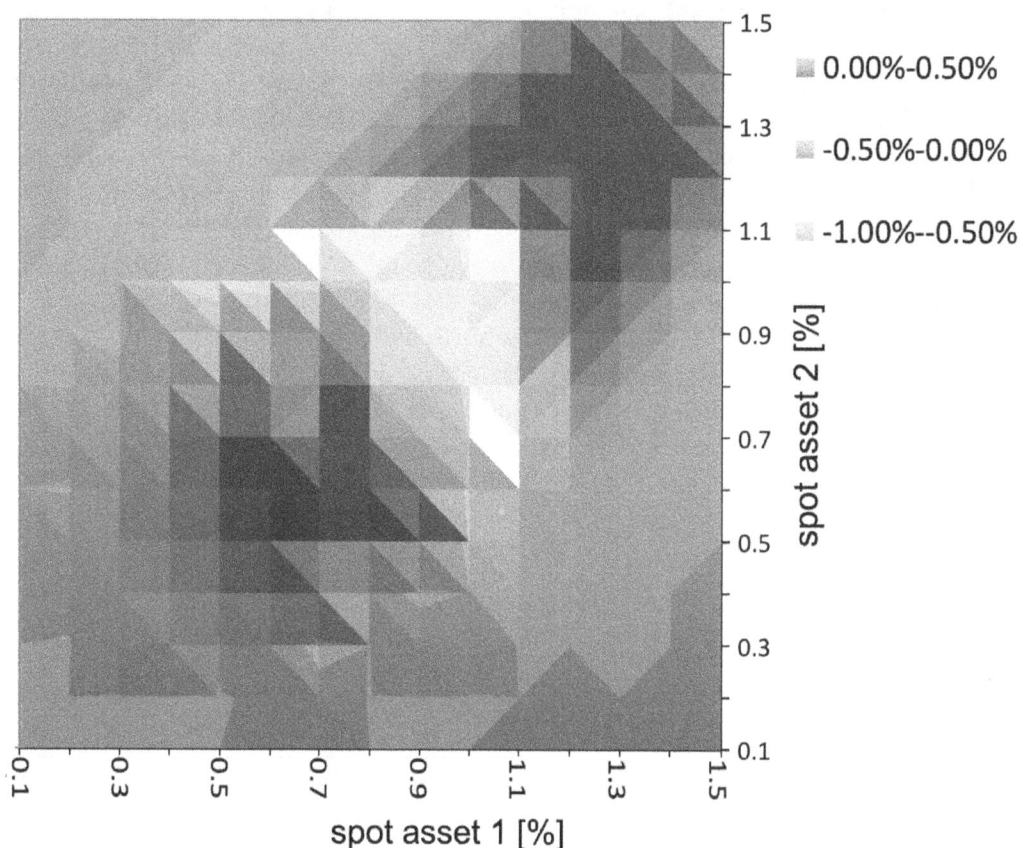

Figure 5.9: Sum of the cross-gamma as a contour plot of a long 1 year worst-of knock-out option position on two assets with a barrier at 70%. The cross-gamma switches sign between the top right and bottom left valley / peak, respectively.

5.3.5.3 Outperformance option

In the outperformance option, the payout is typically the linear outperformance or spread of one asset over another. For example, an outperformance call on two assets would pay

$$C_{\text{outperformance}} = \max\left[0, \frac{S_{i,T}}{S_{i,0}} - \frac{S_{j,T}}{S_{j,0}} - K\right]. \tag{5.20}$$

Depending on the strike, the outperformance may be ATM (K=0) or OTM (K>0). The holder is here short correlation, *i.e.* the probability of the payoff increases when the assets disperse.

Things get even more interesting when considering the outperformance in the form of a digital, *i.e.*

$$D_{\text{outperformance}} = c \cdot \left(\mathbf{1} \cdot \left[\frac{S_{i,T}}{S_{i,0}}\right) > \frac{S_{j,T}}{S_{j,0}}\right]. \tag{5.21}$$

Hence, if the performance of asset i is better than asset j, the option pays a predetermined coupon c. Close to expiry, the cross-gamma of the outperformance option change signs or flips between the two assets as a function of moneyness. The reason is that if the option is ITM ($P_1 > P_2$) the holder wants them to move in sync. The opposite is true for the OTM case. As a consequence, cross-gamma and correlation exposure will switch sign (see Figure 5.10).

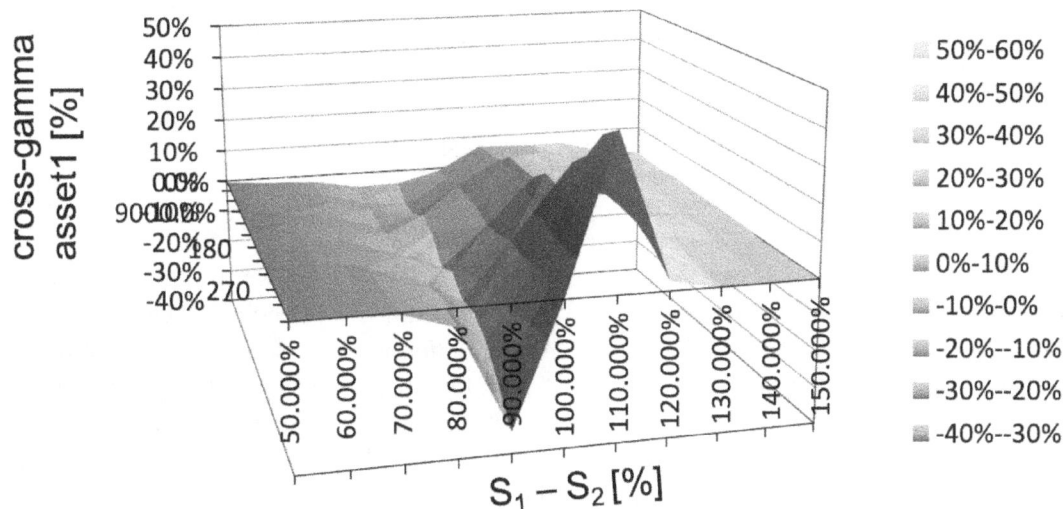

Figure 5.10: Cross-gamma of asset 1 as a function of the performance difference between asset 2 in an outperformance digital option.

If cross-gamma or correlation exposure changes over time, one faces at least two problems. If the contract was priced using a constant (bid or ask) correlation assumption, then there was a potential misprice. Moreover, the correlation risk figure remains somewhat arbitrary in certain spot regions. As a consequence, one cannot measure the correlation sensitivity of the option by a simple variation of the constant correlation parameter. Therefore, it is advisable to not only determine correlation exposure as an average over all paths at inception but also take into account scenario analyses. In case the scenario analyses show significant correlation exposure changes, it is advisable to add a (cash) reserve on the pricing to offset potential future re-hedging costs.

In the case of a basket outperformance option

$$C^B_{\text{outperformance}} = \max\left[0, \frac{B_{1,T}}{B_{1,0}} - \frac{B_{2,T}}{B_{2,0}} - K\right], \tag{5.22}$$

one is dealing with the two correlation exposures

- inter-correlation: correlation between the basket B_1 and B_2
- intra-correlation: correlation between the components in baskets B_1 and B_2

The inter-correlation exposure is quite evident as the holder is short correlation. However, the intra-correlation exposure is a function of the basket volatilities and may *change*.

5.3.6 Cross-gamma smoothing

As was shown, worst-of options may lead to increased dynamic hedging costs because basket components can switch their positions throughout the trade lifetime (*e.g.* best becomes worst, etc.). The position switch drives changes component greeks (*e.g.* vega) and leads to the need for rebalancing the hedge overlay. One way of smoothing out these undesired effects is to book the worst-of as a rainbow option, which (linearly) converges to the correct worst-of payout at expiry. The rainbow option is a multi-factor derivative whereby different weights are assigned to its components. The equation below shows the synthesis of the worst-of performance via a rainbow option for a three component basket as

$$
\begin{aligned}
wof_{N,t} = \text{rainbow}[&70\%\text{worst-of} + (t \cdot (30\%T))\text{worst-of} \\
&+ (20\% - t \cdot (20\%T))2^{nd}\text{worst-of} \\
&+ (10\% - t \cdot (10\%T))3^{rd}\text{worst-of}] \; .
\end{aligned}
\tag{5.23}
$$

In other words, instead of pricing an option as a full worst-of, it is priced as a *time-scaled* blend between the worst, 2nd worst and 3rd worst. As the option reaches expiry, the weight linearly approaches the full weight of only the worst-of such that the correct payout is guaranteed (see Figure 5.11). Such a rainbow 'worst-of' has a lower price at inception and the buyer of a worst-of put makes a loss if it is booked as a rainbow 'worst-of' since the latter has less value compared to the former. This technique is effectively an overhedge, designed to smoothen the cross-gamma until expiry. While this will, in general, reduce P/L variance, it is vital to bear in mind that the real correlation exposure of the book is somewhat hidden. In other words, the actual delta against the worst-of is by design underestimated. It is therefore advisable to keep track of the missing shadow delta due to the overhedge.

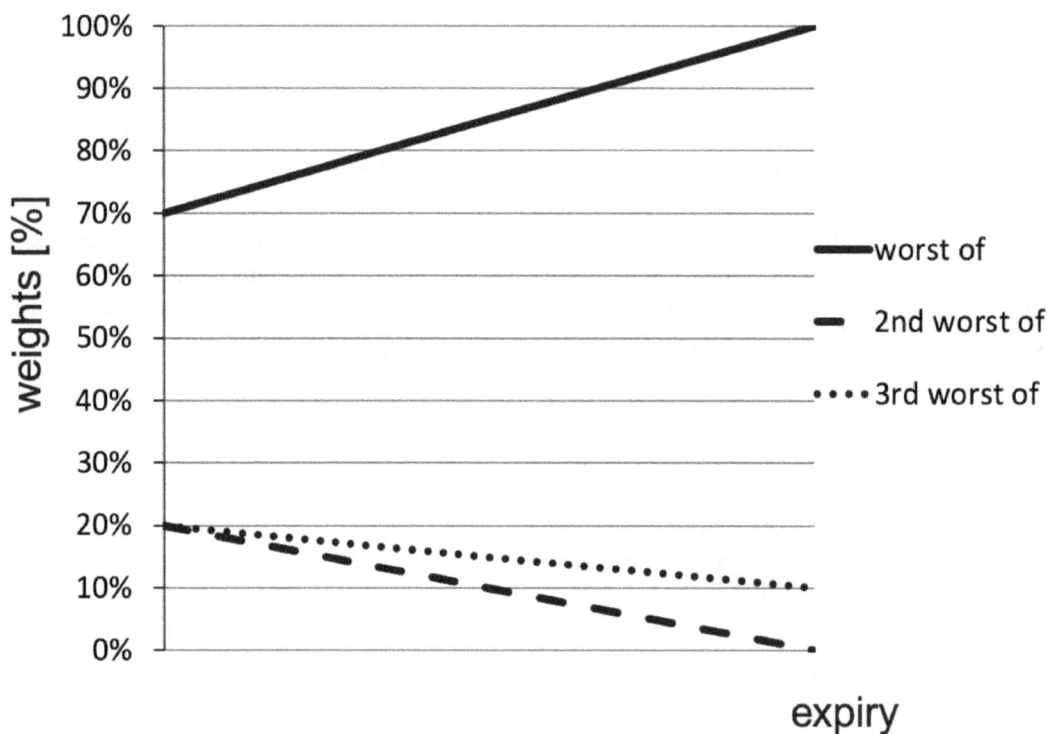

Figure 5.11: Rainbow worst-of correlation exposure as a function of time to expiry.

5.3.7 Correlation marks

Effectively, there are three approaches one can mark asset-asset or other correlations (*e.g.* FX-equity for Quanto and composite trades):

- mark the book correlation in line with some historical correlation level
- mark the book based on implied correlation levels derived from market multi-factor option quotes
- do both (with a preference for implied levels if liquidity is sufficient)

On the equity index side, things are typically a lot easier because the market for multi-factor option quotes is more liquid compared to *e.g.* the single stock business. In fact, on the index it is possible to mark via implied correlation quotes (*e.g.* SX5E/SPX, SX5E/NKY, SPX/NKY) for maturities up to 5 years. On the single stock side, what is typically done is to calculate historical pairwise realized correlation levels, which are then shifted to be in line with quotes from the market.

Correlation products marked at different correlation levels lead to different greeks and, as seen earlier, the carry of the book largely depends on the level of correlation it is marked. Therefore, it is often necessary to adjust a historical correlation matrix to be marked in line with the dynamics of the market.

The so-called *lambda approach* is a way to shift (historical) correlation while making sure that the resulting correlation matrix remains positive definite. Lambda λ is a real number between 0 and 1 and applied in the following way

$$\rho^*{}_{ij} = \rho^{\text{historic}}{}_{ij} + \lambda \cdot (1 - \rho^{\text{historic}}{}_{ij}) . \tag{5.24}$$

Note that $\frac{\partial \rho^*_{ij}}{\partial \lambda} = 1 - \rho^{\text{historic}}{}_{ij}$. For $\lambda = 0$, the historical correlation level is recovered and for $\lambda = 1$, the correlation is shifted to unity. Trading desks define a lambda for both bid & offer level, whereby the book itself is marked at mid or close to the offer side (in case of an overall short correlation position).

Apart from the positive definite invariance, the lambda approach also makes sure that low historical correlation pairs are shifted (upwards) more in proportion compared to higher marked pairs (see Figure 5.12). Since asset correlation in financial markets is typically positive even for cross-asset cases, assuming too low correlation is often detrimental to many modeling use cases (*e.g.* asset management whereby a pivotal ingredient to successful portfolio optimization is diversification in theory).

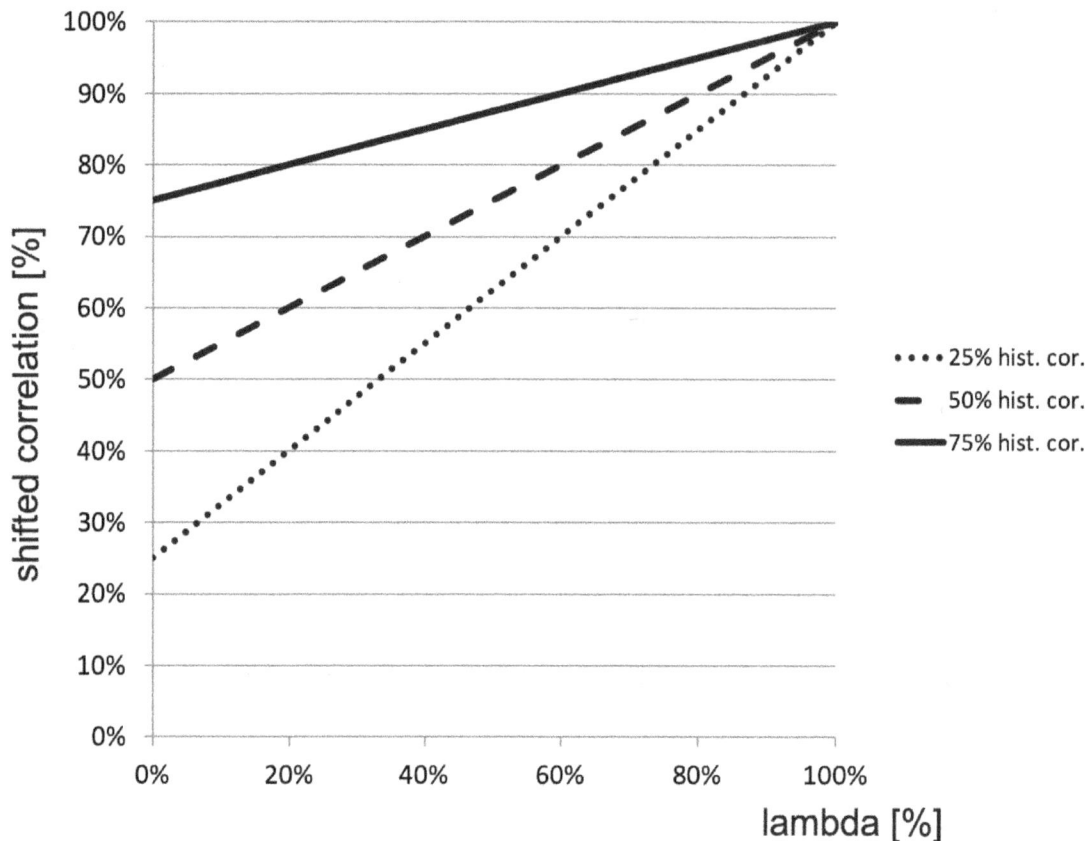

Figure 5.12: Lambda approach to bid / offer the correlation in a trading book.

The typical lambda ranges are between 0.2 and 0.9. Lambda levels are determined from market quotes on correlation structures such as Call vs. Calls, outperformance options, dispersion quotes, etc.. The problem is that there is typically no quote for a single pair, *i.e.* the implied lambda is valid for the whole basket. Also, the lambda parameter is usually not constant across all stock pairs. For example, different sectors (*e.g.* Automobiles vs. Financials) typically trade at different lambdas. The lambda approach works fine for correlation baskets of five or more stocks but bid/offer levels for *e.g.* two-factor outperformance option quotes must be analyzed with more care. As discussed before, implied correlation exhibits a term structure (see also 5.3.8); to be consistent, the same must be valid for the lambda parameter. Given these limitations and the fact that correlation is notoriously unstable, it is advisable to book a correlation reserve against highly sensitive trades.

Another advantage of using the lambda transformation is that it facilitates the perturbation of the correlation marks numerically to obtain the resulting P/L impact on the portfolio. Recall the definition of the correlation delta for a portfolio as $\frac{\partial P}{\partial \rho}$. Unfortunately, taking the derivative directly may lead to numerical issues as well as invalid correlation matrices (*i.e.* violation of positive definiteness [166]). One practical advantage of the lambda approach is that the perturbation can be done instead as

$$\frac{\partial P}{\partial \rho} = \frac{1}{1 - \rho^{\text{historic}}} \frac{\partial P}{\partial \lambda} \, . \tag{5.25}$$

The aggregation of correlation delta is (similar to volatility) not exactly trivial. While it is certainly possible to do a simple summation, possibly unwanted netting effects might offset unrelated risks (*e.g.* short correlation delta on the financial sector vs. long correlation delta on the non-cyclical sector). Hence, the overall correlation exposure might look flat, but in reality, the book is running large inter-sector or other correlation risks. Therefore, it is advisable to calculate sector-based correlation risks and other more granular metrics. Alternatively, a sum of the absolute correlation delta (long and short) will at least give an idea of the gross exposure.

The correlation market shows similar characteristics like the volatility surface, *i.e.* there is a correlation term structure and a correlation skew. On the index side, it is possible to measure the term structure directly from identical market quotes of different maturity. For single stocks, there are typically not enough quotes to determine the term structure directly. However, it is possible to back out the implied correlation levels between an index and its components for different maturities up to five years with decent accuracy. This index/component implied correlation is a good indicator of the correlation term structure. Applying different lambda parameters for different maturities is technically possible, but not every bank is doing this currently. However, it is clear that quoting the same correlation trade for a 1 month or 5-year maturity is quite different. In fact, in this case, it is possible to argue that the 1-month trade should be priced independently at the current realized correlation levels.

5.3.8 Implied Correlation

From the price of any multi-factor option, it is possible to back out the correlation level by taking assumptions concerning all other parameters (*e.g.* volatility, dividends, etc.). Similar to volatility, the obtained metric is called *implied* correlation. In the case of index versus index components there exists a relationship from which the implied correlation can be calculated as well given by

$$\rho_{\text{implied}} = \frac{\sigma_I^2 - \frac{1}{N^2} \sum_{i=1}^{N} \sigma_i^2}{\sigma_{\text{components}}^2 - \frac{1}{N^2} \sum_{i=1}^{N} \sigma_i^2} \, . \tag{5.26}$$

Taking following approximation for the mean component variance

$$\sigma_{\text{components}}^2 = \frac{1}{N} \sum_{i=1}^{N} \sigma_i^2 \approx \left(\frac{1}{N} \sum_{i=1}^{N} \sigma_i \right)^2 \, , \tag{5.27}$$

finally yields

$$\rho_{\text{implied}} \approx \frac{\sum_{i<j} \sigma_i \sigma_j \rho_{ij}}{\sum_{i<j} \sigma_i \sigma_j} \, . \tag{5.28}$$

Under certain limit conditions, the expression for the implied correlation can be approximated further as

$$\rho_{\text{implied}} \underset{N \to \infty}{=} \left(\frac{\sigma_I}{\sigma_{\text{components}}} \right) \approx \frac{\sigma_I^2}{\sigma_{\text{components}}^2} \, , \text{ if } \frac{w_{max}}{w_{min}} = O(\sqrt{N}) \, . \tag{5.29}$$

Figure 5.13 shows the implied correlation within a basket of components as a function of the volatility levels. Note that it is in theory possible to trade an implied correlation higher than 100%. Such trades were indeed sometimes possible until specialized dispersion desks became operational (before 2000) and eliminated this arbitrage opportunity.

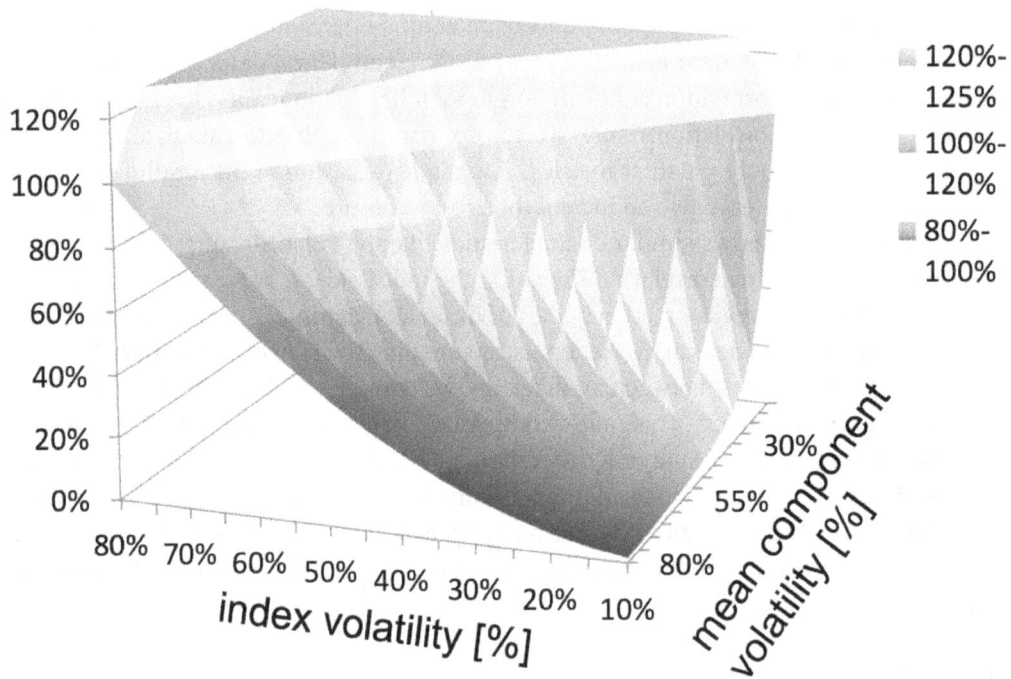

Figure 5.13: Plot of the implied correlation with respect to index / basket volatility and mean component volatility.

Similar to volatility, implied correlation can be an indicator of forward-looking market stress. This view can be rationalized considering that operators tend to buy disproportionate amounts of index volatility vs. the components in preparation for adverse market conditions.

5.3.9 Correlation Skew

It is common knowledge that realized correlation tends to increase during sell-offs or market crashes significantly. In other words, similar to volatility, realized correlation and spot levels show an inverse relation historically. Figure 5.14 illustrates the inverse spot-correlation relationship for the S&P 500 Index. It is visible that correlation increases with lower spot levels in agreement with common knowledge.

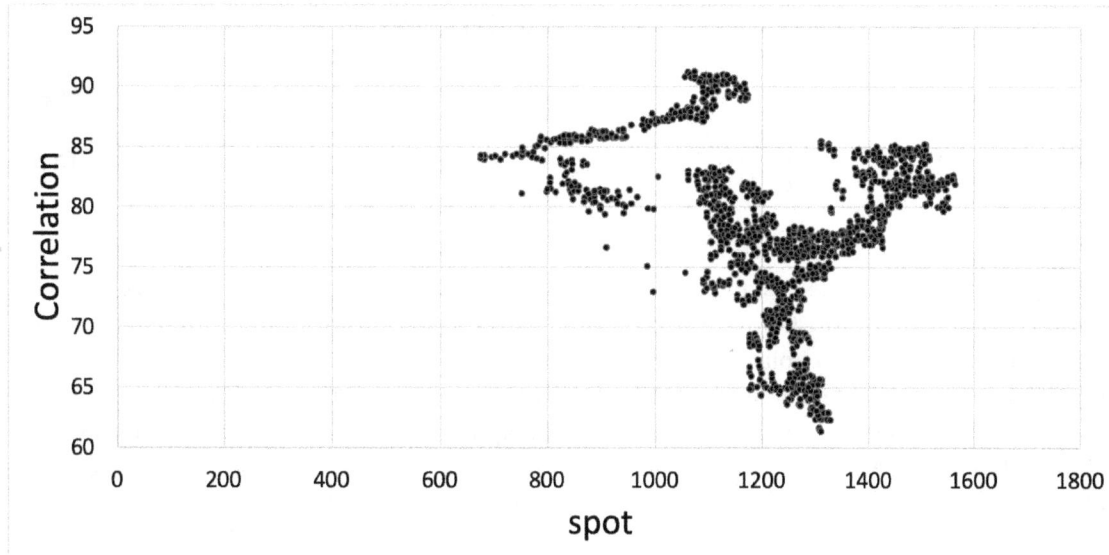

Figure 5.14: Plot of the weekly log returns of the S&P 500 Index from 2004-2010. The realized correlation is consistently higher for lower spot levels.

During these times of distress, short correlation / co-variance / cross-gamma positions suffer in carry unless the book correlation mark is increased, or the trading desk has implemented a directional delta-bias before. It should therefore not surprise that correlation quotes are skewed in the strike space as well. For example, an OTM worst-of put (*i.e.* short correlation exposure) will lose value in a market crash since correlation increases. This so-called *correlation skew* is similar to volatility skew, *i.e.* for different spot (strike) levels dealers will quote different correlation levels. For example, traders normally quote an OTM basket option at a *higher correlation* compared to an ATM basket.

Correlation skew modeling aims to introduce a state/spot dependent correlation, *i.e.* the correlation used in the pricing/valuation adjusts according to the spot level. However, even before trying to model this relation explicitly, it is worth thinking about a more straightforward approach that can be used at least for pricing purposes. Recall that the index or basket implied volatility skew is typically larger than the average skew of the components. The heuristic explanation for the increased index skew is the fear of systemic risk during crashes. In order to quantify the effect, the measure $D(K)$ is introduced as the spread between the average volatility of the components and the index/basket volatility given by

$$D(K) = \overline{\sigma} - \sigma_B . \tag{5.30}$$

The trick is now to realize that if the component-basket spread D remains *constant* it will naturally also generate correlation skew. For the case of a two stock basket, the volatility as a function of strike is given by

$$\sigma_B(K) = \overline{\sigma} \cdot \sqrt{\frac{1+\rho}{2}} . \tag{5.31}$$

The implied correlation is then given by

$$\rho_{\text{implied}} = 2 \cdot \frac{\sigma_B^2}{\overline{\sigma}^2} - 1 . \tag{5.32}$$

Expressing the basket variance with the component-basket spread yields

$$\rho_{\text{implied}}(D, \overline{\sigma}) = 2 \cdot \frac{(\overline{\sigma} - D)^2}{\overline{\sigma}^2} - 1 . \tag{5.33}$$

If the spread D remains constant, the implied correlation increases whenever the average component volatility increases. To illustrate this approach, consider again a basket of two components each with a volatility of 30%, a volatility skew of 2% for a 10% move in strike marked at a constant correlation of 60%. Table 5.1 shows that by keeping the ATM (100%) volatility spread between basket and components *constant* in the pricing, the approach generates a correlation skew (last column). Hence, the ATM spread D = 30% - 26.83% = 3.17% is kept constant to generate the basket volatility $\sigma_{B,\text{const. D}}$. As a result, ρ_{implied} rises with decreasing strikes. Hence, for pricing purposes, it

strike	$\overline{\sigma}$	$\sigma_{B,\text{const. cor}}$	$\sigma_{B,\text{const. D}}$	ρ_{implied}
50%	40.00%	35.78%	36.83%	69.60%
60%	38.00%	33.99%	34.83%	68.00%
70%	36.00%	32.20%	32.83%	66.30%
80%	34.00%	30.41%	30.83%	64.40%
90%	32.00%	28.62%	28.83%	62.30%
100%	30.00%	26.83%	26.83%	60.00%
110%	28.00%	25.04%	24.83%	57.30%
120%	26.00%	23.26%	22.83%	54.20%
130%	24.00%	21.47%	20.83%	50.70%
140%	22.00%	19.68%	18.83%	46.50%
150%	20.00%	17.89%	16.83%	41.60%
160%	18.00%	16.10%	14.83%	35.80%
170%	16.00%	14.31%	12.83%	28.60%
180%	14.00%	12.52%	10.83%	19.70%
190%	12.00%	10.73%	8.83%	8.30%
200%	10.00%	8.94%	6.83%	-6.70%

Table 5.1: Generating correlation skew via a constant volatility spread D.

is relatively trivial to adjust for missing correlation skew.

5.3.9.1 Local correlation Model (LCM)

As discussed before, it is impossible to match the implied index correlation skew with a constant *spot-invariant* correlation matrix between the components. Figure 5.15 shows the mismatch between the index implied volatility for a given put or call strike versus what is generated by the corresponding constant correlation component basket. Low strike regions are underestimated in terms of implied volatility while strikes above the ATM regions are too rich.

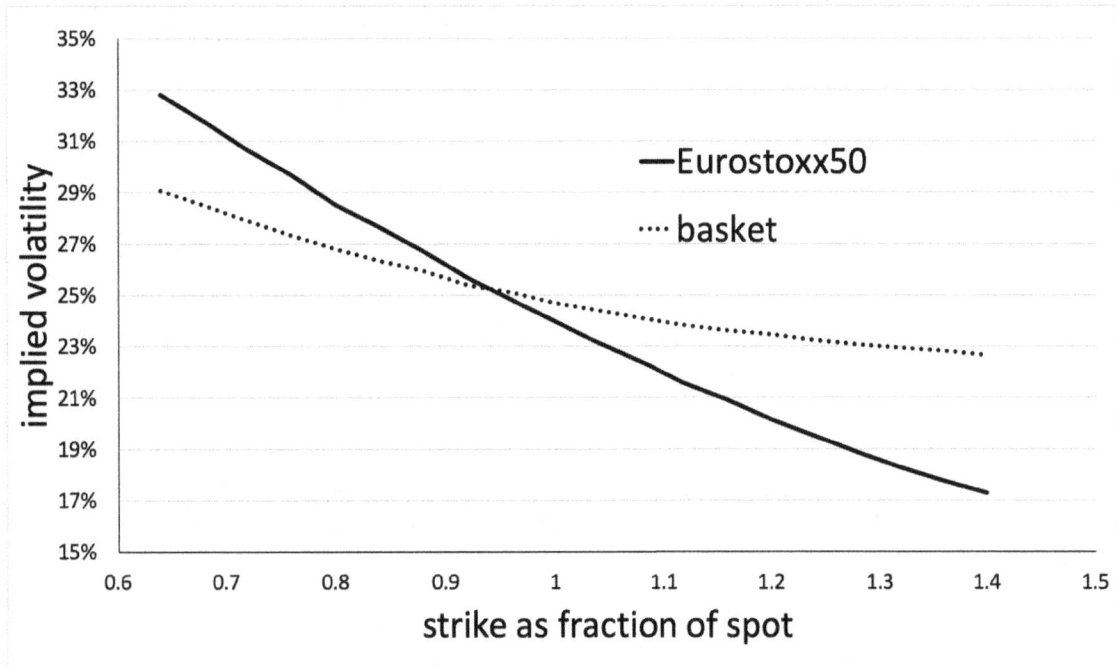

Figure 5.15: Euro Stoxx 50 implied volatility versus basket component volatility (puts and calls, correlation = 0.7) as a function of strike.

Even if one were to vary the constant correlation parameter, it is simply impossible to obtain a satisfactory fit (see Figure 5.16).

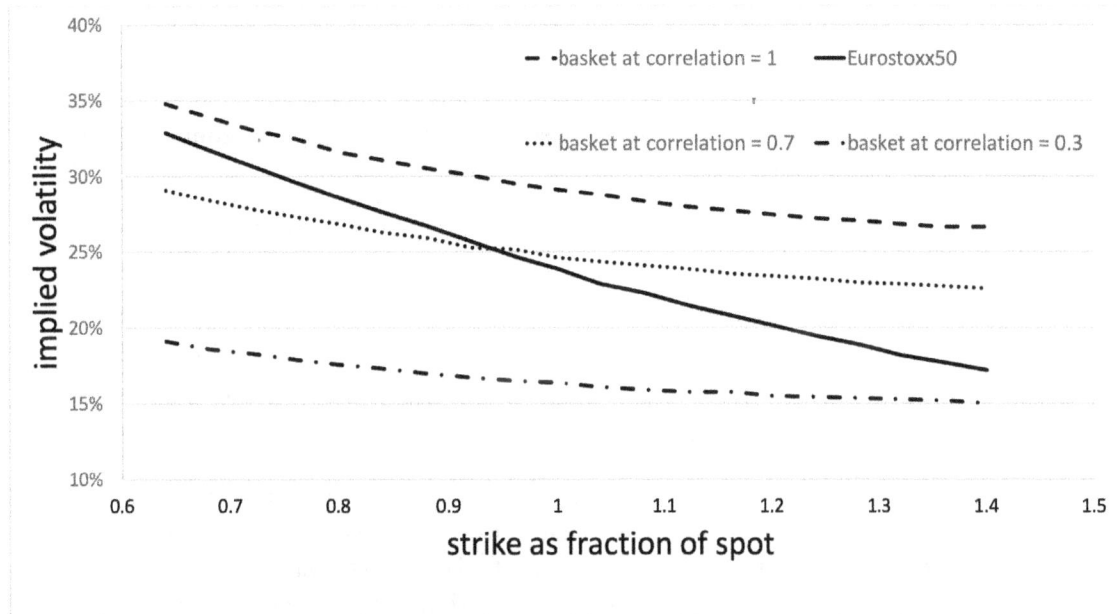

Figure 5.16: Euro Stoxx 50 implied volatility versus basket component volatility (puts and calls, correlation = 1.0 (dashed line), 0.7 (dotted line) and 0.3 (dotted-dashed line)) as a function of strike.

However, it is possible to extend the LV framework to incorporate a deterministic yet (locally in spot) dynamic correlation matrix [167, 168, 169, 170]. These types of model extensions are commonly called Local Correlation Models (LCM). The LCM allows the pairwise correlation coefficient to vary as a function of spot and time given by

$$dS_{i,t} = \mu_i S_{i,t} dt + \sigma_{i,S_{i,t}} S_{i,t} dW_{i,t} , \tag{5.34}$$

with $dW_{i,t} dW_{j,t} = \rho_{i,j}^{\text{local}}(t, S_{i,t}, S_{j,t})$ for $i \neq j$. Here $\rho_{i,j}^{\text{local}}(t, S_{i,t}, S_{j,t})$ is a local correlation function between the assets $S_{i,t}$ and $S_{j,t}$. This class of models is typically *non-parametric*, *i.e.* it uses the correlation skew embedded in observable index variance as a model input parameter and enforces the matching as a constraint.

The setup of most non-parametric LCMs is to seek a local correlation function which matches the imposed index variance $\sigma_I^2(t, T_t)$ as

$$\left(\sum_{i=1}^{N} w_i S_{i,t} \right)^2 \sigma_I^2(t, S_t) = \sum_{i,j=1}^{N} w_i w_j S_{i,t} S_{j,t} \sigma_i(S_{i,t}) \sigma_j(S_{j,t}) \rho_{ij}(t, u) . \tag{5.35}$$

In order to reduce the dimensionality due to the local variance constraint arising from $\frac{N(N-1)}{2}$ correlation pairs, the trick is to express the pairwise correlation via a convex combination of two correlation matrices and a lambda parameter as

$$\rho_{ij} = \lambda(t) \rho_{ij}^{\text{center}} + \kappa[1 - \lambda(t)] \rho_{ij}^{\text{up}} , \tag{5.36}$$

with $\kappa = 0, 1$. More specifically, one defines $\lambda = \frac{1}{1+u^2}$ and solve for the local variance constraint as a function of the state variable u, depending on the choice of κ. What effectively happens in the model is that the correlation matrix $\sum \rho_{ij}$ shifts as a function of the state variable u. This shift allows, in turn, to replicate the index implied volatility as a function of strike via the index components whereby the mode is systematically increasing the correlation among the constituents for lower strikes. Figure 5.17 shows the corresponding plot of the LCM model fitted to the Euro Stoxx 50 skew before. It is apparent that the fit is satisfactory apart from very extreme strike regions.

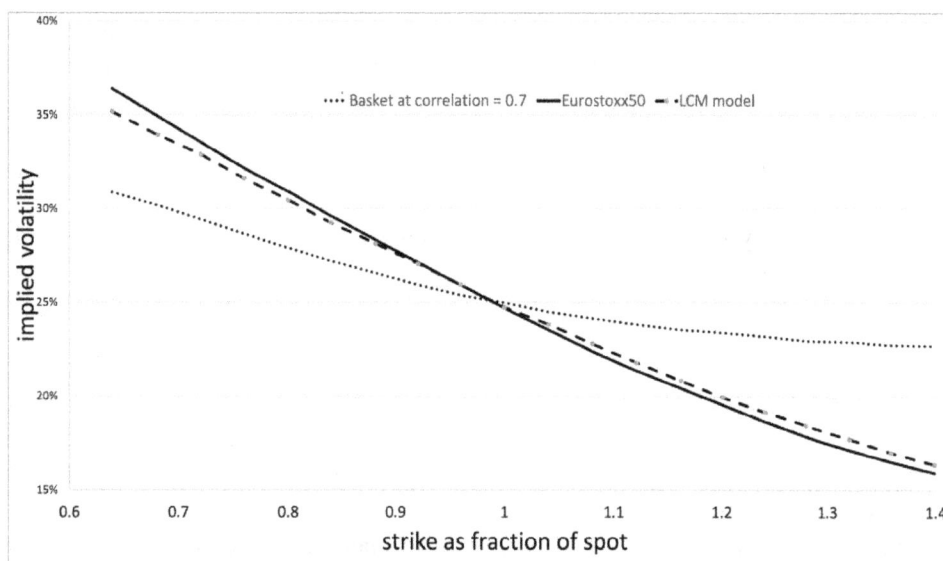

Figure 5.17: Euro Stoxx 50 implied volatility (solid line) versus basket component volatility (puts and calls, correlation = 0.7 (dotted line)) and the local correlation model (dashed line) as a function of strike.

If the method is then applied to *e.g.* best-of and worst-of options, the respective prices are increased and decreased versus the equivalent constant correlation approach. This phenomenon is expected since *e.g.* the frequent short exposure for sell-side desks in worst-of puts suffer from increasing correlation levels. While this is not taken into account in a constant correlation model, the LCM dynamically increases the component correlation to match the respective index variance and in turn, lead to a *lower* price. The advantage of LCM approaches like the one above is that it is

- a non-parametric model, *i.e.* uses correlation skew embedded in index variance as an input
- relatively straight-forward to implement
- relatively moderate in terms of computational expense
- ideal to assess shadow delta on trading books marked at a constant correlation

The critical challenge is, as usual, to deal with correlation matrices ensuring that they remain positive-definite at all times for all levels of the spot.

5.3.9.2 Correlation Switching Model

One issue which is not solved by LCM-type models is that they do not necessarily quantify re-hedging costs for structures that exhibit cross-gamma sign switches (*e.g.* outperformance digital). In other words, while correlation in LCM rises/falls with falling / rising spots, it does not help to quantify cross-gamma sign instabilities in a confined spot region. In those cases, for pricing, it is advantageous to be able to bid/offer correlation as a function of the local cross-gamma exposure to find a maximum for the option value.

In a Monte Carlo model, it is possible to shift the correlation by adding another stochastic driver to our assets inside the MC simulation such that

$$S_i^* = \sqrt{1 - \lambda} S_i + \lambda Z \,, \tag{5.37}$$

where Z is an additional Gaussian variable independent of the stochastic driver for S_i. It follows that

$S_i^* \cdot S_j^* = (1 - \lambda)\rho_{ij} + \lambda$ [4]. The lambda parameter is here only a function of state and possibly time. It is now possible to for example decrease the original instantaneous correlation matrix by adding additional Brownian drivers defining a correlation matrix with a minimum correlation so that

$$S_i^* = \sqrt{1 - \lambda} S_i + \lambda Y_i , \qquad (5.38)$$

with $Y_i^* \cdot Y_j^* = P_{\min}$. Finally, changing the correlation matrix inside the Monte Carlo simulation from the original matrix P to the minimum matrix $P_{\min}$ is done via

$$S_i^* \cdot S_j^* = (1 - \lambda)P + \lambda P_{\min} . \qquad (5.39)$$

Hence, given a bid and an offer matrix, it is possible to switch between them by adjusting the performances inside the simulation. The switch itself is triggered by defining a bid/offer lambda. In the example of the outperformance digital option, the bid/offer lambda trigger would be a function of the moneyness of the option.

For example, consider pricing an offer for an outperformance digital on two assets A (vol = 30%) and B (vol = 20%), which pays the notional in case the performance of A is larger than B in one year. The exposure is long correlation at inception, and the pricing is done at bidding the correlation at a level of 50%. The price for the option with this constant correlation is approximately 46%. Now let the correlation vary between a lambda of 0% and 40%, equivalent to a correlation of 50% (bid) and 70% (offer). Whenever the option is ITM / OTM (daily sampling) the correlation is triggered to switch from bid/offer to offer/bid. This switch results in a price of approximately 51% with the uncertain bid/offer correlation limits above. While the bounds (50% / 70%) might be conservative, it is possible to find a maximum price for this particular bid/offer correlation pair.

There are payoffs for which it is impossible to determine exact drivers for correlation switches in the payout *a priori*. In these cases, the only indicator is cross-gamma switches. The uncertain correlation model [171, 172] offers a way to assess these types of situations, but the extension to more complicated payoffs is not straightforward.

5.3.10   Correlation Vehicles: Call vs Call

The Call vs. Call (CvC) or Option-Basket-Basket-Option (OBBO) is one of the main instruments to hedge out correlation exposure. It consists of a long/short basket call position against a short/long position on the individual basket options, *i.e.* a dispersion trade. At inception, the weightings are typically chosen to give a vega neutral package at inception

$$\sum_i^N w_i \left(\max \left(0, \frac{S_{i,T}}{S_{i,0}} - K \right) \right) - \max \left(0, \sum_{i=1}^N w_i \frac{S_{i,T}}{S_{i,0}} - K \right) , \qquad (5.40)$$

whereby K is the strike in percentage return (*e.g.* 15% for 115% strike calls with respect to the ATM level). It can be shown that payout at expiry is equivalent to

$$\sum_{sgn(S_{i,T}/S_{i,0}) \neq sgn(\sum_{i=1}^N w_i S_{i,T}/S_{i,0}} w_i |r_i - K| , \qquad (5.41)$$

whereby $sgn(x) = 1$ if $x > 0$, else -1. This means that the payout is always positive. By convention, the CvC buyer is long the component calls and short the basket.

---

[4]The operation is here on two vectors in Euclidian space for which the inner product denoted by $\cdot$ is defined.

The advantage of the CvC is that it can be traded on a bespoke basket to match the correct book exposure, especially on large individual trades. Unfortunately, the premium of the CvC package is very low, *i.e.* a large notional needs to be traded to hedge out a significant portion of the correlation exposure. There is somewhat of a path dependency over the lifetime while also the optimal weighting scheme is not clear either. One is also potentially facing pin risk at expiry if the components trade close to the strike, *i.e.* the trades often need to be unwound before. The setting of the strike is also crucial.

As a CvC buyer (short basket, long options), the trader makes money if the underlyings disperse well around the strike of the call options. For example, in the case of an ATM CvC, the optimal outcome is to have large positive and large negative performances on the components whereby the basket call expires exactly at the strike. If all stocks go up on average, the payout is zero since the basket loss is offset by the gain on the components. If the strike is OTM (*e.g.* 110%), the payout is zero unless some underlyings outperform the strike. It can be concluded that an OTM strike is a good idea for takeover stocks, whereas for an equally balanced basket between expected over and under-performers an ATM strike is sensible.

5.3.11 Correlation Vehicles: Dispersion Option

The dispersion option is an instrument that pays out the directly realized dispersion of a basket of components at expiry. For example, the dispersion call takes the form

$$\max\left[0, \left(\frac{1}{N}\sum_{i=1}^{N}|r_i - r'|\right) - K\right],\qquad (5.42)$$

where r_i is the individual component return and r' is the average return over all components. A long position in a zero strike dispersion call ($K=0$) is long volatility and short correlation. Similar to a regular ATM option, the premium increases approximately with the square root of the duration. The zero-strike dispersion call is linear in dispersion and therefore relatively easy to risk manage. In a way, the zero strike dispersion call is an optimal CvC whereby the basket strike is chosen to be the one at expiry in foresight. Therefore, the premium of the zero strike dispersion call is also much higher. The dispersion option is also relatively insensitive to the basket size in a backtest, *i.e.* a 2 stock or 10 stock basket rarely makes a big difference. As the strike increases, the cost of the dispersion option falls.

5.3.12 Correlation Vehicles: Variance Dispersion

The Varswap dispersion (vardisp) consists of a long/short position on a basket variance swap against a short/long position in variance swaps on the basket components [5]. Just like for the CvC trades, different weighting schemes exist. The generic payout is given by the difference below as

$$\mp\sum_{i=1}^{N}w_i \cdot N_i \cdot \sigma_i^2 \pm N_B \cdot \sigma_B^2 - \underbrace{K}_{\substack{\text{residual strike,} \\ \text{typically zero}}}.\qquad (5.43)$$

The advantages are that, similar to a co-variance swap, the typical exposure in co-variance risk can be traded out. Moreover, the strike dependency is not an issue. Unfortunately, it is not possible to

---

[5]Alternatively, the trade may be set up as a straddle dispersion, *i.e.* straddle of the index versus straddles in the components. However, similar to the CvC setup, the trade picks up delta and vega over the lifetime.

perfectly offset the residual vega. Hence, undesired volatility of volatility exposure can build up significantly over the lifetime for a long basket position and the positive (correlation) P/L on large correlated (downside) market moves might not offset the loss on the vega of the components.

The issue with the volatility convexity can be a real problem in these trades. Define the hedge ratio as the ratio between index and component volatility to make the trade vega neutral at inception. As correlation increases (*e.g.* in a market crash), the hedge ratio turns such that the index volatility dominates for apparent reasons. For a short position on the index (*i.e.* equivalent to a short correlation exposure) this can be a significant (negative) contributor to the P/L of the trade overall. Another way to look at this is to recall the proxy implied correlation formula $\frac{\sigma_I^2}{\bar{\sigma}^2}$. Assuming that the single stock volatility stays constant and correlation changes one obtains

$$\Delta\rho = \frac{2\sigma_I}{\bar{\sigma}^2}\Delta\sigma_I = \frac{2\sqrt{\rho}}{\bar{\sigma}}\Delta\sigma_I \ . \tag{5.44}$$

For example, at a correlation of 40% and an average component volatility of 25%, a 1% increase in correlation leads to 0.2 points increase in index volatility, *i.e.* $2\cdot\sqrt{40\%}/25\% = 5; 5\cdot0.2 = 1$. In other words, the trades will exhibit an adverse coupling between correlation and volatility exposure.

5.3.12.1 Correlation Vehicles: Dispersion weighting

Dispersion trades typically involve trading components against the component basket in order to buy or sell correlation. However, in these trades, it is in general also required to agree on the respective vega weighting between the two legs (components vs basket). Three typical weighting schemes are used

- Vega weighting (equal): the index vega is set to be identical to the sum of the component vega.
- correlation weighting: the index vega multiplied by its volatility is equal to the sum of the component vega weighted by their respective volatility.
- Gamma weighting: the index vega multiplied by its gamma is equal to the sum of the component vega weighted by their respective gamma.

The different weighting schemes are also a consequence of the fact that index versus component volatility typically trades at different levels. This discrepancy means that the average component volatility is higher than the index volatility, *i.e.* the diversification effect within the index reduces the overall volatility. As a consequence, an equal vega-weighted (vega-neutral) dispersion trade means that the correlation buyer (long index / short components) earns theta on the overall portfolio and be short gamma overall as a consequence. In case of volatility weighting, the overall vega is not flat, *i.e.* the component vega is less than the index vega, which implies that the correlation buyer is long vega, long gamma but typically theta flat overall. The gamma weighting (component vega in excess of index) is in turn gamma flat, short vega and long theta. In general, only the volatility weighting, which is by construction theta neutral at inception, provides actual correlation exposure between implied and realized correlation. Therefore, it is the recommended approach unless a particular view is to be built in.

It is important to re-iterate that dispersion trades implicitly carry volatility convexity risk [173]. Again, dispersion trades mean that one is ultimately trading spreads in volatility between a basket and its components. However, because there is, in general, a strong correlation between index volatility and correlation, the trade acquires a short volatility exposure as volatility rises and a long volatility exposure as volatility drops. Hence, for a long dispersion trade (short index / long components), a stress scenario with a correlation increase will, in addition, lead to a loss when the trade turns net short vega. Conversely, a decrease in correlation would be accompanied by a loss in volatility, which limits the gains made on the decorrelation. Hence, long dispersion also means short volgamma. It is also for this reason that dispersion trades are quoted several correlation points above the level of a correlation swap (see below), which tends to be more in line with the historical realized correlation.

On a less technical note, it must be stressed that a short dispersion position can also end up in an adverse P/L situation even if correlation increases overall. This scenario can arise because the basket components carry idiosyncratic risk, *i.e.* M&A events, bankruptcy or scandals may significantly impair the P/L of the total trade in a single event.

5.3.13   Correlation Vehicles: Correlation Swap

Similar to variance or other moments, correlation can be traded directly via a CFD. The correlation swap [174] provides exposure to the average pairwise correlation of a pre-determined basket of assets.

Analogous to a moment swap, the payout of the correlation swap is the notional amount multiplied by the difference between the swap strike and the subsequent realized average pairwise correlation on the basket of underlyings given by

$$P/L = N \cdot (\text{realized correlation} - K) \,, \tag{5.45}$$

where N is the notional and $K=0,1$ the strike. Correlation swap strikes tend to trade at historically realized levels of correlation of the relevant basket of assets, as opposed to trading at the level of the implied correlation backed out from the index. It is important to define the measure of the realized correlation exactly when one is dealing with asynchronous time zones. For example, it is common to measure the correlation between different time zones as 3-day or 5-day log returns. Also, dividends are taken into account or adjusted for, which may lead to a decrease in the correlation given that the ex-dates are not typically the same for all components.

While the correlation swap offers a linear payout, correlation is not additive, and it is not clear how to model, price or let alone *hedge* them. Depending on how the swap is modeled and *booked*, the P/L over the lifetime, which is a function of realized and implied correlation weighted by the volatility in a specific period, can be more volatile than naively anticipated. This becomes obvious from the mark-to-market correlation expression $\rho^{\text{mtm}_{ij}}$ between time t and expiry T ($t_0 < t < T$) for two assets i and j given by

$$\rho^{\text{mtm}_{ij}}(t,T) = \frac{\frac{t}{T}\rho^{\text{realized}}\sigma_i^{\text{realized}}\sigma_j^{\text{realized}} + \frac{T-t}{T}\rho_{i,j}^{\text{implied}}\sigma_{i,T-t}\sigma_{j,T-t}}{\sigma_{i,t}\sigma_{j,t}} \,. \tag{5.46}$$

Here the correlation during a time of higher volatility counts more towards the average.

5.3.14   Correlation Vehicles: Co-variance Swap

Co-variance Swaps (co-var swaps) [175, 176] were partially introduced because the performance of correlation swaps did not always satisfy the expectation for hedging out correlation risk embedded in structured products desks [177]. Co-var swaps have the same mechanics as correlation swaps, but the payout is the co-variance of the assets. The co-variance between two assets is given by

$$covar_{ij} = \rho_{ij}\sigma_i\sigma_j \,. \tag{5.47}$$

The equation shows that the co-var swap has direct exposure to both correlation and volatility. The P/L is typically expressed as

$$P/L = N \cdot (\text{realized pairwise co-variance} - K) \cdot 100 ,\qquad(5.48)$$

whereby the co-variance swap strike K is the level of the (average pairwise) co-variance. The co-var is normally quoted as a percentage, which explains the factor 100 at the end of the equation. Contrary to correlation swaps, co-var swaps are typically quoted as log returns over a longer period, *i.e.* between 3 and 20 days. Note that the difference in observation days can make a significant difference in the observed realized co-variance. In general, the co-variance measured with longer holding periods is higher than that for shorter holding periods.

Similar to variance, co-variance is additive, *i.e.* time-weighting of sub-periods to calculate the total co-variance is possible. The sensitivity for a co-var swap to future co-variance decreases linearly until zero at expiry. Similarly does the sensitivity to correlation decrease with time, but as volatility increases the co-var swap tends to get longer correlation. For sell-side exotics desks, reducing correlation exposure indirectly via co-var swaps matches the actual risk profile of the books more closely since the exposure is rather to co-variance and not correlation itself.

Practical Tips 5.3.1 Questions to ask your quants / risk system support:

- How is the correlation delta calculated?
- How is the mark-to-market process for the correlation? Does it follow a price testing approach via *e.g.* Totem? [a]
- What is the correlation skew exposure of book?
- How does the correlation sensitivity of the book change in an extreme scenario (*e.g.* spot -25%)?
- What ratio of diagonal- to cross-gamma is the book running?
- How does the system take care of the integrity of the correlation matrix?
- How do we calculated historical correlation (across different time zones)?

---

[a]https://ihsmarkit.com/products/totem.html

6. Interest Rates & Interest Rate Derivatives

6.1 Introduction

Interest Rates (IR) are a broad topic and covering this is in merely one chapter is very challenging. However, the idea is again to provide relevant knowledge about the theoretical background, available instruments, and develop an awareness of essential topics. As an example for the latter, consider one result of the MBS crisis in 2007-2009, whereby even derivative traders outside the fixed income world were affected by *e.g.* diverging LIBOR / OIS spreads. Even on derivatives desks that are not specialized in interest rates trading, the rates exposure can be significant, and cannot be ignored.

The previous chapters were mainly concerned with derivatives trading from an equity asset class perspective. In equities, as well as in many other asset classes such as Foreign Exchange or Commodities, the underlying is typically a unique instrument, *e.g.* the spot equity price or commodity future. This is different in IR since many independent instruments are normally combined to make up the yield curve (YC). In other words, the resulting dynamics of the underlying YC is often much more complex, which consequently leads to a more abstract picture.

IR provide a link between the present value (*PV*) and the future value (*FV*) of cash. The individual rate is typically quoted in per annum (p.a.) convention even if actual maturity terms on an instrument do not match. IR reflect the preference for money now as opposed to money in the future (time value of money) and may often also exhibit a (separable) credit risk component. The *FV* is linked to the *PV* by means of discounting or a discount factor (*DF*). Hence, for a *FV* = 1.02 and a *PV* = 1.00, the *DF* is given by *DF* = 1/FV = 1.00/1.02 = 0.9804. In general,

$$FV_t = \left(1 + r/n\right)^{n \cdot t} , \tag{6.1}$$

where r is the interest rate quoted typically in per annum (p.a.) units, n is the number of compounding periods per year and t time. The p.a. quoting convention is the by far most used form of indicating the interest rate or yield for a particular product. However, note that p.a. convention is not necessarily equal to the *annualized* interest rate. Annualization aims to approximate the interest amount assuming it was paid in a single transaction on an annual basis, even if the actual payment frequency (p_f) is higher. The transformation between the p.a. rate ($r_{p.a.}$) and the annualized rate ($r_{a.r.}$) is given by

$$r_{a.r.} = \left(1 + \frac{r_{p.a.}}{p_f}\right)^{p_f}. \tag{6.2}$$

All other things being equal, a higher payment frequency (*e.g.* quarterly versus yearly) is more profitable for the receiver since the proceeds may be re-invested more often. This observation is in line with the common sense view that receiving money sooner is better than later.

Finally, in the case of continuous compounding ($n \Rightarrow \infty$), $FV = 1 \cdot \exp(r \cdot t)$, which one might recall from high school mathematics. Note that continuous compounding is generally not used for any financial instrument. However, because of the convenient mathematical properties, it is used for most modeling purposes.

A seemingly trivial concept, which is nonetheless essential when dealing with interest rates is the so-called day count (convention) . The day count reflects the number of days in a year for the interest calculation and varies between currencies. While the majority of currencies (*e.g.* EUR, USD) use a 360 day convention/basis (actual days / 360), others use 365 (*e.g.* GBP, YEN; actual days / 365). As a consequence, GBP 100 and USD 100 at 10% interest over 180 days will earn differently (*i.e.* GBP $100 \cdot 10\% \cdot 180/365$ =GBP 4.94 versus USD $100 \cdot 10\% \cdot 180/360 =$ USD 5.00). Another important day count basis is 30/360, which is the norm for the Eurobond and US corporate bond markets. Hence, in this convention every month has 30 days by definition.

In addition to payment frequency, annualization, and day count, it is necessary to define the exact payment dates in the respective interest rate schedule. The payment schedule distinguishes between business days and non-business days (*e.g.* market holidays or weekends) and incorporates a rule book determining how to modify the payment schedule given the occurrence of the latter. As one might expect, business days are geography dependent and are typically aggregated in case the trade references two or more geographies. There are two main ways of adjusting the schedule in case of a holiday, either going forward to the following business day (*i.e.* 'modified following') or backward to the preceding day ('modified previous'). Depending on the market move for a particular interest rate fixing, the impact of rolling forward or backward can be significant. The same is true in the case of equity fixings irrespective of whether it is for the final observation date of a vanilla option or potential barrier trigger in the case of an exotic derivative. For example, in case of an interest rate product with a fixing schedule ending on a Saturday, the modified following convention would move the observation date to Monday compared to Friday in the case of the backward roll. The potential P/L impact can be substantial also in case there is a term mismatch between the trade and a potential hedge.

6.1.1 Spot versus Forward rates

There are two key rates which make up the foundation in Interest Rates: the spot and the forward rates. As the name implies, the *spot rate* refers to an interest rate for a pre-defined period starting now. The *forward rate* on the other hand refers to an interest rate starting in the future for a pre-defined tenor. For example, the 3x6m forward rate is the interest rate starting in 3 months from now and ending in 6 months from the future start date. Spot and forward rates need to be in sync, *i.e.* cash deposited at the 6 month spot rate needs have the same future value as if it were deposited at the 3m plus 3m forward. Table 6.1 shows an example for deriving the spot rate for market observed forward rates. For example, the FV for period $n = 3$ is calculated as $FV_3 = (1 + fwd_{rate,1}) \cdot (1 + fwd_{rate,2}) \cdot (1 + fwd_{rate,3}) = 1.0718$, while the corresponding spot rate equals $Spot_{rate,3} = FV_3 \exp[1/3] - 1 = 0.0150 = 1.5\%$. In this case the spot rate is lower compared to the forward rate, but if the latter where decreasing, the picture reverses.

Period n	Forward Rate	FV	df	Spot Rate	cum. df
1	1.00%	1.0100	0.9901	0.0100	0.9901
2	1.50%	1.0252	0.9755	0.0125	1.9656
3	2.00%	1.0457	0.9563	0.0150	2.9219
4	2.50%	1.0718	0.9330	0.0175	3.8549
5	3.00%	1.1039	0.9058	0.0200	4.7608
6	4.00%	1.1481	0.8710	0.0233	5.6318

Table 6.1: Example of calculating the spot rate equivalent for observed annually compounded forward rates. The cells are calculated via $FV_n = \prod_{i=1}^{n}(1 + fwd_{rate,n})$, $Spot_{rate,n} = FV \cdot \exp[1/n] - 1$ and $df_n = 1/FV_n$.

6.1.2 Money market instruments

The term money market (MM) refers to borrowing/lending money for 1 year or less via various typically very liquid instruments. MM instruments in the United States make up the most important market and trade at different rates:

- fed funds target rate: the market rate at which commercial banks in the US charge each other overnight for funds to satisfy their reserve requirements set by the FED [1]. The FED sets the rate as a target. FED funds drive many other short-term rates. In Europe, the ECB set a similar target rate.
- discount rate: the rate at which FED charges member banks for overnight loans. Set higher than the FED funds rate, typically 100 basis points (bp; 1bp = 0.01%)
- repo market: repo refers to 'repurchase agreement' and in this case for the sale and repurchase of treasury securities.
- commercial paper (CP) rates: CP is debt sold by large corporations providing short term funding. CP is the equivalent of US government treasury bills (T-bills).
- Eurodeposits ('depos'): eurocurrency is currency held in banks outside the jurisdictions of the currency's home country, *e.g.* eurodollars are dollars held outside the FED influence.

In Europe, the European Central Bank (ECB) [2] sets various EUR central bank rates ranging from the marginal lending facility rate, the primary refinancing operations rate and to the deposit facility rate. These rates are decided upon every month. The Bank of England (BoE) sets the GBP Bank Base Rate [3] in monthly meetings by the Monetary Policy Committee (MPC). Finally, in Japan, the Bank of Japan (BoJ) sets the basic discount rate and basic loan rate for the JPY in an *ad hoc* frequency [4].

Note that U.S. Treasury Bills are issued at a discount to the face value. This means that if one buys a USD 1'000 face value Treasury Bill with 200 days maturity from today at a discount rate of

---

[1] https://www.federalreserve.gov/monetarypolicy/openmarket.htm

[2] https://www.ecb.europa.eu/stats/policy_and_exchange_rates/key_ecb_interest_rates/html/index.en.html

[3] https://www.bankofengland.co.uk/monetary-policy/the-interest-rate-bank-rate

[4] https://www.boj.or.jp/en/statistics/boj/other/discount/index.htm/

4.5%, then the discount is given by: USD $10'000 \cdot 0.045 \cdot 200/360 =$ USD 25. Hence, the price is USD 1000 - USD 25 = USD 975 and the yield $25/975 \cdot 365/200 = 4.68\%$. This is the so-called U.S. Treasury convention.

6.1.3 LIBOR

LIBOR stands for 'London Interbank Offered Rate' and is a key benchmark interest rate. In general, IBOR indices are proxies for unsecured interbank lending of which LIBOR is probably the most well-known. Despite an effort to move away from LIBOR, it remains arguably the most important rate in the market. Note that LIBOR is not a traded rate since it is determined indirectly by estimating tradable levels. In this sense, LIBOR is the rate at which contributing banks believe they can raise unsecured funding, *i.e.* it is a proxy for unsecured interbank lending. The LIBOR rate is set for 10 different currencies, and tenors at 11 am London time, thereby reflecting the availability of the corresponding funds in European markets.

The LIBOR calculation is carried out by the Intercontinental Exchange (ICE) [5] on behalf of the British Banker's Association (BBA) whereby 16 contributing banks are chosen for the four major currencies (USD, GBP, EUR, CHF, YEN, *i.e.* USD-LIBOR, GBP-LIBOR, EUR-LIBOR [6], CHF-LIBOR, JPY-LIBOR, etc.). For the remaining currencies between 8-12 contributors are used. As a general principle, after the quotes are collected, the 25th percentile of the highest and lowest submission are discarded. The remaining quartiles of the quotes are averaged and published as the days LIBOR fixing [7]. The LIBOR fixings are determined each business day for a set of maturities/tenors up to 12 months while the banks' money market desks deliver the required LIBOR quotes. The process is repeated for each tenor (*e.g.* 1M, 3M, 6M, etc.) until all respective LIBOR fixings are computed and made available by the LIBOR panel for all covered currencies.

Effectively, the LIBOR rate carries a similar function as the fed funds rate (see 6.1.2 above). USD-LIBOR is the essential benchmark, and it trades above the corresponding 3 month Treasury bills (T-Bills). The spread is commonly known as the *TED spread* and an indicator of general credit risk perception in the economy. The long term average of the TED spread is approximately 40bp; during the MBS crisis in 2008 it increased up to 450bp.

Note that the accrual periods of the LIBOR rates, *i.e.* the dates corresponding to the specific LIBOR tenors, do not need to be in line with the previous LIBOR fixing. In other words, the start date for a new LIBOR tenor (the so-called LIBOR spot) may differ from the respective previous LIBOR fixing, *i.e.* there is a fixing lag. LIBOR fixings typically exhibit seasonal effects around the end of quarter or end of year period given that the lending capacity tends to be constraint around the reporting periods for banks. Finally, LIBOR fixings following central bank meetings often depict higher volatility since participants only act after the decision before potentially adjusting rates.

Following the 2008/09 financial crisis and several related scandals around LIBOR fixing manipulations [178], various regulators have decided to push for phasing out the LIBOR reference rate (see [179] for an extensive overview). In other words, the regulators are pushing for new risk-free rates to replace LIBOR. In the US and UK, the authorities have selected the Secured Overnight Financing Rate (SOFR) and Sterling Over Night Index Average (SONIA) as the risk-free rates for the

---

[5]https://www.theice.com/iba/libor

[6]Note that EUR-LIBOR is not identical to EURIBOR. EURIBOR is very similar to LIBOR but established by the European Banking Federation. For trading and fixing EUR short-term interest rate futures (STIR) and options, EURIBOR is effectively the standard.

[7]Note that the LIBOR fixing is sometimes also called the LIBOR reset rate as it by definition resets floating to fixed cash flows

USD and GBP markets, respectively. The New York Federal Reserve [8] is already publishing SOFR which is based on transactions in the Treasury repurchase market, where banks and investors borrow or loan Treasuries overnight. In the United Kingdom, SONIA is the OIS rate (see 6.6) for unsecured transactions in the GBP market. The UK financial regulator also declared that it urges banks to migrate to the SONIA family of interest rates at the end of 2021. Regulators for the Eurozone and Japan are still to decide on their risk-free rate. The transition to the new benchmark curves is not a trivial undertaking [180, 181]. Apart from the logistical impact, such a transition involves across various functions and departments in a financial institution, and there also remain various modeling issues to be sorted out. One key issue is that LIBOR is a forward term rate, *i.e.*, the cash flows for transactions can therefore be calculated at the beginning of a respective period upfront. Hence, picking a backwards looking rate including payment in arrears, as it is currently been proposed [182], would change the perspective significantly. Therefore, it remains to be seen at which point LIBOR indeed ceases to be the key reference point in the interest rate universe.

6.2 Forward rate agreement (FRA)

One of the fundamental OTC interest rate products is the forward rate agreement (FRA) [22]. The FRA is a contract between two parties agreeing on a future fix interest rate. Recall that a *forward rate* is simply an interest rate agreed upon today which applies to a period in the future. Hence, contrary to a spot rate, which starts today and ends after some time, the forward rate starts in the future and ends in the future. The standard notation for this transaction is YxZ, *e.g.* 0x3m for the 3-month spot date and 3x6m for the 6 months rate forward starting in 3 months. The FRA is thereby an IR derivative in which one party pays a fixed rate and receives a floating rate equal to some underlying reference rate. The reference rate is typically LIBOR, and the contract is ultimately cash settled. FRAs trade for a variety of periods (days to several years) and are quoted as a pair of numbers (Y x Z). The first number refers to the start month and the second to the end month, counting from the current month. For example, a 3x6 FRA is the FRA starting in 3M and ending in 6M from now, *i.e.* 3 months forward, 6 months FRA. 'Buying the FRA' means buying the rate (paying fixed), *i.e.* the FRA buyer is long the forward rate and makes money if this rate rises. 'Selling the FRA' means selling the rate (receiving fixed), *i.e.* the FRA seller is short the forward rate and makes money if this rate falls. As a concrete example, consider a 3x6 FRA at 1.5%, notional $1m, 3M USD-LIBOR as the reference rate The FRA buyer has agreed to 'borrow' $1m at 1.5% 3M from now. In 3m from now, the FRA expires. Take the assumption that the 3M LIBOR now fixes at 1.75%. The buyer had agreed to 'borrow' at 1.5%, but market rates are now 25bp higher. The seller will therefore pay the buyer 25bp, *i.e.* $0.0025 \cdot \$1m \cdot \frac{1}{4} = \$625$. The payment is due in 3M after the FRA expiry (or in 6M from now), but the discounted value is paid *now*, *i.e.* $625/(1 + 1.5\%/4) = \$622$. Note that although the transaction is referred to as 'borrowing', no actual borrowing (or cash transfer) takes place. The FRA present value (PV_{FRA}) itself from the holder point of view is given by

$$PV_{FRA} = df_{i-1} \frac{N \cdot dcf_i(r_i - R)}{1 + dcf_i r_i} \, , \tag{6.3}$$

where df_{i-1} is the discount factor of the present day with respect to the valuation date i of the expected fixing r_i, dcf_i the *day count fraction* (also sometimes called coverage or year fraction) between i and $i-1$, N the FRA notional and R the FRA rate. Hence, in practice, two parameters

---

[8]https://www.newyorkfed.org

need to be predicted, *i.e.* the expected future rate r_i and the expected discount factor for the payment date of the contract. The schematic representation of a FRA date schedule is given in Figure 6.1. Note that the payment occurs at the *start* of the observation period, which is a problem in case the shift away from forward looking rates such as LIBOR indeed takes place [183].

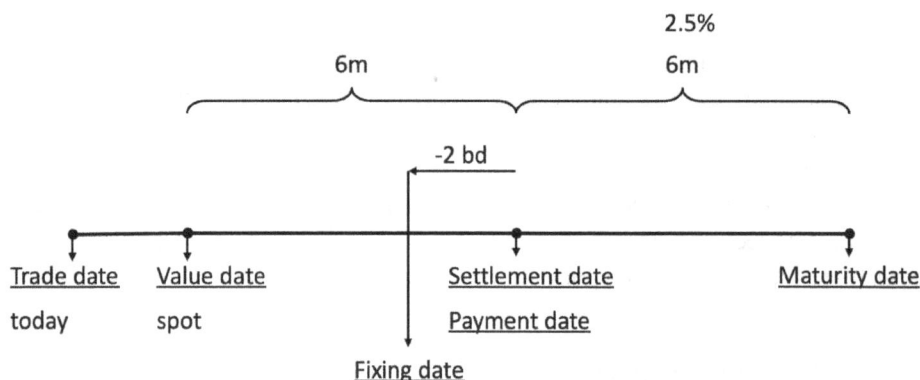

Figure 6.1: Schematic illustration of the date schedule for a 6x12 FRA at 2.5%.

Hence, in trading a FRA the counterparties agree to a rate today applied to a period starting in the future. For calculating forward rates, the cash flows need to match. For example, the deposit for 6M at the 6M spot rate must have the same future value as a deposit for a 3M + 3M forward in order not to be exploitable for arbitrage.

One can employ FRAs to express views on the future interest rate. Hence, if one believes that the forward FRAs (*e.g.* 6x9, 6x12, etc.) are trading at elevated levels, then it is possible to sell the corresponding FRAs, receive fixed / pay floating and thereby benefit if the floating rate indeed decreases.

Finally, the quoting convention for FRAs is in general given by 'Currency, Index, Start month x End month, roll-date'. For example, a quote for 'USD LIBOR 5x8 22nd FRA' in April refers to a USD LIBOR FRA with value dates from the 22nd of September until 3 months in December.

6.2.1 Interest Rate Delta

The conceptual framework for interest rate delta risk is analogous to the extensive discussion presented in the corresponding chapters for vanilla options on other assets. In other words, the market delta risk quantifies the P/L change of the interest rate instrument V as a function of a change in its underlying interest rate, *i.e.*

$$\Delta_V = \frac{\partial V}{\partial \mathbf{r}} , \tag{6.4}$$

where $\mathbf{r}$ denotes a shift across the *entire* curve. This risk is typically normalized to the movement of the whole curve upwards by one basis point (1 bp) [9]. Hence, if the interest rate curve of a trading book is bumped by 1bp up leading to an observed P/L impact of +USD 50'000, then the outright delta (or *dv01* = dollar value of 1bp, also known as price value of 1bp (PVBP) or PV01) of the book is indeed USD 50'000 p/bp (USD per basis point).

---

[9]1 bp represents 1/100 of a percentage rate, *i.e.* 0.0001 (1bp).

However, things get typically more complicated, given that the underlying interest rate exposure derives from a curve constructed from different tenors. In other words, the aforementioned 1bp bump implies that one conducts a parallel shift of the whole curve. Hence, the parallel shift represents changes in the overall IR market level. Delta exposure resulting from different curves not moving in sync is called (delta) basis risk. More quantitatively, this means that curves move relative to each other by 1bp while the overall IR market level is unchanged. To recap, in the case of outright delta risk, all interest rate curves move in sync. In the case of basis risk moves, some curves move versus each other while the market does not.

6.2.2 Interest Rate Gamma

Contrary to earlier chapters, IR greeks are introduced in the context of actual financial products given that it helps to understand the differences better. Gamma, or convexity as it is often referred to in the context of bonds, is conceptually again not different from the corresponding definition introduced earlier in the context of vanilla options. Applied to interest rate products, one defines gamma risk as the delta change or exposure to increases or decreases to the underlying interest rate by one basis point, *i.e.*

$$\Gamma_\Delta = \frac{\partial^2 V}{\partial \mathbf{r}^2} \ . \tag{6.5}$$

Hence, in case of $\Gamma_\Delta = 10$ in PV01/bp terms, then the delta on the trade will increase / decrease by 10 for every bp that the underlying rate curve r moves up / down. This is illustrated in the context of FRAs given that they only span one period. Note that the generic PV of a FRA is given by

$$V_{FRA} = df_{i-1} \frac{N \cdot d_i (r_i - R)}{1 + d_i \cdot r_i} \ , \tag{6.6}$$

with df_i being the discount factor on date i, N the notional, r_i the published fixing on date i, R the agreed FRA rate and d_i the day count fraction. The key takeaway from the formula above is that the payoff is being *discounted*. It is the discounting, which gives rise to the convexity gamma in the payoff since it depends on the change of the underlying rate. In other words, FRAs, bonds, or swaps do not have fixed basis point values for given rate changes, and therefore, the price/rate (yield) relationship is nonlinear.

Recall the possible FRA trades again: either buy (pay fixed) or sell (receive fixed) the FRA. Consider the case of selling a FRA. If rates go up / down compared to the negotiated forward rate, the seller loses/gains on the mark-to-market of the derivative. However, because the PV is obtained by discounting the cash flow and because the settlement itself is discounted over the whole FRA tenor, the benefit is received by the contract seller for *both* interest rate direction moves. As rates rise, the discount factor decreases, which in turn decreases the loss upon discounting. The opposite is true for the case of decreasing rates, *i.e.* discount factors increase, which consequently leads to a more substantial discounted gain. Hence, as a common rule, receiving fixed on a FRA embeds positive gamma exposure. This effect increases with the tenor and the forward starting period of the instrument given the increased effect of rate changes on the discount factors.

There are effectively two components that create gamma on IR derivatives. On the one hand, as shown above, the IR level movement modifies the discount factors. Derivatives that benefit from falling IR gain positive gamma and the other way around. On the other hand, depending on whether a trade is ITM or OTM, it can gain additional gamma. This gamma component is revisited when discussion interest rate swaps (see section 6.4).

6.3 IR futures

Effectively, IR futures (also known as Short Term Interest Rate or STIR Futures) are exchange-traded FRAs with some subtle differences discussed below. The IR futures are ultimately cash settled unless they are rolled, *i.e.* this is no different compared to equity futures [10]. Futures on 3M LIBOR are listed on exchanges in various currencies (*e.g.* Eurodollar future). Due to the reference to the 3M LIBOR rate, IR futures expire on a 3M basis, *i.e.* March (H), June (M), September (U) and December (Z). STIR futures only settle for value start dates which coincide with International Money Market (IMM) dates. IMM dates are defined to be the third Wednesday of any month. The first four front contracts spanning the first year are known as white contracts and exhibit the highest liquidity profile. The next four contracts are known as red contracts and are typically also liquid.

The quote convention is: 100 – rate, *i.e.* 98.5 means a forward rate of 1.5%. Therefore, when the respective forward rate goes up, the future goes down and vice versa. Futures trading above 100 implies negative interest rates, which quite recently happened for the Euroswiss in 2011 as a result of imposing the EURCHF FX 'peg' by the Swiss National Bank (SNB) (see also 6.14). The SNB thereby declared that it would intervene by selling CHF against EUR in case the EURCHF FX spot were to rise above a level of 1.20. Note that the peg was lifted again in 2015.

The notional for IR futures depends on the currency: USD = Eurodollar futures $1m notional, EUR = EURIBOR futures EUR 1m notional, CHF = Euroswiss futures CHF 1m notional, GBP = Short Sterling 500k and JPY futures 100m. The value of one contract per bp change is: Notional $\cdot$ $0.0001 \cdot 1/4$, *e.g.* for the Eurodollar this means $1m \cdot 0.0001 \cdot 1/4 = \$25$. The factor $1/4$ is derived from the basis, *i.e.* in this case 90/360. Hence, the dv01 of the Eurodollar future is $25 by design. For example, to sell a Eurodollar future at 98.5 means to "borrow" at 1.5% for 3M on the expiry date. Because of the quoting convention, selling a future is like buying the rate. Now, if the future expires at 97.25, *i.e.* the rate has gone up to 1.75%. The seller then makes 25bp, because the future is bought back lower. The final profit is $1m \cdot 0.0025 \cdot 1/4 = \$625$ (or $25 \cdot \$25$).

STIR futures are typically the most cost-effective way of expressing a view on interest rates, especially for the liquid contracts spanning the first year, *i.e.* as mentioned before the so-called front or white futures. However, given that the futures only settle against 3M LIBOR tenors and only for value dates coinciding with International Money Market (IMM) dates, there is less flexibility compared to FRAs. Note that the potential date mismatch between the underlying 3M LIBOR reference rate fixing and the future expiry can result in considerable spread risk and potential losses in case of market stress such as the Lehman default of 2008. Equally important from a risk point of view is the fact that STIR futures have no gamma since they provide a *constant* exposure of $25 per basis point move in interest rates.

6.3.1 FRA versus IR futures recap and convexity correction

It is worth repeating some of the differences illustrated above between FRAs and futures.

FRAs have no specific dates and are not exchange-traded. However, the most liquid tenors are the six-month runs (3-6,6-9,3-9,6-12). FRAs are quoted in terms of interest rates, whereby the quote convention for the future incorporates the rate. For FRAs, day count and IR calculation are usually defined as the same basis as the cash deposit markets of the FRA currency, *i.e.* 3 months on a FRA are not always 90 days.

---

[10]The notable exception being commodity futures which can be physically delivered. Having said that even in the commodity market the vast majority of contracts are rolled, *i.e.* physical delivery is rare.

Since FRAs are not exchange-traded and cleared, counterparties must assess each other's credit risk on their own since FRAs do not have margin requirements. On the other hand, IR futures are marked-to-market daily and subject to margin in- and decrease. The financing of the margin payment is naturally more expensive when rates go up. During the daily mark-to-market process, the profit typically accrues from trade day inception until expiry. Note that the margin is not used for trading the forward rates and only calculated at the expiry of the contract. Given the margining, forward rates are in general lower than the future rates given by the so-called convexity bias [184, 25] as

$$r_{\text{future}} = r_{\text{forward}} - \text{convexity} \,, \tag{6.7}$$

whereby convexity $\sim \frac{1}{2}\sigma^2(T_2 - T_1)$. Here T_1 and T_2 are the future maturity and the maturity of the underlying rate, respectively. More precisely, the correction depends on the volatility of the forward rate, volatility σ of the discount factor and the correlation between the discount factors within the FRA. Hence, the naive assumption of equating the forward rate to 100 minus the futures price is not correct especially for longer-dated contracts and even if the contract dates coincide. The FRA-future convexity bias can be up to 15bp for longer maturities, *i.e.* 5 years and beyond. The exact magnitude of the convexity bias is model-dependent and not trivial to calculate. Finally, note also IR futures are off-balance sheet instruments, *i.e.* the nominal value of the trades are not at risk.

FRAs have no fixed contract notional, but in practice, prices are quoted for a minimum notional of $25m (or equivalent). The FRA benefits are reduced administration hassles due to no (daily) margin calls, including the elimination of cash flows and funding aspects. FRAs are also more flexible concerning dates and therefore allow in principle for more accurate hedges. IR futures, on the other hand, are more liquid in general with smaller bid/offer spreads. In fact, for specific currencies and maturities, the liquidity is significantly more abundant (*e.g.* 2000 3M Eurodollar futures can be traded relatively easily, but an equivalent FRA of 2bn notional is difficult). Therefore, short to medium term interest rate risk on general trading books is typically mostly managed by trading futures. Longer maturity exposure is typically hedged via interest rate swaps.

How is a FRA then be hedged using STIR futures? The principle is that the amount of futures for a given expiry should be chosen such that the respective settlement amount matches as closely as possible. Consider selling USD 100m notional on a 3 x 6 FRA at 4.5% and assume that the period will encompass 90 days. The FRA settlement amount is then given by

$$\frac{USD\ 100m \cdot ((0.0045 + \varepsilon) - LIBOR) \cdot 90/360}{(1 + LIBOR \cdot 90/360)} \,, \tag{6.8}$$

whereby ε denotes the difference between the FRA rate and the forward rate implied by the corresponding futures contract. Assuming that $\varepsilon = 0$, then the respective futures contract then settles at

$$n \cdot (USD\ 1m(0.0045 - LIBOR) \cdot 90/360) \,, \tag{6.9}$$

whereby n is the number of futures contracts such that the FRA and futures settlement amount or dv01 are equal. This is effectively stating that one needs to match the dv01 of the FRA given by

$$n = \frac{dv01_{\text{FRA}}}{dv01_{\text{Futures}}} = \frac{USD\ 100m \cdot 0.0045 \cdot 90/360 \cdot df_{6m}}{USD\ 25} \,. \tag{6.10}$$

Assuming $df_{6m} = 0.99$, one obtains $n = \frac{USD\ 11''250.00}{25} \cdot 0.99 = 450$ (Eurodollar) futures to *sell* in order to hedge the FRA. Therefore, the combined position is long the market on the FRA (*i.e.*

benefitting from a rates increase) and short the market on the futures hedge. Now, as the market rate changes over the trade lifetime, it is clear from the equation above that the resulting discount factor change *only* affects the FRA dv01, whereas the future position is at a constant USD 25 per tick. In the example above, the short FRA position P/L will always be larger than the futures hedge since the discount factors induces convexity. In other words, short FRA means long convexity whereby the futures have no convexity. The combined position is long rates volatility, which is priced in by the convexity correction so as to avoid giving away free optionality (see also discussion on interest rate gamma above under 6.2.2). This is visible in the market prices since 100 minus the future price is typically larger than the forward rate by the amount of the correction.

6.4   Interest Rates Swap & Swap rates

The vanilla Interest Rate Swap (IRS) is an agreement between two counterparties agreeing on a fixed vs. floating rate exchange (typically LIBOR, see Figure 6.2). In case the fixed rate is set to zero, the IRS is also referred to as a *zero-coupon bond (ZCB)*. Receiving/paying the fixed rate in a vanilla swap is thereby equivalent to being long/short a fixed coupon bond.

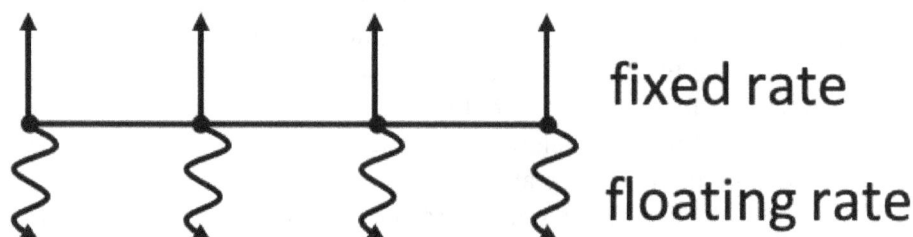

Figure 6.2: Illustration of the fixed vs floating leg flows of an interest rate swap.

Some key terminology regarding IRS is summarized below

- Payer: payer of the fixed rate
- Receiver: recipient of the fixed rate
- Swap rate: the fixed rate
- Basis swap: swap with no fixed rate (both legs float)
- Notional: the principal amount of the trade
- Maturity: duration of the swap
- Tenor: the time between payments (semi-annual is typically the market standard)
- Bullet swap: only one exchange at maturity (*i.e.* like a forward)

The bond par rate (or the IRS swap rate) is the annual coupon, which makes a bond price trade at par (100). Picking up on the example before in Table 6.1, one can calculate another column to represent the annual par rate (see Table 6.2).

Note that both the sum of the product of the forward rates and the respective discount factors up to a period n, and the sum of the respective period n par rate with the discount factors equals 100. Mathematically,

$$\sum_{i=1}^{n} fwd_{rate,i} \cdot df_i = \sum_{i=1}^{n} \text{par rate}_n \cdot df_i = 100 \ . \tag{6.11}$$

Period n	Forward Rate	FV	df	Spot Rate	cum. df	par rate
1	1.00%	1.0100	0.9901	0.0100	0.9901	1.000%
2	1.50%	1.0252	0.9755	0.0125	1.9656	1.248%
3	2.00%	1.0457	0.9563	0.0150	2.9219	1.494%
4	2.50%	1.0718	0.9330	0.0175	3.8549	1.738%
5	3.00%	1.1039	0.9058	0.0200	4.7608	1.978%
6	4.00%	1.1481	0.8710	0.0233	5.6318	2.291%

Table 6.2: Example of calculating the coupon par rate given a set of forward rates and the respective discount factors. The par rate is given by $r_{par,n} = 100 \cdot (1 - df_n)/cum\ df_n$.

This means if one sells/buys the first (equivalent to a Floating Rate Note (FRN, see 12.2) and buys/sells the second cash flow (equivalent to a fixed coupon bond), the par payment of 100 at maturity cancels, and one ends up with a fixed versus floating interest rate swap.

It is sometimes necessary to trade swap maturities that do not exactly match the floating rate schedule. This mismatch means that one might face periods shorter or longer than that of the beginning (or end) of the floating rate. These periods are called *stub* periods. For example, in the case of a short front stub, the first interest rate period is shorter than the floating rate period of the swap. Concretely, a yearly swap starting on January 10th 2015 and ending on April 1st 2020, has its first period from January 10th 2015 to April 1st 2015 following the regular yearly schedule. Hence, it is required to determine the fixing for the first period before switching to the regular schedule. Typically, the rate used to determine the floating rate is then taken from the closest forward curve. The other stub variants are called long front stub, short end stub and long end stub.

In a way, IRS can be considered as a series of FRAs with an identical fixed rate. However, the exact payment mechanics of the IRS legs are more precisely defined by the respective *swap date schedule, i.e.* payment dates, notional amount per period, accrual periods for the day count etc.. The PV of a payer IRS is simply the sum of the discounted fixed and floating cash flows given by

$$PV_{IRS} = N \cdot \left(-R \sum_{i=1}^{T_1} dcf_i df_i + \sum_{j=1}^{T_2} dcf_j r_j df_j \right) . \tag{6.12}$$

The quoting convention is typically 'Currency, Index, Start date, End date, Fixed leg frequency, floating leg frequency, roll date, stub type'. Note that an IRS can also be forward starting, *i.e.* while a '(0Y)10Y' IRS is a 10-year swap starting today, the '5Y10Y' swap is the 10-year swap starting in 5 years. This is equivalent to a swaption (option on a swap) with a 5-year expiry (see swaption later 6.13).

6.5 Asset and Equity Swaps

The asset swap allows two counterparties to exchange an interest floating rate against an asset return. This return may be the price of an equity index or its total return, *i.e.* price plus any other cash flows such as dividends. The most general expression for this exchange is called asset swap, but in practice, the asset is often an equity index such as the S&P or fixed coupon payments of a bond. In case the total return is swapped, the swap is referred to as a total return swap (TRS). Being long or short the swap refers to the underlying asset. The receiver of the asset return is thereby synthetically long the unfunded asset exposure.

Equity swaps trade in terms of spread to LIBOR whereby the quote reflects the cost of hedging and funding the asset leg. A typical quote would be LIBOR-20bp / LIBOR+5bp for the bid/offer. In case a dealer sells the equity swap, the trading desk must purchase the asset in the market after which it can either lend it out and earn the borrow cost or use it as collateral in a repo transaction [11]. In case of being long the equity return, the dealer needs to short the asset to hedge and pay borrow, which explains the sign difference in the bid/offer spread to LIBOR above.

6.6 Overnight Index Swaps (OIS)

An Overnight Index Swaps (OIS) is an IRS where a fixed rate is exchanged for a floating overnight rate. The contract settles at maturity as a CFD between the fixed rate and the compounded series of floating overnight rates. The par fixed rate is equivalent to the market prediction for lending a cash principal at the overnight fix and re-lending that principal, with interest earned, each further day until the swap matures. The overnight fix is then a daily weighted average of the rates from overnight cash trades between selected banks, which is published at the end of the trading day. Despite the fact that OIS is an unsecured rate, the tenor credit risk is minimal due to the overnight settlement mechanics. This makes OIS a natural candidate for the proxy of the risk-free rate following the 2008/09 financial crisis. Central Banks control monetary operations to ensure the overnight fixes are as close as possible to the respective policy rate. Therefore, the OIS is also a predictor of the market's expectation of future CB policy. Overnight fixes are subject to supply/demand pressures of day-to-day cash within the banking system. Therefore, the OIS is also a good indicator of short-term inter-bank liquidity. The lending under the OIS is in principle secure due to the cash flow setup. Overnight interbank lending rates include Eonia (EUR), Fed Funds (USD), Sonia (GBP), Mutan (JPY).

The key advantage of the OIS is that the schedule can be customized and that they are indeed credit efficient given no mismatch of the payment dates. Unfortunately, the liquidity is typically quite poor beyond three years, *i.e.* the product is suitable for the short-end of the rates term structure only. The PV of an OIS from a payer point of view is given by

$$PV_{OIS} = N \cdot \left(-R \sum_{i=1}^{T_1} dcf_i df_i + \sum_{j=1}^{T_2} df_j (\prod_{k=1}^{T_j} (1 + dcf_k r_k) - 1) \right) . \tag{6.13}$$

Note that the compounding feature as given by $\prod(...)$ above means that all daily OIS fixings are required to compute a given periods' cash flows. This feature makes the valuation more complicated.

6.7 Yield Curve

The Yield Curve (YC) is the backbone of money, bond and derivatives markets in any currency. It is constructed by observable market rates and shows whether short-term or long-term rates are higher / lower [185]. The YC is typically quoted against government bond rates and provides a benchmark against which all other rates are measured. Adjustments for credit quality, liquidity are expressed as spreads to the YC rate. The YC also represents market interest rates across all maturities for comparable credit risk. Comparable credit risk instruments include government bonds, deposit rates and swap rates. In principle, YC consist of two types, either par-coupon or zero-coupon

---

[11]Recall that repo is an acronym for *repurchase agreement*, which involves the sales of securities together with the agreement to purchase them back at a later date.

YCs. Par-coupon yields reflect the internal rate of return on a coupon paying instrument whose market price equally 100% of its face value. Zero-coupon yields are yields on non-coupon paying instruments, which can be derived from par-coupon yields. The zero-coupon YC is considered to reflect the actual IR term structure, *i.e.* LIBOR is assumed to be a zero-coupon rate. YCs can be positive (upwards sloping in time) or negative (downwards sloping in time). Whenever the YC is positive, zero-coupon rates are above par-coupon rates (and the other way around).

The Yield Curve (YC) construction is typically done via a process called *bootstrapping* [186]. The process is *in theory* not difficult and entails the following scheme:

- select a range of liquid IR instruments, *e.g.* deposits with different maturities (*e.g.* overnight, 1M,3M etc.), futures up to 2Y maturity and interest rate swaps (fixed vs 6M LIBOR) from 2Y maturity up to 50Y
- select how the instruments shall overlap in their tenors, choose the interpolation method between tenors and correct for possible seasonality effect
- fit a single YC using bootstrapping, splines or other fitting methods

The key equation to determine the swap par rate R_{par} is given by

$$R_{par} = \frac{df(t_0) - df(t_n)}{\sum_j dcf_{j-1,j} df(t_j)} \,, \tag{6.14}$$

whereby $dcf_{j-1,j}$ is the day count fraction between two dates $j-1$ and j. The discount factors for the short term instruments are directly available from the forward rates. The swap rates are typically stripped for every tenor so that each discount factor can be extracted ('stripped') from the previous one using the recursive relation given by

$$df_t = \frac{df_0 - R_t \sum_{i=1}^{t-1} yfc_{i-1} \cdot df_i}{(1 + R_t \cdot dcf_{t-1,t})} \,. \tag{6.15}$$

The technique described above is the legacy. In other words, the idea of deriving a *single* yield curve per currency from the market quotes had to be abandoned so that naive textbook YC bootstrapping techniques (see Figure 6.3 for a stylized example) are not anymore used in practice. This change happened because the respective LIBOR curves fragmented, *i.e.* many intracurve basis spreads (1M vs 3M or 3M vs 6M), as well as the LIBOR/OIS spread, widened significantly [187, 188, 189] to account for the respective difference in credit risk. At the same time, the market started to price in the difference between instruments under CSA with margining and non-margined trades. As a consequence, one now has multiple curves for a single tenor. The subsequent discussion of the modified construction topics is beyond the scope of this book, but the reader can find a concise overview in the literature [190]. The critical message here is that traders need to be sure which discount curve to use for determining the present value of option premia or cash flows. This topic will be revisited in a later section in this chapter.

Finally, note that pricing and valuation in today's multi-curve environment is also different and more difficult. This also includes topics such as how volatility tenors are transformed or how non-standard products (*e.g.* non-standard swaptions) are priced.

6.8 Basic Interest Rate Exposure Hedging

The following section first repeats and extends the previous discussion on the IR delta (see 6.2.1) since this is the foundation. As shown before, practitioners commonly refer to IR exposure resulting

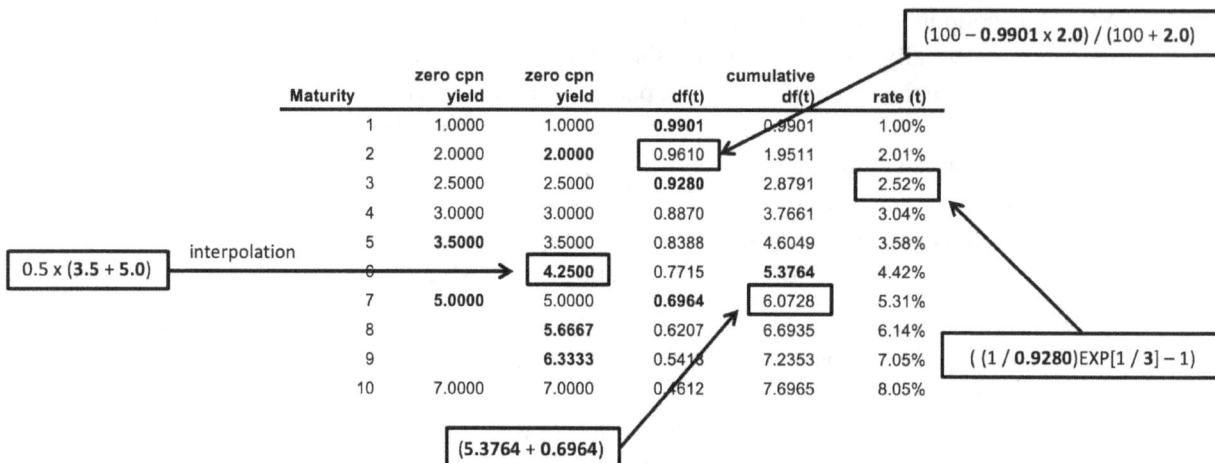

Maturity	zero cpn yield	zero cpn yield	df(t)	cumulative df(t)	rate (t)
1	1.0000	1.0000	**0.9901**	0.9901	1.00%
2	2.0000	**2.0000**	0.9610	1.9511	2.01%
3	2.5000	2.5000	**0.9280**	2.8791	2.52%
4	3.0000	3.0000	0.8870	3.7661	3.04%
5	**3.5000**	3.5000	0.8388	4.6049	3.58%
6		**4.2500**	0.7715	**5.3764**	4.42%
7	**5.0000**	5.0000	**0.6964**	6.0728	5.31%
8		**5.6667**	0.6207	6.6935	6.14%
9		6.3333	0.5416	7.2353	7.05%
10	7.0000	7.0000	0.4612	7.6965	8.05%

Boxes/annotations:
- $(100 - 0.9901 \times 2.0) / (100 + 2.0)$
- $0.5 \times (3.5 + 5.0)$ → interpolation
- $((1/0.9280)\text{EXP}[1/3] - 1)$
- $(5.3764 + 0.6964)$

Figure 6.3: Illustration of a simple Yield Curve bootstrap process resulting in discount factors and interest rate as a function of time.

from the parallel curve moves as 'delta' and quote it in *dv01* terms. dv01 stands for 'dollar value of 1bp parallel shift', *i.e.* the price sensitivity of an interest rate position to a 1 basis point change in interest rates.

The dv01 is often also called dollar duration ($D_\$$) or Basis Point Value (BPV) since it is typically indeed expressed as a cash (dollar) measure per 1 basis point as noted above. Mathematically, the dv01 is defined as the partial derivative of the price with respect to the yield

$$dv01 = -\frac{\partial V}{\partial yield} \,, \tag{6.16}$$

which explains the analogy with the greek delta.

As an example, a dv01 of +USD 1k means that if rates increase by 1bp the position earns USD 1000. Given that IR delta exposure is a function of maturity, dv01 exposure is usually bucketed, *i.e.* risk reports show dv01 exposure in pillars of 1D, 10D, 1M, 3M, 6M, 12M, 24M, etc.. How can a +USD 1k dv01 exposure in the 2-year bucket be hedged assuming the 2y rate is currently 0.63%. Based on the dv01, the exposure is long rates, so to flatten it one enters in a fixed/floating leg IRS where the book receives the fixed/pays the floating leg. The notional of the swap to be traded is approximately given by dv01 / 0.0002 = 1000 / 0.0002 = USD 5m. This is because the dv01 of a 2y IRS is approximately 0.0002. Alternatively, one can trade IR futures. Trading IR futures makes sense for maturities below 2 years since the liquidity is otherwise poor. Recall that the dv01 of one USD IR future is $25. In order to replicate the 2y exposure it is thus required to trade the 2year IR future strip, *i.e.* 8 future expiries with $1000/(8 \cdot \$25) = 5$ futures each.

6.9 Bonds

A bond is a note which specifies the terms of a loan repayment. The word 'Bond' itself derives from the terms 'borrower' and 'lender'. Effectively, a bond is just a series of cash flows (see Figure 6.4), similar to any other IR product. The exact terms of the repayment can be in various forms (*e.g.* floating coupon, fixed coupon, at maturity only, etc.).

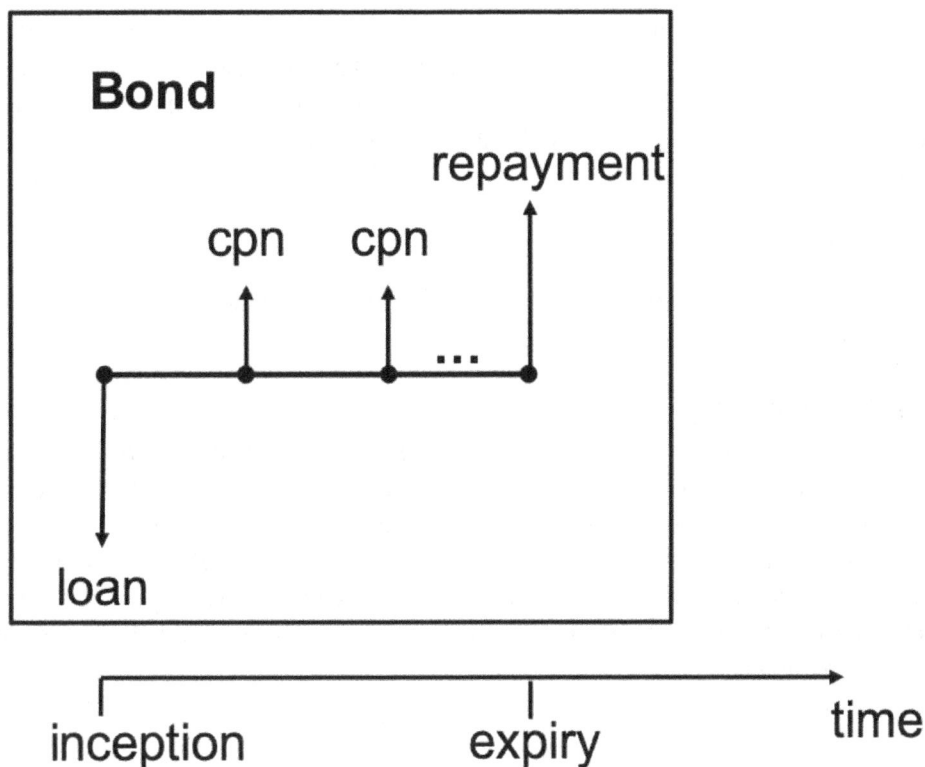

Figure 6.4: Illustration of a simple bond cash flow including loan on principal, coupons and repayment of principle over time.

Various bonds exist such as

- sovereign bonds issued by governments, *e.g.* US Treasuries, UK Gilts, German Bunds, etc..
- agency bonds issued by governmental agencies, *e.g.* Freddie Mac, Fannie Mae, etc.
- corporate bonds issued by companies, *e.g.* Microsoft, Apple, etc.
- municipal bonds issued by states, cities, towns
- samurai bonds issued by a government outside the home country/currency

whereby the most important repayment forms are
- fixed coupon (usually pays an equal amount with regular periodicity, *e.g.* quarterly; coupon can be accreting or declining)
- floating rate (coupon is referenced to a floating interest rate, *e.g.* LIBOR)
- zero coupon (no coupon payment, only notional repayment at maturity)
- perpetual coupon (no maturity of the bond itself, repayment is an infinite annuity)
- callable (issuer has the right to 'call', *i.e.* redeem the bond early; usually at par)
- puttable (the holder can 'put' or give back the bond to force redemption early)

6.9.1 Bonds: Pricing

The theoretical price of a bond must be equal to the present value of all future cash flows. Usually, the price is expressed per 100 face / notional amount (par). However, actual bond purchases may require minimum notional amounts. For example, consider a bond paying a coupon of 5% in one year and 5% + 100% times notional in two years (expiry). What is the theoretical value of the bond? Assume the spot rates for year 1 and year 2 are $r_1 = 1\%$ and $r_2 = 2\%$. The respective discount factors are $df_1 = 1/1.01 = 0.99$ and $df_2 = 1/1.022 = 0.96$. Then the present value price of the bond is then given by

$$PV = 5 \cdot df_1 + 105 \cdot df_2 = 105.87. \tag{6.17}$$

Or alternatively, $PV = 5 / 1.01 + 105 / 1.022 = 105.87$. Hence, the expected cash flows are effectively just discounted at the risk-free rate.

6.9.2 Bonds: Yield to maturity

Yield to maturity (YTM or simply 'yield') is a concept that derives the yield for a bond assuming a *flat* yield curve. Consider the 2 year bond example earlier, which had a *PV = 105.87*. To determine the YTM rate, it is required to solve the following quadratic equation $105.87 = 5/(1+r) + 105/(1+r)^2$ for the rate r. The solution gives YTM = 1.98%. The YTM is the **expected return on the bond** assuming a flat YC. However, the bond return will only be equal to the YTM if the yield curve remains flat over the life time of the bond (or if all coupons could be re-invested at the YTM). The general YTM expression is

$$\text{bond price} = \frac{cpn/n}{(1+r/n)^1} + \frac{cpn/n}{(1+r/n)^2} + \ldots + \frac{cpn/n}{(1+r/n)^{n \cdot t}}, \tag{6.18}$$

with *cpn* being the bond coupon p.a., *n* the number of *cpn* p.a., *t* the time (years) to maturity and finally *r* the YTM p.a.. If the coupon rate equals the YTM then the price of the bond is indeed *100*.

The relationship between the bond price and the YTM is nonlinear. Recall that dv01 is a linear measure, which is why it is commonly called delta. Bond convexity represents the nonlinear relationship between YTM and the bond price. Hence, the dv01 delta provides only a good local representation of the interest rate risk (see Figure 6.5).

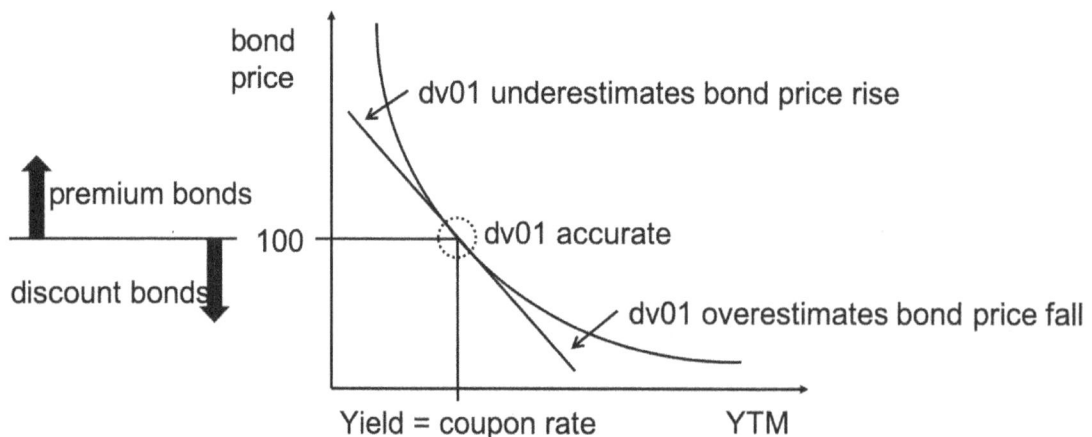

Figure 6.5: Illustration of bond convexity.

Bond quotes may be clean or dirty, whereby the former is the standard. Clean and dirty refers to whether the interest for the current coupon period is ex- or included in the price. In other words, if one sells a bond clean shortly *before* an interest payment, the former holder is still entitled to the accrued interest (AI) for the corresponding coupon period. Hence,

$$P_{Bond,dirty} = P_{Bond,clean} + AI. \tag{6.19}$$

For example, consider a bond paying 3% interest every 6 months. If the bond is sold *clean* 30 days before the coupon payment then the accrued interest the seller is entitled to equals actual days/day count · interest $= 150/180 \cdot 3\% = 2.49\%$.

In case bonds redeem early given callable or puttable features, some additional yield variants are required. The Yield to call (YTC) or Yield to put (YTP) is the respective YTM assuming that the bond redeems early, *i.e.* with a shortened lifetime. Finally, the Yield to worst (YTW) is the lowest yield for a bond between holding it to maturity or any (allowed) early redemption scenario. As a consequence, the YTW is by construction the most conservative YTM measure when dealing with early redemption scenarios. Note that modeling early redemption features of (long-dated) bonds is not trivial and it is often essential to analyze the respective model sensitivity or potential ill-behavior carefully. In other words, it is not uncommon to observe large swings on spreads, yields, and durations (see below) triggered by small price movements for early redeemable bonds.

6.9.3 Bonds: Duration

The generic term of *duration* for fixed income securities or bonds explicitly expresses the lifetime of the security against some metric. The straightforward approach of defining the duration as the time until maturity of the instrument is not optimal because the effect of weighted cash flows versus the repayment of the principle is ignored.

One way of incorporating the weighted average maturity of all cash flows is the so-called Macaulay duration. It is equivalent to the maturity of a zero-coupon bond with the same risk as is shown below. The Macaulay duration of a bond (typically expressed in years) is given by

$$D_{\mathrm{Mac}} = \sum \frac{PV(CF_i)}{V} \cdot t_i , \tag{6.20}$$

whereby $PV(CF_i)$ is the present value of the *i-th* bond cash flow CF, V the current bond price (*i.e.* the present value of all future cash payments of the instrument) and t_i the time (in years) when cash flow i is actually paid. The price change of a bond can then be expressed as

$$\Delta V = - \left[\frac{\delta yield}{1 + yield} \right] \cdot D_{\mathrm{Mac}} \cdot V . \tag{6.21}$$

The Macaulay duration is the point at which the change in the bond price (price risk) and the coupon reinvestment (reinvestment risk) due to yield changes is zero. Recall that the price-yield relationship is nonlinear, *i.e.* at higher yields a change in yield has less price impact.

The other important duration measure is called the modified duration. However, modified duration is a price sensitivity measure, defined as the percentage derivative of price with respect to yield. If the equation above is rearranged one obtains

$$\Delta V = - \underbrace{\left[\frac{D_{\mathrm{Mac}}}{1 + yield} \right]}_{\text{modified duration}} \cdot \delta yield \cdot V . \tag{6.22}$$

The expression in the underbraces represents the modified duration. Consequently, the link to the dv01 is obtained, which can now be expressed as

$$dv01 = V \cdot D_{\text{Mac}}/100 \ . \tag{6.23}$$

These measures allow to set up trades which are dv01 *neutral* assuming a linear response, *i.e.* it only works for small yield moves since the relationship between yield and price is nonlinear. Hence, this is an example of duration convexity again. As a recap, remember the following factors affecting duration

- **Time to maturity**: long time to maturity $\rightarrow$ longer duration
- **Coupon**: lower coupon $\rightarrow$ longer duration
- **Coupon frequency**: lower frequency $\rightarrow$ longer duration
- **Yield**: lower yield $\rightarrow$ longer duration

6.9.4 Bonds: Futures

Bond futures are derivatives which are physically settled instruments of an underlying bond bundle. In other words, upon expiry, the seller delivers a bond matching the contract specifications to the holder of the future. For example, the deliverable bond might be $100'000 notional worth of a 5% coupon treasury note with a remaining maturity between 21 24 months. In other words, there is typically some freedom in choosing which bond to deliver. In case there not an exact match on the coupon, the exchange determines a set of eligible bonds for delivery whereby a conversion factor compensates for the difference in yield. Therefore, the future buyer pays for the delivered bond

$$\$100'000 \cdot EDSP_F \cdot f_{conv} \cdot acc \ , \tag{6.24}$$

whereby $EDSP_F$ is the EDSP of the future, f_{conv} the conversion factor and acc the accrued interest on the bond. Hence, in case of a smaller coupon for the delivered bond, the future buyer pays less. The calculation of the conversion factor is done by re-pricing a potential bond using the theoretical yield (*e.g.* 5% in the example above). However, this methodology is not perfect given that other factors such as maturity and liquidity also differ. This means that despite the conversion, one bond is often cheaper to deliver than others. This bond is called the cheapest to deliver (CTD) bond. As a consequence, the seller rationally chooses the bond which has increased least in value, which is often the one with the lowest duration. In order to quantify the choice further, the term *net basis* is introduced. Note that CTD bond is the bond, which maximizes the return when it is purchased while selling the future, held until expiry and then delivering it against the future.

The net basis is the P/L difference between the bond price and converted future price F

$$\text{gross basis} = P - F \cdot f_{conv} \ . \tag{6.25}$$

The cheapest to deliver bond is typically the one with the lowest gross basis.

6.10 Constant Maturity Swap (CMS)

Following the discussion of duration, it makes sense to introduce the constant maturity swap (CMS). The CMS is an interest rate swap that allows the purchaser to *fix the duration* of received flows on a swap, which explains the use of the term constant. This is accomplished by exchanging the so-called CMS rate, which is the current par swap-rate for a given tenor on the swap yield curve, versus either a fixed rate or a floating rate such as Libor [12]. Hence, the CMS is a floating-to-floating swap (see Figure 6.6).

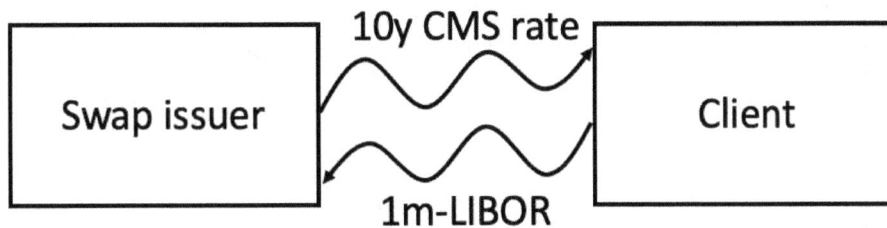

Figure 6.6: Illustration of a simple CMS transaction in which the client pay floating LIBOR and receives a floating CMS rate.

For example, a 5Y CMS - 10Y versus 3M-Libor would mean exchanging the quarterly-fixed 3M-Libor floating leg versus the 10Y par-swap whereby both legs expire in 5 years. Hence, a CMS rate is reset every period to the most recent swap rate of the specified tenor (or the spread between the most recent swap rates of different specified tenors). It is evident that the tenor of the CMS rate does not match the length of the calculation period, and therefore, one cannot merely discount the forward par-swap rates. In other words, while the CMS swap price is simply the difference of the present value of the LIBOR leg (available from the forward interest rates) and the CMS leg, the CMS leg is a function of the CMS rates, which are not equal to the implied forward swap rates. What is required is to make a so-called CMS *convexity adjustment* on top [22], which is a model-dependent valuation adjustment. The description derives from considering the replication portfolio of CMS, which is given by a set of forward swap positions. Plotting the forward swap value as a function of the underlying swap rate shows a convex profile similar to the relation between price and yield for bonds. Hence, the linear CMS rate payoff is replicated with a convex forward swap providing the CMS receiver with a systematic advantage. Therefore, this magnitude, given by the difference in the convexity of the forward swap versus the swap rate, is adjusted for by the CMS payer by shifting the forward swap rate up. The approach of using a convexity correction based on the Taylor expansion of the forward par swap rate [22] is somewhat of a fudge factor to remain in a familiar framework. Therefore, other more advanced methods have been proposed [191, 192, 193, 194]. In practical terms, the convexity lack of the CMS will be visible when trying to hedge it with a vanilla IRS. For example, assume paying the 10Y CMS rate while hedging it with a 10Y IRS. If the 10-year rate *increases*, the CMS swap loses money while the IRS gains, but the amount earned does not offset the loss due to the convexity. This principle is illustrated in Figure 6.7 where the convexity difference shows up in large moves in the swap rate. The approach given by [191] provides an exact CMS replication recipe using swaptions. The exact formalism will be discussed later (see 6.13.3) following the introduction of swaptions.

CMSs are often used to speculate on the steepening or flattening of the yield curve. As an example, for a CMS paying floating Libor versus receiving the 10 year CMS rate, the trade is mostly sensitive to the slope of the curve but not for a parallel shift. Therefore, when expecting a steepening yield curve scenario, one should receive the CMS rate while paying the CMS rate in the case of a potential flattening view.

---

[12]One common variation of the CMS is a constant maturity treasury (CMT) swap whereby one pays the par yield of a Treasury bond, note or bill instead of the CMS swap rate

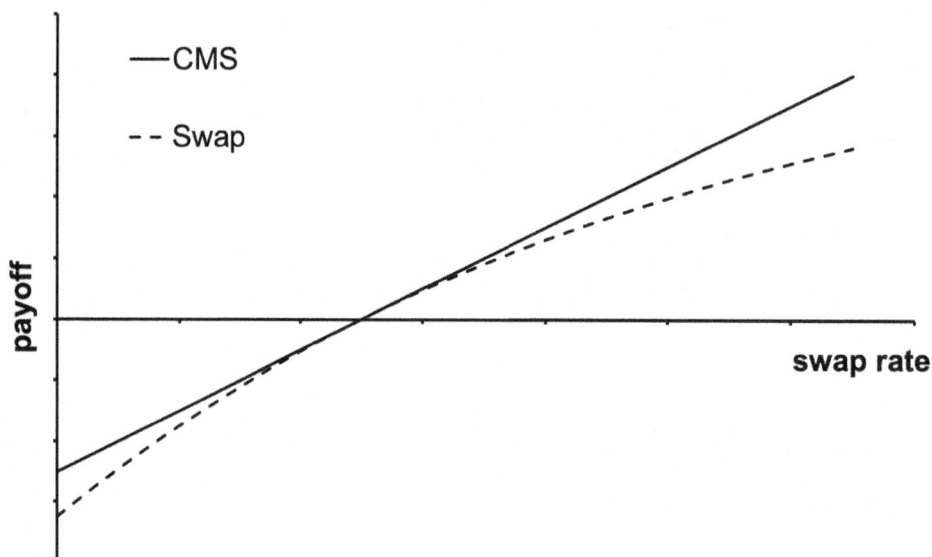

Figure 6.7: Illustration of the CMS payout (solid line) versus a vanilla IRS for equal dv01 at the same rate.

Finally, many interest rate investor products use the CMS rate as the underlying index. While the CMS rates may differ from the underlying yield curve significantly, the CMS itself is a clearly defined in terms of its fixing. This topic will be revisited when discussing CMS spread options and steepener/flattener notes (see 6.13.4).

6.11   Interest Rates: Basis risk / collateral discounting

Before 2008, the interest rate landscape was relatively straightforward for non-specialists. More concretely, this meant in practice that everyone discounted cash flows using the appropriate LIBOR rate by default, which was considered the risk-free rate. However, during and after 2008, the so-called LIBOR / OIS basis increased significantly, *i.e.* the difference between these two interest benchmark quotes. Moreover, different LIBOR tenors (*e.g.* 3m vs 6m) started to display different term premia. Recall that LIBOR (lending) is purely unsecured, *i.e.* the LIBOR curve embeds credit risk. On the other hand, OIS (lending) is effectively secure, *i.e.* the OIS curve is nearly risk-free. The difference between the two rates is called the LIBOR / OIS spread or LIBOR / OIS basis. Before 2008 this basis was typically small but exploded during the liquidity crisis. This effect was because operators realized that an ITM OTC derivative contract carries significant counterparty risk given that the expected cash flows are only realized if the counterparty does not default. Moreover, clearing houses demand that collateral is posted against short ITM listed positions. Note that clearing houses or CCPs do not necessarily have the same margin or collateral requirements, which can result in different funding, liquidity and ultimately capital costs. Nevertheless, the interest received on the collateral is typically the respective OIS rate. Before the crisis, it was assumed that any swap-linked cash flow could be funded or reinvested at LIBOR. Therefore, LIBOR was considered the appropriate discounting rate by default. Today all clearing houses have effectively switched to OIS discounting. Hence, OIS has become the market standard for collateralized trades. Another way of looking at this is to realize that the future value of a derivative transaction discounted to today must be in line with the collateral plus the interest earned. This is because the balance between the collateral and the mark-to-market value of the derivative position need to be in line. In other words, the cash flow is funded through the collateral and therefore this funding needs to be in agreement with the rate used for discounting. This analysis will become clearer in the example within the next section.

6.11.1 Interest Rates: LIBOR / OIS Basis

As discussed before, the LIBOR / OIS basis is defined as the difference between a LIBOR fixing and an OIS of equivalent maturity. Due to cash flow differences between the two products, the basis provides a measure of market inter-bank liquidity and, therefore, also banking sector confidence. In the OIS case, the loan principal is theoretically returned with interest to the lender each day. For LIBOR (lending), principal and interest are returned only at maturity. Therefore, the OIS is a less risky investment as the lender would receive back their cash each day before subsequently re-lending it. As a consequence, the OIS should always trade at a lower rate than an equivalently dated LIBOR rate. The difference between these rates (*i.e.* the basis) is the extra premium demanded by the lending bank for leaving their deposit with the counterparty until full maturity, *i.e.* a compensation for credit risk. One key LIBOR / OIS basis is the 3m LIBOR - 3m OIS spread, which is also known as the *LOIS spread* [195].

It is possible to express a view on or hedge against the LIBOR / OIS basis using a FRA in combination with a forward-starting OIS position. Hence, for the same notional one would pay a FRA, receive OIS and therefore benefit in case the spread widens. There is typically also a strong correlation between the FRA / OIS spread and the credit spread for financial institutions. In times of a severe crisis, it is a general proxy for credit spreads and can sometimes be used to implement views on the credit markets more cost efficiently compared to trading dedicated credit instruments directly.

The LIBOR / OIS spread increase has significantly changed how collateralized and uncollateralized derivative transactions are priced. In practice, this means that future derivative cash flows are not anymore LIBOR discounted *by default*. Instead, cash flows in collateralized trades are discounted at the respective OIS rate. Moreover, cash flows in non-collateralized trades are discounted at the rate at which each bank can borrow.

In other words, before the financial crisis, the credit markets were liquid, and it was assumed that every institution could borrow at LIBOR. During and after the crisis, it was realized that non-collateralized trades should be funded at the rate at which the bank's treasury desk can borrow money. Because banks fund at different levels, there is no universal benchmark.

For example, assume paying fixed 2% on a $100m notional 1 year IRS versus 3 month LIBOR. Fixed cash flows are exchanged annually while LIBOR, and the current swap rate is 2.5%. Clearly, the swap is ITM because the current rate is *higher*. How much collateral must the counterparty post against this? If the position is offset by entering a new 2.5% swap, the floating legs cancel, and one can expect to receive 0.5% annually. If this mark-to-market value is discounted using LIBOR the value amounts to $(0.5\% \cdot 100m)/(1 + 2.5\%) = \$488k$. Hence, using LIBOR, 488k is enough to insure against *default* of the counterparty. However, is this enough if instead an OIS rate of 1% is received on the collateral? Unfortunately, not, because the very same calculation now requires posting collateral equivalent to $495k. Therefore, the appropriate discounting rate when marking the collateralized swap is the OIS rate [196]. It follows that the impact of switching to OIS discounting for the mark-to-market valuation of an IRS is

$$\text{Impact} \approx (\text{LIBOR} - \text{OIS}) \cdot \text{dv01 of annuity with per-period payments}(R - r) \cdot \text{Notional} , \quad (6.26)$$

whereby R is the fixed swap rate and r the par swap rate. For example, when the LIBOR curve is

50bp higher than the OIS curve, then switching from LIBOR to OIS discounting means moving down the discount rate for this annuity by 50bp.

Hence, ITM / OTM swaps gain/lose under OIS discounting as long as LIBOR-OIS spreads are positive/negative. Books that run many offsetting positions are very likely to be unaffected by the switch in discounting. Directional traders will however certainly see an impact. Given the general drop in rates over the last years, most 'receive-fixed' swaps initiated in the past are likely ITM and the other way around. In theory, insurers are naturally fixed receivers on the long end of the YC and should benefit from positions initiated in the past.

6.11.2 Interest Rates: LIBOR / LIBOR basis

The LIBOR / OIS basis is not the only basis a trader can be (unknowingly) long or short. The LIBOR / LIBOR basis swap is exchanging floating cash flows whereby the floating legs refer a different LIBOR index. Given that LIBOR is equivalent to an unsecured deposit rate, there must be a growing credit risk premium embedded when extending the lending or payment duration. In other words, lending money for three months must be more *expensive* than rolling the equivalent notional three times for a one-month duration each.

Basis spreads and their corresponding trades are commonly referenced with the letter 's'. This convention has two legs, the 'spread leg' and the 'flat leg'. The spread is added to the 'spread leg', which is usually the leg with the shorter underlying tenor. The payment frequency is typically determined by the longer underlying tenor, with compounding applied. Hence, spreads (basis) are quoted against the shorter underlying tenor, while the longer tenor determines the payment. For example, a USD 3s1s basis swap has USD 1M LIBOR as the spread leg and USD 3M LIBOR as the flat leg. Payment is every 3 months, with the one month leg compounded. The positive 3s1s basis is then the result of the compounded 1-month rate being *less* than the 3-month rate reflecting the smaller credit risk on the shorter tenor.

Another essential basis within intra-currency basis swaps is the 3M / 6M swap basis (6s3s). Imagine entering an OTC transaction of a 12 month zero-coupon IRS in EUR, receiving 3 month LIBOR on EUR 1m. To hedge the exposure, a 12M zero-coupon IRS in EUR is traded, which pays 6M LIBOR on EUR 1m. The dv01 or outright delta exposure is flat, but is the position fully hedged? The answer is no because one is still exposed to the basis delta (see also 6.2.1). If one receives the floating payment in 6M instead of 3M, the position is running a higher credit risk because the counterparty might default *before*. This difference is reflected in the 3M / 6M basis spread, which widened significantly in and after 2008. Hence, if one hedges rate exposure by not paying attention to the coupon payment frequency, then this can lead to a non-deliberate buildup of large 3M / 6M (or other) basis risks.

Banks typically have a funding mismatch between the assets and liabilities. In other words, banks naturally receive funding on a 3-month basis while the assets are tied up to 1-month receivables. In order to alleviate the mismatch, banks can buy a 3s1s basis swaps (paying 1M compounded over 3M, receiving 3M) to lock in the current spread between the asset vs. liability funding. Analogously, corporate funding is often linked to 6 month LIBOR whereas assets are tied up to 3M funding. Again, buying a 3s6s basis swap can hedge or lock in the current spread to not run into a funding crisis when the spread widens.

6.11.3 Interest Rates: cross-currency basis and swaps

Another subtle issue and hidden exposure can arise from the cross-currency (XCCY) basis. In a XCCY swap, each leg of the swap is denominated in a different currency whereby the principal amounts are exchanged at maturity or inception. Consider the example in Figure 6.8. A US investor has exposure on a 10m EUR bond paying EURibor+100 but does not want the FX risk. Therefore, he enters into a XCCY swap, receiving EUR 10m today in exchange for the equivalent amount in USD ($14.2m; USDEUR FX rate = 0.7). Hence, the investor pays EUR-LIBOR, receiving USD-LIBOR on the notional on a floating-for-floating setup. At expiry, the investor receives USD 14.2m and pays EUR 10m. The investor can thereby lock in 100 bp less any USD funding spread to LIBOR *without* FX risk. The flow is equivalent to exchanging Floating Rate Notes (FRNs) (see 12.2) paying LIBOR.

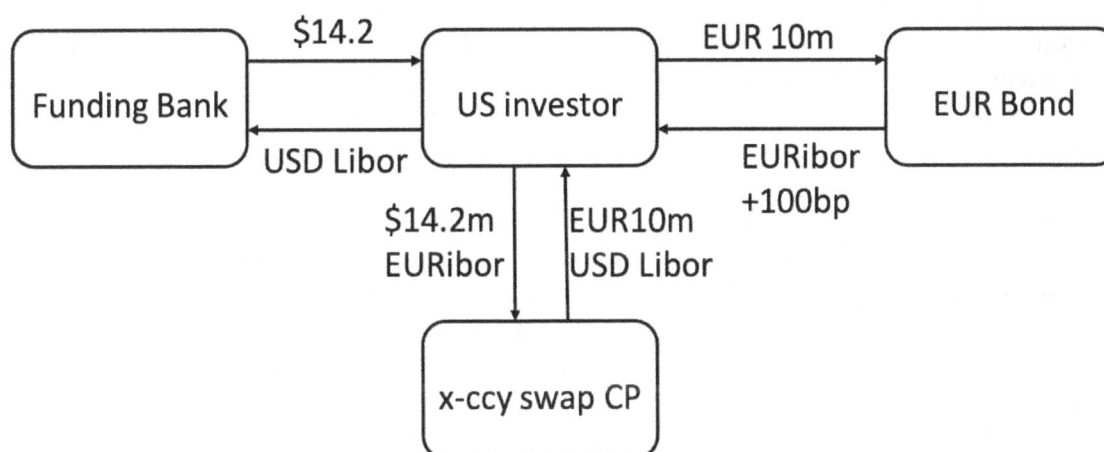

Figure 6.8: Example of a xccy swap transaction.

Hence, the steps are effectively

- (*i*) exchange of principal at spot FX rate
- (*ii*) exchange of FRN paying LIBOR
- (*iii*) exchange of principal at maturity at spot FX rate

The G7 convention on the direction of any XCCY spread is that it is against USD-LIBOR. Hence, for a quote of **REC/PAY +1.0/-1.0** of a particular tenor, if one is paying 3m-USD LIBOR then this means receiving *e.g.* 3m-EURibor - 1.0, and if one is receiving 3m-USD LIBOR then this means paying 3m-EURibor + 1.0. This means that in this example the *basis-swap spread* is zero, which is the equilibrium value under LIBOR discounting given the equivalence to a FRN. If the quote on the same currency pair is **REC/PAY -5.0/-6.0**, then the spread is negative, *i.e.* -11 on aggregate. This is what happened during the last financial crisis for EURUSD LIBOR [13] and is typically also still the reality today [197] for many currencies against the USD. The cause for basis swap spreads to diverge from zero is typically a supply/demand imbalance, and in a time of crisis, investors will increasingly convert money into safe-haven currencies such as the USD.

This issue gains in importance also because collateral is often posted in USD, even if the underlying trade is *e.g.* in EUR. The XCCY basis for a given currency pair reflects the funding differential in those currencies. Any rational counterparty prefers to post collateral in the currency

---

[13]The EURUSD 3m basis swap following the Lehman Brothers collapse in September 2018 reached levels of -200 bps.

for which the funding costs are *cheaper*. Funding in USD, as opposed to EUR, is historically and currently more expensive because of the EURUSD XCCY basis (*i.e.* negative on a 3-year trade). Hence, for a EUR trade for which one needs to post USD collateral, there is a loss due to the funding difference. As mentioned before, collateral must be discounted at the respective OIS rate, which implies that the basis swap is not zero and close to the LIBOR-OIS difference between the respective currency pair. This has important implications on how the yield curve for a particular currency must be constructed when for example the collateral currency differs from the swap currency.

6.12 Interest rate models

Following the definition of the yield curve and the introduction of various linear instruments, it is natural to wonder how to model the movement of the future rate. Consequently, in order to price interest rates derivatives (IRD), it is required to specify the underlying stochastic process, *i.e.* to choose a model. At the beginning of the book, some elementary short rate models were mentioned already (see 2.1.5). In these models, the interest rate curve is a model output as a function of the respective parameters. The drawback of the short-rate models is they only capture one part of the curve by definition.

The entire dynamics of the forward rate curve can be represented by models in the so-called Heath–Jarrow–Morton framework [151]. This model family is often split onto low dimensional models such as the Cheyette model [198, 199] and high dimensional models such as the Libor Market Model (LMM) [200, 201]. The original LMM cannot incorporate volatility smile/skew, but various extensions have been proposed to deal with this. LMM treats a set of forward rates as a basket and relies on Monte Carlo methods, *i.e.* it entails a computational expense. Given the basket structure, LMM requires a correlation framework between the forward rates. The effective dynamics are given by

$$\frac{df_{i,t}}{f_{i,t}} = v_{i,t}dt + \sigma_i \sum_{j=1}^{n} \frac{\sigma_{i,j}}{\sigma_i} dW_i \, , \tag{6.27}$$

where the loading factors $\frac{\sigma_{i,j}}{\sigma_i}$ incorporate the correlation given by $c_{ij} = \frac{\sigma_{i,j}}{\sigma_i}$ as

$$\mathbf{C} \cdot \mathbf{C}^{\mathbf{T}} = \rho \, . \tag{6.28}$$

The correlation is typically also defined as a term structure represented by a functional form such as an exponential, *e.g.* $\rho(\Delta T) = \lambda + (1 - \lambda) \cdot \exp[-\beta \Delta T]$. Note that this functional is equivalent to the lambda correlation mark process discussed earlier (see 5.3.7). The LMM is then calibrated to market quotes of interest derivatives such as caps/floors or swaptions.

The last model to be briefly mentioned is the interest rate local volatility model [202, 203, 204], which is a rather new development. The equity LVM (see 3.1.4) cannot be immediately translated to the interest rate world because the required derivatives with respect to the option maturity are not available ($\frac{\partial C}{\partial T}$). In other words, whenever option prices at different maturities exist for the same underlying, the forward process is identical, and the canonical Dupire approach [94] works out of the box. In interest rates, the respective forward processes for different options are typically different. The exact mechanics on how the Dupire framework is modified in the context of interest rate derivatives is beyond the scope here. Nevertheless, given the advantages of the LVM approach in capturing smile/skew effects in the underlying volatility surface easily, this development is very likely going to be pursued further.

6.13 Interest Rates: Swaption

The swaption is an option to enter an interest rate swap at a fixed rate specified by the contract. Here a *payer swaption* is then the option to enter a swap paying the fixed rate and the receiver swaption the other way around. Hence, the payer/receiver swaption is given by

$$N \cdot \max[I \cdot (R_{t,T} - K), 0] \cdot A_{t,T} , \tag{6.29}$$

with $I \pm 1$ denoting payer/receiver, $R_{t,T}$ the forward swap rate at swaption expiry t and $T - t$ being the swap tenor. $A_{t,T}$ is either the PVBP annuity or cash annuity depending on whether the swaption is physically or cash settled. More on this difference at the end of this section.

The swaption is the IRS derivative counterpart of the vanilla option whereby the IRS is the asset and the swaption the option. Hence, to hedge the delta of the swaption, one trades the IRS as the underlying asset. In order to hedge the other basic greek exposure (*e.g.* gamma, vega) in a swaption portfolio, it is required to trade other swaptions against it. Moreover, more complex digital or exotics options on swap rates or spreads will typically be hedged (among other things) using swaptions. Swaptions are can be priced using the Black-76 [38] model and the swap forward rate of the underlying swap. The quoting convention is typically 'Expiry, Swap, Strike, Type', *e.g.* '3M, 5Y, 1.5%, Payer' is a payer swaption on a 5Y IRS with a strike at 1.5% expiring in 3 months. However, swaptions can also be written on forward starting swaps, *e.g.* '3M, 2Y5Y, 1.75%, Payer' is a payer swaption expiring in 3 months on 5-year swap forward starting after 2 years. Alternatively, the SABR model is often used (see 6.13.1 for a more detailed discussion) and effectively by now also the default model. Note that even if various models agree on the same price, the derived greeks may differ significantly [205].

Swaption volatilities for the forward swap or LIBOR rate are quotes in bps whereby the underlying volatility surface exhibits the familiar non-constant term structure and variation in strike space. As a result, the constant volatility assumption of the Black-76 model is as usual ignored by using the respective implied volatility to match the market quotes. The volatility surface is constructed between the swap forward tenor, the swap expiry and the respective strike space. Hence, this is a fairly large calibration space and results in a so-called *swaption (volatility) cube* given by the swaption expiry dates, the strikes and the underlying swap tenor [206]. Figure 6.9 shows an illustration of the volatility cube components (adapted from [207]) [14]. Fitting a consistent, interpolated, and arbitrage-free volatility surface is not a trivial undertaking. Note that the obtained swaption volatility also requires a transformation in case the underlying swap is nonstandard. These differences include for example changes in payment frequency or the day count. What is effectively done is to find the equivalent standard forward swap rate and strike to match the non-standard swaption parameters.

If one ultimately derives a volatility surface like the one in Figure 6.9 then this does not yet contain all information needed to price swaptions on forward starting swaps. Hence, in order to price a 1Y5Y5Y swaption (*i.e.* a swaption expiring in 1 year on a 5-years forward starting 5 year swap), some assumptions need to be made. In other words, the curve will have a volatility for the 1Y5Y and 1Y10Y swaptions, but not the 1Y5Y5Y. Simply blending the two volatilities will not properly take into account the correlation between the 1Y5Y and the 1Y5Y5Y rates nor the respective dv01. The expression to calculate this forward variance is given by

$$\sigma_{1Y5Y5Y}^2 = \left(\left(1 - \frac{dv01_{1Y10Y}}{dv01_{1Y5Y5Y}} \right) \right)^2 + 2 \left(1 - \frac{dv01_{1Y10Y}}{dv01_{1Y5Y5Y}} \right) \cdot \rho \, \sigma_{1Y5Y} \sigma_{1Y10Y} + \left(\frac{dv01_{1Y10Y}}{dv01_{1Y5Y5Y}} \sigma_{1Y10Y} \right)^2 ,$$

---

[14]Note that it is also possible to fit a local volatility model on the implied volatility of the swaption quotes [204].

$$\text{(6.30)}$$

where ρ denotes the correlation between the two swaption rates. The correlation parameter assumption obviously accounts for a large difference in the derived volatility.

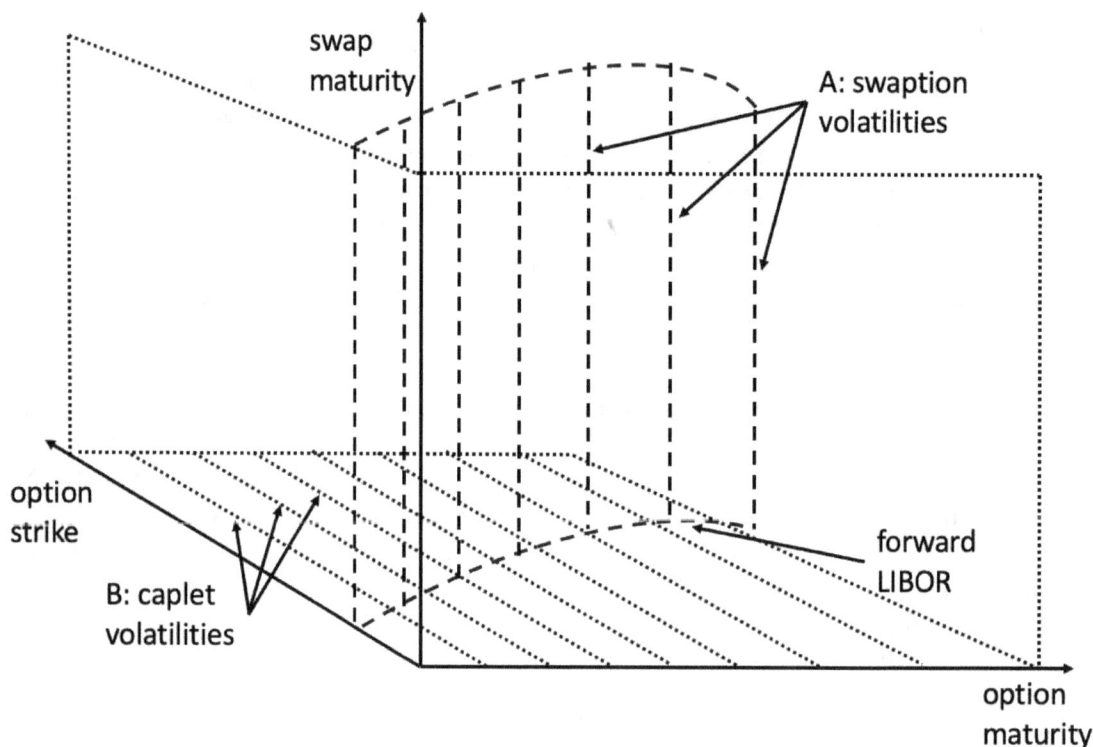

Figure 6.9: Illustration of the swaption volatility cube construction.

An exotic variant of the vanilla swaption is the Bermudan swaption [208]. This Bermudan swaption gives the holder the right to exercise into a swap on pre-defined dates. The main two variants are the bullet and accreting/amortizing Bermudan swaptions whereby the latter exercises into an accreting/amortizing notional swap with pre-determined notional term structure. For example, a yearly Bermudan swaption 10Y into 5Y with strike 3% means that in 5 years the payoff is a European swaption on a 10 year swap with strike 3%, in 6 years the payoff is a European swaption on a 9 year swap with strike 3% and so on. The critical parameters are the forward volatilities of the remaining swap rates and in the case of accreting/amortizing swaptions also the respective correlations. Note that the vega exposure for an accreting/amortizing Bermudan swaption changes with the shape of the yield curve. This also means that the pricing requires a multi-factor model. Since the bullet swaption is effectively a series of European swaptions, the lower valuation boundary has to be the most expensive in the series. In other words, the difference between the most expensive European swaption and the Bermudan is the P/L to manage over the lifetime.

Finally, given recent events [209], it is required to discuss the difference between physical and cash settlement for swaptions. As the name implies, physical settlement of an ITM swaption means that the owner enters into the respective underlying swap. Until recently, the European market convention was mainly to use cash settlement, *i.e.* an ITM swaption receives the cash amount on the settlement day calculated under the assumption of the flat yield curve for the entire life of the reference swap. In a nutshell, while the physical settlement price valuation is mathematically sound, the cash-settlement is often an approximation [210, 211, 212]. Hence, it is vital to consult with the quant team to understand how the settlement is modeled.

6.13.1 Interest Rates: Cap and Floors

The corresponding version of equity vanilla calls and puts in the interest rate world are called caplets and floorlets, respectively. More precisely, a caplet is a call on an interest rate (*e.g.* LIBOR) payable at the end of the period. Alternatively, a caplet can be viewed as a put on a bond, *i.e.* making it insensitive to an increase in rates. The payoff of a caplet/floorlet on a Libor fixing rate $R = L(t_i, t_{i+1})$ in the period $t_i, ..., t_{t+1}$ struck at a strike K is given by

$$N \cdot dcf \cdot \max[I \cdot (R - K), 0] , \tag{6.31}$$

with N being the notional value, K the strike, dcf the day count fraction in relation to the reference rate and $I = \pm 1$ denoting caplet or floorlet, respectively. Caplets and floorlets can be priced using a variant within the BSM framework, the so-called Black-76 [38] model. However, similar to equities or FX, caplets/floorlets with different strikes required different implied volatility inputs in order to match the observed prices in the market. The underlying asset for the caplet is the implied forward rate. Caplets and floorlets can in principle be traded like options on interest rates futures whereby the respective call on the future is a floorlet and the other way around given the (inverse) quoting convention for the futures. Hence, an interest rate future call at a strike of 98% pays off if the reference rate is below 2% at expiry, *i.e.* this is equivalent to buying a put on the rate effectively.

A series of caplets or floorlets is then called a Cap or a Floor for a common strike K, *i.e.*

$$Cap(t, K, t_a, t_b) = \sum_{i=a}^{b-1} caplet_i(t, K, t_i) \text{ and } Floor(t, K, t_a, t_b) = \sum_{i=a}^{b-1} floorlet_i(t, K, t_i) , \tag{6.32}$$

whereby t_a to t_b denote the covered time period. Strikes are usually quoted in absolute terms, *e.g.* 1%, 2% etc.. The ATM strike is then equal to the strike of the swap rate for the respective period, which is often used as a quote reference point for other strikes.

Caplet and floorlet volatilities are not directly quoted in the market. Instead, caps/floors are available as market quotes across a range of strikes and maturities. The process of deriving caplet/floorlet volatilities consistent with the respective cap/floor quotes in the market is a process called *stripping*, which is similar to the bootstrap principle when constructing the YC (see 6.7). This extraction process is not exactly straightforward since caps/floors are for example not always quoted versus the same LIBOR reference (*e.g.* 3M versus 6M).

Apart from the canonical Black-76 model, the local volatility approach can also be transferred to interest rates [213, 203]. Alternatively, one can resort to a stochastic volatility model such as the SABR model [214, 215, 216, 217, 218]. The latter is effectively the industry standard volatility model in vanilla interest rates derivatives and will be briefly described below. SABR stands for 'stochastic-alpha-beta-rho model' whereby the greek letters denote the calibration parameters in the model. In the SABR model [214], the forward price is given by

$$dF_t = \sigma_t F_t^\beta dW_1 \text{ with } F(0) = f , \tag{6.33}$$

and

$$d\sigma_t = \alpha \cdot \sigma_t \cdot dW_2 \text{ with } \sigma_0 = \sigma , \tag{6.34}$$

with the correlation between the stochastic drives given as usual by $dW_1 dW_2 = \rho dt$. The parameters are bound by $\alpha \geq 0$ and $0 \leq \beta \leq 1$. The parameter ρ defines the correlation between forward and volatility, and, as usual, controls the tilt of the volatility skew/slope. α describes the curvature/convexity by means of the volatility-of-volatility. During the calibration process (*e.g.* when fitting to swaption quotes), the β parameter is often fixed first. It is advisable to observe the parameter variation and stability carefully during the calibration process since this is prone to large deviations especially for different maturities. In order to remedy this problem, the so-called dynamic SABR model was introduced [214, 219] whereby the parameters are allowed to vary. The calibrated SABR model embeds a particular volatility skew dynamics which is a function of β. This is commonly referred to as the SABR 'backbone' [214, 220] and defines how the ATM volatility moves with the forward. Hence, the discussion here is the interest equivalent of the skew dynamics section earlier (see 3.1.5). The SABR model can be calibrated such as to follow sticky strike or sticky delta dynamics or a mixture of both. However, traders tend to prefer sticky strike dynamics when calculating deltas.

It seems intuitive that caps and swaptions are related [221]. Recall that a cap is effectively just a series of options on different forward rates. Similarly, the swaption is effectively an option on a portfolio of different forward rates. The link between the two is the correlation between the individual forward rates, which is the common asset in both markets [222]. This is also why the caplet volatilities are part of the volatility cube construction in Figure 6.9.

6.13.2 Interest Rate cross-gamma

Cross-gamma was previously defined as the risk resulting from correlated derivative payouts such as basket options (see 5.3). The same mechanics is also possible in interest rate derivatives, *i.e.* one might trade a basket option on the average of different swap term rates subject to a pre-defined strike. The hedge is implementable using swaptions, and the price and cross-gamma exposure is a function of the correlation between them. Nevertheless, it is worth expanding or relaxing this particular cross-gamma definition a bit. In this sense, many people consider cross-gamma as any risk which arises due to a direct or indirect coupling between two (or more) variables. In the context of interest rates, these dynamics are, for example, possible given moves in some part of the same interest rate curve inducing delta changes in other parts. Similarly, changes in FX can induce changes in delta or basis risk. As a simple concrete example, consider a vanilla IRS where one receives fixed and pays 3m LIBOR on a floating basis. To obtain the present value of the swap, both fixed and floating cash flow streams need to be discounted to today. The discount rate is a function of the collateral and be an OIS rate for the respective currency. Hence, there is a possible mismatch between projecting future cash flows based on LIBOR and discounting those via OIS. Hence, cross gamma risk comes into play because the delta of the LIBOR IRS changes if the OIS rate moves.

6.13.3 CMS replication

Given the discussion on swaptions it is now possible to work through the replication of the CMS (see 6.10). Recall that there is a convexity difference between a vanilla IRS and its respective CMS counterpart visible in Figure 6.7 for large movements in the swap rate. The vanilla IRS is composed of a payer and receiver swaption struck at the respective swap rate. Similarly, the CMS swap is composed of a long CMS cap and a short CMS floor. The trick is now to realize that the CMS cap can be replicated with one ATM payer swaption and a *series* of OTM payer swaptions with increasing strikes to match the missing convexity gap. In similar spirit, for a long CMS floor the hedge is to go long one ATM receiver swaption and short a series of OTM receiver swaptions with decreasing strikes. This principle is illustrated in Figure 6.10. The replication [191] is model independent and achieved via (*i*) a long ATM payer and a series of long OTM payer swaptions, and (*ii*) a short ATM receiver and a series of long OTM receiver swaptions.

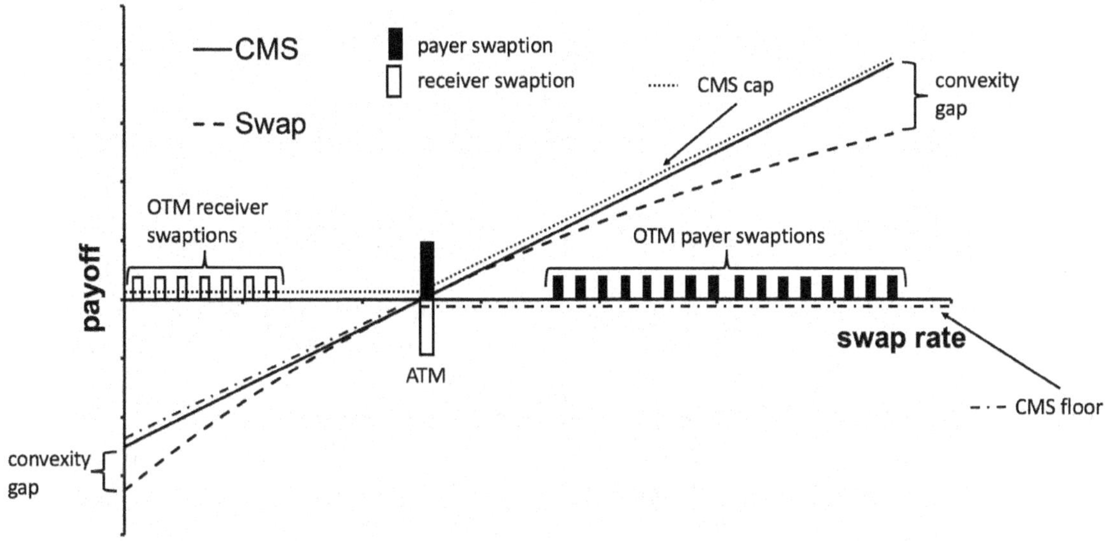

Figure 6.10: Illustration of the CMS swap (solid line) replication with a payer/receiver swaptions (solid and transparent rectangles). The CMS cap (dashed line) and floor (dashed-solid line) are also shown.

The strike weighting is chosen such as to offset the CMS dv01 along the swap rate on aggregate. Since the replication involves OTM swaptions, it is important to do the valuation with a pricing model (such as SABR above) which can fit the respective skew/wings in the implied swaption volatility accurately [192]. In the case of any model (but especially SABR), it is critical to understand how the calibration of the wing region behaves in case of large volatility moves. It is therefore not unusual to apply additional smoothing techniques in the wing regions of the SABR volatility surface.

Finally, while the swaption replication is certainly the approach which is theoretically most appealing, one can obviously also delta hedge the forward curve maturity buckets using vanilla interest rate swaps, FRAs or STIRs.

6.13.3.1 CMS options

Recall from the analysis above that the CMS caplet can be replicated using a portfolio of payer swaptions [191]. This finding can as well be translated to the replication of more complicated payouts such as CMS caps, floors or spread options for which also a correlation assumption between the two rates needs to be taken. CMS rates are naturally correlated with each other whereby closer CMS maturity rates tend to also show a higher correlation as one would intuitively expect. In the case of CMS rate behaving lognormally, the classical Black-76 framework can be used for pricing a vanilla payoff.

CMS spread options are more challenging [223] and the discussion below is admittedly not very deep. As an example, consider a 10Y-2Y call paying

$$\max[w_1 \cdot CMS_{10Y} - w_2 \cdot CMS_{2Y} - K, 0] , \tag{6.35}$$

whereby w_1, w_2 denote the respective weights. The process is given by

$$\frac{df_{CMS_1}}{f_{CMS_1}} = \mu_{CMS_1} dt + \sigma_1 (\rho dW_{CMS_1,t} + \sqrt{1-\rho^2} dW_{CMS_2,t}) \tag{6.36a}$$

$$\frac{df_{CMS_2}}{f_{CMS_2}} = \mu_{CMS_1} dt + \sigma_2 dW_{CMS_1,t} . \tag{6.36b}$$

What is intuitively required is the volatility of the 1Y-2Y and the 1Y-10Y swaption as well as an historical correlation estimate between the respective forward rates [224, 213].

Note as well that there is a natural arbitrage condition between calls on the rates and the spread options given by [225]

$$\max[r_1 - k_1, 0] - \max[r_2 - k_2, 0] \leq \max[r_1 - r_2 - k_3] \leq \max[r_1 - k_1, 0] - \max[k_2 - r_2, 0] , \tag{6.37}$$

where $k3 = k_1 - k_2$. Hence, to statically replicate the 10Y-2Y CMS spread at strike K, one can sell a call on the 10Y rate and buy a call on the 2Y rate at the corresponding strike combination which is cheapest for the package in comparison for the call on the spread.

However, the calibration of the model is challenging given requirements to be consistent between the CMS market itself, the CMS cap/floor quotes and potential CMS spread option prices. This is irrespective of whether one is using a Black-76 model, a bi-variate model, or a full-fledged multi-factor term structure representation. The simplest pricing approach is to treat the spread itself as the random variable and realize that the total variance is then given by

$$\sigma^2 = \sigma_1^2 - 2\rho \sigma_1^2 \sigma_2^2 + \sigma_2^2 , \tag{6.38}$$

whereby ρ denotes the correlation between the spread component variances [224, 226]. This parameter can then be used as an input to price the CMS spread caplet under a Bachelier (normal) process. Hence, the pricing is effectively only a function of the (flat) correlation parameter, which can be estimated from spread option quotes.

The copula approach is the most common model for pricing spread options whereby both bivariate Gaussian and t-copula models have been used [227] assuming that the spread is normal. The price is then obtained by numerical integration of the spread option payout and the probability density function joined by the copula. Alternatively, given the dependency on multiple (LIBOR) rates, one can consider resorting to a Libor market model type of valuation model [228, 229]. However, the implementation, calibration complexity and computational cost is obviously higher.

Since the modeling assumption and options above are quite diverse, it should not surprise that the pricing can be quite different. Hence, it is advisable to understand the valuation model in detail so as to gain awareness of the approximations taken.

6.13.4 Interest Rates: Steepeners and Flatteners

Steepeners and Flatteners fall into the category of yield curve spread trades. As the name implies, YC spread trades are a bet on the yield differential between two different maturities of a bond issuer such as the difference between the yield of two US treasuries of different maturity. Since this spread can go either way, there are also two instruments available. The flattener profits when the yield differential decreases or narrows. Hence, one sells the spread to put on a flattener (short front leg vs. long back leg). Conversely, the steepener profits when the yield differential increases or widens. Hence, one buys the spread to execute a steepener (long front leg vs. short back leg). Both strategies can easily be implemented by trading interest rate futures for the respective legs. Alternatively, bonds can be used, *e.g.* a flattener trader would short 2 year bonds versus a long position in 10 year bonds. Again, given the higher sensitivity of the 10 years bonds to yield changes, this strategy will in its naive implementation only work is the YC flattens without shifting higher in absolute terms as well. Assuming a delta (dv01) neutral setup between the respective front and back legs, these strategies allow to trade on the expectation of the YC slope perturbation. Note that even on a dv01 neutral trade, depending on the rate differential between the front- and back legs, flatteners and steepeners may not be carry neutral.

Steepener and flatteners can also be by based on CMS curves. For example, a steepener structure might be set up as follows

$$cpn = \min[\max[mult \cdot (CMS_{10Y} - CMS_{2Y}), floor], cap] , \qquad (6.39)$$

whereby *mult* is a leverage multiplier on the CMS spread. Hence, working inwards on the payout above, the final coupon is capped, and the spread cannot go below a floor, all of which are pre-set. Ultimately, the exposure to hedge is again a spread option.

6.13.5 Interest Rates: Spread range accrual

This section discusses IR product hedging aspects incorporating digital risk in light of real events during the 2008 EURO yield curve inversion [230, 231, 232]. The product family involved in this discussion is the so-called spread range accrual (SRAC). The SRAC is a structured swap or note which is typically referencing the spread S between 2 rates (r_1 and r_2) of the same curve such as the CMS 30Y and the CMS 2Y. At the end of a repeating observation period (e.g. each month or quarter), the payoff for this kind of CMS range accrual to the structure holder is given by

$$R \cdot \frac{n}{N} , \qquad (6.40)$$

where R is a fixed rate, n the number of days when the fixing of the reference spread $S = r_1 - r_2$ was above a pre-defined strike K, and N the total number of days in the observation period. Hence, from the seller point of view, the payoff looks like the horizontally flipped image of the digital option payoff illustrated in Figure 3.15 whereby the x-axis denotes the spread. The strike K can be zero whereby spreads such as CMS 30Y - CMS 2Y, CMS 30Y - CMS 10Y or CMS 10Y - CMS 2Y are common. The motivation for buying such as structure lies in the fact that the earned fixed rate on the range accrual is larger than the equivalent swap rate of same maturity.

For the structure seller, the risk management is relatively straightforward as long as the spread is above the strike. Similar to the discussion before on digital and barrier options, the (daily) discontinuity is decomposed into a barrier shift ε. More concretely, one is selling a cap at strike $K - \varepsilon$ and buying a cap at K, both leveraged with the factor $\frac{R}{\varepsilon}$ reflecting of the bet. In other words, the discontinuity is replicated using vanilla instruments, *i.e.*, in this case, the cap. The delta for this type of digital is as usual negative for the seller and can be hedged using swaps. Consequently, if the curve flattens and the spread gets smaller, traders will trade CMS steepeners to hedge the exposure. Above the strike, vega (and gamma) will be positive and can be hedged with swaptions. The steepener hedging activity can lead to a vicious cycle catalyzing the flattening of the yield curve further. As this happens and in case the spread falls below the strike, gamma and vega exposure reverses sign on the digital. The long gamma turns into short gamma and will, in turn, flip the delta to be positive at a time when the spreads are offered, and traders need to unwind steepeners for flatteners.

6.13.6   Interest Rates: Target Redemption Notes (TARN)

Target Redemption Notes (TARN) belong to the class of early redeemable structures (as known as autocallables), which will later also be discussed in the context of Structured Products. These structures pay a periodic coupon to the note holder whereby the structure terminates early at par if the sum of the coupons reach a pre-determined target. The coupons themselves can be structured in many ways, *e.g.* range accrual type payoffs (see above) are possible. Other possibilities are reverse floaters (also known as inverse floaters), whereby the coupon is the leveraged difference between two rates such as

$$cpn_i = \max[l_i \cdot (R_i - F_i), R_{min}] , \tag{6.41}$$

with l_i being the leverage factor, R_i a pre-set fixed rate, F_i the reference floating rate (*e.g. LIBOR or CMS* and R_{min} a minimum rate. The name reverse floater derives from the fact that the holder benefits from a decrease in the floating rate. Effectively, one is buying a fixed interest bond and selling a FRN, *i.e.* in this vanilla setup the pricing is similar to a FRN. However, the structures are often long-dated and also callable by the issuer, *e.g.* 30y total maturity, callable after 10 years. Other features involve cumulative coupons whereby the previous coupon is added to the current one. Under these conditions, it should not surprise that the pricing and hedging of these products is complex [233] whereby the exposure is typically both with respect to caplets/floorlets as well as swaptions. Hence, a jointly-calibrated multi-factor LMM model is necessary. The vega exposure can be complicated

6.14   Interest Rates: Negative Interest Rates

One fundamental issue interest rate derivative pricing had to deal with since the last financial crisis is negative rates in currencies such as EUR and CHF. Given its foundation, the Black model assumes that interest rates are strictly positive since the forward rate is a lognormally-distributed random variable [15]. Therefore, alternative volatility models such as normal volatilities and displaced diffusion volatilities were introduced.

In the normal model [234], the asset dynamics are given by

$$dS_t = \sigma_N dW_t , \tag{6.42}$$

wherein the rate may indeed become negative. The volatility σ_N used to match an observed price in the market is then called normal volatilities.

The other simple way to treat negative rates is the displaced diffusion model (DDM), which is governed by the following equation

$$dS_t = (S+b)\sigma dW_t , \tag{6.43}$$

whereby b is the so-called displacement parameter. The pricing via DDM is very similar to the Black model, which is why it is sometimes also called the shifted Black model. Both models have closed-form solutions offering fast pricing, which is why market participants were willing to subscribe to these quick fixes. Note that a similar exercise is possible for the SABR model [217] in the context of normal volatilities.

---

[15]Note that the same is true for the BSM model when *e.g.* modeling equity price diffusion

Practical Tips 6.14.1 Questions to ask your quants / risk system support:

- How is the YC constructed? Which instruments are used, how is the curve interpolated, etc.?
- YC construction: are inter-currency and cross-currency basis swap spreads replicated by the curve?
- Check whether the book is running some hidden basis risks (3M/6M) and check how cash flows are discounted (LIBOR vs OIS).
- Check how the dv01 exposure is calculated: is the system bumping the YC pointwise or is it possible to bump it by instrument exposure? The latter is computationally more expensive but often a better indicator of the exposure.
- Are there some large IR future exposures which might introduce noise because their mark-to-market adjustment is in general intraday (*i.e.* faster) than other instruments
- Is your **implied fixing**, *i.e.* the fixing suggested by the YC, in line with the actual LIBOR fixing or do you consistently lose money on the fix?
- What is the main discount curve based on (OIS or LIBOR)? In case it is LIBOR, it is not in line with current market conventions for most cases.
- Check the cash balance of the book and investigate in which currencies you are paying interest on *e.g.* posted collateral.
- Explore the price/yield/spread behavior of long-dated early redeemable fixed-income instruments with respect to potential instabilities. One crude indicator is large differences between modified duration and duration to worst.
- How is the swaption settlement modeled?
- How are spread options modeled?

7. Foreign Exchange and FX Derivatives

7.1 Introduction

All of the previous topics are typically transferable without major adjustments to other asset classes. This means that even if there are differences due to conventions or construction process discrepancies for the forward, most other concepts do apply. In the case of Foreign Exchange (FX) and FX Derivatives, most differences arise from the lack of a natural unique *numeraire* currency. The term numeraire refers to the basic standard by which a value is calculated. For equities or commodities, this unit logically refers to the underlying itself, but for FX there are multiple ways cash can be expressed in terms of exchangeable currencies.

7.1.1 Quoting convention and expiry time

The typical FX quoting convention was already introduced in the sections about Quanto and composite options (see 3.1.6). As a reminder, recall that FX rates are not typically quoted in the newspaper convention, *i.e.* one unit equivalent of a reference in all other currencies. Instead, currency pairs are quoted as **CC1CC2**, which is the number of units of CC2 (known as the domestic currency, *i.e.* the quote currency) required to buy one unit of CC1 (known as the foreign currency). The respective multiplier is then the spot rate s_t at time t. Note that precious metals such as gold, which are typically treated as currencies as well, have the same convention and are always CC1 by convention. Hence, 'XAUUSD' refers to the amount of USD to buy one unit of gold (*e.g.* one ounce). Similarly, 'USDJPY' refers to the amount of YEN to buy one USD. A spot transaction at today's rate s_0 refers to exchanging N_d units of domestic currency into N_f units of foreign currency given by

$$N_d = s_0 \cdot N_f . \tag{7.1}$$

The actual day on which the payments are made and settled is the so-called *value date*. For example, a spot transaction today with value date T+2 means settlement in two business days. Note that the concept of value date also applies to other financial instruments or contracts in general. The convention for denoting a long position in a currency (spot) trade always refers to CCY1, *i.e.* long 5m USDJPY means 5m USD has been bought and the equivalent amount of JPY sold.

For FX derivatives, four different quote conventions exist:

- domestic per foreign (d/f)
- foreign per domestic (f/d)
- percentage foreign (%f)
- percentage domestic (%d)

This is again because the numeraire is not uniquely defined. Of course, all four quoting conventions must yield the same relative price to avoid arbitrage. However, the presence of quote conventions leads also to different conventions for the underlying derivative greeks as shown in the following section.

One of the main advantages of FX markets is that they operate 24/7. This characteristic, in turn, translates to better liquidity risk profiles compared to other classes in general. However, when the market never closes, it then naturally raises the requirement to define trade inception, observation dates and expiry dates for contracts also in terms of actual date time. Those date times are so-called *cutoff times*. In general, the cutoff time is set to 3pm local time with respect to the contractually referenced trading venue. As usual, no rules without exceptions, *i.e.* for New York the cutoff time is 10am EST and for the ECB 2:15pm CET. Hence, paying attention to the cutoff time venue for a given contract is a must.

7.1.2 BSM and greeks in FX

The BSM framework is also valid in the FX world. However, there are some amendments, which are discussed as follows. First, let $V(s_t, t)$ be the value of a derivative subject to the performance for an FX rate s_t. The corresponding BSM partial differential equation is then given by

$$\underbrace{\frac{\partial V}{\partial t}}_{\Theta} + \frac{1}{2}\sigma^2 s^2 \underbrace{\frac{\partial^2 V}{\partial s^2}}_{\Gamma} + (r_d - r_f)s \underbrace{\frac{\partial V}{\partial s}}_{\Delta} - r_d V = 0 \ . \tag{7.2}$$

Hence, apart from the introduction of the foreign and domestic interest rate terms (r_f and r_d, respectively), the expression is identical. Similarly, the SDE is given by

$$ds_t = (r_{d,t} - r_{f,t})s_t dt + \sigma_t s_t dW_t \ . \tag{7.3}$$

The notion of option delta in the FX world is identical to the definition before, *i.e.* the sensitivity of the derivative price in relation to a change of the underlying price. However, given different quoting conventions for the option value (see above), there are also different conventions to express the option delta in. The *points spot delta* $\Delta_{s,pips}$ indicates the amount of foreign currency units to hold, in order to hedge an option with one unit notional of foreign currency versus K units of domestic currency. Hence, this is equivalent expressing the delta as a percentage of foreign currency.

On the other hand, the *percentage spot delta* $\Delta_{s,\%}$ denotes the change in option value in percentage foreign currency with respect to a change in percentage foreign currency spot. In other words, $\Delta_{s,\%}$ is the points spot delta adjusted for the foreign currency premium in percentage terms given by

$$\Delta_{s,\%} = \Delta_{s,pips} - V_{\%f} \ . \tag{7.4}$$

This *premium adjustment* represents the required delta correction resulting from paying the option premium in foreign currency. In a way this is analogous to the potential premium FX hedge required when trading composite options (see 3.1.6). Both conventions can also be expressed in forward terms, *i.e.* the delta references the options future/forward value ($\Delta_{F,pips}$ and $\Delta_{F,\%}$, respectively). This convention has increased in popularity given the absence of discounting necessity. A more extensive and detailed treatise on the different conventions and conversions can be found elsewhere [235, 236].

Luckily, the FX market has agreed to an overall delta convention with respect to the currency pair quote. This means that if the premium currency is in CCY2, then no premium adjustment is applied and $\Delta_{s,pips}$ is used, and the other way around.

7.1.3 FX volatility models

The main class of volatility models used in FX derivatives were already introduced earlier. From canonical BSM (strike adjusted) constant volatility approach, local volatility, stochastic volatility to local-stochastic volatility, all models are all transferable and are being used depending on the respective payout [237]. The rationale for using one model over the other is again based on determining the payout sensitivities to volatility convexity, forward skew and stochastic process dependencies (see Figure 3.28). Nevertheless, there is one method not yet mentioned which originated in the FX modeling world. The so-called vanna-volga approach [238, 239] is still sometimes used for constructing volatility surfaces given only a limited set of option quotes. What is need are three option quotes for a given maturity T: the 25% delta put and 25% call (*i.e.* risk reversal, long call / short put), the ATM straddle and the 25% delta wing butterfly (*i.e.* long OTM put / short ATM straddle / long OTM call). From the previous chapters, the reader will recognize the risk reversal as a measure of skew/smile and the butterfly as an indicator of kurtosis. The management of exotic or even OTM vanilla derivatives is highly dependent on those two sensitivities, which are of course not captured by the BSM framework explicitly. Hence, the exotic option can be thought of as the sum of the BSM price and the costs for vanna and volgamma. This is the basis of the motivation for the vanna-volga method whereby the approximations for the vanna and volgamma costs are given in the literature [239] as well as the implied volatility surface as a function of strike. Note that the vanna-volga method does often not match prices of a stochastic-local-volatility model, which is a result of not being able to fit the skew/smile consistently especially for extreme cases. Therefore, the market standard of using a stochastic volatility or stochastic-local-volatility model is clearly preferred.

7.1.4 FX correlation

Given that FX is quoted in pairs, there are constraints on the values a pair can take with respect to others. For example, if USDJPY is 100 and EURJPY is 110, then EURUSD must be 1.1. Otherwise, there is an arbitrage opportunity in the respective *triangle*. The pairing also induces another coupling, which is represented by the relation between implied volatility and correlation. In the case of a geometric Brownian diffusion process for n FX pairs given by

$$ds_t^i = (r_{d,t}^i - r_{f,t}^i)s_t^i dt + \sigma_{i,t}s_t^i dW_t^i \,, \tag{7.5}$$

with $i = 1,...,n$. Picking up on the stylized three currency pair example above and setting $s_t^1 =$ USDJPY, $s_t^2 =$ EURJPY and $s_t^3 =$ EURUSD with $s_t^1 \cdot s_t^2 = s_t^3$, one obtains for the instantaneous correlation

$$\rho_{ij,t} = \frac{\sigma_{3,t}^2 - \sigma_{1,t}^2 - \sigma_{2,t}^2}{2\sigma_{1,t}\sigma_{2,t}} \,. \tag{7.6}$$

As a consequence, correlation does not need to be estimated and the risk can be hedged directly by trading volatility.

The example above holds for triangular markets, *i.e.* for pairs which share one common currency. Hence, how to for example determine the correlation between GBPJPY and EURUSD? In order to do so, it is required to introduce more pairs from which the correlation is then inferred consistently. The process can be pictured geometrically as a four-sided tetrahedron whereby each corner represents the respective currency pair component (EUR, USD, GBP, JPY) [240]. The number of edges in the tetrahedron then correspond to the currency pairs and/or implied volatilities required (see Figure 7.1). Combinatorically, this leads to 15 correlation coefficients whereby 12 can be estimated using the triangulation method above. The correlation to be solved for (GBPJPY versus EURUSD) is the respective pair of $\rho_{3,4}$ within Figure 7.1 and is given by

$$\rho_{3,4} = \frac{\sigma_1^2 + \sigma_6^2 - \sigma_2^2 - \sigma_5^2}{2\sigma_3\sigma_4} . \tag{7.7}$$

It follows that this method is only applicable if there is a large enough market between the required currency pairs.

While the approach above appears to solve a major estimation problem, it insinuates that FX pairs trade only with one implied volatility (per expiry). Hence, it does not take the volatility smile into account and is therefore not *a priori* suitable for pricing payouts which are sensitive to the smile. The extension to a multi-factor setting is then equally involved as in other asset classes. In other words, the model needs to fit the market for both spot FX rates (*e.g.* $s_1 = CCY1/CCY2$ and $s_2 = CCY1/CCY3$) and the cross-rates (*i.e.* $s_3 = CCY2/CCY3 = s_2/s_1$) while preserving the above-mentioned triangulation symmetries. One such model within the Heston family is reported in the literature [241]. Unfortunately, the calibration for a pure stochastic volatility model such as the multi-factor Heston is very challenging. As a remedy, the same authors present a Heston local correlation model [242] based on a previous single-factor implementation [114], which offers better calibration properties. While the further analysis and technical discussion of these models is beyond the scope of this book, it should be clear that the investment in modeling and calibration is far from trivial.

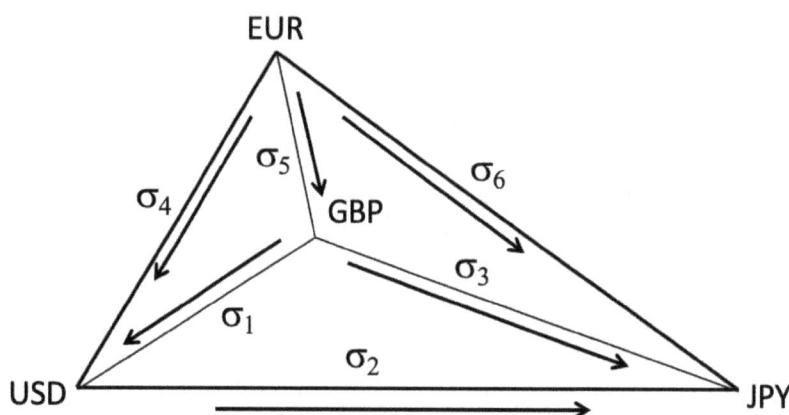

Figure 7.1: Illustration of the FX tetrahedron used to derive correlation between pairs with uncommon currencies.

7.1.5 FX carry

It is possible to discuss carry trades also in the context of interest rates, but given the embedded FX risk the topic is discussed here. The principle of a *carry trade* refers to earning the interest differential between two currency rates, *e.g.* USD versus BRL. In other words, one buys the currency with the higher rate and sells the lower rate to earn the differential. In its simplest implementation, this strategy can be executed by trading the respective forward. Recall that if the exchange rate at time t is given by s_t and the forward rate by f, then the payoff at forward expiry is $S_T - f$ with

$$f = s_0 \cdot \exp((r_d - r_f))T \ . \tag{7.8}$$

The equation above is the risk-neutral forward rate, which does not necessarily need to reflect the spot price in the future. Hence, if an investor believes that the spot will remain at the current level irrespective of the forward interest rate differential, then the transaction makes sense. Note that based on uncovered interest parity (UIP) [243], the low yielding currency should depreciate to account for the rate differential. As a consequence, if an investor borrows USD to buy the higher yielding currency (*i.e.* BRL in the example above), it is clear that one is exposed to USDBRL FX risk until the loan is repaid. An alternative implementation is to trade an ATM forward call- or put(-spread) depending on whether the current spot is above or below the forward. Carry trades often belong to the category of investments which work great until they don't [244]. Hence, small carry P/L gains over calm markets may suddenly be wiped out in a few days following a large dislocation. This does not qualify interest rate carry as a bad investment but illustrates that the risk management needs to be active.

7.1.6 FX swap

The foreign exchange swap is similar to a cross-currency swap (see 6.11.3) in terms of conventions. The FX swap exchanges a FX spot and a FX forward, both of which are agreed on at trade inception. For example, in a EURUSD swap one buys spot / sells forward EUR 3m versus USD 10m with 5 (forward) points [1] and a spot of 1.15. This means that on the spot date one receives EUR 10m EUR and pays 11.5m USD. At spot plus 3 months, one pays back EUR 10m and receives USD $(1.15 + 0.0005) \cdot 10m = 12.505m$. The FX swap is effectively a trade on the interest rate differential since the amounts paid and received offset the FX exposure almost perfectly. The spot part is called the *near leg* and the forward part the *far leg*.

7.1.7 Power-reverse dual-currency (PRDC) options

Power-reverse dual-currency (PRDC) options and its variation make up a large portion of the exotic FX derivative market. Originally introduced in 1995 [245], these derivatives are effectively interest rate carry instruments. The structure pays a series of coupons over a time interval $t \in t_0, ..., T$ if a pre-defined future exchange rate is closer the current spot versus the forward given by

$$cpn_i = \alpha_i \cdot \max\left[N_d\left(\frac{s_{T_i}}{s_0} cpn_f - cpn_d \right), 0 \right] , \tag{7.9}$$

where α denotes the accrual period (annual, semi-annual etc.), N_d is the notional in domestic currency, and cpn_f and cpn_d (with $cpn_f > cpn_d$) is the coupon in foreign and domestic currency,

---

[1]The forward points are sometimes also referred to as swap points.

respectively. The equation can be rewritten as

$$cpn_i = \alpha_i \cdot \frac{N_d cpn_f}{s_0} \max \left[s_{T_i} - s_0 \frac{cpn_d}{cpn_f} \right] . \tag{7.10}$$

Hence, this is a strip of call and put options. The coupons are financed against a domestic interest rate, whereby the investor receives the coupons in foreign currency. Historically, the canonical currency pair for these structures has been USDJPY, *i.e.* for an initial fixing $s_0 = 110$ the investor benefits linearly if the JPY depreciates further against the USD or if USDJPY does not decrease. Note that the power coupon payout is typically also capped at a certain level, which then turns the option into a short call spread instead of a call for the option seller. Short call spread means that the trader is short the USDJPY (ATM) call and long the upside cap. Hence, there is not only vega but also skew exposure, which was clearly visible in the USDJPY option market for years. The problem is as well that the structures tend to be very long dated, *e.g.* 10 years or above. However, the assumption of constant interest rates over this long time is very risky. In other words, the USD and JPY rates need to be modeled stochastically using for example a Vasicek type of model (see 2.1.5). This has led to the so-called three-factor modelling approach whereby the FX rate is treated as lognormal and the interest rates driven by one-factor Gaussian processes. However, in order to treat the FX skew risk properly more sophisticated models are required [246, 247]. Variants of PRDCs include target redemption structures, which can redeem/terminate early. These derivatives will be discussed later in the context of Structured Products in more detail (see 9.1.7). In summary, the risk components on these structures are fairly diverse ranging from FX smile/skew risk, correlation between interest rates and the skew of the implicit interest rate option (*i.e.* swaption) component. Hence, a careful investigation of the modeling assumptions is warranted.

8. Commodities & Commodity Derivatives

8.1 Introduction

Commodities differ from many other asset classes in that they are often physical entities that can also be physically delivered. Physicality implies a production lifecycle as well as storage requirements, which is why the commodity forward is modeled differently compared to other asset classes (see 2.1.4). Commodities can be classified in the following groups:

- Grains: corn, wheat, rice
- Oil and meal: soybean
- Livestock: beef, pork, poultry
- Food: cocoa, coffee, sugar
- Textile: cotton
- Forestry: lumber, pulp/paper
- Metals: gold, silver, copper, aluminum
- Energy: crude oil, gasoline

Given the inherent dependency on the production cycle, commodities require arguably more macroeconomic product knowledge compared to other asset classes. The requirement of specialist knowledge within each commodity sub-domain also means that this chapter only scratches the surface and is by far not a complete synthesis of the respective topics. As a consequence, some fields such as carbon trading, weather derivatives, or network bandwidth trading are not discussed at all. However, most of the principles from the earlier chapters can be applied with only small adaptions.

The list above provides a coarse classification of various commodities. Similar to trading sectors in equities, the respective markets often require specialist knowledge as well as a sound understanding of macroeconomic and geopolitical relations. Precious metals and their derivatives such as gold are often classified as FX products and can be priced using very similar approaches. What is also identical is that the respective implied volatility parameterization is done by deltas and not absolute strikes. Base metals are often known for their coupling to the economic cycle whereby especially copper often serves as a price gauge for the global economic sentiment [248]. The rationale is that as demand for base metals increases given more economic activity, prices will naturally rise and vice versa. Crude oil, natural gas, and coal make up the core group of energy commodities. Similar to copper, the demand for crude oil is often a proxy for future economic activity. The major crude oil future/forward contracts are West Texas Intermediate (WTI) and Brent, whereby the former is referenced to a physical shipment point in Cushing/Oklahoma in the United States. This region is a convenient location for many pipelines connecting oilfields in the Gulf coast with consumers in North America. Brent is named after an oilfield of the coast of Scotland in Europe. Finally, energy power is also directly traded as electricity. Electricity differs from the other energy commodities in that it cannot be effectively stored in inventories despite progress in battery technology. This constraint suggests that spot and forward markets are often very decoupled. The spot market often exhibits large spikes and is therefore often modeled using a jump-diffusion process [249].

8.1.1 Commodity forward

Similar to FX derivatives, a sound understanding of the forward is critical to trading this asset class. Therefore, some definitions from the section on asset forwards (see 2.1.4) will be repeated and extended.

The commodity basis risk is defined as the difference between the spot price S_t and the forward/future price $F_T(t)$ between the respective time interval $[t...T]$ given by

$$basis_{t,T} = S_t - F_T(t) \, . \tag{8.1}$$

Only approximately 1% of futures contracts are delivered physically, which is then denoted by an exchange for the physical agreement which specifies the location and price of the delivered asset. Otherwise, the future/forward contract is cash settled or rolled before expiry. The forward price $f_T(t)$ for expiry T is related to the spot price via

$$f_T(t) = S_t \exp[(r - y)(T - t)] \, , \tag{8.2}$$

whereby y denotes the *convenience yield* [250] on the commodity if it is storable (a notable exception being electricity). The form of the equation above is equivalent to the equity spot-forward relation whereby the dividend yield replaces the convenience yield. The convenience yield is typically split into two components

$$y = y_b - c \, , \tag{8.3}$$

whereby y_b denotes the benefit of holding the asset and c the storage cost. Note that y_b is negative for the holder of a forward contract since there is no benefit until the actual physical delivery. The whole forward curve across all maturities T is then given by [251]

$$f_T(t) = S_t \exp[(r + c - y_b)(T - t)] \, . \tag{8.4}$$

In the case that the exponent above is negative, the curve slopes downwards and is said to be in *backwardation*. The opposite shape is called *contango*. Hence, if potential supply shortages due to structural reasons or geopolitical conflict (*e.g.* military conflict in the middle east) arise, the forward curve goes into backwardation. The expression above assumes a time-invariant convenience yield. However, this is not realistic if seasonal effects [252] play a role. As a consequence, when taking these observations as well as structural supply/demand constraints into account, the forward modeling becomes more complicated (see for example [253]). Alternatively, in the case of predictive seasonal effects (*e.g.* natural gas in winter given the demand for heating), the forward curves can be de-seasonalized. The simplest way of de-seasonalizing a forward curve is to apply some moving average regression [252, 24].

8.1.2 Stochastic Process

The construction of a forward does not yet allow for the valuation of commodity derivatives on its own. Hence, a stochastic process is required that appropriately describes the underlying dynamics. The BSM framework is only applicable to the pricing of *spot* commodity options *if* the underlying GBM process represents the spot price evolution appropriately. This decision is typically a function of the lifetime of the option in the sense that it effectively assumes that the convenience yield is constant.

The classic approach to pricing commodity contracts is the Black-76 model [38], which applies to the price of one underlying future $f_T(t)$. It follows a driftless lognormal process given by

$$df_T(t) = \sigma f_T(t)dW_t \ . \tag{8.5}$$

Given the mark-to-market mechanics for futures, it makes sense that this P/L implicitly covers for the absence of the drift term. Recall that the Black-76 model is also widely used for pricing vanilla interest rate derivatives such as caplets, floorlets or swaptions (see 6.13.1 and 6.13, respectively).

Contrary to equities, commodity prices do not grow or decline over time as their dynamics is often more characterized by a mean reversion process. The non-stationary Black-76 model does not incorporate these dynamics and is therefore only an approximation, but in many situations the model converges to the same price [254] as mean reversion process models which are discussed next. The canonical approach to modeling mean reversion in finance is the already mentioned Ornstein-Uhlenbeck process [110]. Within the commodity world one key model is the two-factor Gibson-Schwartz process [255] given by

$$\frac{dS}{S} = (r - y_t) \cdot dt + \sigma_S dW_t^S \ , \tag{8.6}$$

with

$$dy_t = (\kappa(\theta - y_t) - \sigma_y)dt + \sigma_y dW_t^y \ , \tag{8.7}$$

and

$$dW_t^S \cdot dW_t^y = \rho dt \ . \tag{8.8}$$

In the equations above, the reader will recognize the same parameterization as in the Heston stochastic volatility model, *i.e.* κ being the mean-reversion speed and θ, in this case, the long-term value of the convenience yield. Similar to Heston, the model is not market complete as the two stochastic drivers cannot be hedged with the same underlying. The model was initially proposed for the oil market but can be applied to other seasonal commodity time series as well.

A mathematically equivalent two-factor model was introduced by Gabillon [256] whereby the future spot price is mean reverting to a long term average L_t following log-normal diffusion as well. The dynamics is given by

$$\frac{dS}{S} = \kappa \ln(\frac{L_T}{S_t}) \cdot dt + \sigma_S dW_t^S \ , \tag{8.9}$$

with

$$\frac{dL_t}{L_t} = \mu_L dt + \sigma_L dW_t^L \ . \tag{8.10}$$

One key advantage in this approach is that it is not required to model the convenience yield dynamics as it is capture implicitly by the coupling between the short- and long-term price dynamics. The forward price is then given by

$$F_T(t) = A_T(t) S_t^{B_T(t)} L_t^{1-B_T(t)} \, , \qquad (8.11)$$

with

$$A_T(t) = \exp[\frac{1}{4\kappa}(\sigma_S^2 + \sigma_L^2 - 2\rho_{S,L}\sigma_S^2\sigma_L^2) B_T(t)(1 - B_T(t))] \, , \qquad (8.12)$$

and

$$B_T(t) = \exp[-\kappa(T-t)] \, . \qquad (8.13)$$

The model can also be extended to incorporate the option market volatility smile [257] to provide a more realistic representation for path-dependent derivatives.

Finally, it should not surprise anymore that effectively all previously discussed models can also be translated to the commodity world. Whether local volatility [258], Heston stochastic volatility [259] or local stochastic volatility [260] there is no principle reason why any of those approaches might not apply to modeling the price and volatility dynamics of path-dependent commodity derivative.

8.1.3 Volatility surface

While equity option strikes are often skewed to the left (see 2.22), commodity options are often skewed to the right, especially in the context of energy derivatives. In other words, market participants often consider the impact of a price increase riskier compared to a decline. For example, a supply disruption can cause a massive price spike which justifies the shape of the surface. This phenomenon effectively the inverse implied leverage effect compared to the equity market.

8.1.4 Spread Options

Spread options were already discussed in the context of interest rate derivatives (see 6.13.3.1) and are given by the generic difference

$$S_1(t) - S_2(t) - K = s(t) - K \, , \qquad (8.14)$$

where $s(t)$ denotes the spread at time t. However, these derivatives are also frequently used in commodity markets [261] whereby the spread can refer to differences in the prices of the same commodity at two different locations (location spreads), or between the prices of the same commodity at two different points in time (calendar spreads), or between the prices of inputs to, and outputs from, a production process (processing spreads), as well as between the prices of different grades of the same commodity (quality spreads) [261]. There are also various exchange-listed spread options between e.g. heating oil / crude oil and gasoline / crude oil crack spreads. Crack spreads are spreads between crude oil and refined oil products, e.g. gasoline. The gasoline crack spread is for example given by the difference in the gasoline price and the crude oil price.

A special case for spread options is the case for which the strike is zero, i.e. $K = 0$. This so-called Margrabe option assumes log-normal dynamics for both underlyings (S_1, S_2), and has then an analytical solution [262]. In the case of $K \neq 0$, various approximations exist [263, 264, 265], but some of them (such as the Kirk approximation) are not very good for low strikes (i.e. close to

ATM). Moreover, all of these approximations will typically not take into account the volatility or correlation smile/skew [266]. Especially for high correlation, the impact of the volatility surface is not negligible. Hence, it is advised to compare the approximate price with a full-fledged Monte Carlo simulation using a richer volatility model [266] or even a jump diffusion process [267].

Finally, a brief discussion on the relationship between correlation and vega for spread options. While the spread option will always gain value in the case that the spread volatility increases, the overall vega can go down as a function of the correlation and individual volatilities of the components. This generic relationship is given by [268]

$$\frac{\sigma^2_{spread}}{\sigma^2_1} = S^2_1 - \rho \frac{\sigma_2 S_1 S_2}{\sigma_1} \, . \tag{8.15}$$

The equation above shows the coupling between of the spread variance and the individual volatilities (in this case shown for asset S_1). In order for the spread variance to decrease, the second term requires a positive correlation and $\rho \frac{\sigma_2}{\sigma_1} \frac{S_2}{S_1} > 1$. This also means that while the delta hedge of the spread option is relatively straightforward, hedging the vega can be very path-dependent.

8.1.5 Swing Options

Swing options are derivatives on which the contract volume can vary. For example, the buyer of a swing option agrees to buy a fixed amount of crude oil (base amount) and has an option to raise or decrease the required quantity (swing) within a preset limit for the agreed strike price. A swing contract with M days to expiry would allow the holder to exercise $m \leq M$ swings at a rate of one per day. If $m = M$, the pricing is equivalent to a strip of m European options with corresponding strikes and maturities. If $m < M$, then the pricing reflects an optimal exercise problem equivalent to pricing m early exercise options. For $m = 1$, the price is an American option. Hence, the swing option lies between a European and American option. It is recommended to value these option using least-squares Monte Carlo [269, 270]

8.1.6 Commodity swap

The commodity swap exchanges the floating commodity price against a pre-determined fixed price. The settlement difference can be either on a periodic basis or at expiry. The long swap position then pays the difference of a future fixing $f_{fix,i}$ versus the strike given by

$$V_i = f_{fix,i} - K \, , \tag{8.16}$$

whereby the value V_0 of the swap today is the discounted risk-neutral expectation of the sum of the n fixings as

$$V_0 = df \cdot \mathbf{E} \left[\frac{1}{n} \sum_{i=1}^{n} V_i \right] \, . \tag{8.17}$$

Commodity swaptions are analogous to IR swaptions in that they offer the holder the option to enter in a forward swap [271]. Similarly, a long position in the swaption reflects the right to pay the fixed price, *i.e.* the payer swaption is equivalent to a call on the underlying swap given by

$$V_{payer,t_0} = \max[V_{float,t_0} - V_{fixed,t_0}, 0] \, , \tag{8.18}$$

whereby V_{float} and V_{fixed} denote the floating or fixed values of the swap. This difference is given by the average of the sum of the forward future prices, which needs to be modeled as a stochastic process.

9. Structured Products

9.1 Introduction

In most of the context in this book, Structured Products (SP) refer to securitized investment products containing vanilla or exotic derivatives. This is a very different market compared to more complex securitized structured credit or asset-backed securities. SP exist for the purpose and suitability of retail and institutional investors alike. Effectively almost any kind of payout can be embedded into a Structured Note, *i.e.* these instruments are very flexible. In general, a (retail) structured product contains an interest rate (bond) and an option component. The leading promise of the SP industry has typically been that these products facilitate yield enhancement on client portfolios during times when markets are range-bound, upward trending or only modestly bearish [272]. Hence, unless markets crash hard and fast, SP can provide a yield pick-up versus traditional buy-and-hold or even actively managed portfolios. To be fair, the literature evidence for this promise is still outstanding [273, 274] and market timing is not necessarily easier compared to traditional investments.

In the canonical SP setup, the client buys a structured note at 100% times the invested notional plus a markup/issuance fee. The cash is transferred to the issuer, which emits the note and transfers the embedded optionality to the trading desk to hedge (see Figure 9.1). Note that since there is a net cash inflow for the issuer from the client, SP have also characteristics of funding vehicles. Hence, in addition to earning money on the issuance markup, the bank can raise (committed) funding outside conventional channels. Whether a particular SP cash inflow qualifies as a potential long-term funding source is typically a discussion between the treasury and the trading desk.

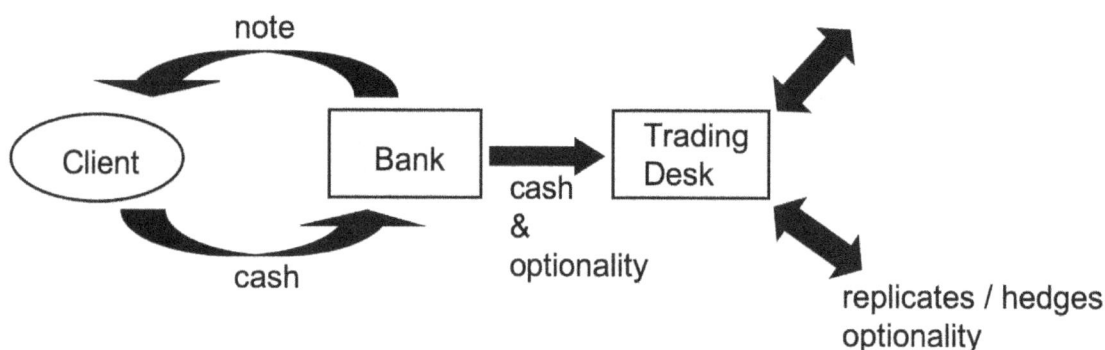

Figure 9.1: Illustration of Structured Product cash flows following issuance.

9.1.1 Structured Products Markets

One can distinguish three main markets for SPs: Europe, US and Asia. These markets are quite different on the retail investor side, both in terms of willingness to take risk as well as average trade maturity:

(*i*) **Europe**: main products are barrier reverse convertibles and trigger-redeemable notes; investors are rather risk-averse; average trade duration beyond 1 year.

(*ii*) **USA**: structured products market not as large since many investors hold equity already; products sold are typically reverse convertibles; average trade duration beyond 1 year.

(*iii*) **Asia**: investors are willing to take risk and switch positions quickly; large market for trigger-redeemable notes; average trade duration below 1 year.

9.1.2 Structured Products: Evolution

The Structured Products market has by now undergone various innovation cycles, resulting in approximately four product generations. Those four generations are:

- **1st generation Structured Products**
  capital protected notes: mountain-range products (*e.g.* Himalaya), rainbow, minimum coupon cliquet, worst-of forward
  non-capital protected notes: reverse convertibles

- **2nd generation Structured Products**
  capital protected notes: cheap compounding cliquet, podium, minimum lookback cliquet, reverse put cliquet, top rank call, ICB, certificate plus

- **3rd generation Structured Products**
  worst-of target redemption, trigger redeemable, callable notes

- **4th generation Structured Products**
  volatility products, leveraged notes, bespoke dispersion trades, implied versus realized skew 'arbitrage', tail event capture

The most commonly traded structures today are many variants of (barrier) reverse convertibles and trigger redeemable / autocalls. Both product classes may from time to time have a significant impact on the volatility market due to hedging activity. Note that some exotic options embedded in Structured Products have already been discussed in previous chapters (*e.g.* cliquets 3.1.10, double-no-touch 3.1.9.6). Therefore, the reader is also referred to the analysis presented there.

9.1.3 Structured Products: Mountain-range option Himalaya

Mountain-range options are a class of structured products on an underlying asset basket. The structures often aim to lock in the individual performance peaks over time so that the overall performance ideally resembles the 'skyline' of a mountain range. The large variety of these structures makes a generic analysis impossible. Moreover, risk sensitivities may vary significantly as a function of the specific payout. Therefore, the following analysis illustrates the issues by a more thorough analysis of the Himalaya payout and its variations. Nonetheless, in general, when faced with a mountain-range type of payout, one can assume that the structure is at inception long correlation, long volatility and short dividends from the note holder point of view.

As an example of mountain-range options, the Himalaya structure is considered. The Himalaya is a capital protected product containing a basket of underlyings. The capital protection is achieved by investing the cash from the client into a (zero coupon) bond equivalent to the maturity of the product. The present value of the bond deposit is subsequently used to purchase optionality, *i.e.* in this case, the payout of the Himalaya. The canonical Himalaya payout is the sum of the weighted performances of the respective *best* performing asset in each observation period, after which the asset is *removed* from the basket (see Figure 9.2). Note that performances can also be negative.

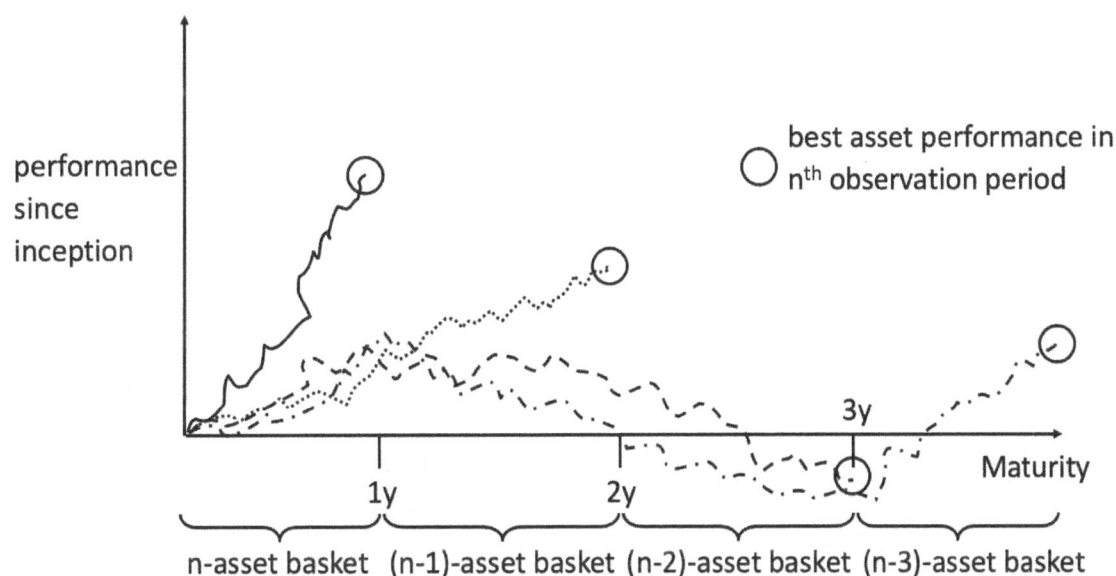

Figure 9.2: Illustration of Himalaya mechanism: each year the best performing asset will be removed from the basket.

The recorded performance in the respective observation periods can, however, take various forms, which determines the correlation sensitivity of the payout. Three cases can be distinguished

- global floor: $\max[\text{floor}_{\text{global}}, \sum_{i=1}^{N}(\frac{S_{n(i),t_i}}{S_{n(i),t_0}} - 1)]$
- global floor and local floor: $\max[\text{floor}_{\text{global}}, \sum_{i=1}^{N} \max[\text{floor}_{\text{local}}, (\frac{S_{n(i),t_i}}{S_{n(i),t_0}} - 1)]]$
- global floor, local floor and local cap:

$$\max[\text{floor}_{\text{global}}, \textstyle\sum_{i=1}^{N} \max[\text{floor}_{\text{local}}, \min[cap, (\tfrac{S_{n(i),t_i}}{S_{n(i),t_0}} - 1)]]]$$

The correlation risk and its hedging is very dependent on the specific form of the Himalaya (see Figure 9.3). While the global floor implies long correlation, the exposure is almost flat for the others. A very similar profile can be observed when plotting the vega against the correlation (not shown), *i.e.* the vega of the global floor Himalaya is increasing with a rising correlation.

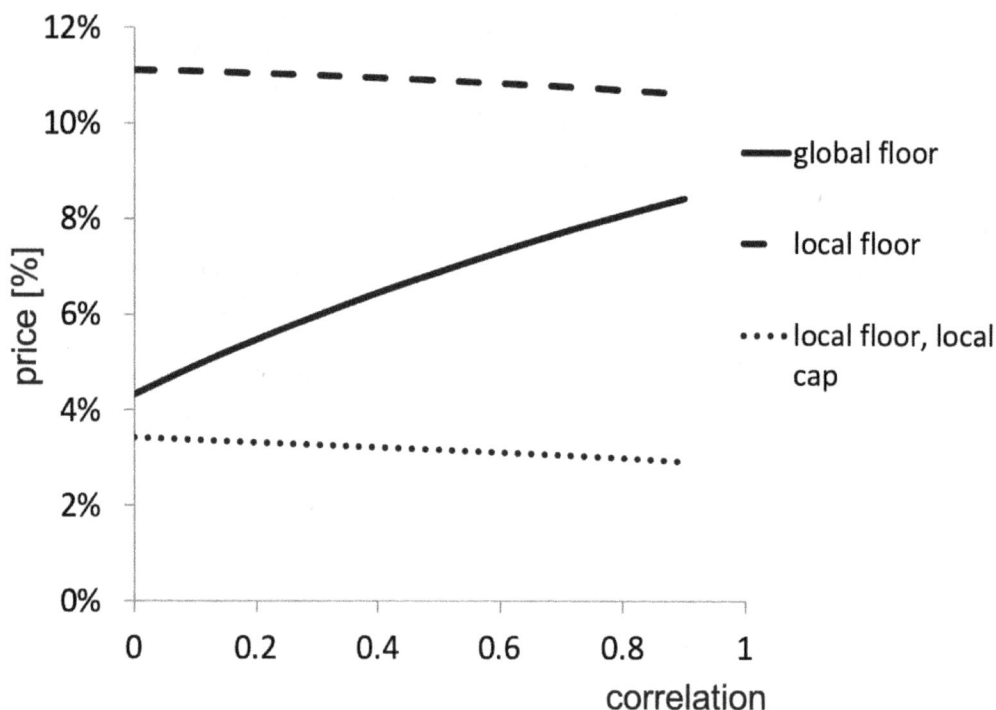

Figure 9.3: Illustration of Himalaya correlation exposure as a function of the payoff (4y maturity, 5 assets, ATM strike): Global floor (solid line), local floor (dashed line) and local floor / local cap (dotted line).

The volatility model used for pricing Himalayas is typically local volatility since the structure does not carry much volgamma. Another subtle issue for the Himalaya can be the scenario for which two stocks with very different volatilities compete for the best. For example, consider two assets with implied volatilities of 20% and 50% competing for the best performer close to the observation date. If the low volatility asset drops from the remaining basket, the price of the option drops significantly compared to the other scenario.

9.1.4 Structured Products: Rainbow structures

Rainbow structures are a generic description for classes of products for which the payout is the sum of the non-equally weighted individual performances. Therefore, these structures show similarities to basket options, which are, however, typically equally weighted. However, because of the non-equal weighting, the rainbow structure may ultimately behave more similar to a best-of or worst-of option. Clearly, with decreasing weight dispersion, the rainbow risk sensitivity converges to the equivalent (equally weighted) basket option. Note that the rainbow payout was previously also discussed in the context of smoothing out cross-gamma exposure (see section 5.3.6). The generic rainbow call/put payout takes the following form

$$\max[0, (r' - K) \cdot \phi] , \tag{9.1}$$

with $r' = \frac{1}{M} \sum_{i=1}^{M} r_{t_i}$, $r_{t_i} = \sum_{j=1}^{N} w_{\mathrm{rank}_j}$ and $\phi = +/-1$ for a call or put, respectively.

For example, the weights on a three component rainbow could be 70% for the best, 20% 2nd best and 10% for the worst performance (note that some of the performance weights can be zero). Rainbow options typically exhibit correlation skew and cross-gamma switches during the lifetime. Often, the inherent problem on rainbow structures is the impossibility of a conservative (constant) correlation mark. For example, consider a call on the second worst of three stocks, *i.e.* weights are: 0%, 100% and 0%, respectively. Now, consider the scenario depicted in Figure 9.4. Since the rankings may change during the lifetime, it is impossible to know which pairs to bid/offer the correlation at inception or even during the trade.

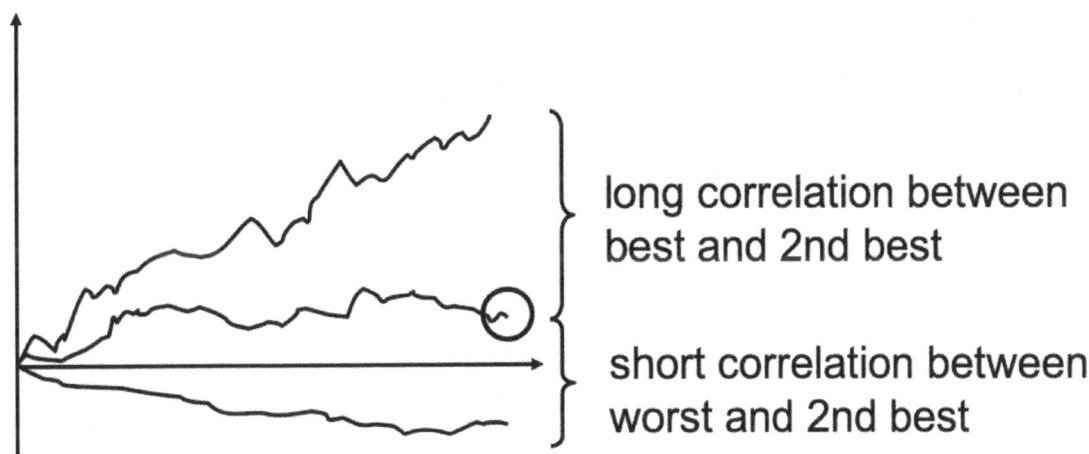

Figure 9.4: Illustration of a rainbow call on the second worst performing asset.

Nevertheless, there are some general rules which related the number of components in the basket, the correlation and the volatility to the expectation value of the worst performing asset. The worst-of expectation value decreases with increasing basket components, decreases with increasing volatility and increases with increasing correlation.

9.1.5 Structured Products: Accumulator

The Accumulator structure [275] allows the purchase of shares at a pre-determined strike, which is below the spot price at inception. Today, these are still popular structures in Asia. In its purest form, the bank will, until maturity (*e.g.* 1 year), deliver daily a specified number of shares on a particular stock at a pre-determined strike price to the client contingent on an upper barrier not being breached by the spot. The latter results in early termination of the trade whereby the so far delivered shares are settled. This also explains why these structures are often called Knock Out Discount Accumulators (KODA), *i.e.* one accumulates shares at a discount until a potential early termination. Hence, as long as the stock trades above the strike, the buyer makes a profit (see Figure 9.5). Accumulators have been in the middle of some controversy whereby retail investors suffered large losses after stock prices declined below the discount levels following the maturity of the structure. As a consequence, the structures became also known as the 'I kill you later' derivatives.

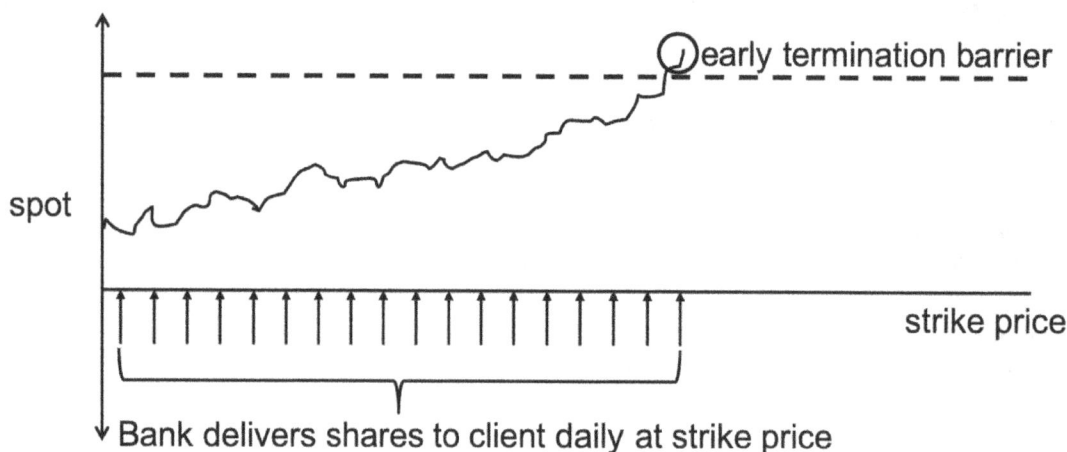

Figure 9.5: Illustration of the canonical share Accumulator structure.

The risk sensitivity is relatively easy to understand:

- The buyer/seller is long/short delta
- The buyer/seller is short/long dividends; in case the settlement is not daily but *e.g.* monthly the contract needs to specify *exactly* who is entitled to the dividends on purchased but not yet delivered shares
- The buyer/seller is net short/long volatility

One way to view the structure is to consider it as a long/short position in a call-spread / put-spread. There exist many variations of this structure, including leveraging the purchase on the upside/downside or ceasing the purchase in case a specific downside barrier is breached (*i.e.* to floor the loss). The opposite structure (decumulator) exists as well, which allows a large shareholder to gradually decrease their holding at a fixed price over a certain amount of time. While some analytical approximations exists [276], it is recommended to resort to a Monte Carlo implementation.

9.1.6 Structured Products: Barrier reverse convertible

The (barrier) reverse convertible is composed of a bond and an embedded put. The put is typically struck ATM and activated on the downside (*e.g.* 60% of ATM spot) via an American barrier. Hence, this is nothing else but the previously discussed American knock-in put (see Section 3.1.9.5). The client typically sells the put to the issuer and is compensated by a (periodic) coupon stream until maturity of the note. In case of no activation of the downside put or an OTM put, the settlement redeems the note at 100%. In case there is an activated ITM put, the settlement at maturity can then either be in shares ('physical') or cash. In the case of the former, any fractional share amount are paid out in cash [1]. In this sense, the payout resembles a synthetic (mandatory) convertible bond (see Chapter 10 later). Hence, the investor risks that the cash investment converts into the asset if the price

---

[1]Note that in the case of a Quanto (barrier) reverse convertible with physical delivery, the potential physical delivery share amount calculation will involve the FX rate at a pre-defined time on the final fixing date (FX_T). The number of shares is then determined as $N_{shares} = $ Note nominal value$/$strike $\cdot FX_T$

breaches the barrier and the put activates. In the FX market, the similar structure is a dual currency deposit/investment (DCD / DCI). Here the investor deposits money in a primary currency for a fixed term and receives an enhanced coupon above market. However, the risk is that the notional converts to a secondary currency at expiry. This conversion is whatever currency is cheaper for the bank to deliver at this point.

Despite the seemingly trivial payout and structure, managing a large barrier reverse convertible book can be challenging. Irrespective of the potential gap risk upon hitting a barrier, the volatility convexity and (theta) carry of the book can be painful. If multi-factor exposure is added via worst-of knock-in puts (see Section 5.3.5.2), the situation does not get more comfortable due to the inherent difficulties of dynamically hedging the embedded worst-of forward exposure.

Traders who claim that managing these type of exposures is trivial are often either only managing a small book and/or benefit from continuous issuance flow so that potential carry losses are mitigated/hidden. It is therefore essential to monitor the carry of a SP trading book closely to understand where any P/L is potentially leaking.

9.1.7   Structured Products: Trigger Redeemable / Autocall

Trigger Redeemable / Autocall structures terminate/redeem early at par plus a coupon in case the underlying asset(s) breach a particular pre-defined barrier. This barrier event is typically on the upside and observed periodically (*e.g.* yearly). The fundamental reason why these trades work is that the expectation value for a trigger event decays rapidly with time (see Figure 9.6). In other words, the upside optionality can be bought cheaply since the expectation value of the trade lifetime until maturity is very high. This matter is further amplified in the case of a low forward, *e.g.* generated through stocks with a high dividend yield or commodities which are in strong backwardation.

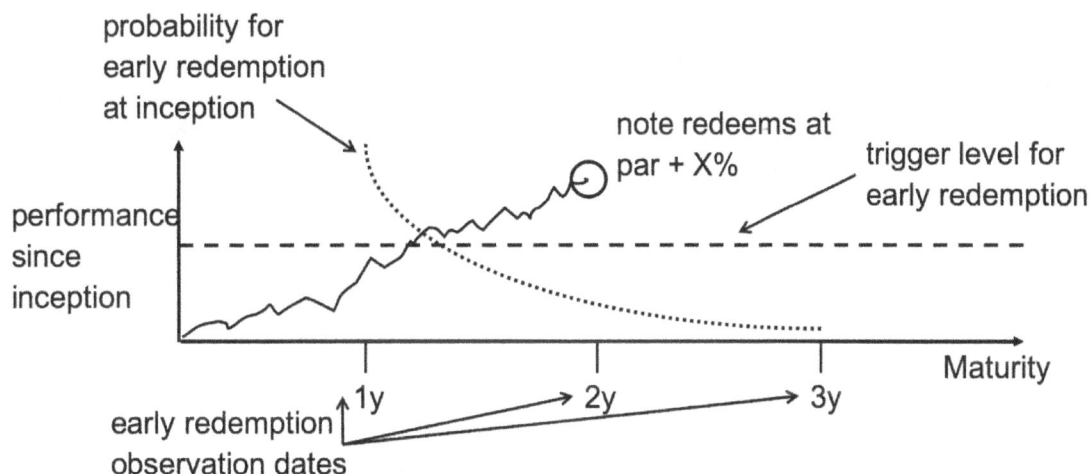

Figure 9.6: Illustration of the trigger redeemable mechanics and redemption probability.

Autocall structures will very often also contain a downside (knock-in barrier) put, which the client is selling. This premium, in turn, is used to finance the upside again partially. Hence, in its most canonical form, the bank is effectively buying a downside put and selling an upside call-spread from/to the client.

There are three main hedging issues with autocallable products:

(*i*) interest rate / equity (IR/EQ) correlation
(*ii*) volatility convexity
(*iii*) spot / volatility correlation inversion

The last two points are somewhat related and may create a vicious cycle, especially when risk limits for operators are tight. As the market moves down, the downside put gains in vega, causing traders to re-hedge by selling vega to maintain a neutral position. This hedging activity can consequently cause volatility to decrease even more, which leads to unusual spot down / volatility down dynamics. Hence, suddenly spot and volatility moves become positively correlated [2]. Similar dynamics are possible in sharp rallies: The downside puts lose vega and reduce the necessity for hedging. As a consequence, the skew steepens, and volatility rises. This trend is enforced in the case of products redeeming early. These dynamics are well known in the industry and have been observed several times [277]. In recent years, dealers have tried to offload some of vega exposure by trading corridor variance swap set in line with the autocall and downside barriers. The corridor refers to the range within which the underlying must trade to keep the swap active. While this sounds good for range-bound markets, trading desks are faced with a vega mismatch in case the autocall gets called and the hedge still remains on the book. In order to remedy this problem, an up-and-out barrier at the autocall trigger level is typically added to the corridor variance so that the hedge disappears in line with the source risk [278] in case the market rallies. Unfortunately, the addition of the additional knock-out barrier leads to model-dependency in the pricing even if the dynamics and replication of the product can be decomposed into a strip of barrier options [143].

The other issue with trigger redeemables is the IR / EQ correlation exposure for the seller of the note. Recall that the redemption date of these trades is not fixed at inception, but rather a function of the underlying asset performance. Reconsider the case from before in Figure 9.7, *i.e.* a four year maturity trade with yearly observation dates.

The IR exposure at inception is distributed along the observation dates as a function of the expected early redemption probabilities at those points. To hedge, the trader buys ZCBs with *decreasing* notional as a function of the autocall maturity.

Assume that spot levels move up. As a consequence:

• the probability for triggering early *increases*
• the trader needs to shift more of the ZCB exposure to the observation dates before maturity

If the IR /EQ correlation is *positive*, then the trader buys/sells the shorter/longer dated ZCB maturity lower, incurring a loss on the longer-dated part. This is because since IR / EQ correlation is *positive*, rates will have gone *up*. Alternatively, bond price levels have gone down. However, this impact is typically higher for the longer-dated maturity bonds. Consequently, the net P/L for the switch is negative. For the converse case(*i.e.* spots go down with positive IR / EQ correlation), one also incurs a loss following the same line of reasoning.

For the case of negative IR / EQ correlation, the seller of the trigger redeemable benefits from possible re-hedging scenarios. Historically, IR / EQ correlation has been positive, *i.e.* the product seller should expect to lose money on this cross-asset cross-gamma risk (*e.g.* the historical correlation between 5y / 10y EUR or USD swaps versus the leading equity indices (S&P 500, Euro Stoxx 50,

---

[2]The same is possible for spot and skew.

probability for
early redemption
at inception

performance
since
inception

ZCB notional
at time bucket t

trigger for
early redemption

1y   2y   3y

Maturity

early redemption
observation dates

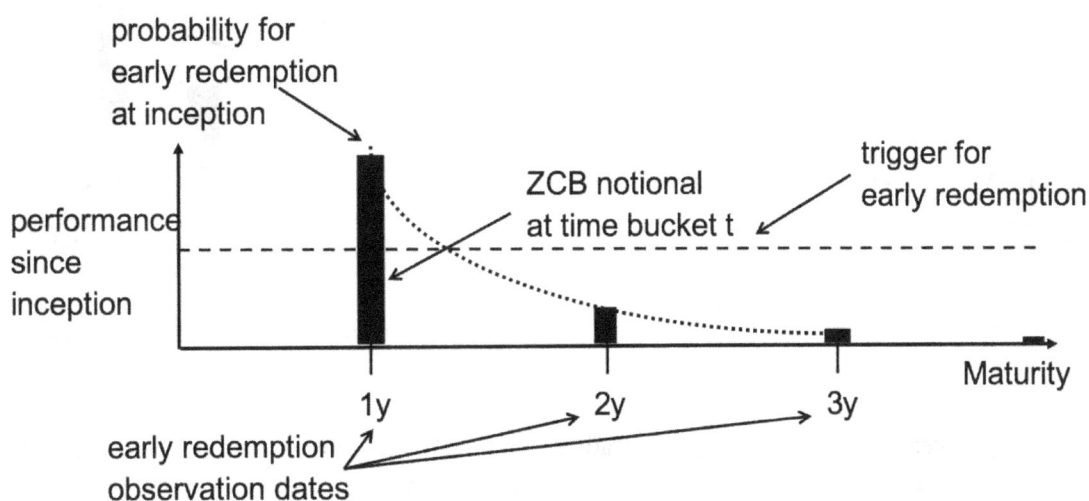

Figure 9.7: Illustration of the trigger redeemable mechanics, redemption probability (dotted line) and zero-coupon bond (ZCB) notional (black rectangles).

and Nikkei) – is around +35%). This risk is dynamically captured using a model that incorporates stochastic rates. Unfortunately, even then it is not clear what kind of hedging strategy to implement. Therefore, instead of using a more elaborate model, one typically charges the IR / EQ correlation price impact up front and manages re-hedging costs via a reserve. The IR / EQ correlation impact is typically between 5-10bp p.a.

Multi-factor trigger redeemables are typically written on the worst-of performing asset, *i.e.* this again means worst-of forward dynamics. In other words, the early redemption is triggered by the worst performer in the basket, which can lead to cross-gamma switches. Consider the case of a two-asset worst-of trigger redeemable close to an early trigger date whereby the redemption amount increases every observation date (*e.g.* $100\% + n \cdot X\%$, where n is the number of times the structure did not early redeem in the past; this is sometimes referred to as a memory autocall). In this case, the value of the structure if triggered *now* needs to be compared to the expectation value of the future cash flows. At inception, the seller is short correlation, but if at some point the present value in case of a trigger event is less than the expectation value in the future (due to the higher redemption payment), it will be an advantage for the seller that the structure early redeems *now* (see Figure 9.8). In both cases, the seller is long correlation, *i.e.* it is preferred to close above the trigger since the present value is smaller than the future expected value. However, if one of the assets suddenly underperforms, the correlation exposure switches sign again.

Figure 9.8: Illustration of the trigger redeemable correlation exposure switches for two assets (solid and dotted black circles).

In recent years, autocalls have been trading with early redemption barriers below the spot at inception. In particular in Asia, structures with the so-called 'Lizard' feature have gained popularity [279]. It is clear that a lower early redemption barrier makes the product more expensive, but the motivation here is to enable clients to invest at a time where markets are trading at a relatively high level so that even in the case of a market correction the product would terminate early. However, also from the dealer's point of view an early knock-out before reaching the level where the downside put knocks in can be advantageous. In the past, trading desks have struggled to manage the common vega convexity issues and structural problems with the downside puts [280], as mentioned earlier. For some markets (*e.g.* structures written on the HSCEI index) even trading the delta can be challenging in terms of liquidity when the market is in distress. The problem is typically also amplified because of the cross-dealer issuance of products with very similar barrier levels, *i.e.* the market is suddenly very concentrated around similar strike levels. Therefore, an early knock-out of some products can alleviate the overall need to re-hedge at the same time. However, it remains to be seen how this eventually turns out in practice.

Some callable structures are callable at the discretion of the issuer. The pricing of this feature is expectedly more complicated even if it 'simply' boils down to comparing the value of the future cash flows (uncalled) to the value of calling early now. These structures can be priced in a conservative way using conventional Monte Carlo by imposing a grid of virtual trigger levels, but it is recommended to resort to backward Monte Carlo such as the Longstaff-Schwartz least-squares algorithm [269] in order to find the true lower bound [3].

Finally, while autocallables have primarily been priced in the past using local volatility models alone, it is advised to assess the impact of stochastic volatility as well given the dual barrier nature. A good choice is a stochastic local volatility (SLV) model [115, 116, 117, 133], but even then analyzing pricing discrepancies is far from trivial especially for (worst-of) multi-factor structures. As recently shown [281], in addition to the already mentioned spot-spot decorrelation effect (see section 5.2.2), there is an effect related to the local spot-spot co-variance which can have an opposite price impact.

9.1.8 Structured Products: Regulation

Retail investors are often not able to opine on the risk/return characteristics of Structured Products or packaged investment products in general. Moreover, even if the payout is understood, the fair value of the instrument at inception and possibly during the lifetime can be opaque to say the least. These problems came to light in a vicious manner during the 2008/9 financial crises when investors

---

[3]In case of structures which are puttable by the client, it is absolutely required to resort to an algorithm like this.

lost money on many products as well as potentially due to the default of issuing entities [282]. As a consequence, various regulatory measures were introduced to contribute to product transparency in the context of consumer protection. For example, in the European Economic Area, as part of the MiFID II (Markets in Financial Instruments Directive II) regulatory directive, many investment products require a KID document (Key Information Document; previously known as KIID, *i.e.* Key Investor Information Document). The KID details product attributes such as fees, risk rating as well as investment profile and covers not only derivatives (*e.g.* ETFs are included, too). If an investment product does not have a KID, it must not be sold to retail investors. In the case of (retail) Structured Products the KID is designed for PRIIPs (Packaged Retail and Insurance-based Investment Products) whereby the definition of content and methodology is provided by ESMA [4]. Note that the provision and maintenance of the PRIIPs KIDs is not trivial since the document is required to be updated throughout the product lifecycle. Finally, although similar initiative have not yet been implemented in other regions such as the United States or Asia, it is probably only a matter of time until regulators align to introduce similar measures.

9.2 Securitization versus Repackaging

Structured Products are securitized collections of derivatives or cash flow assets, providing a dedicated payout. The issuance typically does not require a separate legal entity, especially for retail products, even if the exotic structured credit market often employs Special Purpose Vehicles (SPV) or Special Purpose Entity (SPE). Another way of bundling payouts or cash flow assets is repackaging (also known as 'repacks'). The difference here is that those assets are generally existing securities and derivatives that are repackaged into a different form to meet specific investor needs. Repacks are often more flexible in the sense that they are designed for a particular group of clients. Repacks involve an SPV which is often structured by the arranger as a charitable trust, with shares held by an administrator or trustees on trust for a charity of choice. Repackaging is today often run through dedicated programs and issuance platforms [5] to standardize the process. Common repacks includes asset swaps (see 12.4) whereby the SPV holds some underlying fixed-rate asset and enters into an interest rate swap to exchange fixed for float over the term of the asset. The SPV then issues a floating rate note (see 12.2) to the investor (see Figure 9.9). In this setup, the swap counterparty has exposure to the SPV but not to the investor. In the event of a default on the collateral, the repackaging transaction terminates. The swap counterparty is then normally repaid before the creditors. Other common repacks combine bonds with cross-currency swaps to offer domestic currency bond exposure in a note format or repacking of Credit Linked Notes (CLN). In general, the correlation between the collateral and the assets/cash flows channeled through the SPV is the largest risk to monitor.

---

[4]https://www.esma.europa.eu

[5]https://www.spiresa.com and http://www.standard-repack-documentation.com

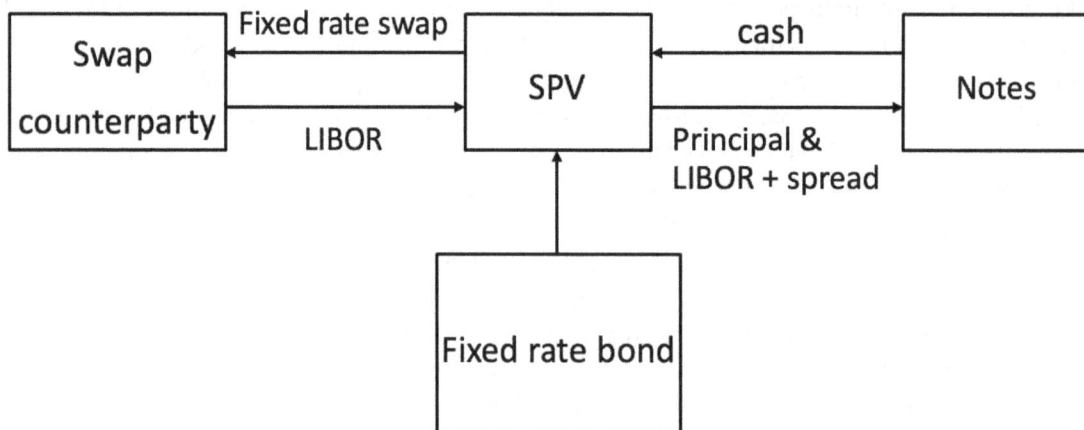

Figure 9.9: Illustration of a generic asset swap repack transaction.

Practical Tips 9.2.1 Questions to ask your quants / risk system support:

- What is the carry of the legacy positions vs. the new issuance of products?
- What is the decay of the upfront margin over the trade lifetime?
- Does the book exhibit an unusual concentration of structures or barrier levels?
- Is there an interest rate basis risk mismatch on funding versus hedge instruments?
- Can the whole book be repriced using a different volatility model or stochastic process?
- Is there a risk concentration on a few trades or is it rather dispersed?

10. Convertible Bonds

10.1 Introduction

Convertible Bonds (CB) are financial instruments, which have both stock and bond character. As a consequence, these securities are often referred to as hybrid instruments. CB issuance dates back to the 1880s where some US railroad companies used the instrument to raise investment capital [283]. Since then, CBs have offered very attractive long-term risk/return characteristics historically compared to other asset classes [284]. In its basic form, the CB holder has the right to convert a bond into a fixed number of the issuer's common stock at a pre-determined price (at maturity). Hence, the CB holder benefits from a price appreciation of the stock while, at the same time, the CB may pay a periodic coupon and redeem as cash at expiry in case it does not convert. The periodic coupon is smaller than for a bond of the same maturity in exchange for upside participation in the underlying. The rationale for the creation of CBs was to combine the benefits of stocks and bonds. For example, a simple prospectus might entail paying 100 for CB, receiving 4% coupon p.a. and at maturity either receiving 100 or 8 shares of common stock.

CB trading often requires paying attention to minute details in the terms and conditions outlined in the prospectus. If those details are not correctly represented in the valuation model, severe mispricing / valuation can occur especially in critical situation such as conversion.

10.1.1 Convertible Bond Basics and Terminology

What makes CB interesting is that they are by construction hybrid instruments between debt and equity. The key drivers determining the CB price are

- Equity parameters, which determine the price of the option to convert from bond to stock
- Interest rates, which determine the underlying bond cash flows
- Credit, which determines the probability of default of the issue

Ignoring the possibility of periodic coupon payments and restricting the discussion to conversion at maturity the following payoff is obtained

$$\max[N, C_r \cdot S_T] = N + \max[0, C_r \cdot S_T - N] , \tag{10.1}$$

where N is the face value of the CB and C_r the conversion ratio. Effectively, this is simply a bond embedded with a call option on the underlying. Via put-call parity the equation above can be rewritten as

$$C_r \cdot S_T + \max[0, N - C_r] \, . \tag{10.2}$$

This means that the CB holder is long C_r shares, including a European put option to sell them in return for the face value of the CB. The CB holder will convert in case the conversion value ($C_r \cdot S_T$) is high enough. In a purely theoretical world (*e.g.* no taxes, etc.), a company cannot really optimize its capital cost by a smart mix of equity and debt. However, in reality, this is possible and a reason why CBs are attractive to the issuer (and investor alike).

The advantages for the CB issuer are

- in case of conversion, shares are issued at a premium compared to the underlying price at issuance (*i.e.* sell equity at a premium if the conversion happens)
- the CB is typically considered as equity by rating agencies
- the CB is typically accounted for as equity (except for coupons)
- the issuance often has little impact on the current stock price
- diversification in the investor space (CB holders typically differ from common shareholders)
- retention of dividends and voting rights unless conversion occurs
- coupon payments are typically lower compared to bonds
- lower cost of debt versus canonical bonds
- earnings dilution postponed until conversion into shares
- often tax efficient compared to issuance of common equity (*e.g.* interest payments on debt are tax-deductible)

The key disadvantages for the CB issuer are uncertainty regarding the outcome (shares vs redemption of the bond notional) and that the CB will be debt on balance sheet until conversion occurs.

Figure 10.1 illustrates the convertible behavior as a function of CB price versus underlying asset price.

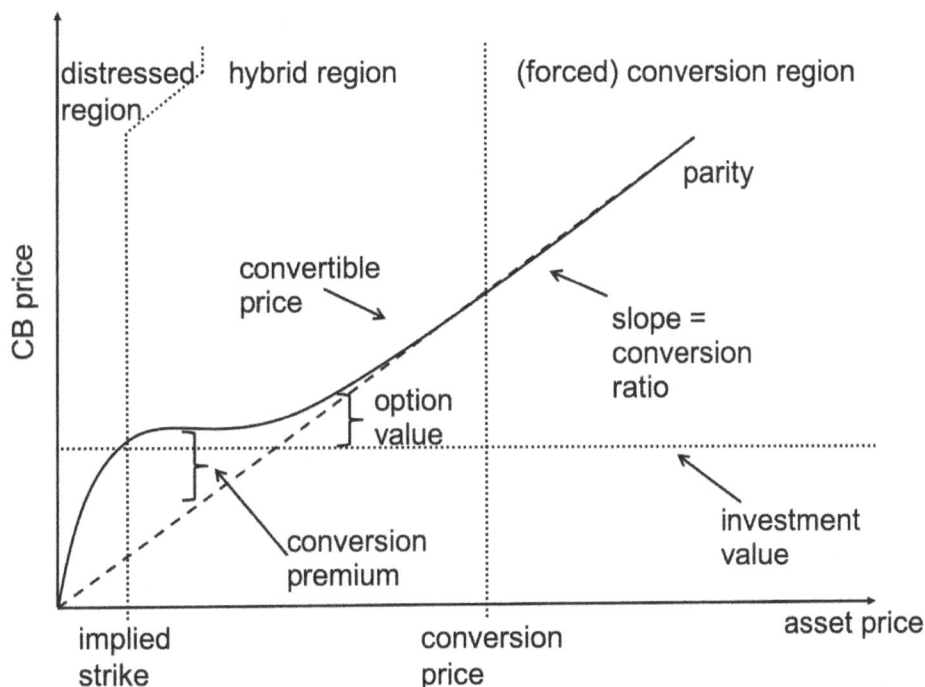

Figure 10.1: Illustration of the various regions for a convertible bond.

Before understanding the stylized dynamics, there is some CB specific terminology to know. These are

- **CB price** P_{CB}, *e.g.* $P_{CB} = 100$. The CB price is bound by the investment value / bond floor and the parity line (see definition below).
- **Investment Value / Bond floor** (B_F): Present value of all bond related cash flows. The price of the convertible is expected to approach this value as the underlying share price falls, *i.e.* this is the lower boundary. Recall: the bond floor itself is not a fixed value and can fluctuate with yields, spreads or issuer quality change.
- **Conversion ratio** C_r: The number of shares into which the CB can be exchanged (can change over lifetime), *e.g.* $C_r = 8$
- **Conversion price** $C_P = \frac{\text{PAR}}{C_r}$: share price above which bond converts, *e.g.* $C_P = 100/8 = 12.5$
- **Parity** (line) P_a: The market value of the shares ($P_{a,t} = S_t \cdot C_r$) the investor would hold if the convertible was converted immediately. Sometimes also called conversion value. In our example, $P_{a,t} = 10 \cdot 8$. Note that the bond component cannot trade below this value.
- **Premium to parity**: The percentage premium the investor is willing to pay for the convertible compared to buying the underlying shares: $\frac{P - P_a}{P_a}$, *e.g.* $(100\text{-}80)/80 = 20/80 = 25\%$
- **Delta** ($\Delta_{\$,t} = n_{CB} \cdot C_r \cdot \Delta_{\%,t} \cdot S_t$: Sensitivity of the convertible price to moves in the equity price
- **Maturity**: CB maturity at inception (usually between 5 and 30 years)
- **Preference**: senior to common stock (typically junior to other debt)
- **Callability**: Some CBs may be called by the issuer at a pre-defined price before expiry
- **Call price**: The amount an investor receives in case the bond is called (early) and the investor forgoes his right to convert (typically 100%). Some issuers retain the right to call before coupon payment without even paying the respective accrued interest.

- **Mandatory CB**: Some CB may convert automatically after a certain underlying price is reached
- **Reset CB**: A CB in which the conversion ratio is reset after a certain underlying price is reached (typically on the downside)

The terms above are just a small collection. The actual contractual elements of a CB issue are represented in the so-called term sheet or prospectus, which often includes additional features such as a soft call, hard call protection or provisional call protection (see section below). Some trading desks specialize in the form of CB prospectus arbitrage whereby they try to find features or hidden optionality which might be exploitable.

10.1.2 Convertible Bond Arbitrage

CB arbitrage (CBA) in general refers to detecting mispricing in one (or more) of the four major CB components. These components are

- default or credit risk (risk on issuer); *e.g.* to hedge a $10m notional CB purchase for the credit risk, one needs to trade a CDS notional of $N_{CDS} = (1 - R) \cdot \$10m$. Here R is the assumed recovery value on the bond. Note that as a proxy hedge, one could also short the stock in excess of the delta to offset credit risk
- IR risk (main risk via bond component); *e.g.* to hedge a 3 year dv01 of +$50k, one could trade a fix vs floating 3y IRS of notional $\$50k/0.0003 = \$166m$ (pay float / receive fix)
- volatility / vega risk (risk from embedded optionality)
- equity / delta risk (risk from embedded optionality)

In case of detecting mispricing, the strategy would be to go long / short the mispriced CB component via a respective market instrument. Hence, one could for example buy a CB and (*i*) short shares, (*ii*) sell calls against the CB optionality, and/or buy protection via CDS. However, note that CBs are securities. This means that while they should, in theory, be in line with market parameters, they may decouple in terms of price dynamics. This can be an opportunity or a source of major pain. Finally, the key to CB trading or arbitrage is often also to know who owns the majority of the CB issuance since this may provide guidance concerning potential future price movements. For example, a CB issuance, which is mostly owned by an investor who is insensitive to mark-to-market P/L often exhibits different price dynamics compared to CB with a diverse and active investor base. This steers the discussion towards liquidity. Picking up on the message in earlier chapters, even the most advanced valuation model does not help if the underlying can hardly be traded. In the context of CBs this means that one should be careful with cases for which one cannot short/borrow the underlying because this means the primary hedging mitigant is gone. Similarly, if the amount of market makers in the CB is very small then this will naturally be problematic in situations of distress. These concerns are even more important today since CB issuance has been on a decline on average over the last 10 years [285].

Nevertheless, CBA is a well-known strategy also run by hedge funds (HF). There are some HF who specialize only in CB trading and CBA. Often CB 'mispricings' manifest themselves in the implied volatility used to price the CB. If a 'cheap' CB is identified, the typical trade is to go long the CB and short the underlying to monetize the arbitrage opportunity. The opportunity can, for example, be free optionality in a delta-hedged strategy by *e.g.* trading the gamma or profiting from alignment with market volatility. In any case, irrespective of the potential market move in the underlying, the strategy presents a viable market-neutral alternative to a traditional fixed income trade. Note that the short position in the underlying makes it necessary to monitor borrow costs closely and that the CB bleeds theta over time since the optionality decays especially if the underlying does not move. Even if there is no apparent mispricing in the CB volatility component, it can often be a great instrument to source long-dated optionality, which has possibly otherwise no liquid market. This activity can be unpleasant for the issuer because it generates downward pressure on the underlying. As a remedy, companies are sometimes forced to use part of the proceeds of the convertible issue to buy back their own shares in the market to offset this dynamic.

CB may also be part of so-called capital structure arbitrage trades (cap-arb, see also 12.5.3). In a typical cap-arb trade, the investor goes long securities of higher capital structure and short securities of lower capital structure within the same company. In a CB scenario, this would exactly mean long the CB and short the equity. Alternatively, it is possible to engage in a convertible asset swap. This involves the purchase of a cheap/distressed CB and selling it to another counterparty in return for the derivative component. In other words, this strategy strips the credit from the equity part of the CB.

Because convertibles carry characteristics of (vanilla) options, large issues may significantly impact the underlying stock price dynamics and the implied volatility surface due to vega hedging activity. This effect may happen close to a conversion day. For example, the Swiss company Swisscom was pinned close to the CHF 450 strike for almost 3 months in 2004/05 before the expiry of the convertible. Following the maturity date, the stock suddenly surged by 4% in only a couple of days.

10.1.3 Convertible Bond Pricing

CB pricing usually involves a numerical approach such as trinomial trees / PDE solver or Monte Carlo. The latter is especially true if the CB contains special features such as American exercise/conversion, callability/puttability, reset in conversion price, etc.. Analytical pricing is possible if the CB can is decomposable into its components, *i.e.* credit and interest rates risk via a general bond valuation approach and optionality risk via a standard option pricing procedure. As a simple example, one can price a canonical CB (void of callability or reset features) using the so-called bond + call option approach. From a valuation perspective, this means

$$\textbf{CB = Bond (IR + credit components) + vanilla call option} \ . \tag{10.3}$$

The bond pricing is effectively just the usual sum of discounted bond coupons using a risky rate curve (see below). The call option can be dealt with as a European call within the BSM framework (C_{BSM}) whereby the conversion price replaces the strike. Finally, one obtains the price for the CB as

$$CB = Bond + C_r \cdot C_{BSM} \ . \tag{10.4}$$

This pricing is useful for a CB which has more bond character, *i.e.* if one is dealing effectively with a little optionality on top of a bond. Note that for a reverse convertible (bond), the investor is short a (European) put and long a bond. The reverse convertible is also a familiar first generation structured product.

The bond component of the CB is simply the sum of the (risky) discounted cash flows, *i.e.*

$$PV(Bond) = \sum_{t=1}^{n} \frac{cpn}{(1 + (r + \lambda))^t} + \frac{par}{(1 + (r + \lambda))^t} \ , \tag{10.5}$$

where λ is the respective credit spread used to obtain the risky rate.

10.1.4 Convertible Bond Features

As already mentioned above, CB often entail various features which can significantly impact the price dynamics and valuation especially in the case of extreme situation or special events. In the following subsections, such common features are presented and discussed.

10.1.4.1 Convertible Bond Call / Put features

The call feature on behalf of the issuer grants the right to call back the CB while at the same time paying the investor a redemption amount K. This early redemption amount is naturally the call strike K. One typically distinguishes between a hard and soft call feature. In the case of the former, the CB is unconditionally callable as the name suggests. The rational trigger for a hard call is whenever the redemption amount is lower than the (expected) continuation value of the convertible. The soft call feature applies only if the parity P_a of the CB reaches a pre-defined threshold $K_\%$ (also known as the call trigger) such that

$$P_a > K_\% = S > K_\% \cdot \frac{N}{C_r} = S > K_\% \cdot C_P . \tag{10.6}$$

This feature is often conditional to a time window, *i.e.* the threshold needs to be breached for a pre-defined number of consecutive (trading/business) days.

The potential put feature of a CB refers to the optionality of the investor to sell the CB back to the issuer at a pre-determined price P_p and also often after a pre-defined date. While the put feature sounds like a sensible downside protection and increases the CB value, the exact utility depends on the credit quality of the issuer. Put and call feature are sometimes also combined so that the respective cost for both issuer and investor alike decreases.

10.1.4.2 Convertible Bond Dividend Protection

Dividend protection clauses were already mentioned in the context of dividend modeling for vanilla options (see 2.2.20.6). As a start, part of the prospectus should define whether dividends are attributed to existing shares or newly create shares following conversion. In the case of the latter. depending on the wording, it is possible that the dividend entitlement is only valid for the following fiscal year.

As explained above, the holder of a CB participates indirectly in the appreciation of the underlying shares. However, compared to a direct equity investment, the dividend and its potential increase, is not passed on. In other words, similar to a vanilla call option the CB value decrease with an increase in the dividend since the forward is lowered. Note as well that the issuer will often compare the call (or forced conversion) option with the subsequent forgone dividend size payments to the CB investors in case this option is not exercised. In any case, one way to offer dividend protection in this case is the so-called *dividend pass through* by which any dividend above a pre-defined threshold is automatically passed on to the CB investor for example by adjusting the periodic coupon payments. Alternatively, dividend increase protection can be handled by adjusting the CB conversion terms (*conversion ratio adjustment*). For example, assuming an absolute dividend threshold of div_t, the new conversion price is given by

$$C_P^+ = C_P \cdot \frac{S - \max[div - div_t, 0]}{S} , \tag{10.7}$$

where S is normally the share price on the ex-div date. Note that potential cross-currency effects for CBs denominated in a currency other than the underlying share (with potential dividend payments in a third currency [1]), need to be carefully analyzed.

---

[1]For example, companies such as Royal Dutch Shell dividend payouts in multiple currencies.

The modeling of the dividend protection clauses is as critical as the dividend modeling itself. This is because the respective terminal stock price distribution is significantly modified and might at some point for large dividend payments, high volatility and long maturity not anymore resemble a standard lognormal diffusion process [79]. In other words, the probability for the stock price to reach zero is increased significantly.

10.1.5 Contingent Convertibles

Contingent convertible bonds ('CoCos', 'CoCo' bonds, or Contingent Convertibles) is an umbrella term for bonds, which are mandatory convertible into common stock upon the occurrence of a pre-defined trigger event [2] [286, 287]. In other words, unless the trigger event occurs, CoCos behave as regular bonds, paying a coupon (sometimes at risk), and would also expire as such. However, the key feature is that the conversion feature makes the debt *loss absorbing*. CoCos used to be popular in the US already before 2007 because until recently, they were treated more favorably on the balance sheet compared to regular CBs (excluded from diluted earnings per share calculation). Following the credit crisis, CoCos became an interesting instrument to improve bank regulatory capital as they could be classified under the Basel III minimum capital requirement up to 2.5% ([4.5% CET1] + (2% Tier 2 and 1.5% additional Tier 1)). CoCo are typically embedded in corporate bonds whereby embedding them into CBs ('CoCoCo' Bonds) is rare [288].
Two main types of CoCos were issued since then:

- (*i*) CoCos converting into common stock after a sharp rally in the underlying without the possibility for cash settlement (*e.g.* Fortis, Unicredito)
- (*ii*) CoCos converting into common stock if the issuers regulatory capital falls below a pre-defined threshold or if the underlying falls below a pre-defined level (*e.g.* Lloyds, Credit Suisse). This is also called the point of non-viability and can sometimes be at the discretion of the regulator.

The advantage of type (*i*) and (*ii*) CoCos is that they do not include a cash redemption in case the trigger event occurred. The only recourse to the bondholder for both CoCo types lies with the pledged shares, which in case of bankruptcy would be effectively worthless. Until then the P/L is effectively the difference between the initial notional and the converted shares. In addition, the face value is typically fully written down with partial write down or staggered write downs being the exception. The exact definition of the capital ratio trigger is critical in determining the CoCo price. This includes the exact reference to the regulatory accords (*e.g.* Basel II vs Basel III) as well as to whether the CoCo obeys the regulatory limits completely ('fully loaded') or whether there is a transitional phase. Type (*ii*) CoCos have the additional risk of converting to common shares in a stressed market regime, which is typically rewarded with a higher periodic coupon payment. The problem here is that upon conversion, additional selling pressure could occur as investors might want to dispose of the converted shares. This is commonly referred to as the CoCo death spiral [289]. It is therefore not yet clear whether the type (*ii*) CoCo is beneficial to the dynamics of the share price in a stressed market. Recent positive findings [290] given an analysis of a vast instrument universe can be misleading given a rather benign market environment over the last years. Both CoCo types were attractive instruments from an issuers point of view because they allowed raising capital in a very tough market (2008/2009). Moreover, at least type (*ii*) CoCos would not dilute shareholders at issuance. Often, part of the CoCo coupons are also tax-deductible. It remains to be seen how large

---

[2]http://www.allonhybrids.com

the CoCo market grows over the next years and how their classification in terms of capital (*e.g.* Tier 1, Tier 2) might change in the future regulatory environment.

The pricing of CoCos is non-trivial and beyond the scope here in detail. Apart from the classic structural model framework [291], the main approaches are market implied models and equity derivative frameworks [284] similar to what was discussed in the context of CBs.

Finally, note that CoCos are not the same CBs even if the semantics sound similar. For starters, the conversion in CoCos is forced with limited upside and unlimited downside. CBs exhibit better characteristics in those attributes. Moreover, the bond floor on the CB as well as the equity upside creates *typically* positive convexity [3]. In this aspect, CoCo bonds have always negative 'gamma'.

Practical Tips 10.1.1 Questions to ask your quants / risk system support:

- How are Convertible Bond modeled and represented in the risk management system?
- Does the CB model align with the other option pricing models used or is it different?
- How is callability and puttability modeled?
- Are there any significant positions in relation to the total issuance?
- Are there any CBs at distressed levels?
- At which volatility level are the CBs exhibiting positive/negative gamma?
- Are the potential liquidity concerns for particular positions?
- What is the impact of large rates increases/decreases on the CB book?

---

[3]Note that in distressed situations negative gamma ($\frac{\partial^2 P}{\partial S^2} < 0$) can also occur for CBs.

11. Corporate Derivatives

11.1 Introduction

Corporate Derivatives (CD) are typically derivative instruments traded by large institutional or corporate clients. This population includes pension funds, insurance companies, corporations, but increasingly also wealthy private clients such as Ultra-High-Net-Worth-Individuals. Often, corporate trades overlap with activity in Equity Capital Markets (ECM), *e.g.* IPOs, refinancing operations (*e.g.* rights issue) or company restructurings. CD can also be used to improve company balance sheets or to provide hedges for employee share option programs (ESOPs). In both cases, the trading desk and sales team interact typically with the treasury department of the client. CD trades often involve sensitive company information. In order to reduce insider trading risk, only a limited number of people are involved in the trade. In other words, similar to IB M&A operations, a Chinese wall is in place, separating regular trading activity from any CD activity. Because of the possibility of sensitive information, CD trades tend to be pitched only to a limited number of competing banks.

CD are typically less complex from a pure derivatives point of view, and many strategies involve vanilla options only. However, the challenge lies in the considerable notional and potential difficulty of hedging (out) the risk entirely. Therefore, CD desks often need to warehouse part of the risk and price for this accordingly. Hence, upfront margins can be larger. Still, it is also clear that not every CD trade ends up making money, *i.e.* to some extent, there are parallels to the venture capital market. It is therefore essential to ideally carry a (broadly) diversified CD portfolio to avoid blowing up on all trades at the same time. Along the same lines, monitoring / simulating stress scenarios can be crucial to survival as well as the upfront incorporation of risk mitigants (to be discussed later). Finally, due to warehousing, CD trades carry more directional and cyclical risk than other trading activity. Therefore, it is equally important to understand and analyze the underlying asset in detail. Finally, corporate trades may be subject to so-called Banking Book treatment. Banking Book trades are transactions which are typically held until maturity and not under a strict mark-to-market valuation adjustment oversight. The opposite is called Trading Book treatment, which is the default setting for derivative trading desks. Operationally, the (daily) fair value adjustment of a Trading Book due to market moves needs to be booked in the respective P/L account of the bank. Banking

Book treatment relaxes this view, but this does not mean that a particular trade is not risk managed or possibly hedged. Rather, P/L variance is minimized in recognition that the fair value is difficult to determine.

11.1.1 Equity Financing

Corporate trades often entail an (equity) financing component, *i.e.* for example, a loan backed by equity collateral. The key metric describing a loan (risk / leverage) is the so-called loan-to-value ratio (LTV) . The LTV is defined as

$$LTV = \frac{\text{drawn loan amount - cash collateral}}{\text{PV of secured collateral}} . \tag{11.1}$$

Here, secured collateral may be shares of a (listed) company. Deviations from the agreed LTV during the trade lifetime may result in margin calls on the loan (*e.g.* LTV > 60% margin call). LTV may also be coupled to a trigger event so that the loan has to be paid back early in case the LTV becomes larger than a pre-defined threshold (*e.g.* > 80%). The main risk for collateralized loans is a shortfall arising from a sudden valuation decrease of the collateral. The term shortfall represents the case for which the loan notional exceeds the collateral value, *i.e.* *LTV > 1*. This situation is often characterized by severe exposure to gap risk since it might not be possible to liquidate the collateral fast enough at a level to recover the loan notional fully.

Vehicles for equity financing include

- equity collateralized bonds
- combination of stock sale and a (total return) equity swap
- combination of prepaid forward, (total return) equity swap and pledge
- repo financing
- stock loan financing (very similar to repo above)
- put and collar backed financing
- (revolving) margin loans (also known as Lombard loans)

The remaining focus is on financing vehicles involving derivatives, *i.e.* more specifically put- and collar backed financing. Note that financing transactions whereby cash (collateralized or not) is effectively leaving the bank also has an impact on the treasury department of the financial institution. In a nutshell, banks need to set aside capital given that they might potentially need to absorb losses (as set out in the regulatory framework of the Basel Accords [1]). The capital adequacy cost of a loan depends on the amount of capital by which it is backed. This amount is typically called the capital charge and needs to be factored in as a cost in the lending margin [2]. In order to manage future capital requirements, it is therefore vital that the treasury department is kept in the loop concerning potential lending transactions.

Finally, before discussing the primary derivative financing vehicle, it is worth pointing out another key risk for corporate loans: early repayment (also known as pre-payment). Quite often corporate financing transactions/loans are pre-payable before maturity. This can be annoying for the lender if the pricing terms have been tightly derived from the expected revenues over the whole lifetime of the trade. The heuristic approach to deal with this risk is the introduction of upfront structuring fees as well as a *make whole clause/provision* linked to a penalty. This way at least

---

[1] https://www.bis.org/bcbs/history.htm

[2] Note that following Basel III (https://www.bis.org/bcbs/basel3.htm), countercyclical buffers and liquidity requirements are set and reset over the life of a loan, *i.e.* the costs can be dynamic.

the minimum costs can be covered. More elaborate approaches include modeling and simulating the loan as a proper credit instrument with state transitions whereby the likelihood of pre-payment increases with a decreasing interest rate environment [292].

11.1.2   Put-(and collar) backed financing

Put (and collar) backed (equity) financings account for a large number of corporate trades. The typical setup is that the borrower buys a put of notional X from the lender on the underlying (often the company itself). The borrower then pledges Y shares to the lender. The lender provides a loan of notional Z to the borrower at a spread to a reference rate (*e.g.* LIBOR + spread). The lender borrows N number of shares to delta-hedge the short put whereby the borrower may guarantee the borrowing cost.

Under this scheme, there is almost no risk for the lender given default of the borrower, *i.e.* the loan notional can be very close to the put strike especially if implied volatility and dividends are low. This large exposure is possible because, given default, the loss on the loan notional Z is perfectly offset by the sum of the value of the pledged shares and the value of the short put (which is now void). Moreover, there is no cash margin requirement for the borrower. Note that although a (corporate) loan is a traditional instrument, it is non-trivial to value properly. Put or collar backed financing avoids some of these complexities due to the implicit collateralization.

For example, consider a client looking for financing backed by 5m shares of company ABC trading at $50 per share (*i.e.* market value $= 5m \cdot \$50 = \$250m$). Based on their funding requirements and market consensus, the bank determines a financing spread on the loan of 3M-LIBOR + 100bp (this is in general significantly lower compared to obtaining financing on a regular uncollateralized loan). To account for the rates risk, a margin of 5% is built in in order to account for the changing exposure, *i.e.* maximum exposure = (5% + 100bp) / 4 = 2.5%. By taking the maximum exposure into account, the bank is willing to finance the loan with a notional equivalent to a put with strike $K - 2.5\%$. The client, on the other hand, is willing to buy the put at strike $K = 90\%$. Then the loan notional is then equal to $\$250m \cdot (90\% - 2.5\%) = USD218.75m$. Assuming the put premium is $30m, the net notional raised by the client equals USD 218.75 – USD 30m = USD 188.75m. Over the lifetime, the client pays 3M-LIBOR + 100bp periodically to the bank, while the bank dynamically hedges the short put at least for its delta. At expiry, the client exercises the put in case it is ITM and repays the loan by possible selling shares in the market.

The advantages of the derivative-backed financing scheme is that

- the loan-to-value (LTV) can be large, *i.e.* LTV approximately equal to the put strike
- the client hedges his exposure to a share price decline
- there are no margin calls
- there is almost no credit risk, *i.e.* tighter financing spread on the loan
- there are no additional credit lines at the bank to be taken up
- potentially weak credit clients may obtain financing on good terms

The disadvantages are mainly that the investor needs to pay the premium on the put and in case of illiquid assets or high volatility (skew), this premium can be expensive. Since the loan is a direct function of the put notional, the lender may not be able to sell a large put notional given illiquid underlyings. Finally, the lender is subject to borrow cost risk on possibly significant short stock positions if the borrow is not locked in via the client at inception.

In the case of a collar-backed financing scheme, the premium disadvantage is partially remedied. Here, the client buys an OTM put, but additionally sells an OTM call against the financing. Hence, part of the premium is recovered by selling the OTM call. Often the respective strikes are chosen to solve for a zero cost upfront (also known as a zero-cost-collar). The drawback is that the client loses the potential upside on the stock performance. For the dealer, the upside call may turn out to be expensive to carry in case the underlying underperforms the implied volatility at the strike, *i.e.* the trading desk is possible paying a large amount of theta at a time when the underlying is not realizing at the implied volatility mark (see also Figure 11.1). Note as well that even if the asset realizes at or above the implied volatility mark trading a large chunk of the underlying every day in the market to cover the theta is not necessarily a trivial undertaking. Hence, determining the correct hedging costs at inception and during the trade until expiry is challenging given the large notional.

In practice, many of the pricing parameters are determined by heuristic rules such as the maximum gamma exposure at expiry in relation to the average daily trading volume (ADTV) of the asset. Also, the amount of skew benefit (difference in implied volatility level of the short put position versus the long position in the call) to grant to the client in the pricing. Moreover, collar positions with an aggregate delta lower than a certain threshold (*e.g.* 40%) are typically not quoted. For longer-dated collar (or put-backed) financing trades dividends can become relevant. One feature is to include a dividend protection clause such that the client covers any potential loss relating to a change in the actually announced dividend. Note that this implies credit risk in case the client is not able or willing to pay the difference at the time. As discussed above, management of the position close to expiry may be problematic for either trade leg (put or call) given increased gamma exposure in relation to the liquidity of the underlying. One way to mitigate this problem is to embed a clause allowing the lender to '*Asian out*' the settlement price (see also 3.1.3, re-strike, close or somehow roll the position forward (*i.e.* restructuring in general). An alternative approach to circumvent potential pin-risk issues or large gamma at expiry is to modify the strike of the respective options in ways similar to power derivatives (see 4.1.6). Hence, instead of a fixed/hard strike K, the strike is *softened* within a range [293, 154]. The payoff is then given by

$$\begin{cases} 0 & \text{if } S_t < K - x \\ \frac{1}{4x}(S_t - K - x)^2 & \text{if } K - x \leq S_t \leq K + x \\ S_t - K & \text{if } S_t > K + x \end{cases} \tag{11.2}$$

whereby x denotes a barrier shift. Hence, within the range $K \mp x$, the strike is soft and exhibits a constant gamma of $\frac{1}{2}x^3$.

Dealer side: short OTM Put   **Dealer side: long collar**

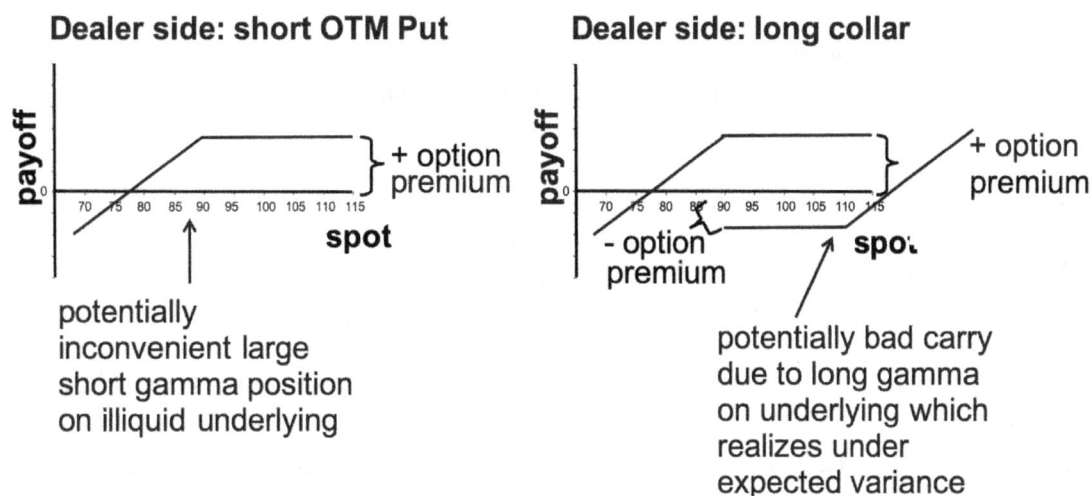

Figure 11.1: Illustration of a large corporate derivative collar exposure from a theta/gamma point of view.

As a side note, collar transactions are also used to build up or protect a (hidden) stake in a company for a M&A transaction. Here the stake is first initiated by buying shares and potentially lower strike calls which can convert to common stock at expiry. On top of this, a collar can be traded to protect the downside and use the linked margin loan to leverage the stake further. This strategy often allows bypassing reporting frameworks, which would otherwise require to disclose a stake early if it exceeds *e.g.* 3% [3]. A recent example in this space is the Geely acquisition of Daimler [4].

Finally, large corporate trades on single stocks or single transaction typify the domain in which pricing by model *alone* should not be the only way of looking at the trade. The more information a trader can gather about the fundamentals of the underlying asset (*i.e.* balance sheet, financial statements, business model, etc.), the respective sector and potential other identical trades in the market, the better. This information is often a much more reliable source for determining the 'pricing' parameters instead of applying only a heuristically derived parameter-based pricing rule approach.

11.1.3 Employee Stock Option Plan (ESOP)

Corporations may incentivize their employees by giving them participation in the company. Employee stock option plans (ESOP) award the right to individual employees to purchase common shares at a pre-defined exercise price. Typically, the exercise price is set to the market closing price or an average up to the grant date of the ESOP. The vesting conditions define if the ESOP is active at the expiry date of the plan (*e.g.* meeting of a company profit target or outperformance of a peer group). The vesting period is the waiting time before the beneficiary becomes entitled to the stock options. Unvested options may typically not be exercised or sold. The exercise period is the time frame in which the ESOP holders may exercise their rights.

The issuer of the ESOP is typically the treasury department of the company. In other words, the treasury is short the ESOP against some employees subject to the vesting conditions. Strategies to hedge the ESOP for the treasury include

---

[3] In case of acquiring a stake via a hybrid derivative structure this threshold is typically a bit higher, *e.g.* 5%.
[4] https://reut.rs/2severF

- purchase/holding of treasury shares is a common way to hedge the exposure. At grant day, treasury buys required shares to offset obligation (either completely or solely the delta). Advantage: easy to implement and transparent. Disadvantage: company resources are used, or financing might be needed; debt/equity ratio worsens; treasury might lose on share premium if the stock goes down
- entering an equity swap treasury pays floating LIBOR+X, receives the total return on own stock equity performance from the counterparty. Advantage: not using cash resources apart from financing on the swap leg. Disadvantage: treasury might lose on the equity swap performance; accounting wise not optimal: liability at inception plus equity entry reducing the balance of the equity section on the balance sheet
- purchase of a call option (and variants thereof) Advantage: treasury knows it cannot lose more than the premium. Disadvantage: call option might not hedge ESOP risk completely

Sometimes, corporates devise ESOPs which are too complex to hedge for its treasury on their own or where the treasury cannot monitor the expectation value of the payoff accurately. A typical example is a peer group outperformance-based share participation scheme. Here the number of shares to be vested is a function of the performance (*e.g.* total return) of the company versus its peers (*e.g.* a group of 30 global competitors). This structure entails a more complicated payout, which also features discontinuities (see Figure 11.2).

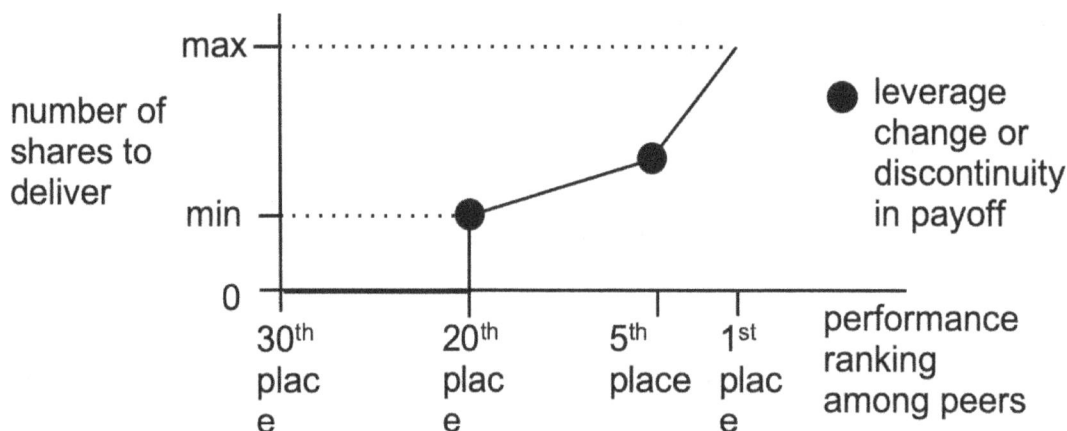

Figure 11.2: Illustration of potential ESOP outperformance option discontinuities.

Roughly speaking, the payout resembles an outperformance or spread option. It is required to have market data for all companies involved and to estimate the correlations between them (spot-spot as well as Quanto correlations in case it is a world basket of peers denominated in different currencies). In terms of delta, the exposure requires to go long the main company and short the peers at inception. Finally, there are some unpleasant discontinuities

- between the 4th-5th-6th place, the delta on the main asset jumps due to the leverage change
- between the 19th-20th-21st place, our delta on the main underlying can drop suddenly to zero in case the ESOP company significantly underperforms (especially close to expiry) → gap risk

Typically, dealers price in this risk (*e.g.* employing applying a barrier shift), which can render this type of option very expensive (since the large notional amplifies the problem).

11.1.4 Illiquid underlyings

Given the potential monetary opportunity with corporate trades, it is sometimes justified to quote on assets that might otherwise be dismissed given liquidity issues. This problem can be typical for some put/collar based financing transactions. Here illiquidity may refer to

- private companies, *i.e.* no ability to trade the asset at all publicly
- poor overall stock volume and/or trading days without any prints
- poor order book depth
- (consequently) large bid/offer spreads
- poor tradable option volume
- poor correlation to related indices or sectors making it difficult to offset risk with a proxy

To make matters worse, illiquid underlyings often exhibit all of these features combined. It is also common for these stocks to be more often in a jumpy rather than diffusive regime. Recall that the latter breaks the BSM (dynamic replication) framework in theory (as well as in practice typically). As a rule of thumb, any asset below $25m daily trading volume can be considered illiquid if it is part of a potentially large payoff discontinuity. Alternatively, trading suddenly more than 10% of the average daily trading volume will not get unnoticed in any asset class.

What can one do on a short gamma position where it is not possible to frequently delta hedge due to illiquidity? One option is to not dynamically hedge, *i.e.* take a view. The trade then becomes directional, and the BSM dynamic replication framework is irrelevant. Besides, one can try to trade a spread in the strike or maturity space (*e.g.* trade the closest possible listed expiry even if there is a mismatch in the aggregate exposure). One can also try to figure out whether the stock price is trending or mean reverting. In the case of the former, one can take a delta bias in the direction of the trend or follow the stock performance tightly with the delta hedge. In the case of the latter, the delta is adjusted only close to close (if at all). One can also trade delta only in a pre-defined band (*e.g.* based on daily breakeven volatility). Another possibility is to book the trade with a strike shift or volatility overhedge to suffer less from the short gamma. In the latter case, one takes advantage of the fact that an increase in volatility reduces the gamma. Finally, one can try to (proxy-) hedge out vega risk using a similar index or stock (typically in the same region/sector with a high correlation in spot or volatility to the base asset). Clearly, the latter introduces dispersion or basis risk but might be sufficient enough to cover systemic market risks.

Practical Tips 11.1.1 Questions to ask your quants / risk system support:

- What are the scenario risks which potentially impact the loan collateral most?
- What is the process/workflow to enforce the collateral following a shortfall?
- Is there any jurisdiction risk potentially hindering the enforcement of the collateral?
- Is there gap risk exposure and what are the main drivers?
- Are all trades under mark-to-market valuation or treated as banking book trades?

12. Credit Risk

12.1 Introduction

The default of a counterparty against a trading transaction is called counterparty credit risk. Credit risk can be substantial and must be quantified as well as monitored actively. Typically, the credit risk of a bank against clients/counterparties is monitored by a designated credit desk with the credit risk management (CRM) department.

The most important components of credit risk are:

- **Arrival risk**: the uncertainty of whether a default occurs or not for a given time horizon. The measure of arrival risk is the *probability of default*
- **Timing risk**: the uncertainty about the precise time of default. The underlying random variable is the time to default, and its risk is given by a probability function for the time of default
- **Recovery risk**: the uncertainty of the severity of the losses if a default happens. Hence, the uncertainty is the actual payoff that a creditor receives after a default. The market convention is to express the recovery rate of a bond or a loan as the fraction of the notional value
- **Market risk**: risk of changes in the market price of a defaultable asset, even if no default occurs. Apart from other market factors, market risk is also driven by changes in timing and recovery risk (or at least changes in the market's perception of these risks)
- **Market price correlation risk**: risk of defaults (and defaults likelihoods) correlate with price movements of defaultable assets. Default correlation risk is an additional risk component introduced when the risk of joint defaults of several obligors is considered

12.1.1 Default Symmetry

One issue with credit risk is the inherent asymmetry between potential losses. Depending on the *Present mark-to-market Value* (PmtmV) of an outstanding position there are two cases:

(**i**) PmtmV > 0: The defaulting entity will very likely be unable to settle to commitment. This outcome implies a loss equal to the PmtmV less any recovery value (possibly zero).

(**ii**) PmtmV < 0: The claim is still owed to the defaulting counterparty, and one is legally obliged to settle the amount at the PmtmV.

In other words, one loses when the PmtmV against the defaulting counterparty is positive but does not gain if it is negative. Effectively, this is like a short option on the exposure given by $\max(0, PmtmV)$. Therefore, a key parameter to assess this risk is the volatility of the PmtmV or the volatility of future cash flows. The *Potential Future Exposure* (PFE) is an estimate of the PmtmV in the future. Similarly, the *Expected Exposure* (EE) represents the average of only positive PmtmV future values. Figure 12.1 plots both measures for the normal distribution. Analogous to IR risk, credit risk is globally measured as CS01, *i.e.* the dollar value of 1bp shift parallel in the respective credit curve(s).

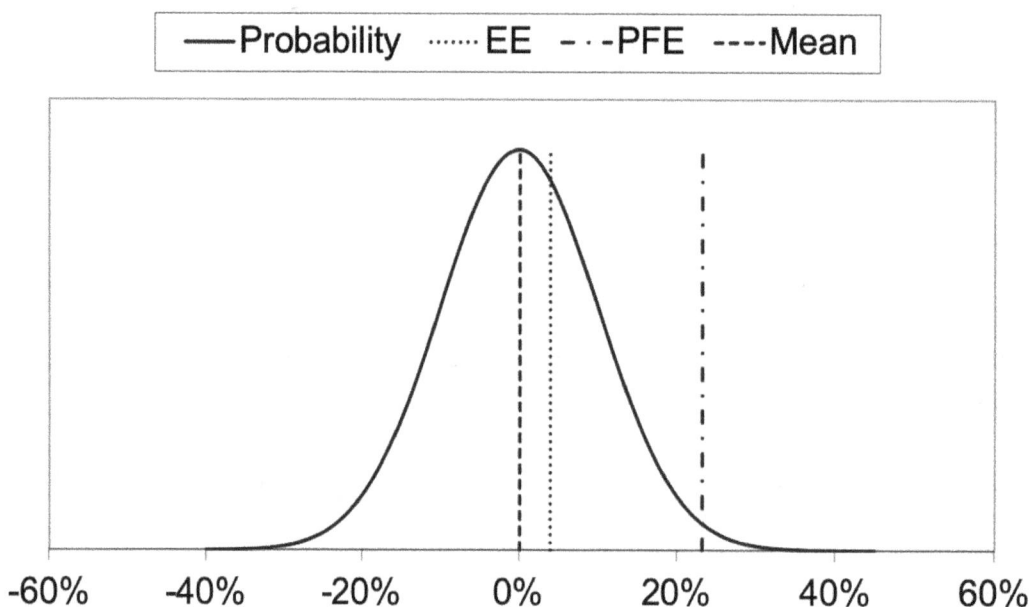

Figure 12.1: Plot of the expected exposure (EE, dotted line), potential future exposure (PFE, dashed-dotted line) for a normal distribution (zero mean, 10% std) for a 99% confidence level (α).

The in-house credit line is the maximum value that the PFE against a specific counterparty must not exceed when taking all current transactions into account. Hence, upon making a trade, it has to be checked that this credit line is not already breached. The credit line is not a static barrier but typically adjusts with the dynamics of the PFE. Even a straightforward credit line model takes into account the default probability, expected recovery rate, the rating agency downgrade probability, and the counterparty correlation. It is possible to increase/reduce the credit line by hedging instruments such as CDS, collateralization, netting, etc.. (see Figure 12.2).

Counterparty credit risk may be controlled using various methods such as

- **Diversification**: making sure that exposure is spread across different counterparties
- **Netting**: the ability to legally offset positive and negative PmtmV upon default
- **Collateral**: holding cash or liquid non-risky assets against the PmtmV
- **Hedging**: trading instruments such as asset swap or credit default swaps (CDS)

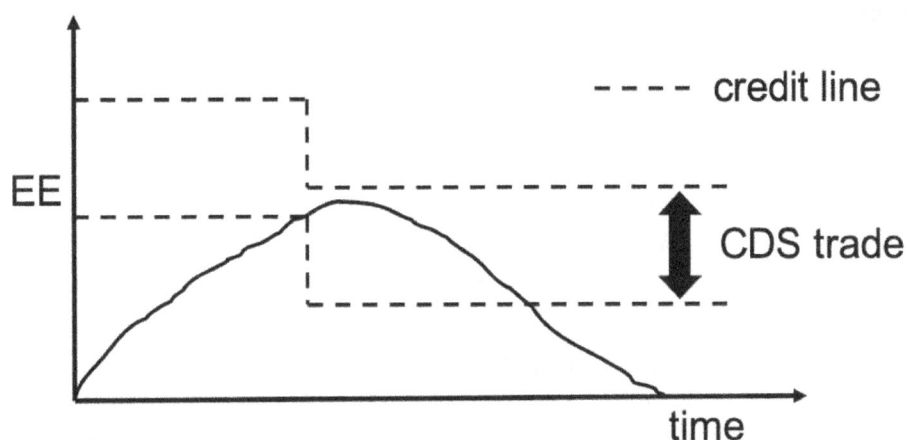

Figure 12.2: Plot of the credit line (PFE) and expected exposure and its respective reduction given a trade in an instrument reducing the exposure.

- **Selectivity**: trading with solid or strongly collateralized counterparties (governments, SPVs) only; note that the 2008 crisis showed that entities prior thought to be risk-free were effectively not (*e.g.* monoline insurers)
- **Clearing house**: the entity which effectively acts as a guarantor to all trades (by imposing collateral/margin); the problem is that the clearing house needs to be able to risk manage its exposure well; as a result, not every OTC instrument is yet cleared

12.1.2 Collateral

The collateral to be posted as a function of PmtmV is defined in the collateral agreement. The collateral agreement determines base currency, agreement type (one way or two way), collateral type (cash, sovereign securities, bonds, equities, etc.), margin call frequency (vanilla/repo products typically intraday, swaps daily), threshold (*i.e.* the amount of uncollateralized exposure, which is not margined), possibly interest rates payable on collateral (OIS, LIBOR) and haircuts (discount applied to collateral deterioration, *i.e.* zero for cash, but some % for debt).

The Credit Support Annex (CSA) is the amount of uncollateralized exposure. It is common to couple terms of the collateral agreement to the credit quality of the counterparties such as:

(*i*) credit rating
(*ii*) credit spread
(*iii*) equity market value
(*iv*) net asset value (*e.g.* for hedge funds)

In general, any OTC trade is associated with a CSA agreement defining, for example, which collateral is allowed and how potential collateral can be substituted (see also Chapter 15). Closely related to the CSA is the so-called *netting* agreement, which effectively governs the collateral management process. As an example, the netting agreement defines which trades make up a collateral unit.

12.1.3 Credit Markets

The credit markets consist of two main investment instruments:

(*i*) loans
→ issuers: corporate, government, commercial banks
→ facilities: term loans, revolving loans or bespoke
(*ii*) bonds
→ issuers: governments ('sovereign bonds'), corporate ('credit-sensitive') In the year 1999, the

original ISDA documentation [1] on credit derivatives was released. After that, the credit derivatives market saw explosive growth in the years leading up to the global financial crisis of 2007-09. Credit Default Swaps (CDSs) accounted for much of the growth. By the end of 2007, there was over $62tn in notional amounts outstanding. This figure had more than halved by the end of 2009. The most common form of CDS is the single-name CDS, where protection is bought (and sold) on a single reference obligation. 'Exotic' forms of CDS include basket CDSs, equity default swaps, zero-recovery CDSs, and credit swaptions. The credit derivatives market underwent substantial change in 2009 with the implementation of the so-called CDS Big Bang [2] and Small Bang Protocols [3], as well as the introduction of new CDS trading conventions. The goal of these changes is to enhance the infrastructure of the CDS market to achieve same-day trade matching, the elimination of offsetting trades, and centralized clearing.

12.2 Floating rate bond/note (FRN)

The concept of a Floating Rate Note (FRN) (also sometimes referred to as a Floating Bond) was already alluded to in the discussion of fixed versus floating interest rate swaps (see 6.4). In addition, the floating rate bond/note (FRN) is presumably also the oldest credit derivative. This is because the cash flows of a FRN and a CDS (to be covered later, see 12.5) are effectively identical. Typically, bonds pay a fixed stream of coupons (*e.g.* US treasuries). The FRN pays coupons that *reset* or *float* in relation to the respective current benchmark interest rate (see Figure 12.3). The reference rate is as usual, typically LIBOR. The FRN itself then pays LIBOR + spread whereby the spread is a function of the issuer's credit rating. For AA-rated credit, the spread is typically zero.

The pricing of an FRN is straightforward. Effectively, it just requires calculating the price from the underlying forward rates (ignoring the spread to the forward rate at the moment). Note that the FRN is insensitive to changes in the interest rate because it 'floats', *i.e.* any IR change is immediately passed on to the price which is therefore always at par.

Figure 12.4 illustrates the sensitivity of an interest rate move on the FRN. Ignoring that the price changes somewhat because the first coupon is fixed, the FRN is effectively *insensitive* to rate moves versus a standard fixed coupon bond. Recall that for a common bond, as rates rise, the discount factors get smaller, and the bond price falls as a consequence. In the FRN, this is exactly offset by the expected future cash flows.

One common use case for hedging FRN rate exposure is to employ a FRA (see 6.2) to lock in the respective borrowing or lending costs. Consider the hypothetical example of an investor who is long a FRN receiving 3M LIBOR + X aiming to transform the floating rate exposure into a fixed

---

[1] https://www.isda.org
[2] https://www.isda.org/traditional-protocol/big-bang-protocol
[3] https://www.isda.org/traditional-protocol/small-bang-protocol

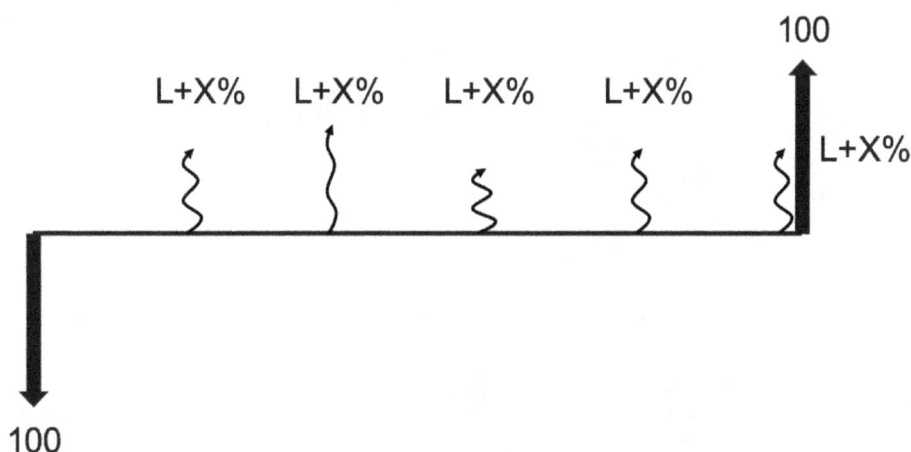

Figure 12.3: Illustration a floating rate note cash flow.

rate. All that is required is to sell a FRA (receiving fixed) against the same or another counterparty with the same payment schedule, and the rate will be locked in. Note that this trade incorporates additional credit risk unless it is cleared and margined by a central clearing house.

12.3 Credit Spreads, ratings and risk premia

Before 1995, credit risk was measured versus treasury curve spreads. By the early 1990's, the reference became increasingly LIBOR, *i.e.* the LIBOR curve became the benchmark instead of some government bond curve (see Figure 12.5). After 2008, as discussed previously, LIBOR is not necessarily the curve to use by default.

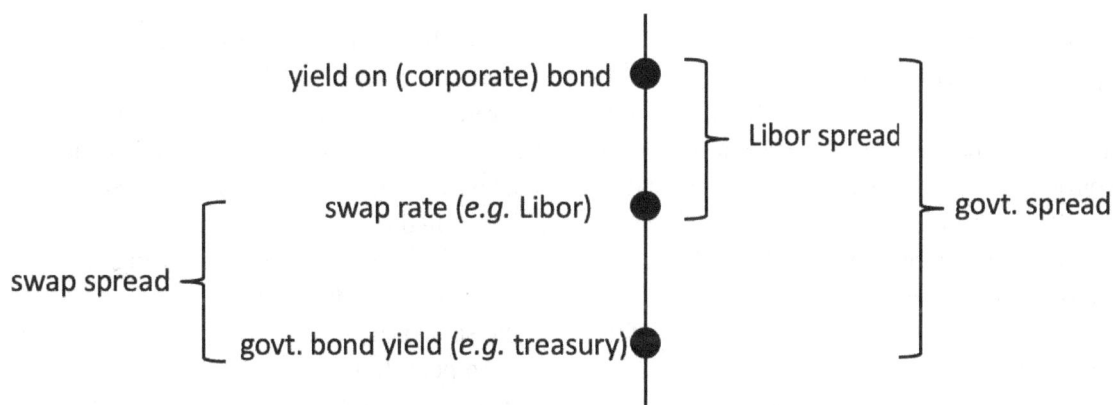

Figure 12.5: Illustration of various credit spreads.

Nonetheless, the spread between the bond yield and swap rate (*e.g.* LIBOR) should more or less be in line with the respective CDS spread of the underlying asset. In order to interpret the credit spread more easily rating agencies such as Moody's, Fitch, or S&P provide so-called standardized ratings, which allow assessing the credit quality and potential default risk quickly. The demarcation

rates go up

year	forward	FV	df	forward x df		year	forward	FV	df	forward x df
1	1.000	1.010	0.9901	0.990		1	1.250	1.0125	0.9877	1.235
2	1.500	1.025	0.9755	1.463		2	1.750	1.0302	0.9707	1.699
3	2.000	1.046	0.9563	1.913		3	2.250	1.0534	0.9493	2.136
4	2.500	1.072	0.9330	2.333		4	2.750	1.0824	0.9239	2.541
5	3.000	1.104	0.9058	2.718		5	3.250	1.1175	0.8948	2.908
6	3.500	1.143	0.8752	3.063		6	3.750	1.1595	0.8625	3.234
				12.479						13.752
			100 x df5	87.521					100 x df5	86.248
			FRN price	**100.00**					FRN price	**100.00**

$FV_3 = (1.010 \times 1.015 \times 1.020)$

$df_3 = 1 / FV_3$

price unchanged

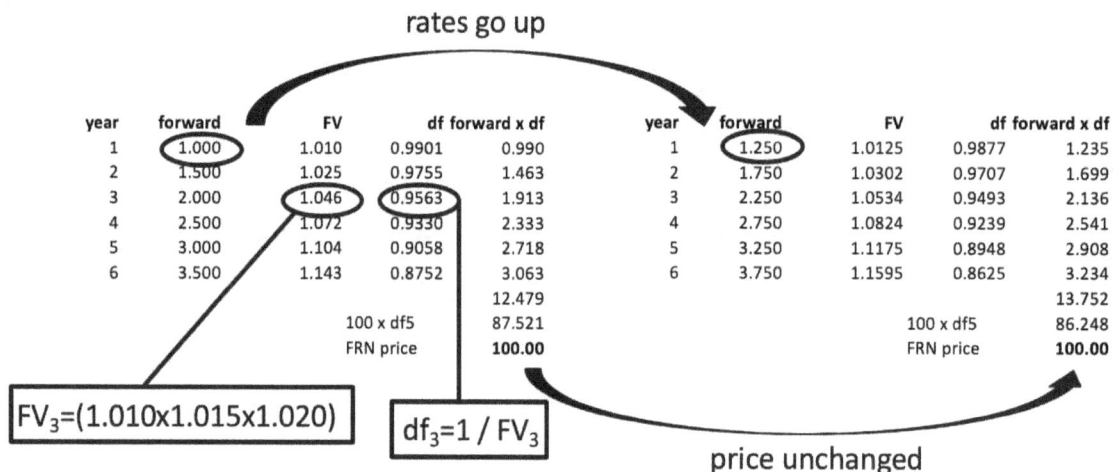

Figure 12.4: Illustration of the floating rate note price sensitivity with respect to interest rate movements, *i.e.* the price is insensitive to a change in the underlying interest rate.

line between 'solid' investments (investment grade) and the opposite (non-investment grade) is an important guideline for many professional investors.

Ratings can be obtained by mapping key fundamental multiples or ratios (*e.g.* operating income, EBITDA, etc.) to a rating table whereby historical data is used to 'calibrate' the mapping. As a further development, models such as KMV [294] pioneered a more quantitative approach. The KMV model and extensions [295] essentially require three parameters:

- **Company value**: value of the company today
- **Company debt**: debt of the company today
- **Implied volatility**: implied volatility of the company backed out from the option market

From these inputs, the model calculates the expected default frequency (EDF) using a lognormal approach. One of the key success stories of the model was the prediction of the Enron crisis [296]. The company Enron had an AA rating 6 months before its 2011 bankruptcy filing while trading at $80. In the KMV model, Enron was in the highest default category by that time because the convergence of asset value to debt level had increased, and the implied volatility exploded.

Related to the discussion about default risk is the so-called risk premium [297]. Since people often mean different things when talking about risk premia contemplate the following example. Consider a (quasi risk-free) 1-year government bond yielding 2% today. Assume a corporate bond of similar maturity has a 3% chance of default over the same time period. What should the yield on the bond be? In a risk-neutral world, one seeks compensation for the default risk, *i.e.* one requires to obtain a yield so that the expectation value compared to the risk-free bond is the same. Hence, the expected payoff is: $(0.97) \cdot (100) + (0.97) \cdot \text{coupon} = 102$. Solving for the coupon gives coupon $= 5/0.97 = 5.15$, *i.e.* a 3.15% spread over the risk-free rate. However, due to *e.g.* liquidity constraints, there is an additional *premium* for risk. Quantifying this risk premium at any given time is effectively the holy grail in asset management since it allows investors to objectively assess where to allocate capital best in a risk-adjusted manner. In other words, knowing the risk premium ex-ante is effectively being able to say where the market is going.

In the prior example, zero *recovery* was assumed in the event of a default. This is typically not the case since potential assets will be liquidated and the proceeds distributed to the creditors in accordance to the seniority of their debt claim. The difference between a complete default is called the *recovery rate* (RR). In the example above, for the case of a RR > 0, the expected payoff is given by $(0.97) \cdot (100) + (0.03 \cdot RR) + (0.97) \cdot \text{coupon} = 102$. Assuming a RR = 50 (*i.e.* 50%) the calculation yields $97 + 1.5 + 0.97 \cdot \text{coupon} = 102$, *i.e.* coupon $= 5.5/0.97 = 5.67$ (*i.e.* 3.67 spread).

Estimating recovery rates is anything but trivial. The long-term average recovery rate for senior investment grade debt is approximately 50% with a standard deviation of about 25% [298]. Recovery rates for corporate debt are more reliable than those of sovereign obligations because there is more data. Another crucial factor is the *time to recovery* since the bankruptcy proceedings may take several years before any decision is taken. From the *RR*, the so-called Loss given default (LGT) can be calculated, defined as $LGD = 1 - RR$. Credit spreads may be derived from default probabilities (PD) and the other way around. However, the inverse problem is more challenging since the credit spread also entails the risk premium, which typically leads to overestimating the default probability. Another problem is that there is no common opinion as to whether implied risk-neutral or historical PD should be used. The proponents of implied PD argue that one should use the probabilities implied from the actual hedging instruments. The advocates of historical PD say that implied PD is an amalgam (PD+RR+risk premium) at best and that *e.g.* CDS spreads react highly nonlinear to the level of PD [299]. In other words, when the market turns against an asset, the CDS price may change significantly. This coupling creates problems or at least significant volatility when estimating *e.g.* loan reserves or credit value adjustment. Under Basel III [4], the CDS spread volatility is a crucial determinant of the capital requirements. It is not yet clear whether this will lead to even more volatility due to positive feedback from the increased hedging activity of CVA desks in the future [300].

12.4 Asset Swap and Asset Swap Spread

Before discussing the arguably most known credit instrument (credit default swap, see 12.5) it is worth to mention another similar instrument, *i.e.* the asset swap. Consider a company, which does not issue FRNs but only fixed coupon bonds. Assume that an investor wants to trade the credit of the company, but without exposure to LIBOR. Before the credit default swap (CDS), the solution was a *synthetic FRN*, which is called the *asset swap*. In the asset swap, one buys the fix coupon bond (*e.g.* at par, funded at LIBOR) and swaps the cash flows into a floating rate with the help of a 3rd party such as a bank. As shown in Figure 12.6, the net coupon is 1% and should equal the hypothetical FRN spread. This spread is called the *asset swap spread* (ASW), which is reflective of the actually traded spread. The only problem for the asset swap is that in case the bond defaults, the fixed/floating swap legs are still alive.

---

[4]https://www.bis.org/bcbs/basel3.htm

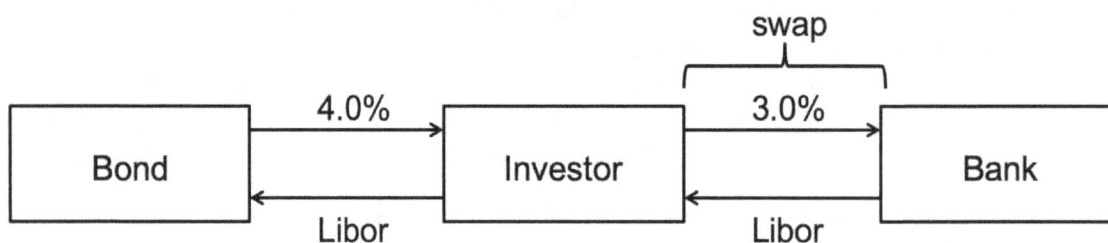

Figure 12.6: Illustration of a synthetic FRN or asset swap.

Another metric in this domain is the *Option-Adjusted Spread* (OAS). The OAS [5] expresses the spread of a fixed-income security rate to its risk-free rate of return, which also takes into account any embedded optionality (*e.g.* a callable feature). The latter makes this spread typically model-dependent. The difference between the ASW and OAS is often little for smaller spreads but increases with a rise in the volatility used to model the option component.

12.5 Credit Default Swap

Around 1995, Credit Default Swaps (CDS) emerged because it was cumbersome to add another IRS transaction on top of the bond. Hence, the CDS was introduced to isolate the credit spread, and the asset swap market died as a consequence. Effectively, the CDS is the most basic credit derivative [301]. CDS are OTC instruments with underlying ISDA documentation and increasingly cleared by exchanged such as ICE [6]. Typically, one party buys credit protection from another for a period between 1 and 10 years. The premium is paid as an annuity (bps p.a.). If a credit event occurs the trade terminates, and the protection seller will either (*i*) buy the underlying obligation at par or (*ii*) cash settle the respective difference.

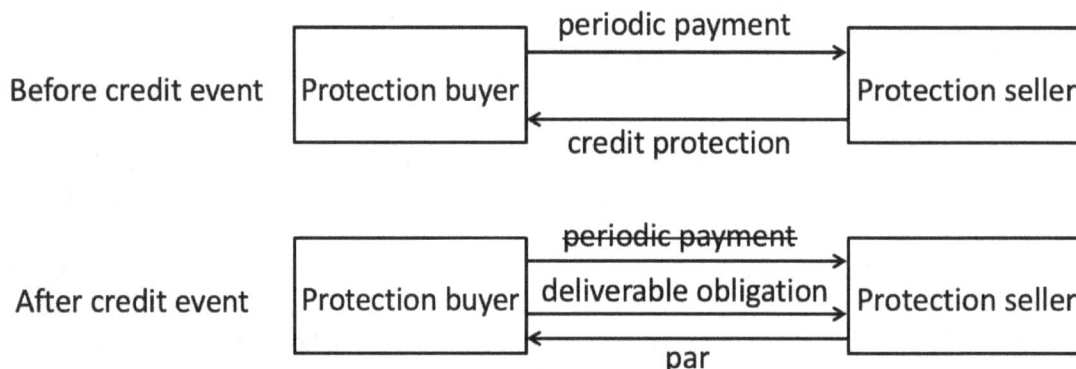

Figure 12.7: Illustration of the CDS payment mechanics.

Buying / Selling credit protection resembles a short/long position in credit risk. This convention sounds confusing at first but is based on the view that the protection seller benefits if the credit

---

[5]Related to the OAS is the Zero-Volatility Spread (ZVS), or Z-Spread given by $Z - spread = OAS + optionality$.
[6]https://www.theice.com/clear-credit

quality of the underwritten asset improves. Hence, the seller is long the credit risk in the sense that he profits if the risk improves. The advantage of a CDS is that one can also use them against loans. This good for commercial banks, which can reduce their exposure to a specific sector. Otherwise, there are effectively two uses for CDS:

(*i*) hedging credit risk: allows free up of credit capacity, easier to buy credit protection than shorting bonds, credit risk can be transferred without borrower consent

(*ii*) investing in credit: taking a view, alternative to direct bond/FRN investment, easier to trade compared to illiquid bonds, more flexibility concerning maturity, access to leverage (CDS is unfunded) For example, a $10m notional CDS gives protection against bonds with a par value of $10m. There is an interesting discussion as to whether this hedge is perfect in theory given that the default risk cannot be hedged by trading the underlying asset. For all practical purposes, the assumption here going forward is that the hedge is perfect, but the interested reader is invited to explore the literature further [302].

If one compares the CDS cash flows to the FRN, then it should be clear now that the CDS is effectively an *unfunded* FRN, *i.e.* there is no investment of the principal at inception.

12.5.1 CDS Pricing

Risk-neutral CDS pricing is straightforward, *i.e.* one effectively just uses a binomial model. Consider the example in Figure 12.8 for a *single period* CDS. Assume the discount rate is 5%, *i.e.* $df = 1/(1+0.05) = 0.952$. The reference asset coupon equals 6% with 50% recovery rate (RR). Finally, the marginal probability of default PD is 2% in each period.

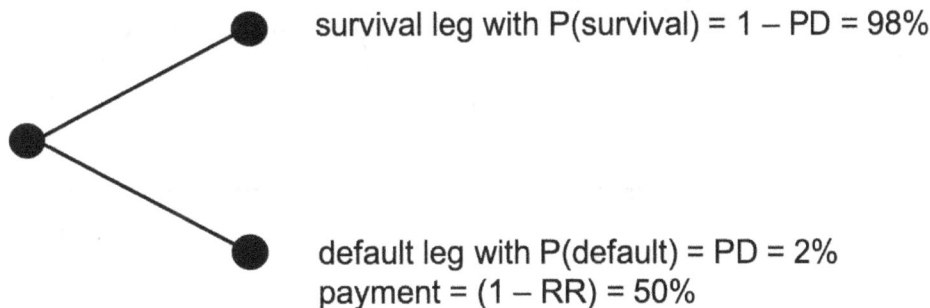

survival leg with P(survival) = 1 − PD = 98%

default leg with P(default) = PD = 2%
payment = (1 − RR) = 50%

Figure 12.8: Single period CDS pricing example.

Setting the two payment legs equal to each other so that the swap value is zero one obtains

$$\text{spread}_{CDS} \cdot (1 - PD) \cdot df = PD \cdot (1 - RR) \cdot$$
$$\text{spread}_{CDS} = \frac{PD \cdot (1 - RR) \cdot df}{(1 - PD) \cdot df} = 1.02\% \tag{12.1}$$

If this is extended to two periods (Figure 12.9) one needs to extend the survival and default legs accordingly and match them, *i.e.*

$$\text{survival} - \text{spread}_{CDS} \cdot \pi_1 \cdot df_1 - \text{spread}_{CDS} \cdot \pi_2 \cdot df_2$$
$$\text{default} PD_1 \cdot (1 - RR) \cdot df_1 + PD_2 \cdot (1 - RR) \cdot \pi_2 \cdot df_2 \tag{12.2}$$

with $\pi_1 = 1 - PD_1$ and $\pi_2 = (1 - PD_1) \cdot (1 - PD_2)$. Solving for the CDS spread then gives

$$\text{spread}_{CDS} = (1 - RR) \cdot \frac{PD_1 \cdot df_1 + PD_2 \cdot \pi_1 \cdot df_2}{\pi_1 \cdot df_1 + \pi_2 \cdot df_2} \, . \qquad (12.3)$$

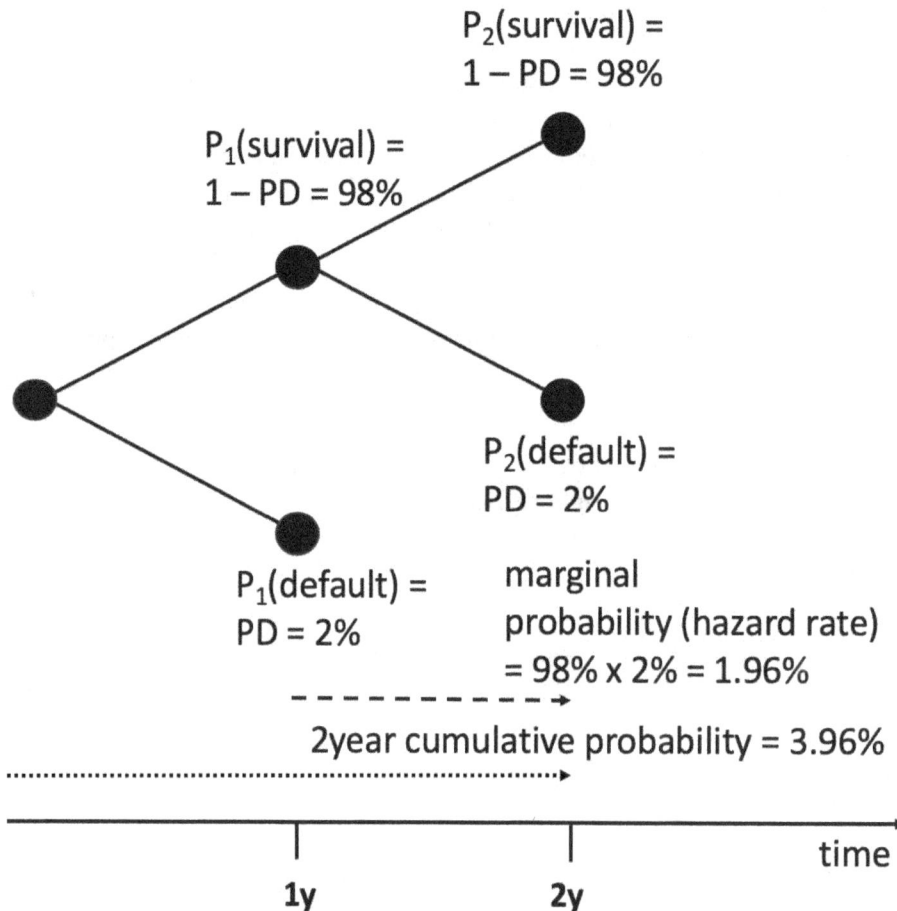

Figure 12.9: Two period CDS pricing example.

The configuration at the default payment can take the following forms:

- 100 + coupon $\rightarrow$ spread paid on default
- 100 + coupon $\rightarrow$ spread not paid on default
- 100 $\rightarrow$ spread paid on default
- 100 $\rightarrow$ spread not paid on default

Typically, the third configuration is used. The prior representations assumed physical settlement on the CDS, which is how all single-name CDS were typically settled in the past. However, when *e.g.* Lehman Brothers declared bankruptcy in 2008, there was an assumed ratio of *150bn outstanding debt versus* 400bn CDS [303]. Despite the presumed mismatch, the settlement processes have typically been very smooth. In September 2006, the ISDA introduced an auction-based protocol for CDS cash settlement. All contracts on CDS indices (itraxx, CDX) are currently cash settled. Note that recovery value determination can take years, which is why the insurer normally takes care of it.

Finally, for the case of settlement at 100 and spread paid upon default, one obtains the following formula for multiple periods

$$\text{spread}_{CDS} = \frac{(1-RR) \cdot \sum_{t=1}^{N} (\pi_{t-1} \cdot PD_t \cdot df_t)}{\sum_{t=1}^{N} (\pi_{t-1} \cdot PD_t \alpha_t^{\text{spread CDS}} \cdot df_t)} + \sum_{t=1}^{N} (\pi_{t-1} \cdot \alpha_t^{\text{spread CDS}} df_t) , \tag{12.4}$$

with α = accrual factor for the CDS and $\pi = \prod_{j=1}^{t} (1 - PD_j)$.

12.5.1.1 Hazard rate

The *hazard rate* h at time t is the probability of default in a small interval dt. Another expression for the hazard rate is default intensity. The hazard rate is related to the cumulative default probability $F(t)$ via

$$F(t) = 1 - \exp[-h \cdot t] = 1 - s(t) , \tag{12.5}$$

with $s(t)$ being the *survival probability*. An approximate relationship between hazard rate and CDS spread is given by the so-called *credit triangle* [304]

$$h \approx \frac{\text{spread}_{CDS}}{(1-RR)} . \tag{12.6}$$

It follows that

$$F(t) = 1 - \exp[-\frac{\text{spread}_{CDS}}{(1-RR)}] = \frac{\text{spread}_{CDS}}{(1-RR)} \cdot T . \tag{12.7}$$

In other words, it is possible to approximately back out the default probabilities implied by a CDS spread in the market. Note that the above formula typically overestimates the historical default values significantly when compared to representative data from rating agencies [305]. Finally, the CDS spread, assuming a recovery rate of zero, is quite similar to the observed OAS spread.

year	CDS spread (bp)	F(t)	annual default probability
1	100%	1.65%	1.65%
2	150%	4.88%	3.22%
3	200%	9.52%	4.64%
4	250%	15.35%	5.84%
5	300%	22.12%	6.77%

Table 12.1: Example of a CDS spread calculation.

12.5.2 CDS: varia

Some key details are essential to be aware of when engaging in a CDS trade. First, there are potentially subtle details about the contract itself. For example, it is crucial to make sure that the CDS contract refers to the correct legal reference entity one is trying to buy protection against. Large corporations often operate a complex network of different branches and entities, which may issue bonds independently from the parent. If the CDS does not refer to this entity, a default might not immediately imply. In a now famous example [7], debt in the Dutch cable operator VodafoneZiggo [8]

---

[7] https://www.bloomberg.com/opinion/articles/2019-01-15/sometimes-cds-is-on-the-wrong-company
[8] https://www.vodafoneziggo.nl

had been moved to another entity, rendering the original entity-referenced CDS contracts worthless without many investors even noticing. Moreover, the correct succession has to be defined on the contracts, *i.e.* what happens in case of mergers/takeovers or other corporate actions. Finally, it is also essential to know what happens to the CDS if the company buys back all its debt.

The declaration of a credit event itself is not always straightforward, or there might be significant delays in the settlement. In general, a credit event includes

- default on bond/loan payment subject to a minimum pay requirement (*e.g.* $1m); note that failing to pay utility bills (gas, power etc.) does in general not constitute a credit event
- bankruptcy in general

On the contrary, rating agency downgrades, widening of CDS spreads, or devaluation of currencies for sovereign debtors do normally *never* constitute a credit event. In the case of bonds, loans, or debt restructuring, the restructuring may also trigger a credit event subsequently. However, as seen in the case of Greece in 2012 [306], there can be much uncertainty.

In the case of physical settlement, the deliverable obligations (*e.g.* bonds) need to be carefully defined as well. Typically, deliverable obligations

- must not be subordinated concerning the reference obligation
- have a maturity limited to a maximum of 30 years
- must not be contingent
- must be in an acceptable currency
- need to be assignable in case of a loan

Moreover, the buyer of the insurance has *de facto* the so-called cheapest to deliver option. The cheapest to deliver option relates to the fact that while in theory upon default, all deliverable obligations should trade at the same recovery rate, it must not necessarily be so. In other words, recovery rates may differ, and the protection buyer can choose to deliver the obligation, which is at the time trading the cheapest. The CDS spread should, in principle, price this in, *i.e.* the protection seller must be compensated for this risk and consequently discount the average recovery rate additionally.

Some of the CDS contract issues above were standardized and solved in 2009 based on their region (North America vs. Europe). Features of the Standard North American CDS (SNAC [9]) are

- fixed coupons and initial cash flows
- fixed coupons are: 100bps (investment grade), 500bps (speculative grade)
- initial cash flows:
  (*i*) cash flow > 0 (long position pays) if fixed coupon < CDS spread
  (*ii*) cash flow < 0 (long position receives) if fixed coupon > CDS spread

The Standard European CDS (SNEC [10]) features

- fixed coupon of 25bps, 100bps, 500bps or 1000bps
- 300bps and 750bps for re-couponing old trades
- otherwise, cash flows as in SNAC

Under SNAC / SNEC cash settlement and the auction process is fully pre-determined [11].

---

[9] http://www.cdsmodel.com/cdsmodel/documentation.html?

[10] http://www.cdsmodel.com/cdsmodel/documentation.html?

[11] www.creditfixings.com

12.5.3 CDS: Capital Structure Arbitrage

One application for using CDS as a trading instrument is capital structure arbitrage (cap-arb). Cap-arb is founded on the Modigliani–Miller theorem [307], which states that the value of a company is invariant to how it is financed. The term *capital structure* itself denotes how a firm finances its assets. This may be via equity issuance, debt, or other securities. In classical cap-arb, one tries to trade a firm's equity against its debt by taking a position in the asset volatility. For example, in 2005/2006, the implied volatility of supermarket retailer Sainsbury's [12] was trading unusually low compared to Tesco [13] (Tesco being the much larger company). As a trade, one could now buy Sainsbury's stock as well as the CDS, or buy CDS on Sainsbury's and sell CDS on Tesco. Since there was an expectation of a leveraged buyout (LBO) the sensible idea is to follow the former strategy. Indeed, the CDS and asset implied volatility exploded following that given the LBO a change in the capital structure of the company was likely to follow [14]. As a result, the investment made a profit on both the equity rally as well as the spike in the CDS spread.

Another example where things did not turn out so well is the recent case of the French supermarket chain Casino [15]. Casino is part of a larger group structure whereby its parent company therein is Rallye [16]. When Casino ran into business troubles, investors began as usual to short the stock to profit from an expected decline in the asset price. At the same time, some hedge funds additionally sold CDS on Rallye assuming that the latter would survive if it came down to bankruptcy considerations [17]. However, exactly the opposite happened as Rallye started to negotiate its debt going forward. In other words, the capital structure play did not work out at all.

12.5.4 CDS: Cash Bond Basis

Note that a CDS can be replicated by long and short positions in cash bonds by the protection seller and protection buyer. In turn, they can borrow/lend the reference obligation in the repo market such that

- The premium leg of the CDS with a long position in the reference obligation combined with a fixed-for-floating interest rate swap and
- The payout leg with a short position in the reference bond and a repo agreement to borrow the security

The replication of the CDS legs involves several steps and is, therefore, operationally intensive. Recall that the Z-spread is the yield spread of a bond referenced to the zero-coupon swap curve, rather than riskless zero coupon bond yields inferred from US treasuries. The Z-spread often also reflects the asset swap and CDS equivalence when comparing cash bond spreads with CDS premia. The basis or spread between cash bond implied credit spread and the respective CDS is called the cash-CDS basis, Cash Bond Basis or CDS-bond basis. Note that extracting the implied credit spread from the corporate bond spread is only trivial if the company had issued a FRN with the same maturity as the CDS. Since this is typically not the case, one needs to apply a methodology such as PECS [308] to extract the spread from fixed rate bonds. Even if the asset swap and CDS are in theory through the no-arbitrage requirement equivalent, the CDS versus cash bond basis can be

---

[12]https://www.sainsburys.co.uk

[13]https://www.tesco.com

[14]https://reut.rs/2JQPica

[15]http://www.casino.fr

[16]http://rallye.fr

[17]https://www.ft.com/content/7c66a3c6-8141-11e9-9935-ad75bb96c849

substantial [309]. This discrepancy can arise due to differences in calculating the basis (*e.g.* Z-spread vs. I-spread etc.), market forces or funding, among others.

12.5.5 CDS Indices

A CDS index is a measure of the performance of a pre-selected group of CDS quotes (or premiums). CDS indexes allow investors to buy and sell protection against default on baskets of CDS. There are several principal 'families' of CDS indexes:

(*i*) iTraxx [18]: the iTraxx brand name, which is owned by the International Index Company (IIC). The Markit Group collects CDS quotes for the index-constituent names on behalf of the IIC. iTraxx indexes cover credit derivatives markets in Europe, Asia, and Australia. Currencies: EUR, JPY, USD.

(*ii*) CDX: The CDS IndexCo [19] administers the CDX indexes which are marketed by Markit. CDX indexes cover credit derivatives markets in North America and the emerging markets. Currencies: USD, EUR. New series' of iTraxx indexes launch every March and September. The standard maturities are three, five, seven, and ten years (5- and 10-year only for the Crossover and Sector Sub-indexes). In October 2006, the IIC and Markit introduced LevX, an index of CDSs on European leveraged loans. At the time of writing, there are two LevX indexes - LevX Senior (75 CDSs) and LevX Subordinated (45 CDSs). In 2007, a North American leveraged loan CDS index (LCDX North America) containing 100 names was introduced.

The credit indices currently trade as OTC mainly. EUREX has introduced futures, but they are not very liquid (the same is true for ETFs). A respective index is created with an initial price of 100, including a fixed coupon. Buying/selling the index is like trading a bond. Hence, if one buys the index, one takes on the credit exposure of the credit portfolio, *i.e.* buying/selling the index is equivalent to selling/buying protection. As a consequence, the quarterly coupon is paid/received by the protection buyer/seller.

12.5.6 Credit Linked Note (CLN)

The Credit Linked Note (CLN) is effectively a credit default swap embedded into a debt issue. The issuance is typically routed through a *Special Purpose Vehicle* (SPV), which is independently collateralized. Hence, contrary to a CDS, the CLN is normally fully collateralized. Similar to the CDS, the CLN pays a coupon composed of a reference rate plus the CDS spread reflecting the issuer. The investor buys the note at 100% and receives the periodic coupon streams until redemption at par if there is no credit event. The CLN is not traded OTC and allows retail investors to speculate on credit. Otherwise, the mechanics are identically to a (fully funded) CDS transaction.

12.5.7 Equity Credit Relation

Intuitively, asset volatility, asset price, and credit spread must be related. The classical approach for this link is the Merton model, which equates the default event to the crossing of a virtual downside barrier on the asset value (or price) [291, 310]. In other words, the default probability of an individual company derives from a knock-in barrier put option. The barrier is thereby set equal to the option exercise price, which is the value of the outstanding debt of the company. If the value of the

---

[18]https://ihsmarkit.com/products/markit-itraxx.html
[19]http://www.indexco.com

company's assets goes below the debt level, it automatically triggers the default event following the assumption that the debtor is insolvent if he cannot meet his financial obligations.

Another standard model to provide the link between default probabilities and observable equity market data is given by [311] and is equivalent to the CreditGrades model [312]. CreditGrades is arguably the most well-known publicly available commercial structural model. As the writing implies, this model is also conceptually based on the original Merton structural model [291]. Hence, in the same spirit, the asset value is assumed to follow the typical geometric Brownian motion process

$$dAV_t = AV_t v dt + \sigma_{AV} AV_t dW_t \, , \tag{12.8}$$

where AV denotes the asset value at time t. The asset value is typically assumed to have no drift ($v = 0$) assuming that the company issues debt to keep the leverage level constant over time. The default barrier $B_t = LD$ is given by the product of the expected recovery rate averaged over all debt classes L' and the debt per share D. The evolution itself is then modeled as a stochastic process and is given by

$$LD = L' \cdot D \exp[\lambda Z - \lambda^2/2] \, , \tag{12.9}$$

where Z is the mean and λ the standard deviation characterizing the underlying lognormal distribution. Given an uncertain recovery rate, the default barrier can be hit unexpectedly, resulting in a jump-like default event. Hence, the model default event immediately occurs when the asset value breaches the default barrier.

The approximation for the survival probability P_t is given by

$$P_t = \Phi\left(-\frac{A_t}{2} + \frac{\ln(d)}{A_t}\right) - d \cdot \Phi\left(-\frac{A_t}{2} - \frac{\ln(d)}{A_t}\right) \, , \tag{12.10}$$

where $A_t^2 = \sigma^2 t + \lambda^2$, $d = \frac{AV_0}{L' \cdot D} \exp[\lambda^2]$, $AV_0 = S_0 + L' \cdot D$ and Φ denoting the cumulative normal distribution. Finally, the asset volatility is approximated as $\sigma_{AV} = \sigma \frac{S}{S + L' \cdot D}$. Note that to now calculate the implied credit spread, one needs to know the actual recovery rate R, which is credit specific. The recovery rate can be different because, for example, R for an unsecured debt obligation is typically lower than $\bar{L}$ because the latter also includes secured debt with a higher recovery rate. Hence, this reflects a model parameter mismatch. Nonetheless, taking into account this limitation one can calculate the final credit spread given R and P_t as

$$CDS_{\text{spread}}(0, T) = r \cdot (1 - R) \frac{(1 - P_0 + H)}{P_0 - P_T \exp[-rT] - H} \, , \tag{12.11}$$

with $H = \exp[\frac{r\lambda^2}{\sigma^2}] \cdot (G(T + \frac{\lambda^2}{\sigma^2}) - G(\frac{\lambda^2}{\sigma^2}))$. The function G is given by

$$G_T = d^{z+0.5} \cdot \Phi\left(-\frac{\ln(d)}{\sigma\sqrt{T}} - z\sigma\sqrt{T}\right) + d^{z+0.5} \cdot \Phi\left(-\frac{\ln(d)}{\sigma\sqrt{T}} - z\sigma\sqrt{T}\right) \, , \tag{12.12}$$

with $z = \sqrt{0.25 + 2r/\sigma^2}$. The original model above is designed to work with historical estimates for the equity volatility, but it can be modified to work with implied volatility [313] and stochastic volatility models as well [314].

The quality assessment of relating equity market parameters to the credit world and the other way around is such that it is not perfect but that there is an apparent positive correlation. Whether or not these modeled relationships can be used for relative value trades (*e.g.* low barrier knock-in put versus CDS) should be a very case-specific decision.

The alternative to the structural model approach which avoids the need to specify a barrier level triggering default is a reduced form model [20]. Here the default is seen as a random event and modeled as a Poisson (jump-to-default) process. However, the problem with the Poisson model types is that they often do not calibrate well to the current equity market parameters. An alternative model which has been frequently used in this context is the Constant Elasticity of Variance (CEV) model [315, 316, 317, 318]. The dynamics governing the CEV model are given by

$$dS = \mu S dt + \sigma S^{\alpha} dZ, \tag{12.13}$$

whereby α is the so-called elasticity term. Note that the stochastic part of the CEV model corresponds to the SABR model with $\alpha = 0$ (see 6.13.1). Unlike in the BSM model, the asset price can go to zero in the CEV model, which constitutes the desired property in case of default. In other words, within a reduced-form model, the probability of default is the probability that the share price hits zero over a time horizon T. The fundamental motivation behind the CEV model is that it is possible to account for the negative relationship between asset prices and volatility by setting the parameter $\alpha < 1$ [21]. Another way of looking at this is to realize that the CEV process mixes a lognormal process ($\alpha = 1$) with a normal process ($\alpha = 0$). Note that while this is a useful and straightforward parametric extension of BSM, the CEV model is typically not able to fit the skew for the full term structure and is therefore not widely used in practice. Moreover, the volatility dynamics implied by the model are not in line with BSM [319].

The calculation of the default probability in the CEV model then goes as follows. The model is calibrated to observed option market prices for the equity in question using a sensible maturity range (*e.g.* 6 months, 12 months and 24 months), *i.e.* the parameters σ and α are estimated using the least squares fitting approach. Then the probability of default is set equal to the probability of the share price reaching zero. In the CEV model, the option pricing formula is expressed in terms of the non-central chi-square χ^2 distribution [320]. In other words, contrary to BSM, the share price is not governed by the standard normal distribution but via the χ^2 distribution, which is more skewed. Therefore, given a fit of the model parameters to the option market, the χ^2 distribution can be derived so that for a given time horizon T the probability of default prior to T is given by $Pr(S_T = 0, t < T) = 1 - \chi^2$. Finally, the CDS price in the CEV model is given by the rebate price in time to expiration [321].

12.5.8 Equity Default Swap (EDS)

Another financial instrument related to the equity-credit relation [322] above is the so-called Equity Default Swap (EDS) [323, 324, 317, 325]. The EDS is effectively the equity counterpart of the CDS whereby an 'equity' event is defined as the decline of the equity stock market price below a pre-defined barrier (*e.g.* 30%). Upon triggering the barrier, the holder receives a fixed payment determined by notional N and recovery rate RR as

$$N \cdot (1 - RR), \tag{12.14}$$

and the trade terminates. Contrary to the CDS world, the recovery rate for an EDS is fixed, *i.e.* typically at 50%. Throughout the trade, the options pay a fixed or floating coupon/spread reflective

---

[20]Reduced form model denotes any model which uses a simpler/reduced form process to model the dynamics.

[21]Note that for $\alpha = 1$ the model recovers BSM dynamics.

of the risk of the equity event. Hence, one is dealing with an American style downside digital. The EDS spreads are typically higher than their CDS variant given that an equity event, as defined above, is more probable than a credit event. Obviously, at some barrier level, the two prices should converge. The EDS pricing given the low barrier is challenging from a volatility surface calibration point of view and also requires assessing the impact of stochastic volatility, possibly in combination with a jump-diffusion process. However, the amount of benefit traders price in using more sophisticated models is as often a function of the market itself. The advantage of an EDS is that the trigger event is clearly defined including the fixed recovery rate. EDS pricing is possible within the CEV model family and analytical formulas are available in the literature [324].

12.5.9 Credit Default Obligation (CDO)

The emergence of Credit Default Obligations (CDOs) and other structured credit vehicles is often attributed to have been a significant driver of the 2008/09 financial crisis [326]. Indeed, it is hard to argue against the view that these products contributed to the credit cycle boom. However, if properly understood and used, these financial products can deliver performance for a professional investor [327].

Consider a portfolio of 100 bonds, each of which has a 1% default probability for the next year. This portfolio is equivalent to an S&P rating of BB to B (low investment grade). Now the three portfolios are split as follows:

- Portfolio A has 10 bonds
- Portfolio B has 15 bonds
- Portfolio C has 20 bonds

However, instead of assigning the bonds to each tranche at *inception*, one does it at *maturity* as a function of their redemption level:

- Portfolio A contains the first 5 defaults (equity tranche)
- Portfolio B contains the next 10 defaults (mezzanine tranche)
- Portfolio C contains default after the first 15 (senior tranche)

What is then the chance that the senior tranche ever experiences a default? Even without a thorough mathematical analysis, one can guess that the default probability for the senior tranche is reasonably low if

- the defaults are reasonably independent
- there is perfect correlation, then the rating of each tranche is identical (*i.e.* B) and the default probability of the equity trance is $1 / 5 = 20\%$

20% default probability sounds high, but this is fine as long as the investor is fairly compensated for the risk. Similarly, the assumption that all components do not all blow up at the same time is critical here. The remains of a defaulting company are often the equity alone, and then it might even be in the interest of the equity tranche holder to take over some of the defaulting companies. The mezzanine tranche pays a small spread because if the defaults are uncorrelated, there is only a small chance of 6 defaults. The senior tranche is *effectively* risk-free again under the assumption of no highly correlated defaults. The risk *tranching* process above also facilitates access to more funding sources. In reality, there are more than three tranches, and especially during the years 2007-2009 default correlation was **not** independent.

The securitization boom did, in a way, start with Enron [296] who provided the market with various examples of what financial engineering can do. Following the early innovation, assets that have been securitized so far include car loans, mortgages, credit card receivables, etc.. As far as mortgages go, the central mistake was to assume that subprime mortgages behave similarly as prime mortgages. However, even based on intuition alone, subprime defaults must show a higher correlation. Hence, mortgage-backed securities (MBS, the CDO analogue) created access to mortgages that should otherwise never be granted. To some extent, the structured credit industry transitioned from a bespoke OTC product to a flow product without being generally challenged on some of the key underlying assumptions.

Another simple securitization example goes as follows. Combine 100 different USD 100m loans in a very diversified portfolio. The structuring desk then delivers them into an SPV, which is typically independently capitalized. The SPV can now issue debt, which is guaranteed by the loans. Again, a tranching process is applied whereby the USD 200m of the equity tranche takes the first losses. Hence, the remaining USD 800m of the bonds do not lose any money until USD 200m is lost. Now assume a 1% p.a. default probability with a recovery rate of 40%, *i.e.* the loss given default (LGD) is 1-40% = 60%. What is the rating of the equity tranche? The expected loss (EL) on the $1bn is $EL = PD \cdot LGD \cdot \$1\text{bn} = 1\% \cdot 60\% \cdot \$1\text{bn} = \$6m$. The EL of USD 6m on the USD 200m tranche is $6/200 = 0.03 = 3\%$. The default probability for the tranche is then $PD = EL/LGD = 0.03/0.6 = 0.05 = 5\%$. The rating of the equity tranche is thus dependent on how the market prices the 5% p.a. default probability. The default probability of the remaining tranche (*i.e.* 80% of the portfolio that kicks in after 20% loss) is effectively zero, *i.e.* super-senior or AAA.

13. Trading Strategies

13.1 Simple strategy types

Several trading strategies or trade types have already been introduced in the earlier chapter within the context of various derivatives, *e.g.* interest rate carry (see 7.1.5) or capital arbitrage (see 12.5.3). Given the cross-asset setting in this book, the following short paragraphs will focus on general trading strategies as well as position sizing instead of the implementation of specific views (*e.g.* buying commodity futures due to smaller expectations of crop harvests given dry weather conditions).

All cross-asset derivative trades can be characterized across at least two main dimensions: (*i*) theta earning / paying implying short / long gamma and (*ii*) net long / short volatility. Whether one prefers to be theta earning / paying is clearly a matter of market conditions but also of personal trading style. Theta paying corresponds to more active trading behavior since one needs to monetize the gamma. Trading long gamma consistently well is a skill and will also entail more trading costs in terms of slippage and fees even if it is not required to cross the bid/offer spread. Directional trades are often best implemented with forwards. Having said this, at low implied volatility it can be beneficial to replace the underlying with calls of the same delta to benefit from the convexity of the latter. The inverse is true when volatility or skew is high, *i.e.* selling puts to replace the underlying can be a good way to monetize expensive volatility levels. These strategies can also be implemented with risk reversals (*i.e.* short put, long call) in order to benefit from selling skew. Sometimes these strategies are referred to as cash extraction trades.

Very often various strategies need to be combined in order for the trading book to not suffer in theta/carry. For example, since buying protection via volatility or puts in general has a cost, running a net short volatility position against long short-dated puts can be a good compromise. Moreover, since longer-dated options are typically priced higher given steady market demand for protection, this combination can offer good opportunities. Another classic combination is *call overwriting* in case the book is long the underlying structurally in general. Call overwriting means to systematically sell short-dated OTM calls in order to collect the premium and improve the theta carry of the book. This strategy has also the advantage of not being detrimental in a crash scenario. Note that buying volatility to purely hedge a long position is likely to be overpriced and might additionally not offer the desired level of correlation in a crash situation.

The strike of the option is another key determinant for the success of a derivative strategy. This means that while cheap OTM might look attractive they also have low delta, *i.e.* the convexity only kicks in for large moves. This is why ITM options will deliver higher returns for regular market moves. Along those lines, relative value trades aim to identify assets or asset components, which are either expensive or cheap compared to historical metrics in isolation or in relation to other assets. For example, the current spread between the realized variance of two assets might be wide compared to their historical average so that one would trade the spread in order to speculate on convergence over time. Alternatively, under the assumption of a particular volatility model, it might be possible to find components in the respective variance risk premium which looks overpriced [328]. Risk premia trading strategies have in general been popular in the market for some time now. The promise is to dynamically allocate risk towards the best investment styles (interest rate carry, trend following, value and momentum) in a cross-asset setting. The implementation can again often be done using derivatives.

Special situation trades center around particular events such as earnings announcements or corporate actions. For example, expressing a view on the probability of an unexpected event following a corporate reporting day or central bank communication is a common trade setup.

13.2   Cost-of-carry and roll-down

When managing a derivatives book and implementing trading strategies it is important to be clear about the contextual meaning of cost-of-carry and roll-down. As already established in the introductory chapter (see 2.1.4), the classical cost-of-carry with reference to the commodities market is zero for other derivatives. However, there are clearly costs relating to funding, refinancing, margin, capital, which need to be measured and quantified closely. Hence, for practical purposes these costs make up the cost-of-carry for a derivatives book. The other concept is *roll-down*. In the commodities world, cost-of-carry and roll-down are often used in the same context and denote for example the convergence of the future price to the spot price at expiry of the former. In the interest rate world, (positive or negative) roll-down can for example be seen as the convergence of a forward FRA rate to the respective interest rate reference assuming that the yield curve remains *static*. This analysis should also be applied when analyzing curve trades (flatteners/steepeners) in order to ideally benefit from positive roll-down for the scenario when there is no curve move. Benefitting from positive roll-down is also a well-known strategy in the volatility index world (see 4.1.3). Since the VIX future term structure [1] is typically in contango, buying the front months versus selling the back months will generate positive roll yield.

13.3   Position sizing

Trading strategy decisions are typically based on incomplete information, which means some of them turn out to be wrong. In the worst case, the trading desk then needs to cut the losses, which usually means to reverse/exit the position. The latter can be very costly for illiquid positions or large bid/offer spreads in general. Hence, sizing the position correctly at inception and dynamically during the trade lifecycle can be of critical importance.

Arguably the most prominent position sizing schemes are based on or derived from the Kelly (Growth) criterion [329] . The underlying formula determines the optimal portfolio percentage

---

[1]http://vixcentral.com

allocation to individual trades given their respective ratio of success ('edge') to failure probability ('odds') as well as the associated gain or loss. In other words, it tries to assess the amount of money to dedicate on an individual trade in relation to the potential P/L. The exact formula is given by

$$A_P = (P_{size} \cdot DD_{P_{max}}) \cdot \left(Prob_{base} - \frac{Prob_{stress}}{P_{base}/L_{stress}} \right), \qquad (13.1)$$

where A_P is the portfolio allocation notional of the trade in question, P_{size} the portfolio size, $DD_{P_{max}}$ the maximum tolerable portfolio drawdown, $Prob_{base}$ the probability of the base case, $Prob_{stress}$ the probability of the stress case, P_{base} the profit in the base case and L_{stress} the loss in the stress case.

As an example, consider $P_{size} = \$100m$ with a maximum tolerable drawdown of $DD_{P_{max}} = 10\%$. A prospective new trade is estimated to be characterized by $Prob_{base} = 55\%$, $Prob_{Stress} = 45\%$, $P_{base} = 15\%$ and $L_{stress} = 5\%$. The notional allocation to this trade is then $A_P = (\$100m \cdot 10\%) \cdot (55\% - \frac{45\%}{15\%/5\%}) = \$4m$ or 4% of the total portfolio.

There several issues with the approach above. While the allocation is mathematically optimal, the output is strongly dependent on the assumptions of the input parameters. Moreover, it does not take into account the correlation between the other trades in the portfolio. In other words, if several success/failure probabilities are positively correlated, then one is adding implicitly more risk to the portfolio than assumed. Finally, the formula does not account for different time frames or investment horizons as it is based on a binary outcome.

14. Scenario Risk and Value at Risk

14.1 Introduction

Operating a trading desk involves managing risks. These risks need to be identified, measured, reported, and controlled. In a bank, these tasks are independently carried out by risk management (RM), legal & compliance, and product control (PC). The key risks concerning trading desks are:

- **Market risk**: Risk of large P/L variance due to mark-to-market valuation adjustment.
- **Counterparty Credit risk**: Risk of counterparty credit rating deterioration or default.
- **Funding and liquidity risk**: Risk of funding stress or liquidity issues for positions.
- **Operational risk**: Risk of wrong bookings, modeling, or trading system outages.
- **Reputational risk**: Risk of reputational damage due to unauthorized or fraudulent trading activity.

Market, credit, and liquidity risk has already been covered to some extent when discussing greeks and their behavior. The assessment of these risk factors is typically done separately by dedicated market and credit risk (*e.g.* Credit Risk Management, CRM) teams. Funding and liquidity risk is also a concern for the treasury department, which typically takes a more holistic view of the refinancing/funding requirements of the financial institution as a whole. The role of Product Control is to make sure that the valuation and potential valuation adjustments or reserves against positions are justified and in line with market practice. This task is often not trivial and depending on the liquidity profile of a particular trade, a topic of frequent discussion between the trading desk and the PC officer. The monitoring of operational risk, including topics such as incorrect or late trade bookings, is often split across various functions such as the trading chief operating officer and again PC. Finally, reputational risk topics range from concerns about the nature or counterparty of individual trades [330] to the numerous rogue trading scandals reported in the past [331].

Before discussing risk measures in detail, it makes sense to wonder what actually makes a good metric from a statistical perspective. The following attributes are important:

- **Translational invariance**: if a fixed amount is added to all scenarios, then the risk changes by that fixed amount

- **Monotonicity**: a portfolio with consistently worse performance than others measures more risk
- **Positive homogeneity**: doubling the portfolio size results in twice as much risk measure
- **Subadditivity**: if portfolios are combined, the risk measure must take into account diversification benefits

14.1.1 Scenario Risk and Stress Testing

Scenario risk aims to simulate the behavior of the trading book under various market (stress) scenarios. The possible scenarios to run are limitless, and one needs to define what is most relevant and realistic for the respective book/exposure. The most common scenario is P/L impact analysis as a function of market parameter perturbations such spot and implied volatility ladders (-30%, -20%,...0%..., +20%, +30%). More complicated scenarios include specific variations of market data in order to proxy the impact of a future market scenarios (*e.g.* EU breakup = spot -30%, volatility +30%, correlation +20%, USDEUR +30% etc.). Moreover, various stress tests corresponding to extreme historic market conditions (*e.g.* 2008) are routinely replayed to examine the impact on the books (*e.g.* oil shock 1970s, stock market crash 1987, GBP currency crisis, emerging market default 1998). The information obtained from these simulations can then ideally be used to improve the book dynamics in times of stress by adding hedges. The reason why it makes sense to include ladder levels up to -40% / +40% is not because one necessarily expects movements of this magnitude on one single day, but because it might be required to hold the position due to liquidity constraints longer than expected (*e.g.* in this case up to -40% in spot). As a matter of fact, (il)liquidity risk [332] is often the most critical risk driver for a book. Given insufficient data, it is also challenging to model.

The ability to define bespoke scenarios is, in particular, useful for conducting stress tests. Stress tests should, among other things, reflect macroeconomic scenarios (*e.g.* stock market crash, emerging market default, oil crisis) and be designed as a shock to capture this information. As a start, it is useful to obtain a spot ladder (-20%, -15%,...,+15%, +20%) for the P/L and the most critical greeks. In the case of the delta, it is also useful to weight it additionally as a function of the respective daily volume so that illiquid underlyings thereby obtain higher importance. It is essential to make sure that scenarios and greeks are defined in the same way so that they are in line. If this is the case, then *e.g.* the reported delta is in line with the derivative of the spot ladder around the ATM region. Finally, convexity in variables such as volatility of volatility needs to be carefully measured as well since not all risks are represented in the spot level movement alone.

As mentioned before, when dealing with illiquid assets, the scenario risk should include measures that relate the delta exposure against the daily trading volume. This coupling is required because trading delta up to 30% daily volume to rebalance or even exit a trade can be a problem. Moreover, the trading volume may dry up, *i.e.* the situation could get even worse. The issue might get even more troublesome if one adds a short gamma position into the mix. Finally, other market participants may quickly sense that there is 'blood in the water' and try to corner a problematic position even further. The recent loss within the CIO department of JPMorgan illustrates this problem accurately [333]. In this particular case, market participants noticed a dislocation between the skew and spread level of a particular CDS index arising from the JPMorgan position and started betting against it to force a reversion to the mean. While the trades initially did not work, the pressure both from media and market ultimately forced JPMorgan to unwind their positions at a significant loss.

14.1.2 Value at Risk

Value at Risk (VaR) tries to answer the question of how much one can lose on a given position in case the market behaves in a certain way. More precisely, VaR is defined as the maximum likely loss of a portfolio over a specified time horizon (possibly ranging from days to several years). The probability for this loss is given by a so-called confidence level (typically >95%). VaR is then normally quoted in cash terms, *e.g.* USD lost. If VaR is positive/negative, it implies a loss/profit. More formally, VaR at confidence level p is defined as the $100 \cdot p\%$ quantile of the underlying loss distribution. Losses exceeding VaR are called *VaR exceptions*. For example, a daily VaR measure at 95% confidence level states USD 5m. This metric means that in 95 out of 100 days, one can *statistically* expect a loss of at most USD 5m. VaR is often criticized by academics and practitioners alike for valid reasons. Most criticism centers around unrealistic assumptions of the return distribution. Despite the (valid) criticism, VaR is still how trading desk risks are predominately quantified and presented to senior management.

14.1.2.1 Value at Risk: Advantages and Disadvantages

One principal reason for the adoption of VaR is that it is easy to understand, *i.e.* the units are in potential 'money lost'. VaR can also be applied to effectively any portfolio/position consistently, and the aggregation across different portfolios is easy. VaR can take into account correlations between different risk factors (*e.g.* dividend exposure against volatility) and collapse them into one measure.

On the negative side of things, VaR takes no account of losses larger than specified, *e.g.* the 95% confidence level loss does not contain information about the remaining 5% loss (which is typically larger). Hence, VaR does not provide information about the (size of the) *tail losses*. In the case of a position with a highly improbable substantial loss, VaR does typically not detect the risk, *i.e.* the size of the position can *in theory* grow infinitely. Expressed more technically, this means that VaR is not a sub-additive measure, *i.e.* the risk of the sum is always smaller (or equal) to the sum of the risks. For these reasons, VaR can, in principle, be manipulated, since the risk of *e.g.* selling large numbers of deep OTM options might go undetected.

14.1.2.2 Value at Risk: Toy Example

Consider the toy example of two profitable trading desks. The task at hand is to assess which desk is more profitable in a risk-adjusted manner. From the average trades the following statistics is derived:

- Trading desk **A**:
- Average trades per day = 100
- Successful trade makes +10.05, losing trade is -10.00 on average
- Probability of win = 0.5, *i.e.* expected P/L over one trading day: $100 \cdot (0.5 \cdot \$10.05 - 0.5 \cdot \$10) = \$2.5$

- Trading desk **B**:
- Average trades per day = 100
- Successful trade makes +50.30, losing trade is -10.00 on average
- Probability of win = 1/6, *i.e.* expected P/L over one trading day: $100 \cdot (1/6 \cdot \$50.30 - 5/6 \cdot \$10.00) = \$5$

Hence, desk A makes a small profit every other time on average while desk B has fewer winning trades, but if they do, it pays off significantly. It is of interest to assess the following questions:
(*i*) Which trading desk does one want to invest more?
(*ii*) Which trading desk operation is less risky?

(*iii*) How much capital should one commit?

(*iv*) What is a reasonable rate of return as a function of the committed capital?

Figure 14.1 shows the associated probability distribution for the number of winning trades. The probability distribution is here modeled as a binomial distribution yielding the discrete probability distribution of the number of successes in a sequence of n independent experiments.

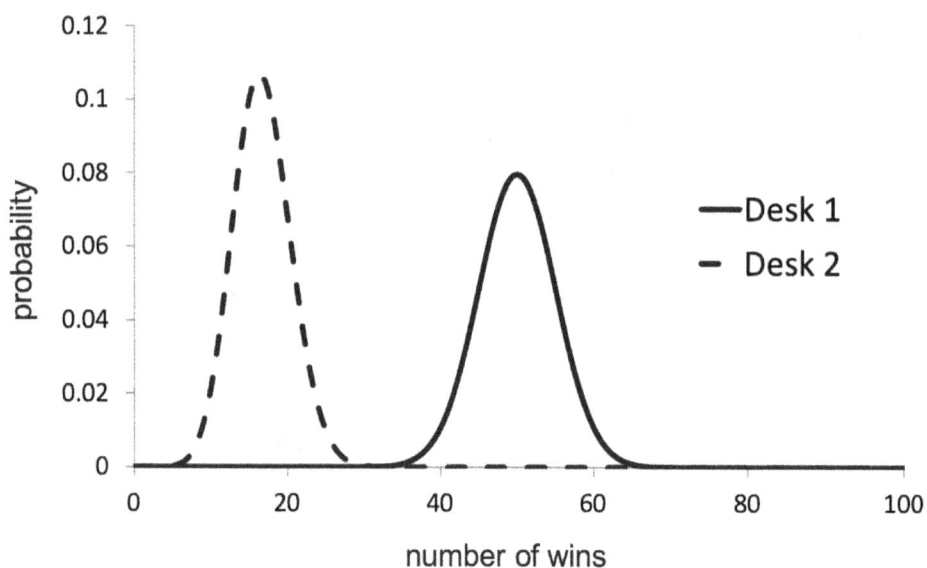

Figure 14.1: Probability distribution for the number of winning trades for desk A and desk B.

Given the probability distribution it is now possible to determine the P/L given a particular number of winning trades. Using the formula for the standard deviation $\sigma_{bd} = \sqrt{n \cdot p \cdot (1-q)}$ of the binomial distribution with p and q denoting the probability of wins and losses, respectively, one can plot the *cumulative normal distribution function* (CNDF). The revenue distribution at 1% of the CNDF is by definition the (daily) VaR at 99% confidence interval. For trading desk A this is $231 and for trading desk B $518 per day as shown in Figures 14.2 and 14.3, respectively.

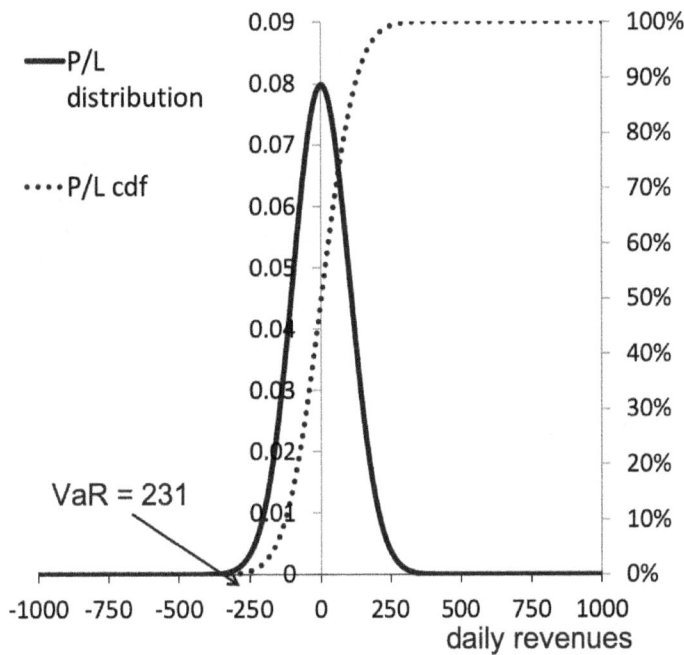

Figure 14.2: Daily expected revenue and cumulative distribution for trading desk A.

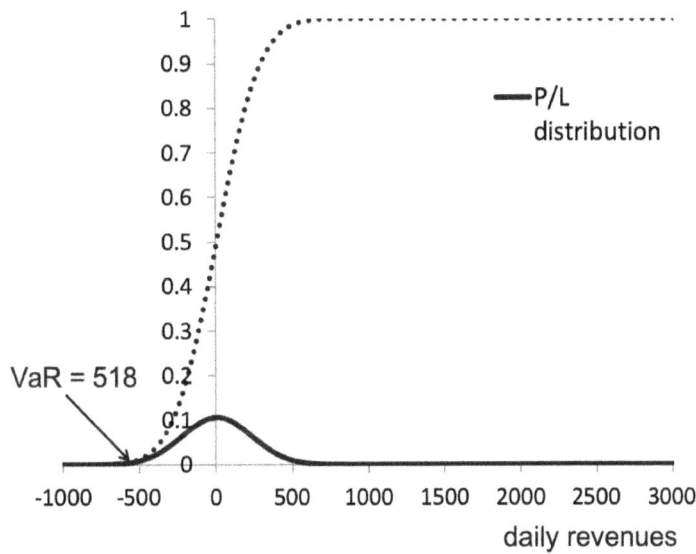

Figure 14.3: Daily expected revenue and cumulative distribution for trading desk B.

One way to look at the profit and risk questions posed above is indeed via VaR. First, one determines risk-adjusted returns for the two desks by normalizing the expected daily revenue by the respective VaR.

(*i*) Desk A: RVaR = 2.5 / 231 = 1.08%

(*ii*) Desk B: RVaR = 5.0 / 518 = 0.97%

Hence, trading desk A provides the better risk-adjusted return, *i.e.* less capital is required to run the business in a sustainable way.

Trading desk A is expected to lose more than 231 at 1% of the time, *e.g.* 2-3 days within 1 year; any loss exceeding 231 is then a VaR exception. Assume that one does not want to lose more than expected with a probability of 1 in 1m. For this threshold, the probability of losing more than 480 is approximately 1 / 1m, which is statistically roughly 4.77 standard deviations below the expectation of 2.5 (26 wins and 74 losses). Multiplying 1 / 1m by the number of trading days (252) gives 0.025%, which is equivalent to the annual rate of default for this specific business. Hence, the total capital of 2 times VaR implies an expected default frequency of 0.025%, which is equivalent to a historical AA+ rating [298].

Assuming a cost ratio of 70% and a tax rate of 35% one obtains:

(*i*) annual revenue: $(2.5 \cdot 252) = 630$
(*ii*) cost ratio: $630 \cdot 0.7 = 441$
(*iii*) pre-tax profit: $630 - 441 = 189$
(*iv*) net profit: $(1 - 0.35) \cdot 189 = 122.85$

The annualized return on capital is then 122.85 / 480 = 25.59% and 22.7% for trading Desk B, respectively. Hence, risk-adjusted return and return on capital are better for Trading desk A. Obviously, several assumptions are taken in the analysis above. As one might guess, the main one is the choice of a normal distribution for modeling the P/L statistics.

The example above can be generalized to calculate the VaR of a portfolio P for a particular confidence interval given its net asset value (NAV), expected return and expected volatility as

$$VaR_{cash} = NAV_P \cdot \left([E[r] + E[\sigma] \cdot z] \right), \tag{14.1}$$

whereby z represents the value defining the percentage area from minus infinity to z for the respective confidence interval in the normal distribution. Taking an example of a $10m NAV portfolio with zero expected daily return and 0.5% expected daily volatility one obtains a daily VaR at 99% confidence of $10m \cdot (0\% + 0.5\% \cdot 2.32635) = \$116'317.50$ whereby *z=2.32635* corresponds to the respective z-value from the standard normal distribution at 99% confidence.

14.1.3 Value at Risk: Practical application

Consider a portfolio consisting of one asset. Assume the asset price is $30, the average 500-day historical volatility 30% and the correlation/beta to a benchmark index 1.3 with the index volatility quantified at 15%. What is the VaR for this portfolio? First, it is necessary to specify the confidence level and the time horizon (holding period). The asset returns are again assumed to be normal with a mean of zero. The 10 day realized volatility on the asset is then $30\% \cdot \sqrt{10/252} = 5.98\%$. Taking the Basel regulatory framework confidence level of 99% requires finding the return, which is 2.33 standard deviations below zero. Recall that 2.33 std is at the 1st percentile of the normal distribution. Hence, $-2.33 \cdot 5.98\% = -13.92\%$. Recall that the portfolio value is $30. Then $VaR = 13.92\% \cdot 30 = \$4.18$. It follows that one is 99% confident that the portfolio does not lose more than $4.18 over the next 10 days. In other words, there is only 1% change of losses exceeding $4.18 in the next 10 days.

The analysis above determines the asset VaR due to spot moves following the historical volatility. These spot moves can be triggered either due to general (*i*) market risk or (*ii*) residual risk. Market risk relates to how an asset correlates to the market or a representative asset class benchmark as a whole (systemic risk). The Residual risk represents spot moves, which are triggered by news or reports on the asset alone (*idiosyncratic risk*). The Basel regulatory framework requires to split the risk into those components. Hence, how does one decompose the VaR $4.18 into those components? What is necessary is to calculate the impact due to the sensitivity (beta) with the market, *i.e.* one conducts the same analysis above for the benchmark index. The 10 day benchmark volatility is: $15\% \cdot \sqrt{10/252} = 2.99\%$. Then $2.33 \cdot 2.99\% = 6.97\%$, *i.e.* $6.97\% \cdot \$30 = \$2.09$. Hence, the VaR of a $30 portfolio invested in the market benchmark *alone* is $2.09. Recall that the asset has a correlation/beta coefficient of 1.3 to the benchmark. Beta is a statistical measure of the sensitivity of an asset's return to the market (*e.g.* a stock index), *i.e.* effectively the slope based on linear regression as specified in CAPM [334, 335, 336]. It follows that the market VaR component is $1.3 \cdot 2.09 = \$2.72$. In other words, \$ 2.72 is the VaR of $1.3 \cdot \$30 = \$39$ invested in the benchmark. Finally, the residual VaR component is given by the squared difference as: $\sqrt{4.18^2 - (2.72)^2} = 3.17$. Note that it is required to take the difference after squaring because VaR (*i.e.* std) itself is *not additive*. Squared VaR (*i.e.* variance) is additive as long as the components are independent, which is assumed here.

Effectively, the calculation above is based on decomposing the total variance into the market and the residual variance as

$$
\begin{aligned}
\sigma_{\text{total}}^2 &= \beta^2 \sigma_{\text{market}}^2 + \sigma_{\text{residual}}^2 \\
\sigma_{\text{residual}}^2 &= \sqrt{\sigma_{\text{total}}^2 - \beta^2 \sigma_{\text{market}}^2}
\end{aligned}
\tag{14.2}
$$

Hence, with the numbers above the same result is obtained, *i.e.* $\sigma_{\text{residual}}^2 = \sqrt{0.3^2 - 1.3^2 \cdot 0.15^2} = 0.2280$ p.a.. Finally, for the residual $VaR = 0.2280 \cdot \sqrt{10/252} \cdot 2.33 \cdot 30 = 3.17$. Note that this is only true if the market and residual risk are indeed *uncorrelated*, which is rarely the case. To hedge the market risk, one needs to sell the benchmark for a cash notional of $1.3 \cdot \$30$ to hedge against the long position on the asset. The essential question is, as usual, how often assets follow a normal return distribution. The honest answer is that they often do until they suddenly do not. As a consequence, the missing risk component in the tail of the normal distribution must be assessed by running (extreme) scenario risk.

Consider now the same portfolio whereby another asset is added so that one obtains the following composition: 1 times Asset A (spot = $30, vol = 30%) and 2 times Asset B (spot = $50, vol = 18%). Assuming a correlation of 40% one gets

$$
cov_{ij} = \rho_{ij} \cdot \sigma_i \cdot \sigma_j = 0.4 \cdot 0.3 \cdot 0.18 = 0.0216 .
\tag{14.3}
$$

The portfolio volatility σ_P of a position of one asset each is

$$
\sigma_P = \sqrt{w_1^2 \cdot \sigma_1^2 + w_2^2 \cdot \sigma_2^2 + 2 \cdot w_1^2 \cdot w_2^2 \cdot cov_{12}} \approx 17.79\% .
\tag{14.4}
$$

As expected, the portfolio blend exhibits lower volatility compared to the individual components alone. The 10-day portfolio volatility is obtained by the usual scaling relation, *i.e.* $17.79\% \cdot \sqrt{10/252} = 3.54\%$. The 1st percentile of the 10 day distribution is then given by $-2.33 \cdot 3.54\% =$

-8.25%. Finally, the total portfolio VaR is given by $8.25\% \cdot \$130 = \$10.73$. It is also possible to calculate the beta of the portfolio β_P for a representative benchmark to get the general and residual VaR component. Assuming a beta of 1.3 and 1.0 for asset A and asset B, respectively, one obtains

$$\beta_P = w_1 \cdot \beta_1 + w_2 \cdot \beta_2 = \frac{30}{130} \cdot 1.3 + \frac{100}{130} \cdot 1.0 = 1.069 \; . \tag{14.5}$$

Recall from the first example that the 1st percentile of the 10-day benchmark volatility is 6.97%. Then, for the market VaR one obtains $6.97\% \cdot 1.069 \cdot \$130 = \$9.69$ and for the residual VaR $\sqrt{(10.73)^2 - (9.69)^2} = \$4.61$.

The residual VaR is now *smaller* than the market component. The total VaR for a portfolio of 2 units of asset B is only $2.33 \cdot (0.18 \textit{x} \sqrt{10/252}) \cdot \$100 = \$8.35$. This so-called diversification benefit will then often be shown in a VaR report as

- Asset A (1x): 4.18
- Asset B (2x): 8.35
- Diversification benefit: 10.73 - (4.18 + 8.35) = -5.10
- Total VaR: 10.73

Note that the VaR numbers are not additive and that the total portfolio VaR is *less* than the sum of the individual VaRs due to the diversification effect.

The Basel Committee requires different levels of reserves to be held against systemic and residual VaR. For systemic VaR, the regulation requires a multiple of a minimum of 3. For residual VaR, a multiple > 3. For example, the reserves could be equal to (3 x general VaR) + (4 x residual VaR). The multiples serve as a cushion beyond VaR and are supposed to account for extreme (tail) events. How does one then come up with the multiples in the first place? This analysis can be done via backtests but understand that this remains only as good as the historical data and the lookback period used.

To recap, VaR quantifies the maximum loss on a position or portfolio if holding it for a specific time for a specified confidence level. For example, a 10-day VaR of $100m at 99% confidence means that the portfolio should not lose more than $100m over 10 days. Alternatively, if the position is held for 10 days, the losses should not exceed 100m at 99% of the time. Moreover, there is only a 1% chance that the portfolio loses more than $100m over the next 10 days. These metrics are all true assuming *normal* market conditions. Finally, it is essential to specify how the VaR is calculated (historical, model, etc.) while the choice of the holding period should ideally reflect the time required for a full liquidation of the portfolio or trading book.

In general, there are three ways to calculate VaR.

- **Analytical**: requires making assumptions about the win/loss probabilities; this assessment is difficult for portfolios with optionality
- **Historical**: requires determining the return distribution based on historical events
- **Monte Carlo**: simulates the profit/loss probabilities assuming a certain stochastic process for the evolution of the portfolio

In a (multivariate) normal return distribution world, all three methods result in the same number. In practice, experience has shown multiple times that this is not the case.

Historical simulation is arguably the VaR calculation method, which is applied most often. It works by retrieving the historical time series and constructing a return histogram for the portfolio in question (*e.g.* 1 times asset A and 2 times asset B as in the portfolio example above). Assuming a history of 5 years with daily portfolio returns, one then determines the point which cuts off the lower 1% of the distribution. This cutoff is then the VaR if one multiplies it with the overall notional. Assuming that for the portfolio in question, the return is -6.69% then the historical VaR is $130 \cdot 6.69\% = \$8.69$. The 10-day VaR is then obtained by scaling as $\$8.69 \cdot \sqrt{10} = \$27.50$. The advantages of the historical simulation are

- no assumption about the underlying return distribution required
- no estimation of (co-)variance required
- able to deal with effectively any portfolio including derivatives

The disadvantages are

- it is computationally expensive
- potentially lacks historical data for some assets
- the history might not be an accurate representation of the future
- the resulting historical VaR does not provide estimates about the probability of experiencing losses of different sizes (*e.g.* if VaR is $50m, what is the probability of losing $100m?)

The lookback period for historical VaR is another crucial component. In practice, financial institutions typically use a sliding window between 3 to 5 years. In other words, today, extreme stress scenarios, such as 2008, are not anymore considered in the default VaR model. It is therefore advisable to run point-in-time scenarios in parallel to obtain an estimate of potential tail losses. Another discussion should be whether one must weigh the data points equally or whether it is better to give more importance to the present or past? There might also be some new trades/instruments in the portfolio which might obscure the picture in the sense that they contain risk which is not represented in a past historical time series analysis of returns (*e.g.* merger/arbitrage positions, credit defaults, etc.). Finally, it is crucial to know whether the historical VaR is calculated using a full revaluation method or using some approximations. As the name replies, full revaluation means that the current portfolio is indeed recalculated completely at every point in time. This approach is computationally more expensive and entails also challenging requirements on model robustness as well as historical market data coverage. Typical approximations to the full revaluation approach are based on a Taylor series expansion of the derivative exposure, *i.e.* one considers a 'Delta-Gamma-Theta' type of sensitivity analysis approach to proxy the P/L impact upon spot moves. However, this approach may underestimate risk in the case of nonlinear or digital payouts when the greeks change rapidly. Therefore, it should not be surprising that a full revaluation approach is in principle always to be preferred [337].

Monte Carlo VaR generates 'random' portfolio configurations by letting the spots evolve according to a pre-determined stochastic process. The advantages are that

- the method is very flexible
- it can use various correlation, volatility models and stochastic processes
- it can do sensitivity analyses based on various conditions at inception
- it might provide a better representation of the future than historical simulation

The disadvantages are that Monte Carlo VaR is

- computationally expensive
- computationally very expensive if one aims to simulate all relevant risk factors *independently* (volatility, dividends, interest rate, spots, etc.)
- that it is not clear which stochastic process is the most accurate reflection of reality (jump diffusion + stochastic volatility?)

However, even given the difficulties above, there is still a critical test one can do to evaluate the respective model performance. This test is a so-called VaR model backtest, *i.e.* examining how well the model predicts actual maximal losses given a certain confidence level. In a VaR backtest, typically 1 day VaR and 99% confidence level are used. Any backtest loss exceeding the VaR is called a VaR exception. While VaR exceptions are to some degree expected, it is clear that fewer exceptions are in principle to be favored. On the other hand, observing no VaR exceptions at all can be an indication that the firm is not using the capital adequately or that the model is inaccurate. Alternatively, one could argue that the VaR number is too conservative in the sense that it is just a too large barrier due to which the actual risk dynamics are not anymore necessary to fully understand. From a purely 99% confidence level point of view, one should expect 1% exceptions over time (subject to some variation).

In 2008, VaR at all banks showed many VaR exceptions compared to the years before. This observation is reflective of the common knowledge that VaR works well under normal markets, but not during times of distress. Hence, other tools are potentially necessary. As discussed before, one issue with historical simulation is that once the considered simulation window passes an extreme event, it is not anymore included. Basel II [1] tries to deal with this by introducing a stressed VaR measure. Here the VaR is specifically calculated during historical stress periods such as 2007-2009. Furthermore, a 10-day VaR at 99% confidence level computed over 12 months of stress is reported. The portfolios in question are then replayed with the historical data. As a side note, capital charges (see also 15.1.5) are also calculated by taking into account the stress VaR.

14.1.4 Expected Shortfall and Tail Risk

VaR provides us with the maximum loss expectation if a tail loss does not occur. Discussing tail risk in the context of VaR makes sense given that this is precisely the component the latter is missing by design assuming normal return distributions. However, as it has been repeatedly stated before, it is common knowledge that the assumption of normal returns is unrealistic in some market regimes. For example, when comparing the S&P 500 Index return history with a Brownian diffusion process of identical volatility (26.5% p.a.), it is apparent that a canonical diffusion process does not capture many upside and downside tail events (see Figure 14.4) [338].

---

[1]https://www.bis.org/publ/bcbsca.htm

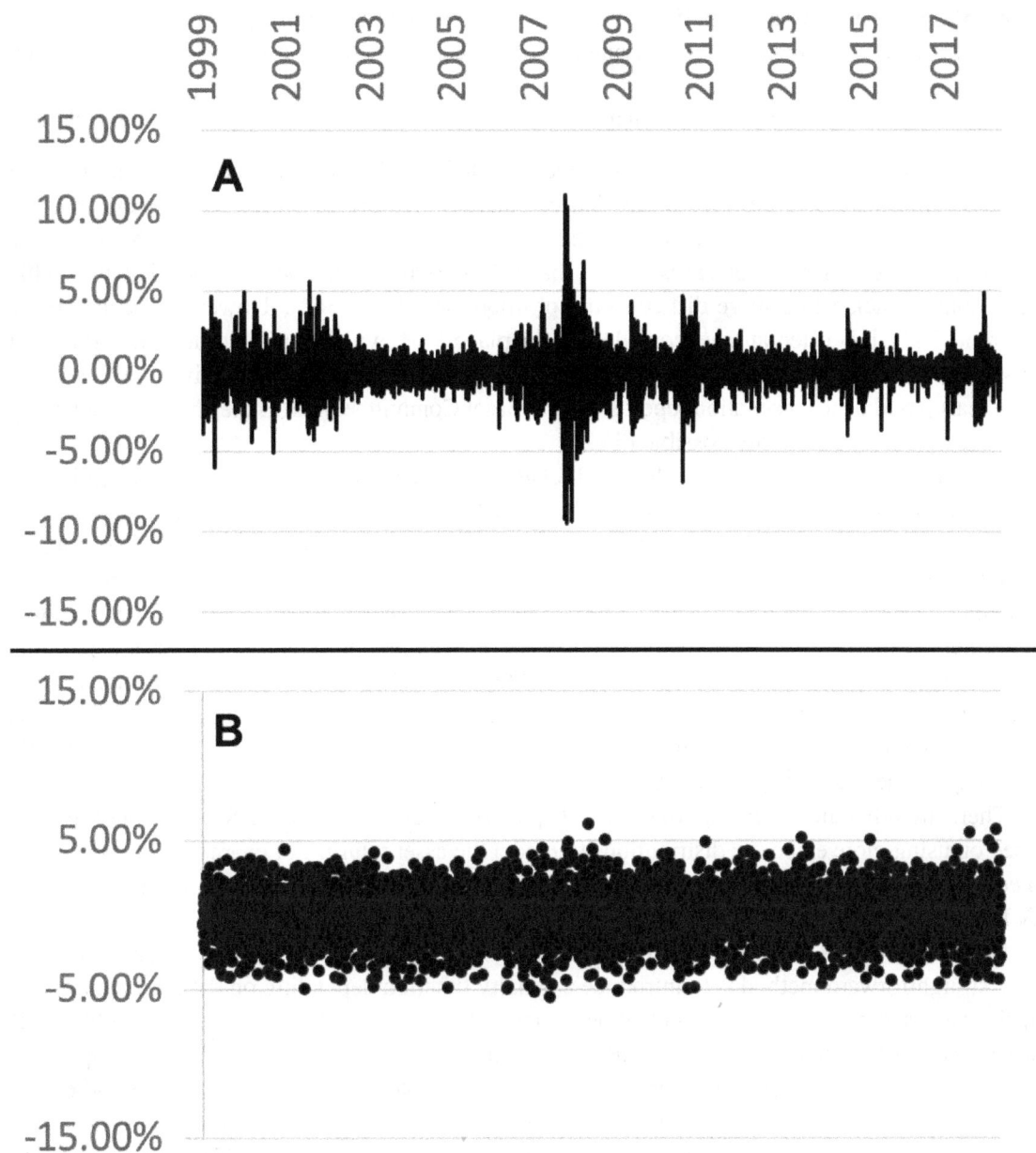

Figure 14.4: S&P 500 index returns versus a Brownian diffusion process with the same average volatility.

This outcome is not surprising given that any mean field approach typically results in loss of granularity. In other words, as one averages out the daily returns, the average will at some point not be representative of individual events possibly exceeding it.

Tail risk is traditionally defined as rare events or Black Swans [339], which

- sample extreme outcomes in the tails of the underlying return distribution
- exhibit market returns (on the downside) above *e.g.* three or more standard deviations
- are not always predictable

- exhibit a market drawdown in excess of x% (*e.g.* x% loss in a day)
- can express the magnitude and dynamics of the current economic market cycle (expansion overheating collapse recovery)
- can express the magnitude and dynamics of the current volatility regime (high or low volatility)

The tail estimate within VaR framework is called expected shortfall (ES) or conditional VaR (CVaR). The calculation of ES follows from the VaR calculation, namely by taking the average over the losses beyond VaR. For example, at 95% confidence level, the ES is calculated by taking the average of returns in the worst 5% of cases. Note that ES, as opposed to VaR, is not elicitable [340], which makes backtesting more difficult but not impossible [341, 342]. However, because ES is coherent [343], it is often at least considered to replace VaR, which, on the other hand, does not satisfy this property in all cases. The ultimate verdict from a regulatory perspective is still missing, but at least based on a consultation report from the Basel Committee in 2013 the chances of adopting ES more broadly are certainly possible [344].

It is clear that the dynamics of BSM and related models assuming normality are unrealistic in specific market regimes (*e.g.* November 2008, August 2011, etc.). Moreover, there exist scenarios for which the probability for extreme events is also low in more sophisticated models. For example, consider the unexpected inversion of the EUR yield curve in the middle of 2008 where spreads between 30 year / 10 year and 10 year / 2 years yields got close in a few days [231]. The event was an unlikely scenario and consequently hard to pick up even in any model. However, it is possible to model this via stress tests, and this is arguably the only way a sizeable adverse P/L impact from discontinuous payoffs via digital and barrier options can be picked up. Otherwise, there is a high risk of piling up unmanageable concentration risk, which drops below the surface of what is typically picked up by the risk management systems.

There are other alternative approaches [345] to assess tail risk beyond ES, which are typically based on using more elaborate distributions to model the asset return. For example, Extreme Value Theory (EVT) [346, 347] uses a generalized Pareto distribution to model tail events. However, EVT is theoretically sound, the extension to the multivariate case is often challenging as well as the fact that finding a 1 in 100 years event is error prone given lack of calibration data. Another more straightforward method is to introduce a penalty function depending on the market direction (upside versus downside) which is applied on the respective returns [348]. This so-called bubble VaR measure ranges between the canonical VaR metric and a dynamical upper limit. While this approach is certainly based on heuristic assumptions, it is easy to implement, can be extended to other risk types (*e.g.* credit risk) and appears to also provide a countercyclical risk buffer [349]. Another extension to the canonical VaR approach is to use Cornish-Fisher VaR [350, 351], which allows to take into account higher moments. The extension is relatively simple as it effectively boils down to bumping up the VaR standard normal distribution probability function by multiplication with a polynomial series reflecting the higher moments (*i.e.* skew and kurtosis). As usual, straightforward approaches are not without drawbacks. In this case, for large skew and/or kurtosis the Cornish-Fisher approximation of the true distribution's quantile is not good. Moreover, few extreme events can lead to a large error in the estimation of the true (average) skew and kurtosis, which, in turn, leads to large overshooting in the Cornish-Fisher VaR. Despite these shortcomings, Cornish-Fisher VaR is certainly a more conservative VaR measure, which explains its mandatory use in some regulatory reports such as PRIIPS for retail investment products in Europe [2].

The academic literature is skewed towards criticism of VaR-type approaches. But picking

---

[2]https://bit.ly/2kxfNIN

on assumptions of normality does not tell the whole story. Ultimately, risk management must concern itself with projecting the future. VaR is a second moment measure and as such will clearly underestimate future risk in the case markets are calm but also *overreact* in volatile situations. In other words, (stressed) VaR will often overestimate future volatility. Therefore, determining the correct mixture which is both satisfying regulators as well as internal risk limits is challenging.

Fortunately, the underestimation of tail risk and neglect of jumps can be partially hedged out using derivatives. Some vanilla instruments to protect a books against tail risk are:

- short (vega neutral) put spread: short 1 times high strike (*e.g.* ATM) and long 3 times low strike put (*e.g.* 75% ATM) →long skew
- long OTM put: *e.g.* 70 strike (possibly written off, *i.e.* not delta hedged) → timing needs to be good, otherwise expensive; long dividend exposure unwanted
- long OTM put, short OTM call (*i.e.* risk reversal / collar): sale of OTM call offsets part of cost on put, increases exposure to skew and dividends
- long upside call, short delta: long upside call (*e.g.* 110% ATM), short excess delta (*e.g.* 1:2)
- short delta bias: for a given amount of (short) gamma, run delta against it in a pre-defined ratio (1:1, 1:2, 1:3. . .)
- long variance swaps or downside variance swaps

14.1.5 Flash Crashes

Since 2010, financial markets have been exposed to a new kind of extreme event which is the so-called *flash crash* [352, 353]. Flash crashes can be defined as volatile and large market moves in asset prices, followed by reversion, within a very short time period [354]. The occurrence of a flash crash is typically coupled with a dry up of the trading liquidity as well as widening of bid-offer spreads, which acts as an amplifier. A subset within the flash crash family are so-called *mini flash crashes* [355] whereby the asset price bounce (down/up or up/down) happens within microseconds. Flash crashes have been observed in all asset classes and appear to happen more frequently [356]. Various explanations have been proposed for this trend ranging from the adverse impact of algorithmic trading, market structure changes to exchange matching protocols. The impact of flash crashes on derivative traders has various components. The first and primary consequence is the direct impact on the derivative book and its positions. As mentioned in the introductory chapter, the occurrence of uncertain price jumps sizes (see 3.1.14) destroys the BSM replication argument since no hedge portfolio exists even if the underlying is continuously tradable [48]. While this is nothing new in theory, the nature of the flash crash forces (derivative) market participants to even more pay attention to monitoring short OTM positions which may significantly gain in value during such a tail event. The same is true for clearing houses or (discount) brokerage firms in relation to the leverage granted and respective margin required.

Exchanges have two primary ways of dealing with flash crashes. Within the prevention domain one can imagine stricter regulation on algorithmic trading strategies by *e.g.* stringently tracking and eliminating market participants suspected of order spoofing attempts. In the context of market makers, elevating liquidity provision limits in extreme scenarios might be another vehicle. At the same time, so-called *circuit breakers* are already in place, *i.e.* trading is halted for a certain period of time or even ceased in the case an asset drops by a fixed percentage during a trading day. As a measure of last resort, exchanges can also declare a trading day as an *extraordinary market disruption event* after the fact, which often removes the day as an observation date in derivative contracts. However, this is typically reserved for external causes or force majeure events such as natural disasters, terrorist attacks or severe technical failures in the exchange itself. Moreover, two market participants with opposite positions will naturally disagree on the benefit of such a declaration and the communication needs to be fast so that there is no uncertainty regarding potential hedge ratio adjustments.

Finally, the potential increasing occurrence of flash crashes impacts the way traders should look at the classic volatility scaling laws. As stated before, in the absence of autocorrelation between (daily) returns, daily volatility can be scaled up by the square root of time to other time scales (see 2.2.14). But this will underestimate actual volatility dynamics if it is increasingly characterized by elevated kurtosis. This is even more important in the case whereby positions are scaled in relation to some average of realized volatility [357].

14.2 Fundamental Review of the Trading Book (FRTB)

The Fundamental Review of the Trading Book (FRTB) is a set of proposals and measures by the Basel Committee on Banking Supervision (BCBS) [3] to guide the market risk requirements for banks. FRTB is part of the latest iteration of the Basel framework [4] on regulatory capital and is therefore sometimes also referred to as Basel IV. The implementation is currently scheduled for 2022. While some other components of the Basel accords are discussed in the following chapter (see chapter 15), this section concerns itself with the framework around the Trading and Banking book. Recall that both were superficially discussed earlier in the chapter on corporate derivatives (see 11). The FRTB initiative is driven by the observation that the Basel II [5] risk framework did not really work given the systemic fallout from the financial crisis in 2008/98. The reasons were partially given by the enormous growth of the trading books in relation to liquidity, non-adequate risk frameworks such as VaR and the assumption that whatever one can somehow model (internally) can also be marked to fair value and consequently also be traded. The latter point illustrates the framework of securitization, which often also incorporates moving assets from the Banking book to the Trading book *and* thereby also benefitting from capital relief.

Some of the key FRTB measures to improve the past situation is as follows [358]

- Risk metric: move from 10-day VaR at 99% confidence level to 10-day ES at 97.5% to improve the known fact that VaR is not good at quantifying tail losses. This also includes more restrictions on portfolio diversification benefits by imposing strict rules on correlations between asset classes.
- Liquidity horizon: introduce a liquidity horizon in the ES measure per asset class or product reflecting the time required to liquidate the position
- Backtesting: P/L backtesting is required at the trading desk level
- Banking versus Trading Book boundary: more restrictions on which assets can cross the boundary
- Internal models: supervisory review of internal models at desk level including rigorous approval process
- Introduction of Non-modellable Risk Factors (NMRF): the idea of extracting non-modellable risk factors and treating them separately in stress scenarios

---

[3] https://www.bis.org/bcbs/index.htm
[4] https://www.bis.org/basel_framework
[5] https://www.bis.org/publ/bcbsca02.htm

All of the measures above make sense in theory even if the practical implementation (*e.g.* ES backtesting) is challenging [359, 342]. The main criticism is that the approach is still very much centered around a frequentist approach, *i.e.* contrary to *e.g.* Bubble VaR the current level of the market is not taken into account.

Finally, it is worth spending a few lines on the idea of non-modellable risk factors (NMRF). Intuitively, the concept makes sense as there are certainly some risk components which are impossible to model properly. It also breaks the dogma of believing that *everything* can be modelled adequately, which as such is a much better secular approach. *Modellable* risk factors are categorized by attributes such that transactions need to be at a quote which is committed and verifiable by a 3rd party as well as by the regulator. The minimum number of quotes within a calendar year need to be 24 with a maximum of 1 month between the observations. Every risk items outside this definition is a non-modellable risk factor and will be treated separately in how it is capitalized in a stress scenario. In other words, NMRF cannot be offset by other risk factors. The definition rules are strict considering that they do not only include price quotes, but also quotes for less frequently traded risk such as volatility. This means that in the design of a valuation models, quants and traders need to carefully assess how many risk factors or model parameters to include in order to not explode the number of NMRF. The exact treatment of the NMRF stress scenario including a potential relaxation of the initial proposal above is currently being discussed [360] and it will be important for traders and quants to be informed about the direction taken.

15. Valuation Adjustments

15.1 Introduction

The last chapter of this book is dedicated to a series of topics emerging from the fallout of the 2008/09 financial crisis. In addition to the commonly known narrative around excessive borrowing in the loan and mortgage-backed financial sector, the crisis was also catalyzed through an amalgam of sudden refinancing/funding problems, credit counterparty risk issues, and thin capital requirements. As a consequence, various regulatory requirements were launched, which have significantly changed how OTC derivatives are *valued* besides the traditional pricing models described in the chapters before.

The financial sector is highly regulated. In the US alone, banks and thrifts are regulated by multiple federal and state regulators, including the Fed [1], the OCC [2], the National Credit Union Administration [3], the Farm Credit Administration [4], and the Federal Deposit Insurance Corporation (FDIC) [5], among others. In addition, publicly listed banks are also under supervision by the SEC [6]. Banks with investment banking, brokerage and dealership businesses have to follow FINRA rules [7]. Outside the US, banks are typically regulated by national regulators. The primary regulator for European banks is the European Banking Authority (EBA) [8] whereby each country can additionally overlay national regulators, *e.g.* the Prudential Regulation Authority (PRA) in the UK [9], the Federal Financial Supervisory Authority (BaFin) in Germany [10] and FINMA in Switzerland [11]. Similarly,

---

[1] https://www.federalreserve.gov

[2] https://www.occ.treas.gov

[3] https://www.ncua.gov

[4] https://www.fca.gov

[5] https://www.fdic.gov

[6] https://www.sec.gov

[7] http://www.finra.org

[8] https://eba.europa.eu

[9] https://www.bankofengland.co.uk/prudential-regulation

[10] https://www.bafin.de/EN/Homepage/homepage_node.html

[11] https://www.finma.ch/en

Japanese banks are regulated by the Financial Services Agency (FSA) [12] while Chinese banks are governed by China Banking and Insurance Regulatory Commission (CBIRC) [13]. Globally, the Basel Committee on Banking Supervision (BCBS) [14] provides a voluntary regulatory framework on bank capital adequacy, stress testing, and market liquidity risk. The Bank for International Settlements (BIS) [15] is an international financial institution, owned by central banks to establish international monetary and financial cooperation. The BIS also serves as a bank for central banks. Finally, the Basel accords are also administered by the BIS.

When considering banking regulation which impacts derivatives most, one is quickly dealing with capital requirements. Basel III imposes stringent capital requirements for large banks in particular, which are all subject to stress testing. In the US, the Fed introduced the CCAR (Comprehensive Capital Analysis and Review) [16] to ensure bank holding companies possess adequate capital. Similarly, the IMF (International Monetary Fund) [17] conducts the Financial Sector Assessment Program (FSAP) [18], and the EBA stress tests EU banks [19]. Compared to other sectors, banks are traditionally often more leveraged concerning their total equity. The bank's capital ratio is calculated as

$$\text{Capital Ratio} = \frac{\text{Eligible Capital}}{\underbrace{\text{Total Assets} \times \text{Risk Weighting}}_{\text{Risk-weighted Assets}}} \tag{15.1}$$

According to the Basel accords, the Eligible Capital (EC) is divided into three tiers of decreasing quality. The highest quality is called Tier 1 Capital (T1) and is made up of two components namely Common Equity Tier 1 Capital (CET1) and Additional Tier 1 Capital (AT1). Following this, there is Tier 2 and Tier 3 capital. CET1 consists of mainly ordinary share capital and retained earnings. The purpose of the *Risk-weighted Assets* (RWA) is to discriminate between different risk levels on and off the balance sheet assets. It follows that the higher the risk, the higher its weighting. As discussed in the chapter about scenario risk and VaR 14, these risks include credit, market, and operational risk. The RWA further incorporates additional measures such as stressed VaR, incremental risk charges, Effective Expected Positive Exposure (EEPE) for OTC derivatives and Credit Value Adjustments (CVA, see below). According to Basel III, the current minimum requirements for the T1 ratio is 6% of which CET1 is at least 4.5%. For banks, the CET1 is 4.5% plus 2.5% due to a mandatory capital conservation buffer [20]. Moreover, national regulators may increase this further with a discretionary counter-cyclical buffer of up to 2.5%.

Another key metric for all financial institutions is the leverage ratio given by

$$\text{Leverage Ratio} = \frac{\text{Tier 1 Capital}}{\text{Exposure Measure}}, \tag{15.2}$$

which is currently set to a minimum of 3% by Basel III [21]. Note that different accounting treatments can lead to different results, even for this apparently simple ratio. The Exposure Measure is typically

---

[12] https://www.fsa.go.jp/en

[13] http://www.cbrc.gov.cn/english/index.html

[14] https://www.bis.org/bcbs

[15] https://www.bis.org

[16] https://www.federalreserve.gov/supervisionreg/ccar.htm

[17] https://www.imf.org/external/index.htm

[18] https://www.imf.org/external/np/fsap/fsap.aspx

[19] https://eba.europa.eu

[20] https://www.bis.org/bcbs/basel3/b3summarytable.pdf

[21] https://www.bis.org/bcbs/basel3.htm

the sum of the replacement cost and the potential future exposure times a multiplier, which should reflect the exposure in a default situation [22].

The canonical business model for banks is to lend out money for longer duration and finance this via short-term borrowing. Given that the yield curve is usually upwards sloping, banks make more money on the higher interest earned versus what they pay short term. This mechanism works all well until a potential liquidity crisis in which short term borrowing becomes difficult. This respective experience during the 2008/09 financial crisis led to the introduction of two Basel III liquidity ratios: (*i*) the Liquidity Coverage Ratio (LCR) [23] and (*ii*) the Net Stable Funding Ratio (NSFR). The LCR refers to highly liquid assets held by a financial institution to meet short-term obligations over 30 days. Highly liquid assets are classified into three levels - Level 1, Level 2A and Level 2B - subject to a 0%, 15%, and 50% haircut or discount, respectively. The LCR is then calculated as the *ratio* of high quality liquid assets (HQLA) divided by a financial institution's total net cash outflows over a 30-day stress period given by

$$\frac{\# \, \text{HQLA}}{\text{total net cash outflows over a 30-day stress period}} \geq 100\% \, . \tag{15.3}$$

The NSFR is the ratio of stable funding resources (available stable funding) divided by the medium-term needs of the bank (required stable funding) given by

$$\frac{\text{available stable funding}}{\text{required stable funding}} \geq 100\% \, . \tag{15.4}$$

As a requirement, the NSFR must be higher than 100%. Each one of the bank's funding sources (*e.g.* deposit, long-term debt etc.) has a stability coefficient, depending on the probability that the bank can maintain such a source for an extended period during an idiosyncratic stress event. Note that the ratio calculations above also discriminate between the quality of the assets. In general, three quality levels are distinguished

- Level 1: Assets which are liquid and provide a regular unbiased mark- to-market mechanism for determining the fair value (*e.g.* equities, bonds, funds, listed derivatives)
- Level 2: Assets which do not have regular market pricing, but whose fair value is marked-to-model (*e.g.* OTC derivatives, IRS)
- Level 3: Assets whose fair value cannot be determined by using market inputs or measures (*e.g.* complex loan transactions, complex derivatives, structured mortgages)

Depending on the classification of the asset, a haircut is applied to reflect possible deviations from the realistic fair value before calculating the liquidity ratios. Note that the different asset quality levels do also result in different funding costs at the treasury level because of the reduced funding availability.

The treasury of a bank is required to calculate, forecast, maintain, and manage the ratios and metrics cited above. The critical link between derivatives and these regulatory requirements are so-called Valuation Adjustments (XVA), which are composed of five main sub-topics

- Credit Valuation Adjustment (CVA)
- Debt Valuation Adjustment (DVA)
- Funding Valuation Adjustment (FVA)

---

[22]https://www.bis.org/publ/bcbs279.pdf
[23]https://www.bis.org/publ/bcbs238.pdf

- Margin Valuation Adjustment (MVA)
- Capital Valuation Adjustment (KVA)

Some of these adjustments are still being discussed in terms of impact, implications, sensibility, and scope. However, in case one is trading derivatives, it is already today necessary to be informed about the issues at stake since they ultimately impact how derivatives are represented from an accounting perspective. Nevertheless, the XVA are then ultimately added to a theoretical or pure value V_{theory}, *i.e.*

$$V = V_{\text{theory}} + XVA .$$ (15.5)

Now, how to derive the V_{theory} based on LIBOR discounting or OIS discounting for *uncollateralized* trades is not so relevant if the respective XVA charges are correct for the respective reference frame [24].

Recall as well that trades are either centrally cleared or OTC. In the former case, the clearing house requires that the initial and subsequent margin is posted against the position to mitigate the default risk. In the OTC case, trades may either be collateralized or not. In the case of collateralization, the collateral mechanics are governed by a Credit Support Annex (CSA). The CSA defines parameters such as the eligible collateral, respective haircuts, calculation methods, dispute resolution, etc.. The CSA may be bilateral (two-way CSA) or unilateral (one-way CSA) [361], *i.e.* depending on whether the CSA governs both or just one of the counterparties. It is vital to be familiar with the CSA terms, especially for large transactions. The CSA is also important on subsequent trade lifecycle events such as novations. A novation is a transaction whereby one of the original trade counterparties steps out and is substituted by another. Alternatively, another institution can step in the middle of the two original counterparties to effectively broker the transaction going forward. Hence, the trade is still alive with the same parameters, but one of the counterparties has changed. What initially appears to be a non-event can, however, lead to adverse P/L impact. As recounted in [362], one investment bank exploited the lack of knowledge about CSAs concerning acceptable currency for posting cash collateral through novations. Hence, one would novate a trade such as to receive reserve currencies (*e.g.* USD) instead of others. Therefore, paying meticulous attention to the CSA in detail can be critical.

15.1.1 Credit Valuation Adjustment (CVA)

Credit Valuation Adjustment (CVA) concerns itself with counterparty credit risk [300, 363, 364] scoring. The measure, as previously introduced in the context of credit derivatives, ultimately concerns itself with the calculation of the credit component within Risk Weighted Assets (RWA). RWA are the banks (or financial institutions) assets as well as off-balance sheet items. These assets carry credit, market, operational, and non-counterparty risk. The counterparty credit risk (CCR) charge within RWA specifies capital requirements for possible (mark-to-market) losses due to a counterparty credit quality deteriorating or even failing. Banks are required to report a fair value credit adjustment for both assets and liabilities. The CVA is then the reserve, or regulatory capital banks must hold against potential counterparty default.

The so-called CVA desk manages the CVA exposure [365]. These desks can extend credit lines or reduce credit RWA exposure by *e.g.* trading CDS. Moreover, CDS spreads (observed in the market) are used to calculate counterparty exposure or the credit RWA component. The fear is that

---

[24]Recall that collateralized trades must be discounted using OIS

the management of the CVA exposure through trading CDS and related credit instruments might result in liquidity issues and increased CDS volatility [366]. This effect is not only a problem for banks: Corporates who enter *e.g.* IR swaps face increased charges due to the CVA as well. The current CVA approach is based on a VaR model where losses are estimated at 99% confidence interval over a 10-day horizon.

Intuitively, a derivative embedded with counterparty risk must always be worth less as the equivalent risk-free part. Therefore, the upfront CVA charge is a positive number (by convention). An approximate expression for the CVA charge sufficient for the level of the discussion here is given by [300]

$$CVA \approx (1 - RR) \cdot \sum_{i=1}^{n} df(t_i) \cdot EE(t_i) \cdot q(t_{-1}, t) , \tag{15.6}$$

where $df(t_i)$ denotes the risk-free discount factor at time t_i, $EE(t_i)$ is the expected exposure (EE) for the relevant dates in the future given t_i and $q(t_{-1}, t)$ the marginal default probability in the interval between date t_{-1} and t. All of the components were encountered before when discussing credit risk (see 12). Evaluating CVA charges for single trades then effectively boils down to estimating the EE over the lifetime as well as the credit spread of the counterparty. Assuming the average EE is constant one can just multiply this with the CDS spread to retrieve a back of the envelope charge or spread [25] The required complexity for the calculation of an (approximate) CVA charge for a single trade versus the calculation of a whole book or even bank exposure is orders of magnitudes easier. This increased difficulty is because potential exposures can be offsetting or are (partially) hedged, *i.e.* one is also dealing with netting effects. Moreover, the estimation of EE can be challenging, given the potential large variety of products in scope. Finally, obtaining reliable quality measures of counterparty default probabilities is far from trivial since the respective benchmark credit markets are not always available or liquid.

There is currently a significant mismatch between CVA charges between US and European systemically important banks whereby US banks incur capital charges which are up to a factor of 7 higher [367]. This mismatch arises partially since US Banks typically have larger OTC exposure. The other reason lies in the European legislature providing CVA capital charge waivers on trades with certain counterparties (*e.g.* pensions funds) [368].

15.1.2 Debt Valuation Adjustment (DVA)

The Debt Valuation Adjustment (DVA) [369] is the counterpart to CVA. It is a positive adjustment taken on the balance sheet to reflect the fair value associated with a possible default of an entity concerning its *own* liabilities. This adjustment appears somewhat counterintuitive or even circular at first sight. As a consequence, it is also the main reason why DVA, which is effectively a funding benefit, is still a matter of debate [370, 371]. One way to look at DVA is to consider it as an extension of the CVA calculation in a bilateral setting whereby one associates a finite probability of default for the own institution *before* a possible default of the other. Hence, if one takes this to the level of a financial institution as a whole one can see a DVA benefit from a widening of the own credit spread. As it so happens, this DVA benefit/adjustment has in the past already been visible in mark-to-market earnings of some banks [372]. From a purely theoretical point of view, one can take the position that this is fine since both CVA and DVA are antagonists in the mark-to-market framework within credit

---

[25]For example, assuming an EE of 5% of the trade notional versus a counterparty CDS spread of 400bps yields a CVA spread or charge of $5\% \cdot 400\text{bps} = 20\text{bps}$.

exposure. On the other hand, one can fear that this could lead to undercollateralization in practice as firms can profit from their debt deterioration. The final verdict remains to be seen in the future.

15.1.3 Funding Valuation Adjustment (FVA)

If DVA is already controversial, the Funding Valuation Adjustment (FVA) possessed characteristics of a religious war at some point [373, 374, 375, 376, 377, 378, 379]. This controversy emerged to a large extent because it challenges or amends the fundamental idea of risk-neutral pricing and discounting. The divide is also a fundamental dispute between academia and industry practitioners. The essential question is whether derivatives and cash flows should be valued at a risk-free rate or the funding rate of the institution. Moreover, the question post 2008/09 is as well what the risk-free rate actually is? In this sense, FVA accounts for all borrowing costs and lending benefits an institution faces when servicing accounts. Concretely, on a single trade, FVA accounts for the excess funding cost for uncollateralized derivatives above the risk-free rate. In other words, it is the cost (or benefit) hedging an uncollateralized trade in the market against the same collateralized one. If one agrees that there is a funding difference in those two transactions (and there clearly is), then it is hard to argue against the concept since it reflects the reality. The FVA charges are by now already reported on banks' balance sheets and have at least in one case exceeded USD 1bn [379].

In order to calculate the FVA charge, it is required to estimate the *Expected Future Value* (EFV) of a given transaction over time, which is effectively the (daily) marked-to-market present value. If the EFV is positive, it needs to be funded and the other way around. The full FVA charge is then given by the sum of the product of the EFV over time with the respective (forward) funding spread (fs) and the survival probability of the trade S (*i.e.* no default of either counterparty) given by [380]

$$FVA = -\sum_{i=1}^{n} EFV_{t_i} \cdot fs_{t_i} \cdot S_{t_i} \cdot \delta t \ . \tag{15.7}$$

Note that discounting at LIBOR (plus a spread) assumes that borrowing as well as lending happens at LIBOR, *i.e.* there is a symmetry. This is not in line with how the market typically operates or how the regulator looks at it (see NSFR or LCR above). Defining the funding curve is done by the treasury department. Since derivatives are not anymore exclusively funded short-term, the treasury department needs to decide how the funding in each currency constructed. It is then at this rate at which uncollateralized trades are typically discounted with *or* at a risk-free rate proxy (*e.g.* OIS) with the FVA adjustment as a spread to OIS added. Note that if one discounted uncollateralized trades at LIBOR, the FVA adjustment is a spread to LIBOR and the trading desk will need to manage the LIBOR-OIS basis. Hence, it is advisable to be informed about the firm's discounting policy for uncollateralized trades.

In terms of funding, the treasury department typically distinguishes between at least two funding levels. First, there is short term carry of a position reflecting the interest cost charge on a daily basis. This cost can be secured (fixed) or unsecured, *e.g.* based on the prevalent overnight funding rate and in accordance with the treasury's funds transfer pricing policy. The other key funding component reflects the cost of long-term debt and is coupled to the dynamic cost of long-term funding in general. Some positions might be eligible for a funding cost haircut if they can be funded in a secured market. This decision is often a topic of discussion between the trading desks and the treasury department. In any case, it is safe to assume that the internal treasury will also not treat lending and borrowing against an internal derivative desk symmetrically. In order to estimate the funding spread of a bank, it can be useful to follow the argument around the LOIS spread proxy [195] for a given maturity T

given by

$$\text{funding spread} \approx CDS + \sigma_{fs}\sqrt{T/2} - LOIS, \tag{15.8}$$

where CDS denotes the bank's credit spread and σ_{fs} reflects the volatility of the funding spread.

15.1.4 Margin Valuation Adjustment (MVA)

Collateralized trades typically require posting of initial margin. In the past, this used to be a constant percentage multiplied with the respective notional at risk at inception. However, there is a clear trend over recent years to move to more model-based approaches. These include VaR or ES estimates at a certain confidence level for a time of 1 or 2 weeks.

The MVA charge is given by

$$MVA = -\sum_{i=1}^{n} EIM_{t_i} \cdot (fc_{t_i} - s_{\text{IM}}) \cdot S_{t_i} \cdot \delta t. \tag{15.9}$$

Here, EIM represents the expected initial margin, fc the funding cost of posting the initial margin, s_{IM} the amount earned on the initial margin and S again the survival probability of the trade. Note that the above sum is not as trivial as it looks given that the EIM needs to be calculated for potentially a large population of trades. Similar to capital valuation adjustments (see next subsection) the practical implementation of the estimates is computationally very challenging.

15.1.5 Capital Valuation Adjustment (KVA)

In the chapter on corporate derivatives (see 11), the impact of the transaction on the capital requirements of a financial institution was already briefly discussed. The concept of Capital Valuation Adjustment (KVA) is, therefore, a generic extension. Since capital costs are a reality and rising due to increasing regulatory constraints, traders need to incorporate this cost when pricing new deals. Any trade effectively generates risk-weighted assets (RWA) against which capital is to be allocated. RWA is part of the regulatory capital terminology. The minimum amount of regulatory capital a firm is required to keep is defined as 8% of RWA by the Basel II Accord. RWA for trading book positions are typically calculated as a function of VaR.

In theory, calculating a capital charge is straightforward in the sense that one merely needs to integrate the expected future capital usage with its respected cost and the probability of default (loss). However, in practice, estimating capital charges *exactly* is not trivial since the vital input of any calculation also requires estimating the amount of capital the trade will consume over its *lifetime*. Moreover, changing capital regimes in the future can alter the cost of a trade booked today. As a consequence, KVA depends very much on the individual bank, *i.e.* banks may have capital regimes or internal return-on-equity (ROE) targets against which the profitability of the trade is benchmarked. In essence, banks calculate a capital charge by blending the impact of a potential loss of a given trade under an appropriate measure such as VaR with the capital percentage allocated against the RWA of the trade and the balance sheet usage. Incorporating balance sheet usage is crucial since there are *e.g.* repo-financing trades with low risk but high balance sheet usage [26] This blended charge is then multiplied with a respective hurdle rate reflecting the actual appetite of the bank to conduct business / allocate capital.

---

[26]Repo desks effectively lend/borrow assets against interest paid over a fixed duration. This business appears low risk, but every transaction typically uses up a unit of the balance sheet, and under Basel III capital ratio and leverage ratio then take a very punitive effect.

15.1.6 Wrong-way Risk

In the discussions about risk and valuation adjustments, the so-called wrong-way risk (WWR) exposure was not yet mentioned. WWR stands for an unfavorable dependency between exposure and credit quality of the trade counterparty. In other words, exposure increases when the credit rating of the counterparty deteriorates, *i.e.* negative correlation. As a stylized example consider a manufacturer of automobiles writing puts on the car sector. If those puts are in the money, there is a high likelihood the car manufacturer is not doing great either since it is very likely to be positively correlated to the sector. Hence, if a bank is both lending money to the car manufacturer as well as the put portfolio trade counterparty, the combined exposure is coupled in the wrong way. Therefore, WWR has a potentially significant impact on the CVA calculation.

Incorporating WWR in the calculations above is typically done by representing the expected exposure (EE) as *conditional* on the default of the counterparty. Recall that *e.g.* for the CVA calculation, the EE was considered to be unconditional. As a consequence, modeling conditionality requires making assumptions on the correlation between the EE and the counterparty default [381].

16. Final remarks

This book has covered derivatives and related products to provide (future) traders or risk managers with the minimum theoretical knowledge required to operate in this domain. It has possibly become apparent that mastering even this minimum is not a small task. Nevertheless, the common denominator for pricing derivatives is practically always the same: model the forward, choose the stochastic process, pick the volatility model and make sure those selections are sensible choices for asset and option payout alike. The next step is simulating and thinking about the parameter sensitivity of the payout. On the replication side of things, drawing the payout and plotting the greeks helps to identify vanilla instruments which can then be used within a hedging strategy.

More complex/realistic models are good, but they often come not for free. Hence, increased 'accuracy' typically correlates with calibration complexity, increased parameter dependency, computational expense, and potential stability issues. Therefore, what is correct and vital for trade pricing must not necessarily be suitable for valuing/running a large trading book. This discrepancy is especially true if markets are volatile or in distress. In these situations, it might be preferable to get robust risk figures from a simpler and well-understood model instead of facing valuation problems due to a more elaborate description of reality. Recall that market parameters in times of distress can be very volatile and extreme, *i.e.* testing new models against historical parameter sets from *e.g.* late 2008 is a good quality assurance measure in the context of model robustness. It is also in these situations when the understanding of model deficiencies in particular for hedge ratios makes a real difference. This is also because, in times of market stress, it is often only possible to hedge first-order risk, *i.e.* in particular the delta. Hence, understanding whether a model over- or underhedges greeks in a particular market environment is crucial. Note as well that the ability to trade the delta in terms of liquidity or slippage often outweighs considerations about the decimal place accuracy of the risk figures.

The mixing of different asset classes within the same payout typically results in *hybrid derivatives* [129]. Sometimes the hybrid character can at first be in disguise (see PRDC structures 7.1.7) and sometimes it is immediately visible if the payout is *e.g.* the maximum of an equity performance and a CMS rate. In general, as one would expect, the pricing and valuation of hybrid structures entail more model complexity and calibration requirements. Therefore, it highly recommended to write down potential scenarios between the respective risk components to identify leading risks as well as a hedging strategy. Quite often it is more sensible to go for a good model that captures the leading risk well instead of trying to find an ultimate solution.

Incorporating theoretical knowledge with a view and understanding of the market domain is another critical path to becoming a successful derivatives trader. Market knowledge about the mechanics and dynamics within a particular domain can make the difference between anticipation and mere reaction. In other words, trading by risk figures, models, or only theory alone will almost certainly fail at some point. Moreover, understanding markets in general and the underlying asset class domain specifically helps to answer possibly the most crucial question of all: How much exposure should be hedged and should one even try to replicate a particular payoff at all? There are situations or trades which should preferably remain on the book *unhedged* if one is comfortable with the risk instead of trying to micro-hedge each risk component dynamically. The latter might, in conjunction with volatile trade dynamics, otherwise result in more losses, especially if the replication strategy is not clear.

Given that derivatives often feature nonlinear payouts, understanding the visible and hidden risks of the positions is critical. Standard approaches of using historical scenarios, (stressed) VaR or market normality assumptions often fail to identify hidden risks. This dilemma can be mitigated by applying scenario analyses even for situations that appear improbable at first sight. Therefore, tail risk scenarios revealing considerable risk exposure must not immediately be discounted by the trading desk and risk management department alike. Being a diligent risk manager means to reduce tail risk actively, and this should be a clear part of the mandate as well. Sometimes even small things like closing out short OTM options prior to expiry can make a big difference. Subsequently, following the last financial crisis, it became inherently important for trading desks to fully understand the impact of their positions at the treasury level of the firm, including the balance sheet. This impact includes derivatives, collateral, loan transactions, and cash positions equally since today banks need very good reasons for supporting trading operations that are only locally profitable. While there are certainly differences in funding costs and capability for balance sheet usage between different trading operations, not understanding the impact of new trades on the firm's capital (cost) does not make sense.

Digitization, automation, and machine learning is also increasingly entering the realm of derivatives trading. While trade execution algorithms, automated market making and algorithmic trading have been around for quite some time, recent initiatives seek to apply advanced machine learning and data-driven techniques to hedging derivatives in general [382, 383]. The advantage of applying advanced machine learning techniques lies in the fact that the parameter space can be increased significantly. This means one can combine the classic paradigm of 'hedging the greeks' dynamically with advanced statistical measures in order to be more reactive. As usual, the statistical analysis only works with a sufficient amount of historical data, *i.e.* for instruments that are not liquid, the approach is difficult and requires to generate simulated scenarios. Nevertheless, the introduction of an increasing amount of artificial intelligence means as well that the skill set of traders who work alongside the machine will need to keep up as well. This evolutionary requirement resonates with the introductory chapter in that traders require increasingly the ability to communicate with the quant teams in the same language so that unintuitive decisions by the machine can be diagnosed efficiently.

In the introduction to this book, it was mentioned that the derivative issuance and trading cycle had undergone a significant downturn since the 2008/09 crisis. However, ten years after the financial crisis global debt has risen significantly and central banks' balance sheets are enormous. Moreover, large inflows into passive investments such as ETFs have contributed to a strong bull market, and the evergreen question of how long this continues before a sharp correction is more relevant than ever. Furthermore, there are countries and regions which have not reached a level of derivative saturation and demand such that the exposure is likely to grow [384]. The combination of worldwide demand for yield in a low-interest-rate environment, a growing middle class, and increasing pension claims might, therefore, constitute the ideal substrate to drive increased derivative issuance in the promise of leveraged returns. If this becomes a reality, it is of utmost importance that regulators, risk managers, and traders alike understand the risks associated with derivative instruments in detail to contribute to a sustainable path for the industry.

17. Questions and Exercises

1. Consider the binomial stock price process in Figure 17.1. Currently, the stock is trading at 100. In 1 year, the stock is either at 120 or 40 with real-life probabilities of $p=0.8$ and $q=1-p=0.2$. Interest rates are 0.5% p.a.. What is the value of the 105 strike **put** today?

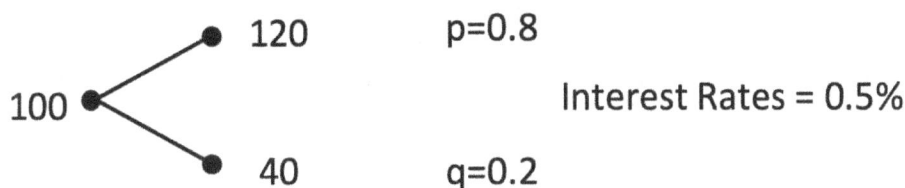

Figure 17.1: Binomial stock price process.

Answer: The forward F of the stock is 100.5. Then the risk neutral probability p^* is calculated as follows: $p^* = \frac{F-S^-}{S^+-S^-} = \frac{100.5-40}{120-40} = \frac{60.5}{80} = 0.75625$. The value of the 105 strike put is then obtained by multiplying the payoff in each state with the risk-neutral probability p^*, *i.e.* $P_{105} = p^* \cdot \max(0,(105-120)) + (1-p^*) \cdot \max(0,105-40) = 0.75625 \cdot 0 + (1-0.75625) \cdot 65 = 15.84375$. Discounting back to today gives $15.84375 \cdot 1/(1.005) \approx 15.76$.

2. On a vanilla option position, you are short $500'000 cash delta ($\Delta^\$$) and long $500'000 cash,percent-gamma ($\Gamma^{\$,\%}$). The asset moves up by +2.0%. What is your predicted P/L? Answer: -$500'000 x 0.02 + 0.5 x 100 x $500'000 x $(0.02)^2$ = -$10'000 + $10'000 = 0.

3. What is meant by the term structure of the implied volatility surface? Answer: The variation of the implied volatility across a specific strike with varying maturity.

4. Which of the vanilla option combination provides the best access to trading the skew of the volatility surface around the ATM (=100% of spot) pivot point? Answer: The 110 / 90 strike risk reversal is the best choice to exploit the skew rotation around the ATM point. This

reasoning assumes the typical equity skew of upwards sloping volatility to the downside and downwards sloping volatility to the upside centered around the ATM region.

5. Which vanilla option combination provides the best access to trading the kurtosis of the volatility surface? Answer: The wings of a wide enough butterfly is very sensitive to kurtosis changes.

6. You are long 100'000 delta hedged European calls on Nestle at strike CHF 50,-. The option expires at CHF 60,-, is cash settled and you want to remain delta hedged / delta neutral on the position. What should be done at expiry? Answer: The long option has a negative delta, *i.e.* to be flat delta you are long physical shares against the derivative. The option expires ITM, *i.e.* the delta is 100%. Therefore, as the option is cash settled, to be flat delta again after the expiry, you need to buy the option amount equivalent in shares into the closing auction.

7. When does the value of a stock drop w.r.t. to its dividend? Answer: The stock drops by the dividend amount on the ex-date.

8. Which instrument is **not** suited for a dividend exposure trade: (*i*) synthetic forward (short call / long put) versus cash delta, (*ii*) dividend swap, (*iii*) long or short put versus cash delta, (*iv*) long or short put spread versus cash delta. Answer: A put- or call-spread does not provide much pure dividend exposure (if at all).

9. You are a market marker for Nestle vanilla options. Nestle is currently trading at CHF 50. You observe the 6-month maturity European CHF 60 strike put option trading at CHF 11.50. What is the value of the corresponding call? Interest rates are 0.5% p.a.. Answer: Via Put-Call parity we have: $C = P + S - K = 11.50 + 50 - 60 \cdot \exp[-0.005 \cdot 0.5] = 1.65$.

10. You notice that the call is priced higher compared to the price implied by Put-Call parity. Which arbitrage strategy do you put in place to make a risk-free profit? Answer: Since the call is too expensive, it is obvious to sell it. In order to not take any position, one needs to effectively engage in a synthetic forward by buying the put and selling shares against it.

11. What happens to the gamma and vega profile on a vanilla option as we move closer to expiry? Answer: Gamma narrows around the strike, while the vega vanishes completely.

12. What happens to the gamma and theta profile on a vanilla option as we move closer to expiry? Answer: Gamma and theta narrow/peak around the strike.

13. Volatility of Volatility refers to which moment of the normal distribution? Answer: The fourth moment of the normal distribution is associated with the volatility of volatility.

14. If the daily volatility of a stock is 2.0%, what is the annualized volatility assuming 252 trading days and Brownian diffusion? Answer: $2.0\% \cdot \sqrt{(252)} = 31.75\%$.

15. What is meant by the expression 'tail risk event'? Answer: A rare event, for which market returns are more than three or more standard deviations. Alternatively, a (daily) drawdown above a pre-defined percentage.

16. What is meant by the expression 'pin risk'? Answer: The risk of having the asset price close on the strike of the option at expiry.

17. Consider a long 1Y maturity ATM put position, which is delta hedged daily on the close. You bought the position at an implied volatility of 20%. At expiry, the stock closes 30% below strike and has realized at a volatility of 25%. Have you made money for sure? Answer: It is not clear, because, for a delta-hedged position, it depends a lot at which time the stock realized the volatility. In other words, the cash-gamma weighting of the difference in implied vs. realized variance is time- and path-dependent.

18. Consider a position of 100'000 options at a strike of 50 for a remaining maturity of 1 year. The underlying company undergoes a simple 1:2 stock split, *i.e.* for every share one more

share is issued. How do you adjust the corresponding option portfolio? Answer: Both strike and number of options need to be adjusted to not change the original moneyness and strike notional. Since we are dealing with a stock split whereby the number of outstanding shares is doubled, the price of each share needs to half to not generate money out of nothing. As a consequence, the strike of the options is halved as well and to keep the outstanding notional constant, the number of options outstanding will double.

19. Consider a long call spread position (long ATM, short OTM). The skew of the volatility surface increases. What is the expected mark-to-market impact on your option portfolio? Answer: Since the skew increased, it can be assumed that the long ATM position has either gained in volatility (or at least stayed constant), while the short OTM upside call have dropped in volatility. Hence, overall, one should expect positive Profit/Loss.

20. Consider a long risk reversal position (long OTM calls, short OTM puts). The skew of the volatility surface decreases. What is the expected mark-to-market impact on your option portfolio? Answer: Since the skew decreased, it can be assumed that the short OTM put position has either lost in its implied volatility mark (or at least stayed constant), while the long OTM upside calls have gained (or stayed constant) in their volatility mark. Hence, overall, one should expect positive Profit/Loss.

21. Given the volatility assumption of the BSM model, which risk sensitivity (greeks) are inconsistent with the model? Answer: Vega and rho are inconsistent because the model assumes these 'parameters' to be constants.

22. Within the Black-Scholes-Merton framework, the sensitivity of an option to interest rates is proportional to the maturity T. Assuming that one knows the sensitivity of the option to volatility, which of the two risks dominates with increasing maturity? Answer: Brownian diffusion assumes a $\sqrt{(T)}$ scaling for the volatility. Hence, IR dominate for longer dated options.

23. Consider a long ATM option position with 1 month to go until expiry. What are the typical greek characteristics? Answer: ATM options with short time to expiry typically exhibit large gamma, theta, and small vega.

24. What is the theta/gamma relation? Answer: $\Theta = -\frac{1}{2}\Gamma^{\$}\sigma^2$.

25. You are short \$1'000'000 cash-percent gamma $\Gamma^{\$,\%}$ on a vanilla option for which you receive \$3'000 each day. You decide only to rebalance your delta in case the daily break-even volatility is exceeded. Calculate the daily and annual breakeven volatility (i.e. the volatility necessary to fully offset the theta P/L) for the asset assuming 252 trading days. Answer: Daily breakeven volatility $= \sqrt{\frac{-(3000)}{50\cdot(-1000000)}} = 0.77\%$. Annualized volatility $= \sqrt{252}\cdot 0.77\% = 12.30\%$.

26. What are the most limiting assumptions in the Black-Scholes-Merton option pricing model in practice? Answer: Liquidity constraints, short selling restrictions, discontinuities, and jumps render the replication argument impractical.

27. Consider the dGamma/dSpot profile in Figure 17.2. Which vanilla option combination does the shape resemble most?

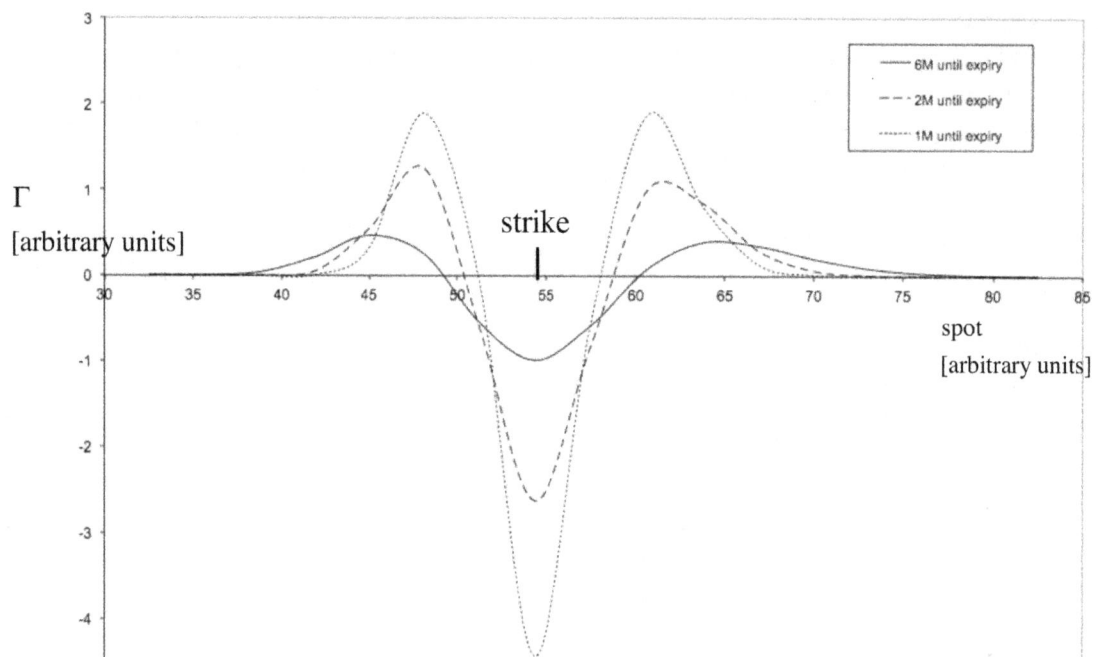

Figure 17.2: Gamma profile.

Answer: The gamma profile depicts a butterfly vanilla combination.

28. Consider the gamma vs. spot profile in Figure 17.3. Which exotic option type does the shape resemble most?

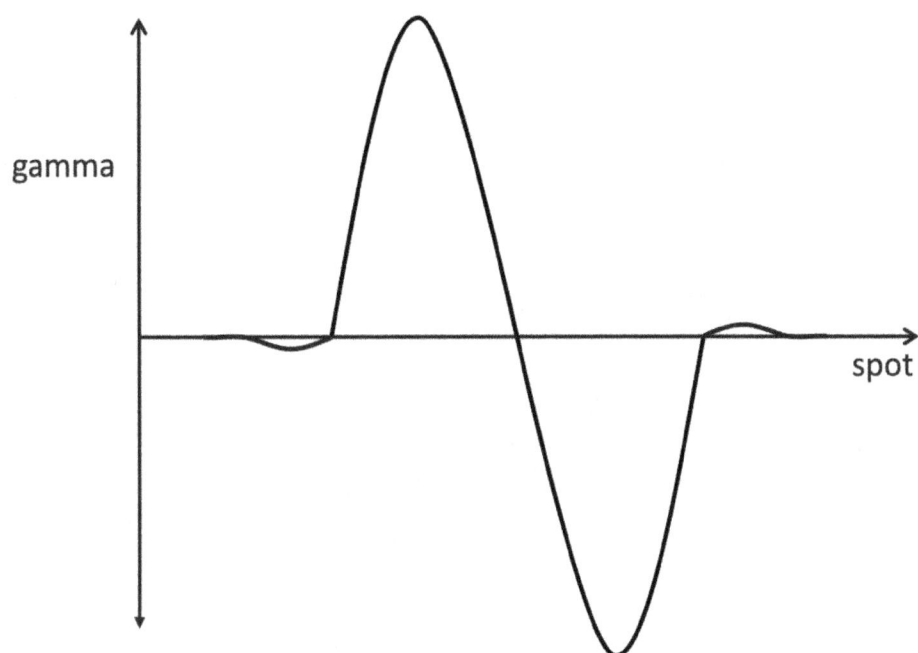

Figure 17.3: Gamma profile.

Answer: The gamma profile depicts a long digital call option.

29. Which volatility surface change does Figure 17.4 illustrate?

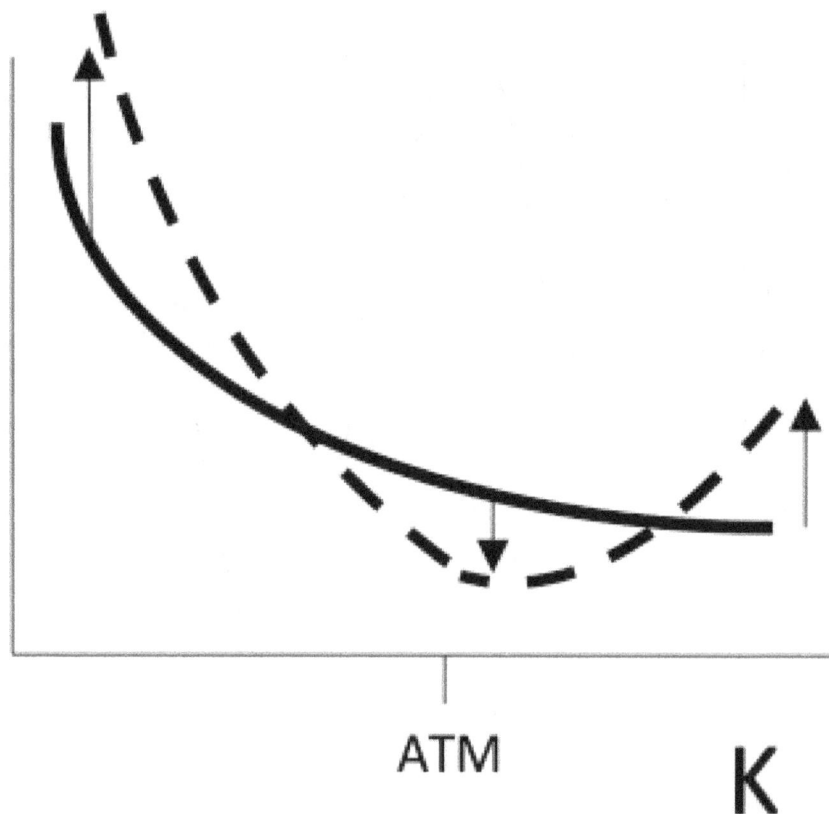

Figure 17.4: Volatility surface change.

Answer: A change in kurtosis.

30. Which spot-volatility (surface) dynamics do the three different lines (A, B and C) in Figure 17.5 illustrate (*e.g.* sticky-strike etc.) and which spot-volatility correlation (*e.g.* positive) does it imply in case of a market down-move (from spot 100 to 90)?

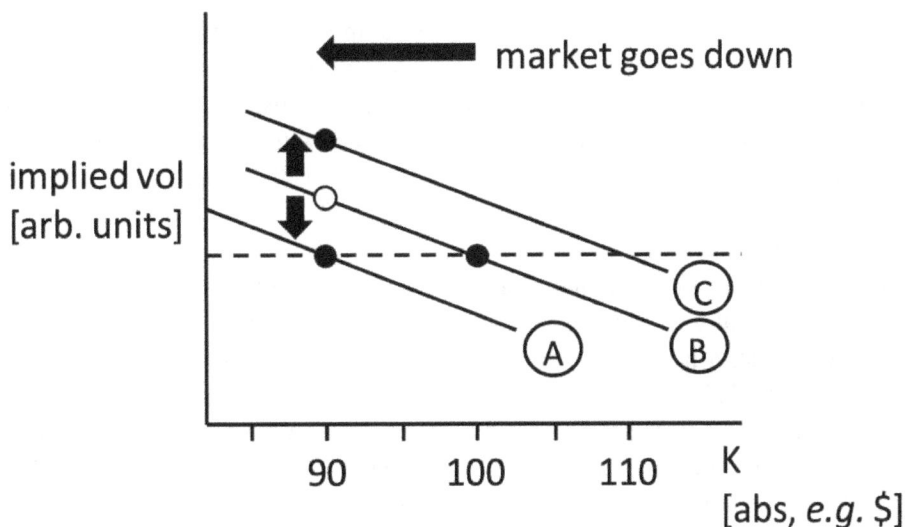

Figure 17.5: Volatility surface change.

Answer: A. Sticky-delta implies a positive spot-volatility correlation, B. sticky-strike implies zero spot-vol correlation and C. sticky-local vol implies negative spot-vol correlation.

31. Your book shows a position in a long 100 strike European call with 1 year time left to expiry. The call is worth CHF 3.10. The implied volatility is marked at 10%, the dividend yield at 10% and interest rate is 0.5%. The current spot is trading at 104. The risk management system shows positive theta, *i.e.* one **earns** theta each day on the position. At first you dismiss the results as a numerical issue but revisit the option 30 days later. At the same spot and identical parameters, the call is now worth 3.15. What is happening, and why? Answer: The dividend yield is larger than the financing cost. Therefore, the call *decays up*.

32. To double check results, you price a 12 month and a 9 month CHF 105 European call (EC). At the current spot of CHF 104 and with the market parameters of the previous question, one gets: 105EC(12M) = 1.00 and 105EC(9M)=1.02. The call with the shorter maturity is more expensive. Is this possible? Answer: Again, the dividend yield is larger than financing cost and the option with the shorter time to maturity and hence less 'time' uncertainty is more expensive, *i.e.* it has a higher probability of ending up ITM.

33. You buy a 1-year maturity European put on a dividend paying stock. What is your **long / short** position on implied volatility, interest rates, dividends, borrow cost (w.r.t. the stock position, not cash)? Answer: The long put position is long volatility, long dividends, short interest rates, and long borrow cost. The latter three sensitivities will lower the forward.

34. You are short a 5% upside digital on Nestle for a (strike) notional of CHF 20m. In order to risk manage the trade, you want to apply a (barrier) shift on the digital. You estimate that you can trade 10% of the daily stock volume (CHF 370m) instantaneously. What is the magnitude of the barrier-shift in % and in which direction do you apply it so that it helps to risk manage the position? Answer: 0.5 x (20m x 5%) / (10% x 370m) = 1.35%. The barrier shift is applied such as to lower the barrier, *i.e.* downwards.

35. You are pricing a downside barrier knock-in put on a single stock, which you will delta hedge. You wonder whether you need to apply a barrier shift to facilitate the risk management. If this is the case, you set out to calculate a barrier shift, which is equal to the historical daily

volatility of the underlying. Assuming 252 trading days, Brownian diffusion and annual historical stock volatility of 35% what is the barrier-shift in % and in which direction is it applied to manage the position best? Answer: For a long position, it is wise to apply a barrier shift because upon hitting the barrier, the option holder will need to sell the stock delta into a falling market. In order to provide a cushion, the barrier is therefore shifted down, which also implies that the option holder carries less physical stock delta against the barrier. The barrier shift is determined as $\frac{35\%}{\sqrt{252}} = 2.20\%$

36. Is the price of an Asian option more or less expensive than the equivalent vanilla and why? Answer: It is typically less expensive because the Asian feature reduces the implied volatility.

37. You are long a delta-hedged Asian call with 10 Asian out dates before expiry. The call is currently slightly ITM. What do you expect to happen to your delta on the Asian out dates assuming the spot stays constant? Answer: Since each Asian date provides more certainty in the final payout, the option increasingly becomes an ITM option and approaches the delta limit of 1. To be completely delta hedged at all times, one therefore sells physical delta against the gain in optionality delta. Moreover, if the option were cash settled, one buys back the full delta on the close of the last Asian date to offset the complete delta drop on the option expiry itself.

38. Which of the following models would be best suited to price an exotic option which is highly sensitive to volatility convexity (*e.g.* reverse put cliquet)?

39. The reverse put cliquet is mostly very sensitive to vega convexity. Only a stochastic volatility model can quantify this risk correctly or at least to some extent.

40. An option pays a certain level of the positive performance of the Nikkei index in USD only if, at the options' maturity, the USD is at a certain prescribed level against the JPY. How would you call such an option? Answer: Quanto Nikkei call contingent on a USDJPY digital.

41. Which of the following is **not** a property of the local volatility model: (*i*) if properly calibrated, perfect repricing of (listed) vanilla options, (*ii*) trivial to calibrate and stable, (*iii*) suitable for pricing light exotic options, (*iv*) intuitive skew dynamics. Answer: Local volatility model implementation do often suffer from calibration issues unless using some regularization tricks. Due to difficulties with calibration, out of the box (Dupire) implementation tend to be relatively unstable, especially in volatile markets.

42. Consider a monthly strike resetting (cliquet) 100 / 110 call spread with a symmetric floor (*i.e.* floor = -cap = -10). What is the highest risk on this option? Answer: The most significant risk on these forward starting call spreads is the forward skew.

43. What is meant by the term gap or exit risk in the case of barrier options? Answer: Gap or exit risk in the case of barrier options refers to the possibility of having to sell/buy physical delta into a falling/rising market.

44. Which long option matches the Profit/Loss profile in Figure 17.6 best?

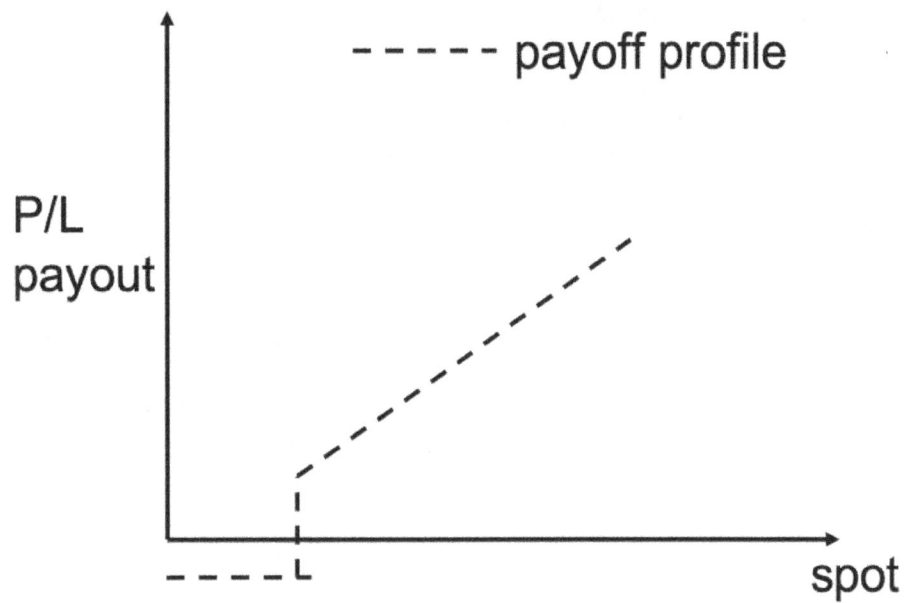

Figure 17.6: P/L profile.

Answer: Upside knock-in call.
Which long option matches the Profit/Loss profile in Figure 17.7 best?

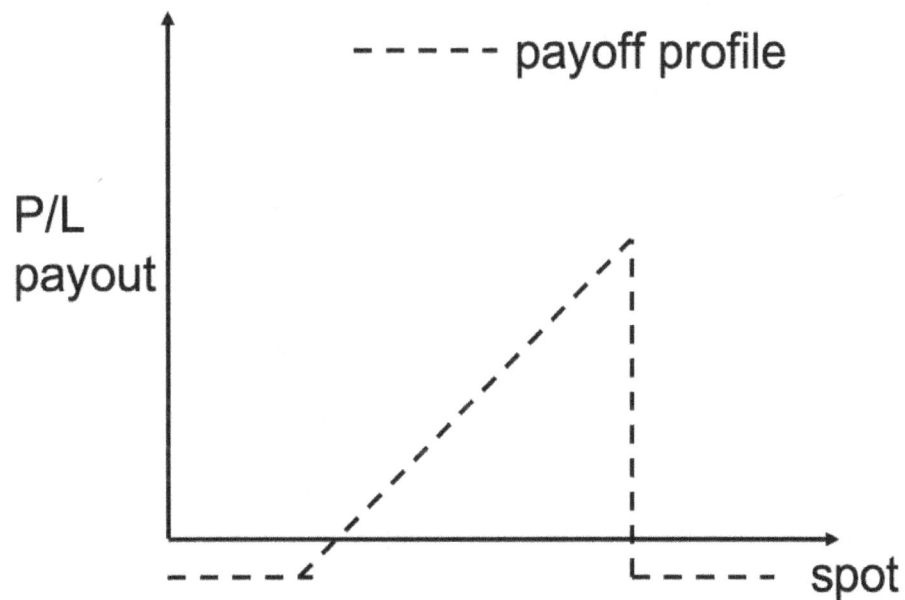

Figure 17.7: P/L profile.

Answer: Upside knock-out call.

45. In the Heston model, which parameters are generating the skew of the implied volatility?

Answer: Skew is generated via volatility-of-volatility and the spot-volatility correlation.

46. You need to price a structure with high sensitivity to forward skew. Which volatility/process model do you chose to assess this specific impact best? Answer: The Independent increment model is best suited to assess the impact of forward skew in isolation.

47. You need to price a structure with has high sensitivity to volatility-of- volatility (*i.e.* volatility convexity / volgamma). Which volatility/process model do you chose to assess this specific sensitivity best? Answer: A stochastic volatility model (*e.g.* Heston) will quantify the impact of volatility convexity best.

48. You are long an American knock-in put on a dividend paying stock. The spot is moving closer to the barrier. What do you expect to happen to your vega and dividend position, *i.e.* do you get longer or shorter? Answer: As we move closer toward the barrier, the vega increases since the proximity drives the option value and increased volatility raises the probability of a barrier hit. On the dividends, an increase at a spot level closer to the barrier naturally has a larger impact as well. Moreover, you hold more of the underlying asset against the barrier in terms of delta.

49. Consider a long position in a 100% strike, 50% barrier downside knock-in put whereby the barrier is observed at maturity only (European). What is the replicating portfolio assuming you can trade a 3% barrier shift for the given size? Answer: The position is replicated by long 1 x the 50% strike put, long 50/3 x 50% strike put, short 50/3 x 47% strike put.

50. What are properties of variance swaps (here we assume zero dividends, zero interest rates and no skew in the implied volatility surface)? Answer: Variance swaps exhibit constant cash gamma, linear variance vega, and resetting delta after each observation period.

51. How can variance swaps be replicated? Answer: Variance swaps are replicated by a continuum of calls and puts weighted by the **inverse** of the square of their strike prices.

52. What are the components or the equivalence of a short variance swap? Answer: The short varswap is equivalent to a position of short underlying, long log contract, short higher order terms.

53. What is the equivalent portfolio of a short log contract? The short log contract is equivalent to a position in a short forward, a long position in call and put portfolio with $1/\text{strike}^2$ weightings.

54. What is meant by shadow or skew delta in case of a variance swap? The skew delta arises due to volatility skew within the weighted replicating vanilla portfolio, whereby the downside dominates due to the inverse strike squared weighting.

55. What is the issue with pricing a capped variance swap? Answer: The variance swap cap needs to be priced as an option on variance, which is model dependent. Not taking into account the cap correctly may have a significant price impact in case the swaps move deep ITM, which is in fact how the problem was initially detected.

56. Consider a long position in a Quanto EUR Nikkei forward (fully delta hedged). Consider the case for which the EURJPY rate stays constant, and the Nikkei spot goes up. What happens to your equity and FX position? Answer: The equity is fully hedged via the offsetting physical (futures) position. However, the impact of the FX dynamics is such that it is necessary to sell EUR and buy YEN to be fully hedged again.

57. What is the issue when hedging a short variance swap position with ATM vanilla straddles? Answer: ATM straddles do not offset the skew and volatility convexity of the variance swap. Moreover, in times of stress, the variance swap market typically dries up quicker compared to vanilla options.

58. Consider a short position in an upside digital. The volatility of the asset is 25%. With respect

to spot level (100), the forward is at 102%, and the strike of the digital is 95%. What is the risk exposure at the inception of the trade? Answer: The delta position is short because we benefit from a potential drop in spot. The digital is already at inception ITM, and the forward is positive, *i.e.* the upside loss is already somewhat limited or contained in the value of the digital; this means we profit from a rise in volatility because it increases the possibility of a drop below the strike. We are also long gamma because we are trading above the digital strike at inception or current spot.

59. What is the definition of the VIX future of maturity T and is the pricing of the future model-dependent? Answer: The price of the VIX future of maturity T is the market's risk-neutral expectation of the return volatility over the next 30 days starting at T. The price of the VIX future is *model-dependent*.

60. In case of positive equity-interest rate correlation, what can be said for the hedging costs on a typical upside (early) trigger redeemable position in case spots move up? Answer: In theory, there will be increased re-hedging costs due to rebalancing of the interest rates exposure hedge.

61. Consider a long position in a \$500'000 vega notional variance swap struck at 15. At expiry, the realized volatility is 25. What is your P/L at expiry? Answer: $\$500'000 \cdot \frac{(25^2 - 15^2)}{(2 \times 15)} = \$6.6m$

62. You are pricing an ATM basket option call and examine the full gamma matrix. What do you expect? Answer: The basket call is long gamma both on the diagonal and cross. The long cross-gamma can be understood because the price increases with increasing correlation (subject to the floor of zero for a call, *i.e.* there is an asymmetry). The long diagonal can be understood because we are still dealing with a long call position even if it is for a multifactor option.

63. You are pricing an ATM basket option put and examine the full gamma matrix. What do you expect? Answer: The basket put is long gamma both on the diagonal and cross. The long cross-gamma can be understood because the price increases with increasing correlation (subject to the floor of zero for a call, *i.e.* there is an asymmetry). The long diagonal can be understood because we are still dealing with a long call position even if it is for a multifactor option.

64. Which inherent problems for multifactor options does the uncertain correlation model allow to assess? Answer: Quantifying switches in correlation and cross-gamma exposure.

65. Consider a short position in a digital outperformance option between assets A and B (*i.e.* we pay X% if A outperforms B at expiry). Close to expiry, what is your correlation position as a function of the outperformance? Answer: A < B: We prefer the assets to move in sync to avoid the payout; hence, long correlation. A = B: rather neutral position, which may quickly change, however. A > B: If the assets continue to move in sync, one needs to satisfy the payoff. Hence, to increase the chance of having no payout, we want the assets to decorrelate. Therefore, a short correlation for the short option position.

66. Is it possible to mark a position in an outperformance digital conservatively using a single correlation number for all scenarios? Answer: cross-gamma or flips in the correlation exposure are typical for outperformance digitals. A conservative correlation mark is only possible for the current local spot position and therefore to some extent meaningless.

67. Consider a short position in an outperformance option between the NKY and the DAX index, *i.e.* you are short the payout $\max[0, \frac{NKY_T}{NKY_0} - \frac{DAX_T}{DAX_0}]$ whereby the subscripts T and 0 denote the index levels at expiry and inception, respectively. What is your correlation position? Answer: The buyer of an outperformance option is typically always short correlation, *i.e.* the opposite

is true for the seller. Now, it is possible that in case of a deep ITM outperformance option, the correlation turns. However, this scenario will (if ever) occur close to expiry when the option has lost most of the correlation sensitivity. Moreover, in a simulation this scenario is typically sampled only very rarely, *i.e.* the impact of switching bid/offer correlations based on moneyness yields minimal extra charge (if any). Hence, pricing this option at a bid correlation is conservative.

68. Assume that the short outperformance option above ($\max[0, \frac{NKY_T}{NKY_0} - \frac{DAX_T}{DAX_0}]$) actually pays out in EUR, which means the NKY is Quanto'ed in EUR. You fully hedge the equity part of the option with NKY and DAX futures and fully hedge the FX exposure via EURJPY cash at inception. What do you need to do in case EURJPY FX moves down (*i.e.* the YEN weakens) for a pure equity-fx cross-gamma perspective? Think about whether you are long or short the Quanto forward to answer this question. Answer: You are short the EUR Quanto forward w.r.t. to the NKY. In case the YEN weakens against EUR (as it is the case today actually due to the inflationary policy of the BoJ), your obligation to deliver the payout in EUR increases. As a consequence, given this FX move, you need to buy more NKY futures.

69. Consider a basket put whereby the correlation between the assets is < 1. Is the price of the option more or less expensive than the sum of the equivalent vanilla puts and why? Answer: A non-unity correlation always reduces the variance of the basket and, therefore, the implied volatility used in the pricing.

70. What is the relation between the price and vega of a basket call versus the basket correlation? Answer: Price and vega increase with rising correlation.

71. What is the relation of the price of a downside barrier worst-of knock-in put versus the correlation of the components? Answer: Price decreases with increasing correlation because the probability of hitting the barrier is lower.

72. What is the dvega/dspot profile of a short worst of forward assuming all components are perfectly correlated? Answer: The worst of forward gains/loses vega with increasing/decreasing spot levels.

73. You are long a worst of downside knock-in option put and examine the full gamma matrix. What do you expect? Answer: A long position in a worst-of downside knock-in put is long diagonal- and short cross-gamma.

74. What is the price versus correlation relationship for a 3 asset worst of call and the cross-gamma for a long position at inception assuming a correlation mark $\tilde{5}0\%$? Answer: The price increases with rising correlation since the downside is floored at zero, and one is effectively dealing with a call. Moreover, a larger dispersion (*i.e.* correlation decrease) increases the probability that the worst of performer contributes in a negative return. As a consequence, the holder of the position is also long cross-gamma. Hence, the latter implies that we benefit from correlated moves.

75. The measured terminal correlation under a non-constant volatility model is typically lower/higher/identical to the instantaneous (input) correlation? Answer: The terminal correlation is typically lower compared to the instantaneous (input) correlation.

76. What is meant by the expression 'correlation skew' in the context of equity or FX multifactor derivatives? Answer: Implied correlation quotes tend to vary as a function of the strike because correlation is not spot invariant, *i.e.* typically increasing with a decrease in the spot level.

77. Is there an issue when using daily close-to-close prices for calculating the historical correlation between asynchronous time series? Answer: The estimate is biased and typically leads to a lower correlation estimate.

78. Consider an index, which for a given strike and expiry trades at 20% implied volatility in the option market. The equivalent average implied volatility of the index components is 25%. What is the back of the envelope implied correlation of the index? Answer: The implied correlation is calculated as $\frac{\sigma_{index}^2}{\sigma_{stocks}^2} = \frac{20\%^2}{25\%^2} = 64\%$.

79. What is the typical relationship between volatility and correlation versus spot? Answer: As spots go up/down, both volatility and correlation have historically for the majority of time moved in the opposite direction.

80. Consider a long position in a worst of downside barrier option. Assuming a dynamic correlation model (*i.e.* correlation changes as a function of spot), will the price typically be lower/higher or invariant compared to a constant correlation assumption? Answer: The probability of a barrier hit decreases with rising correlation. In case we observe the typical negatively correlated spot-correlation dynamics, the price should decrease.

81. What are inherent challenges for multifactor stochastic volatility models? Answer: Stochastic volatility model tend to become very parameter-rich because estimates for inter-asset spot-volatility and volatility-volatility correlations need to be provided. Moreover, merely plugging in some 'sensible' default values does somewhat put the approach in question.

82. You overhear a conversation on the trading floor between some other equity exotic traders. One of them complains that the theta of the equity exotic book has gotten much worse because of the increased short cross-gamma position. What do you think about this statement, *i.e.* do you think it is correct? Hint: Assume that equity-equity correlation is typically positive. Answer: Assuming the correlation between equities is positive, the trading book earns theta on the short cross-gamma terms. Hence, the theta must have worsened either due to increased long gamma on the diagonal or other effects, but certainly not from the increased short cross-gamma position.

83. Consider a fully delta-hedged option portfolio consisting of two assets. The portfolio has zero diagonal but shows $500'000 long cash-percentage cross-gamma ($\Gamma^{\$,\%}$). Asset 1 moves up by 1.0%, asset 2 moves down by 2.0%. What is your expected P/L due to the dispersion? Answer: $2 \cdot 0.5 \cdot 100 \cdot \$500'000 \cdot (1\%) \cdot (-2\%) = -\$10'000$.

84. In order to engage in a long cross-gamma position through a Call vs. Call (*i.e.* CvC, as known as OBBO), which side do you take? Answer: In order to be long cross-gamma, we need to be long correlation and therefore long the basket.

85. Consider a long position in a 3x6 $5m notional Forward rate agreement (FRA) where you agreed at an inception rate of 1.25%. When does the FRA expire w.r.t to inception and what cash flows happen in case of having the rate decrease to 1% after 3 months? Answer: The FRA expires in 6 months, the rates exposure is 3 month forward starting w.r.t. inception and the discounted payment is due after 3 months as $(1.00\% - 1.25\%) \cdot \$5m \cdot 0.25/(1 + 1\%/4) =$ $3'117.

86. What is meant by the expression 'FRA-IR futures convexity bias'? Answer: IR futures are subject to margin/collateral, while FRAs are not. This difference leads to a discrepancy in price.

87. What is the back of the envelope dv01 of a 3 year $10m notional fix vs. floating interest rate swap? Answer: The dv01 of a 3 year swap is roughly 0.0003 or 3bp, *i.e.* $10m x 0.0003 = $3'000.

88. What is meant by the expression LIBOR/OIS basis? Answer: The difference in LIBOR vs. OIS rates due to differences in cash flows causing OIS to be more secure.

89. Collateralized trades should by now be discounted using which rate? Answer: Collateralized trades should be discounted using OIS rates.

90. What is the difference between a credit default swap (CDS) and a floating rate note (FRN)? Answer: The FRN/CDS is funded/unfunded.

91. Which of the following statements about VaR (Value at Risk) is **not** true: (*i*) VaR relies on a Gaussian distribution, (*ii*) VaR is a holistic risk measure, including an estimate for tail losses, (*iii*) VaR can be applied to effectively any portfolio, (*iv*) VaR can be calculated using Monte Carlo simulation. Answer: VaR is not a holistic risk measure since it does not convey any information about the tails of the distribution.

92. Given a daily VaR of $10m at a 99% confidence level, which of the following statements is **not** true: (*i*) in 99 out of 100 days we expect at most a loss of $10m, (*ii*) there is only a 1% chance of losing more than $10m over the next day, (*iii*) the loss exceeding $10m is expected to be capped by 1% of the VaR, (*iv*) the specified VaR number is true for a normal distribution. Answer: VaR contains no information about the loss magnitude exceeding the VaR number.

93. Which is the effect of the VaR number when varying the holding period and the confidence level? Answer: VaR increases with an increasing holding period and confidence level.

18. Glossary

Basis Risk Basis risk refers to the inherent risk when hedging a position by either taking a position in a derivative of the asset or hedging the exposure with a similar or unrelated instrument. Given that neither of the hedges is perfect, the amount of deviation between hedge and source position is typically called the basis risk. In the interest rate world, basis risk typically refers also to intercurve spreads.

Call Option Derivative agreement which gives the holder the right, but not the obligation, to buy a stock, bond, commodity or another instrument at a specified price at or within a specific time (period).

Caplet / Floorlet and Cap / Floor Vanilla option call / put equivalent for interest rate derivatives.

Cliquet Option Derivatives for which the strike periodically resets over the lifetime.

Composite Option Derivative which implicitly includes exchange rate risk between underlying and payment currency of the contract.

Convexity Refers to the measure of the curvature in a relationship between two metrics such as bond price versus bond yield or option delta versus gamma.

Contract for Difference (CFD) Financial contract paying out the difference between a pre-agreed asset level and its actual value at a pre-determined date and time.

Cost-of-Carry Either the cost for physically holding or storing a commodity or the implicit costs of running a derivative position (funding, capital charges, hedging costs, etc.).

Coupon Refers to a cash payment from between two counterparties on the back of a derivative transaction such as an interest rate swap.

Credit Support Annex (CSA) The CSA defines parameters such as the eligible collateral, respective haircuts, calculation method and dispute resolution for OTC contracts.

Derivative Financial instrument for which the price is a function of its underlying asset.

Delta or Option delta Change of the derivative price for a change in the underlying spot price or future.

Delta-neutral Refers to a (derivative) position that is insensitive/neutral to movements of the underlying asset in the first order.

Exotic Options (Exotics) Derivatives with highly path-dependent payoff and P/L profiles. Inherently more difficult to replicate versus vanilla options.

Forward Mechanism to convert spot prices or rates to their values in the future under the consideration of interest rates, dividends, borrow cost, convenient yield or other (asset class-specific) parameters.

Futures (Contract) Exchange-traded equivalent of a Forward.

Gap Risk Risk relating to sudden decreases in asset market value, which in turn may lead to significant losses.

Hedge Trade aimed to neutralize portfolio risk exposure in one or more sensitivity parameters.

Implied Correlation Correlation calculated/implied from financial instruments.

Implied Volatility Volatility calculated/implied from financial derivatives as a function of strike and maturity.

Interest Rates Set of interest marks used to determine how cash flows are discounted or compounded.

Interest Rate Swap (IRS) Financial instrument whereby two counterparties exchange fixed and floating (based on a floating reference rate) interest rate payments periodically.

LIBOR LIBOR stands for "London Interbank Offered Rate" and is a key benchmark interest rate.

Local Volatility (Model) Deterministic implied volatility function as a function of spot and time.

Local Correlation Model Class of local volatility models which allow the pairwise correlation to vary as a function of spot and time.

Long Being 'long' refers to either a position in a financial contract or parameter which makes money if the contract or parameters increases in value (*e.g.* future contract, vega, correlation, etc.).

Overhedge Trade booking techniques or methods aimed to reduce risk or smooth exposure of derivative risk such as discontinuous payoffs.

Pin Risk Risk of an asset price closing exactly at the level of the strike at expiry.

P/L Profit and / or Loss.

Quanto Option Derivative which implicitly hedges out exchange rate risk between underlying and payment currency of the contract.

Put Option Derivative agreement which gives the holder the right, but not the obligation, to sell a stock, bond, commodity or another instrument at a specified price at or within a specific time (period).

Realized Correlation Correlation estimate calculated from historical time series / data.

Realized Volatility Volatility estimate calculated from historical time series / data.

Repo Repurchase agreement, *i.e.* the sale and repurchase of securities at a later date.

Risk Neutral Measure / Pricing Probability measure commonly used in derivative / asset pricing such that the price is the discounted expected value of the future payoff under a unique risk-neutral measure. Hence, the asset risk premium is incorporated in the price.

Short Being 'short' refers to either a position in a financial contract or parameter which loses money if the contract or parameters increases in value (*e.g.* future contract, vega, correlation, etc.).

Spot price Price of an asset today.

Swaption Option to enter an interest rate swap (either physically or cash-settled).

Stochastic Volatility Model Class of volatility models whereby both asset spot and its volatility couple to independent stochastic drivers (with a correlation parameter between them).

Strike The option strike refers to the value below, at or above the underlying price for which the option is OTM, ATM or ITM.

Structured Product Financial instrument combining derivatives in a securitized format for various investor classes.

Valuation Adjustment (XVA) Series of adjustments/charges added or deducted in the pricing of derivative or financial contracts.

Value at Risk (VaR) The maximum expected loss over a specified time interval with a certain confidence level.

Variance Swap CFD exchanging realized variance versus a pre-defined variance strike.

Vega P/L sensitivity of a derivative position concerning changes in the implied volatility mark.

Volatility convexity / Volgamma / Volga Refers to the rate of change in vega concerning a unit change in volatility.

Volatility skew Refers to the fact that implied volatility varies not only across time but also in strike space.

Volatility Swap CFD exchanging realized volatility versus a pre-defined volatility strike.

Term Structure Refers to market data properties or metrics (*e.g.* interest rates, volatility, correlation), which vary in time. A term structure curve then describes the relation of the market property in time (forward-looking).

Yield Curve Curve plotting a respective interest rate versus various maturity buckets of a similar debt instrument.

Yield to Maturity (YTM) The Yield to Maturity is defined as the internal rate of return of a bond, assuming that it is held until maturity.

19. List of acronyms

Acronym	Description
1[...]	Indicator function: 1 if [...] > 0, else 0
1bn	One Billion
1D	One Day
1M	One Month
2M	Two Months
3M	Three Months
6M	Six Months
9M	Nine Months
12M	Twelve Months
1m	One million
10m	Ten million
100m	One hundred million
1Y	One Year
2Y	Two Years
3Y	Three Years
bps	basis points (0.01% = 1 basis point)
AT1	Additional Tier 1 Capital
ATM	At the Money
BCBS	Basel Committee on Banking Supervision
BSM	Black-Scholes-Merton (Model)
CBA	Convertible Bond Arbitrage
CB	Convertible Bond
CCP	Central Counterparty Clearing House
CDS	Credit Default Swap
CET1	Common Equity Tier 1 Capital
CFD	Contract for Difference

CMS	Constant Maturity Swap
CRM	Credit Risk Management
CSA	Credit Support Annex
co-var	co-variance
co-var swap	co-variance swap
cpn	coupon
CVA	Credit Valuation Adjustment
CVaR	conditional VaR
CvC	Call versus Call
dv01	Dollar value of one basis point
DNT	Double-No-Touch
DVA	Debt Valuation Adjustment
$\mathbf{E}[...]$	(risk-neutral) expectation
EDS	Equity Default Swap
EDSP	Exchange Delivery Settlement Price
EE	Expected Exposure
EL	Expected Loss
ESOP	Employee Stock Option Plan
ES	Expected Shortfall
Exotics	exotic options
exp[...]	*e* raised to the power [...]
FRA	Forward Rate Agreement
FRN	Floating Rate Note
FRTB	Fundamental Review of the Trading Book
FVA	Funding Valuation Adjustment
FX	Foreign Exchange
GBM	Geometric Brownian Motion
HQLA	High Quality Liquid Assets
IR	Interest rate
IRS	Interest rate swap
ITM	In-the-money
KVA	Capital Valuation Adjustment
LCM	Local Correlation Model
LIBOR	London Inter-bank Offered Rate
LCR	Liquidity Coverage Ratio
LGD	Loss given Default
LOIS	Spread / difference between LIBOR 3m and OIS 3m
LV	Local Volatility
LVM	Local Volatility Model
MVA	Margin Valuation Adjustment
NAV	Net Asset Value
NMRF	non-modellable risk factors
NSFR	Net Stable Funding Ratio
PC	Product Control
PD	Probability of Default
PVBP	Price Value of a Basis Point, *i.e.* PV01

PV01	Present Value of one basis point
PV	Present Value
P/L	Profit & Loss
PIPS	points spot delta
OBBO	Option-Basket-Basket-Option
OIS	Overnight Index Swap
OTC	Over-the-counter
OTM	out-the-money
Pr[...]	Probability
PRDC	Power-reverse dual-currency derivative
RWA	Risk weighted Assets
RR	Recovery rate
SLV	Stochastic Local Volatility
SPV	Special Purpose Vehicle
std	Standard deviation
STIR	Short term interest rate
SV	Stochastic Volatility
SVM	Stochastic Volatility Model
T1	Tier 1 Capital
T2	Tier 2 Capital
TRS	Total Return Swap
Vanilla	Vanilla option
VaR	Value at Risk
varswap	Variance Swap
volswap	Volatility Swap
WWR	Wrong way risk
XCCY	cross-currency
XVA	Valuation Adjustments (umbrella term)
YTM	Yield to maturity

Bibliography

[1] Louie Woodall. A tale of two CCPs. *Risk Magazine*, (January), 2019.

[2] Mariusz Jarmuzek and Rossen Rozenov. Excessive Private Sector Leverage and Its Drivers : Evidence from Advanced Economies. *Applied Economics*, 51:3787–3803, 2019.

[3] Financial Stability Board (FSB). Global Monitoring Report on Non-Bank Financial Intermediation 2018. Technical Report February, 2019.

[4] Kris Devasabai. If CLO investors flee, defaults could snowball. *Risk magazine*, (December), 2018.

[5] Ognjen Vukovic. On the Interconnectedness of Schrodinger and Black-Scholes Equation. *Journal of Applied Mathematics and Physics*, 3(September):1108–1113, 2015.

[6] Shipeng Zhou and Liuqing Xiao. An Application of Symmetry Approach to Finance: Gauge Symmetry in Finance. *Symmetry*, 2:1763–1775, 2010.

[7] Fischer Black and Myron Scholes. The pricing of options and corporate liabilities. *The Journal of Political Economy*, 81(3):637–654, 1973.

[8] R.C. Merton. Theory of rational option pricing. *The Bell Journal of Economics and Management Science*, 4(1):141–183, 1973.

[9] M. Sprenkle. Warrant prices as indicators of expectations and preferences. *Yale economic essays*, 1(2):179–231, 1961.

[10] Edward O. Thorp and Sheen T. Kassouf. *Beat the Market: A Scientific Stock Market System.* Random House, 1967.

[11] Paul A. Samuelson. Rational Theory of Warrant Pricing. *Industrial Management Review*, 6:2:13, 1965.

[12] Jens Carsten Jackwerth. Recovering Risk Aversion from Option Prices and Realized Returns. *Review of Financial Studies*, 13(2):433–451, 2000.

[13] John H. Cochrane. *Asset Pricing (Revised Edition)*. Princeton University Press, 2000.

[14] Jens Carsten Jackwerth. Distributions and Implied Binomial Trees : A Literature Review. *Journal of Derivatives*, 7(1999):66–82, 1999.

[15] Steve Ross. The Recovery Theorem Journal. *Journal of Finance*, 70(2):615–648, 2015.

[16] Jaroslav Borovicka, Lars Peter Hansen, and Jose A. Scheinkman. Misspecified Recovery. *Journal of Finance*, 71(6):2493–2544, 2015.

[17] Francesco Audrino, Robert Huitema, and Markus Ludwig. An Empirical Analysis of the Ross Recovery Theorem. *SSRN Electronic Journal*, (May), 2014.

[18] Jens Carsten Jackwerth and Marco Menner. Does the Ross Recovery Theorem work Empirically ? 2017.

[19] William F . Sharpe. Mutual Fund Performance. *The Journal of Business*, 39(1):119–138, 1966.

[20] Harry Markowitz. Portfolio Selection. *The Journal of Finance*, 7(1):77–91, 1952.

[21] James Tobin. Liquidity Preference as Behavior Towards Risk. *The Review of Economic Studies*, 25(2):65–86, 1958.

[22] John Hull. *Options, Futures and Other Derivatives*. Pearson Prentice Hall, 7 edition, 2009.

[23] Héylette Geman. *Commodities and Commodity Derivatives - Modeling and Pricing for Agriculturals, Metals and Energy*, volume 20. Wiley, 2005.

[24] Hélyette Geman. *Risk Management in Commodity Markets: From Shipping to Agriculturals and Energy*. Wiley, 2012.

[25] Robert A. Jarrow and George S. Oldfield. Forward contracts and futures contracts. *Journal of Financial Economics*, 9(4):373–382, 1981.

[26] John C. Cox, Stephen a. Ross, and Mark Rubinstein. Option Pricing: A Simplified Approach. *Journal of Financial Economics*, 7(3):229–263, sep 1979.

[27] Paul Wilmott, S Howison, and J Dewynne. The Mathematics of Financial Derivatives., 1996.

[28] Oldrich Alfons Vasicek. An equilibrium characterization of the term structure. *Journal of Financial Economics*, 5:177–188, 1977.

[29] John C. Cox, Jr. Jonathan E. Ingersoll, and Stephen A. Ross. A Theory of the Term Structure of Interest Rates. *Econometrical*, 53(2):385–407, 1985.

[30] John Hull. Pricing Interest-Rate- Derivative Securities. *The Review of Financial Studies*, 3(4):573–592, 1990.

[31] Darrell Duffie and Rui Kan. A Yield-Factor Model of Interest Rates. *Mathematical Finance*, 6(4):379–406, 1996.

[32] Irving Fisher. Appreciation and Interest. *American Economic Association*, XI(4):331–442, 1896.

[33] F. A. Lutz. The structure of interest rates. *Quarterly Journal of Economics*, pages 36–63, 1940.

[34] J. M. Culbertson. The Term Structure of Interest Rates. *The Quarterly Journal of Economics*, 71(4):485–517, 1957.

[35] Burton G. Malkiel. Expectations, Bond Prices, and the Term Structure of Interest Rates. *The Quarterly Journal of Economics1*, 76(2):197–218, 1962.

[36] Samih Antoine Azar. The Pure Expectations Theory and Quarterly Interest Rate Premiums. *Accounting and Finance Research*, 7(1):161–178, 2018.

[37] P. Wilmott. *Derivatives. The Theory and Practice of Financial Engineering*. Wiley, 1998.

[38] Fischer Black. The pricing of commodity contracts. *Journal of Financial Economics*, 3(1-2):167–179, 1976.

[39] S K Mitra. Pricing of Index Options Using Black's Model. *Global Journal of Mangement and Business Research*, 12(3), 2012.

[40] Kenneth J Arrow and Gerard Debreu. Existence of an Equilibrium for a Competitive Economy. *Econometrica*, 22(3):265–290, 1954.

[41] Marek Rutkowski. Complete Markets. In *Encyclopedia of Quantitative Finance*, pages 1–7. Wiley, 2010.

[42] Mark H.A. Davis. Black-Scholes Formula. In *Encyclopedia of Quantitative Finance*, volume 127, pages 1–9. jun 2010.

[43] Aidan Lyon. Why are Normal Distributions Normal ? *Brit. J. Phil. Sci.*, 65:621–649, 2014.

[44] Rama Cont. Model Uncertainty and its Impact on Derivative Pricing. *Mathematical Finance*, 16(3):519–547, 2006.

[45] Elie Ayache. What is Implied by Implied Volatility ? *Wilmott*, (December):28–35, 2005.

[46] Menachem Brenner and Marti G. Subrahmanyam. A Simple Formula to Compute the Implied Standard Deviation. *Financial Analysts Journal*, September-:80–83, 1988.

[47] Peter Jaeckel. By Implication. Technical report, 2010.

[48] Jim Gatheral. *The volatility surface: a practitioner's guide*. Wiley, 2006.

[49] Uwe Wystup. Arbitrage in the Perfect Volatility Surface. *Wilmott*, (September):16–17, 2016.

[50] Roger W Lee. Implied Volatility : Statics , Dynamics , and Probabilistic Interpretation. *Recent Advances in Applied Probability*, pages 1–27, 2004.

[51] Espen Gaarder Haug. Know Your Weapon, Part 1. *Wilmott*, (May):49–57, 2003.

[52] Espen Gaarder Haug. Know your weapon Part 2. *Wilmott*, 2003(3):49–59, may 2003.

[53] Espen Gaarder Haug. *The complete guide to Option Pricing Formulas*. McGraw-Hill, 2008.

[54] Paul Wilmott. Where quants go wrong: a dozen basic lessons in commonsense for quants and risk managers and the traders who rely on them. *Wilmott Journal*, 1(1):1–22, 2009.

[55] Marco Avellaneda, Arnon Levy, and Antonio Paras. Pricing and hedging derivative securities in markets with uncertain volatilities. *Applied Mathematical Finance*, 2:73–88, 1995.

[56] N Taleb. *Dynamic hedging: Managing Vanilla and Exotic Options*. Wiley, 1997.

[57] P. Carr and D. Madan. Towards a Theory of Volatility Trading. In Robert Jarrow, editor, *Volatility: New Estimation Techniques for Pricing Derivatives*. Risk Books, 1998.

[58] Anirban Chakraborti, Ioane Muni Toke, Marco Patriarca, and Frédéric Abergel. Econophysics review: I. Empirical facts. *Quantitative Finance*, 11(7):991–1012, jul 2011.

[59] Jorge Sobehart. Market reaction to price changes and fat-tailed returns. *Risk*, (June):78–83, 2012.

[60] Bence Toth, Zoltan Eisler, and Jean-Philippe Bouchaud. The square-root impact law also holds for option markets. *Wilmott*, (85):70–73, 2016.

[61] Dorje C Brody and Bernhard K Meister. Term Structure of Vanilla Options. *International Journal of Theoretical and Applied Finance*, 10(8):1323–1337, 2007.

[62] Dennis Yang and Qiang Zhang. Drift-Independent Volatility Estimation Based on High , Low , Open , and Close Prices. *Journal of Business*, 73(3):477–491, 2000.

[63] James D. Macbeth and Larry J. Merville. An Empirical Examination of the Black-Scholes Call Option Pricing Model. *The Journal of Finance*, 34(5):1173, dec 1979.

[64] Mark Rubinstein. Implied binomial trees. *Journal of finance*, 49(3):771–818, 1994.

[65] Gregory Brown and Curt Randall. If the skew fits. *Risk magazine*, (April):62–65, 1999.

[66] Scott Mixon. What Does Implied Volatility Skew Measure? *Journal of Derivatives*, 18(4):9–25, 2011.

[67] C. J. Corrado and Tie Su. Implied volatility skews and stock return skewness and kurtosis implied by stock option prices. *The European Journal of Finance*, 3(1):73–85, mar 1997.

[68] Robert Geske. The valuation of compound options. *Journal of Financial Economics*, 7:63–81, 1979.

[69] Vincent Vargas, Tung-Lam Dao, and Jean-Philippe Bouchaud. Skew and implied leverage effect: Smile dynamics revisited. *International Journal of Theoretical and Applied Finance*, 18(4):1–12, 2013.

[70] Stefano Ciliberti, Jean-philippe Bouchaud, and Marc Potters. Smile Dynamics: A Theory of the Implied Leverage Effect. *Wilmott Journal*, 1(2):87–94, 2009.

[71] David Buckle. Portfolio skew and kurtosis. *Risk magazine*, (June):89–90, 2005.

[72] Marco Avellaneda and M.D. Lipkin. A market-induced mechanism for stock pinning. *Quantitative Finance*, 3(6):417–425, dec 2003.

[73] Chris Flood. Call to crack down on multibillion-euro tax tricks as scandal bites. *Financial Times*, (December):1–5, dec 2018.

[74] Louie Woodall. Dealers fear death of dividend risk premia strategy. *Risk Magazine*, page 5, 2016.

[75] Scott Mixon and Esesen Onur. Dividend swaps and dividend futures: State of play. *Journal of Alternative Investments*, 19(3):27–39, 2017.

[76] Harley Bassman. Why do futures markets imply a Depression-level collapse in European dividends ? *Financial Times*, (January):1–11, 2018.

[77] Sascha Wilkens and Jens Wimschulte. The pricing of dividend futures in the European market: A first empirical analysis. *Journal of Derivatives & Hedge Funds*, 16(2):136–143, aug 2010.

[78] Volf Frishling. A discrete question. *Risk magazine*, 2(January), 2002.

[79] Pedro Ferreira and Alain Ouzou. Diving Dividends. *Wilmott*, September(55):16–26, 2011.

[80] Pierre Étoré and Emmanuell Gobet. Stochastic expansion for the pricing of call options with discrete dividends. *Applied Mathematical Finance*, 19(3):233–264, 2012.

[81] Timothy R Klassen. Pricing Vanilla Options with Cash Dividends. *http://ssrn.com/abstract=2634051*, pages 1–28, 2015.

[82] Michael Bos and Stephen Vandermark. Finessing fixed dividends. *Risk magazine*, 7(September):157–158, 2002.

[83] Remco Bos, Alexander Gairat, and Anna Shepeleva. Dealing with discrete dividends. *Risk*, (January):109–112, 2003.

[84] M. H. Vellekoop and J. W. Nieuwenhuis. Efficient Pricing of Derivatives on Assets with Discrete Dividends. *Applied Mathematical Finance*, 13(3):265–284, sep 2006.

[85] Fouad Sahel and Arnaud Gocsei. Matching Sensitivities to Discrete Dividends: A New Approach for Pricing Vanillas. *Wilmott*, 2011(55):80–85, sep 2011.

[86] Stéphane Mysona and Paul Zimmermann. Adjusting Volatility to Discrete Cash Dividends. *Wilmott*, (May):50–55, 2012.

[87] Paul Zimmermann. The Fallacy of Fully Dividend-Protected Stock Options and Convertible Bonds. *The Journal of Derivatives*, (March), 2016.

[88] Kathryn Barraclough, Hans R Stoll, and Robert E Whaley. Stock option contract adjustments : The case of special dividends. *Journal of Financial Markets*, 15(2):1–25, 2011.

[89] Eduardo S. Schwartz. The Valuation of Warrants: Implementing a New Approach. *Journal of Financial Economics*, 4:79–94, 1977.

[90] Nicholas Metropolis and S. Ulam. The Monte Carlo Method. *Journal of the American Statistical Association*, 44(247):335–341, 1949.

[91] Peter Jaeckel and Eckhard Platen. Monte Carlo Simulation. In *Encyclopedia of Quantitative Finance*, pages 1–6. Wiley, 2008.

[92] Raimonda Martinkutė-Kaulienė. Exotic Options: A chooser options and its pricing. *Business, ManageMent and education*, 10(2):289–301, 2012.

[93] David Backus, Silverio Foresi, and Liuren Wu. Accounting for Biases in Black-Scholes. 2004.

[94] Bruno Dupire. Pricing with a smile. *Risk*, 7(1):18–20, 1994.

[95] C. Luo and X. Liu. Local Volatility Model. In *Encyclopedia of Quantitative Finance*, number May. Wiley, wiley edition, 2010.

[96] Emanuel Derman and Michael Kamal. Trading and Hedging Local Volatility. Technical Report August, 1996.

[97] Bruno Dupire. Dupire Equation. In *Encyclopedia of Quantitative Finance*, pages 1–3. Wiley, 2010.

[98] Emanuel Derman, Michael B. Miller, and David Park. *The Volatility Smile*. Wiley Finance, 2016.

[99] H Berestycki, J Busca, and I Florent. Asymptotics and calibration of local volatility models. *Quantitative Finance*, 2(1):61–69, feb 2002.

[100] Rama Cont and José da Fonseca. Dynamics of implied volatility surfaces. *Quantitative Finance*, 2(1):45–60, feb 2002.

[101] Claudio Albanese. Unifying volatility models. *Risk magazine*, (March):94–98, 2004.

[102] Stéphane Crépey. Delta-hedging Vega Risk? *Quantitative Finance*, 4(5):559–579, 2004.

[103] P Jäckel. Quanto skew. (July 2009):1–9, 2009.

[104] J. Marabel Romo. The Quanto Adjustment and the Smile. *Journal of Futures Markets*, 0(0):1–32, 2011.

[105] Ghislain Vong and Mateo Rojas-Carulla. Quanto Derivatives in Local Volatility Models. In *Global Derivatives Conference, Amsterdam*, 2014.

[106] George Hong. Skewing quanto with simplicity. *Risk magazine*, May:1–6, 2019.

[107] J.P. Fouque. Stochastic Volatility Models. In *Encyclopedia of Quantitative Finance*, number 2, pages 1–4. Wiley, 2010.

[108] Steven L Heston. A Closed-Form Solution for Options with Stochastic Volatility with Applications to Bond and Currency Options. *The Review of Financial Studies*, 6(2):327–343, 1993.

[109] Hans Buehler. Heston Model. In *Encyclopedia of Quantitative Finance*, pages 1–9. 2010.

[110] G. E. Uhlenbeck and L. S. Ornstein. On the theory of Brownian Motion. *Phys. Rev.*, 36(5):823–841, 1930.

[111] Wim Schoutens, Erwin Simons, and Jurgen Tistaert. A perfect calibration! Now what? *Wilmott*, 2(March):66–78, mar 2004.

[112] Florence Guillaume and Wim Schoutens. Calibration risk: Illustrating the impact of calibration risk under the Heston model. *Review of Derivatives Research*, 15(1):57–79, jul 2011.

[113] Jim Gatheral. *The volatility surface: a practitioner's guide*, volume 357. Wiley, 2006.

[114] K Said. Pricing exotics under the smile. *Risk*, (November):72–75, 1999.

[115] Carol Alexander and Leonardo M Nogueira. Stochastic local volatility. *Proceedings of the Second IASTED International Conference*, pages 136–141, 2001.

[116] P Henry-Labordere. Calibration of local stochastic volatility models to market smiles: A Monte-Carlo approach. *Risk Magazine, September*, (September):1–16, 2009.

[117] Lorenzo Bergomi. Local-stochastic volatility: models and non-models. *Risk magazine*, August:78–83, 2017.

[118] Dominique Bang. Local stochastic volatility : shaken, not stirred. *Risk magazine*, (December):1–6, 2018.

[119] Yuri F Saporito, Xu Yang, and Jorge P Zubelli. The Calibration of Stochastic-Local Volatility Models - An Inverse Problem Perspective. *arXiv:1711.03023*, pages 1–17, 2017.

[120] Emanuel Derman and Iraj Kani. The Ins and Outs of Barrier Options - Part 1. *Derivatives Quarterly*, pages 55–67, 1996.

[121] Emanuel Derman and Iraj Kani. The Ins and Outs of Barrier Options - Part 2. *Derivatives Quarterly*, pages 73–80, 1997.

[122] Michael Qian. Barrier Options. In *Encyclopedia of Quantitative Finance*. Wiley, 2010.

[123] Jan H. Maruhn, Morten Nalholm, and Matthias R. Fengler. Static hedges for reverse barrier options with robustness against skew risk: an empirical analysis. *Quantitative Finance*, 11(5):711–727, may 2011.

[124] Mark Broadie, Paul Glasserman, and Kou Steven. A continuity correction for discrete barrier options. *Mathematical Finance*, 7(4):325–349, 1997.

[125] Uwe Wystup. Can Vega of a Double- No-Touch Be Positive? *Wilmott*, (March):22–23, 2018.

[126] Paul Wilmott. Cliquet options and volatility models. *Wilmott*, 2002(1):78–82, dec 2002.

[127] Christopher Jeffery. Reverse cliquets: end of the road? *Risk*, October, 2004.

[128] Navroz Patel. The evolving art of pricing cliquets. *Risk magazine*, (July):22–24, 2002.

[129] Marcus Overhaus, Ana Bermudez, Hans Buehler, Andrew Ferraris, Christopher Jordinson, and Aziz Lamnouar. *Equity Hybrid Derivatives*. Wiley, 2007.

[130] Lorenzo Bergomi. Smile dynamics: a theory of the implied leverage effect. *Risk magazine*, (September):117–123, apr 2004.

[131] Lorenzo Bergomi. Smile dynamics II. *Risk magazine*, (OCTOBER):67–73, 2005.

[132] Mark Rubinstein and Eric Reiner. Unscrambling the binary code. *Risk magazine*, 5(1):75–84, 1991.

[133] Pierre Henry-Labordère and Hamza Guennoun. Equity modelling with local stochastic volatility and stochastic discrete dividends. *Risk Magazine*, August:1–6, 2018.

[134] Riaz Ahmad and Paul Wilmott. Which Free Lunch Would You Like Today, Sir ?: Delta Hedging, Volatility Arbitrage and Optimal Portfolios. *Wilmott Magazine*, November:64–79, 2005.

[135] Peter Carr and Roger Lee. Volatility Derivatives. *Annual Review of Financial Economics*, 1(1):319–339, dec 2009.

[136] Carol Alexander, Dimitris Korovilas, and Julia Kapraun. Diversification with volatility products. *Journal of International Money and Finance*, 65:213–235, 2016.

[137] Anthony Neuberger. The log contract. *The Journal of Portfolio Management*, 20(2):74–80, 1994.

[138] Adrien Papaioannou. Variance Swaps And Their Varieties. *Derivatives Week*, XVIII(31), 2009.

[139] Eric Liverance. Variance Swap. In *Encyclopedia of Quantitative Finance*, number 5, pages 1–3. Wiley, 2010.

[140] Wim Schoutens. Moment Swaps. *Quantitative Finance*, 5(6):525–530, 2005.

[141] Douglas T. Breeden and Robert H. Litzenberger. Prices of State-Contingent Claims Implicit in Option Prices. *The Journal of Business*, 51(4):621, 1978.

[142] Benoit Coulombe, Alexander Marini, and Ararat Yesayan. An Analytic Formula for the Delta of Variance Swap. *Wilmott Journal*, 1(3):133–135, 2009.

[143] Amine Ahallal and Olaf Torne. Knocking out corridor variance. *Risk magazine*, (November):2–5, 2018.

[144] Oliver Brockhaus and Douglas Long. Volatility swaps made simple. *Risk magazine*, January:92–95, 2000.

[145] Yong Ren. Volatility Swaps. In *Encyclopedia of Quantitative Finance*, page 1. Wiley, 2010.

[146] Peter Carr and Roger Lee. Realised volatility and variance: options via swaps. *Risk magazine*, (May):76–83, 2007.

[147] Mark Broadie and Ashish Jain. Pricing and Hedging Volatility Derivatives. *The Journal of Derivatives*, 15(3):7–24, 2008.

[148] Peter Carr and Roger Lee. Robust replication of volatility derivatives. *SSRN Electronic Journal*, pages 1–43, 2009.

[149] Frido Rolloos and Melih Arslan. Taylor-Made Volatility Swaps. *Wilmott*, 2017(87):56–61, 2017.

[150] Hans Buehler. Consistent Variance Curve Models. *Finance and Stochastics*, 10(2):178–203, apr 2006.

[151] D. Heath, Robert Jarrow, and Andrew Morton. Bond pricing and the term structure of interest rates: A new methodology for contingent claims valuation. *Econometrica*, 60(1):77–105, 1992.

[152] Anthony Neuberger. The Log Contract and Other Power Contracts. In *The Handbook of Exotic Options*, pages 200–212. McGraw-Hill, 1996.

[153] Peter G Zhang. *Exotic Options*. World Scientific, 1998.

[154] Robert G. Tompkins. Power options: hedging nonlinear risks. *Risk*, 2(2):29–45, 1999.

[155] P. Carr and D. Madan. Optimal positioning in derivative securities. *Quantitative Finance*, 1(1):19–37, 2001.

[156] Karl Pearson. Note on Regression and Inheritance in the Case of Two Parents. *Royal Society*, 58(347-352):240–242, 1895.

[157] C Spearman. The proof and measurement of association between two things. *The American Journal of Psychology*, 15:72–101, 1904.

[158] M. G. Kendall. A New Measure of Rank Correlation. *Biometrika*, 30(1-2):81–93, 1938.

[159] Joël Bun Jean-Philippe Bouchaud and Marc Potters. Cleaning correlation matrices. *Risk magazine*, (April), 2015.

[160] Lorenzo Bergomi. Correlations in asynchronous markets. *Risk magazine*, (November):76–82, 2010.

[161] Takaki Hayashi and Nakahiro Yoshida. On covariance estimation of non-synchronously observed diffusion processes. *Bernoulli*, 11(2):359–379, 2005.

[162] Riccardo Rebonato. *Volatility and Correlation: The Perfect Hedger and the Fox*. Wiley, 2004.

[163] William H. Press, Saul A. Teukolsky, William T. Vetterling, and Brian P. Flannery. *Numerical Recipes: The Art of Scientific Computing*. Cambridge University Press, 1988.

[164] Paul Wilmott. *The Best of Wilmott. Volume 2*. Wiley, 2006.

[165] Matthias R Fengler, Kay F Pilz, and Peter Schwendner. Basket Volatility and Correlation. In *Volatility as an Asset Class*, pages 95–131. Risk Books, 2007.

[166] Mike K.P. So, Jerry Wong, and Manabu Asai. Stress testing correlation matrices for risk management. *North American Journal of Economics and Finance*, 26:310–322, 2013.

[167] Alex Langnau. A dynamic model for correlation. *Risk magazine*, (April):74–78, 2010.

[168] Adil Reghai. Breaking correlation breaks. *Risk magazine*, (October):90–95, 2010.

[169] Julien Guyon. Local Correlation Families. *Risk Magazine*, (February), 2014.

[170] Julien Guyon. Calibration of local correlation models to basket smiles. *Journal ofComputational Finance*, 21(1):1–51, 2016.

[171] Christian Kamtchueng. Uncertain Correlation Model. *Wilmott Journal*, 2(6):317–349, 2010.

[172] Jacinto Marabel. Pricing Digital Outperformance Options With Uncertain Correlation. *International Journal of Theoretical and Applied Finance*, 14(05):709, 2011.

[173] Antoine Jacquier and Saad Slaoui. Variance Dispersion and Correlation Swaps. *papers.ssrn.com*, 2007.

[174] Sebastien Bossu. Correlation Swap. In *Encyclopedia of Quantitative Finance*, pages 1–2. Wiley, 2010.

[175] Peter Carr and Dilip Madan. Introducing the covariance swap. *Risk magazine*, (February):47–50, 1999.

[176] José Da Fonseca, Martino Grasselli, and Florian Ielpo. Hedging (Co)Variance Risk With Variance Swaps. *International Journal of Theoretical and Applied Finance*, 14(06):899, 2011.

[177] Mark Pengelly. Sunk by correlation. *Risk magazine*, (November):1–8, 2009.

[178] Patrick McConnell. Systemic operational risk: the LIBOR manipulation scandal. *The Journal of Operational Risk*, 8(3):59–99, 2013.

[179] Andreas Schrimpf and Vladyslav Sushko. Beyond LIBOR : a primer on the new reference rates. *BIS Quarterly Review*, (March):29–52, 2019.

[180] Robert Mackenzie Smith. Libor transition raises basis risk fear. *Risk magazine*, (June):1–8, 2018.

[181] Nazneen Sherif. Libor switch calls for modelling overhaul , quants warn. *Risk magazine*, (July):1–8, 2018.

[182] International Swaps and Derivatives Association ("ISDA"). Anonymized Narrative Summary of Responses to the ISDA Consultation on Term Fixings and Spread Adjustment Methodologies. Technical report, 2018.

[183] Nazneen Sherif. FRAs won't work with standard Libor fallback, experts say. *Risk magazine*, (March):1–4, 2019.

[184] John C Cox, Jr. Jonathan E. Ingersoll, and Stephen A. Ross. The relation between forward prices and futures prices. *Journal of Financial Economics*, 9:321–346, 1981.

[185] Yolanda S. Stander. *Yield Curve Modeling*. Palgrave Macmillan, 2005.

[186] Leif B.G. Andersen and Vladimir Piterbarg. Yield Curve Construction. In *Encyclopedia of Quantitative Finance*, pages 1–8. 2010.

[187] Marc Henrard. The Irony In The Derivatives Discounting. *Wilmott*, (July):92–98, 2007.

[188] Marc Henrard. The Irony in Derivatives Discounting Part II: The Crisis. *Wilmott Journal*, 2(6):301–316, 2010.

[189] Marco Bianchetti. Two curves, one price: Pricing and hedging interest rate derivatives using different yield curves for discounting and forwarding. *Risk magazine*, (August):74–80, 2010.

[190] Marco Bianchetti and Mattia Carlicchi. Interest Rates After The Credit Crunch : Multiple-Curve Vanilla Derivatives and SABR. *arXiv:1103.2567*, (March), 2012.

[191] Pat Hagan. Convexity Conundrums: Pricing CMS Swaps, Caps and Floors. *Wilmott2*, (March):38–45, 2003.

[192] Fabio Mercurio and Andrea Pallavicini. Smiling at convexity. *Risk magazine*, (August):64–69, 2006.

[193] Guillaume Aubert. Arbitrage-free CMS Valuation — Watch out for the correlations. *Wilmott Magazine*, December:81–87, 2010.

[194] Simon Cedervall and Vladimir Piterbarg. CMS: covering all bases. *Risk magazine*, (March):64–69, 2012.

[195] Stephane Crepey and Raphael Douady. Lois: credit and liquidity. *Risk magazine*, (June):78–82, 2013.

[196] Vladimir Piterbarg. Funding beyond discounting: collateral agreements and derivatives pricing. *Risk magazine*, 2(1):97–102, 2010.

[197] European Central Bank. ESRB risk dashboard. Technical Report June, 2019.

[198] Oren Cheyette. Markov Representation of the Heath-Jarrow-Morton Model. *UCLA Workshop on the Future of Fixed Income Financial Theory*, 1996.

[199] Messaoud Chibane and Dikman Law. A quadratic volatility Cheyette model. *Risk magazine*, (July):68–71, 2013.

[200] Alan Brace, Dariusz Gatarek, and Marek Musiela. The market model of interest rate dynamics. *Mathematical Finance*, 7(2):127–147, 1997.

[201] Farshid Jamshidian. LIBOR and swap market models and measures. *Finance and Stochastics*, 330(January 1996):293–330, 1997.

[202] Dariusz Gatarek, Juliusz Jabłecki, and Dong Qu. Non-parametric local volatility formula for interest rate swaptions. *Risk magazine*, (March):106–110, 2016.

[203] Lingling Cao and Pierre Henry-Labordère. Interest rate models enhanced with local volatility. *Risk magazine*, (March):106–110, 2016.

[204] Dariusz Gatarek and Juliusz Jabłecki. A nonparametric local volatility model for swaptions smile. *Journal ofComputational Finance*, 21(5):35–62, 2018.

[205] Marc Henrard. Swaptions: 1 Price, 10 Deltas, and … 6.5 Gammas. *Wilmott*, (November):48–57, 2005.

[206] Simon Johnson and Bereshad Nonas. Arbitrage-free Construction of the Swaption Cube. *Wilmott Journal*, 1(3):137–143, 2009.

[207] Pat Hagan and Michael Konikov. Interest Rate Volatility Cube: Construction And Use. 2004.

[208] Thomas Roos. Bounding Bermudans. *Risk magazine*, (June):1–6, 2017.

[209] Hamza Hoummady and Matthias Lutz. Cash no longer king in European swaptions. *Risk magazine*, (March):1–8, 2018.

[210] Fabio Mercurio. Cash-settled swaptions and no-arbitrage. *Risk magazine*, (February):96–98, 2008.

[211] Marc Henrard. Cash-settled swaptions:How wrong are we? 2011.

[212] Matthias   Lutz.   Two   Collars   and   a   Free   Lunch. *https://papers.ssrn.com/sol3/papers.cfm?abstract_id=2686622*, pages 1–9, 2015.

[213] Damiano Brigo and Fabio Mercurio. *Interest Rate Models - Theory and Practice*. Springer, 2006.

[214] Patrick S Hagan, Deep Kumar, Andrew S Lesniewski, and Diana E Woodward. Managing Smile Risk. *Wilmott*, pages 84–108, 2002.

[215] Henri Berestycki. Computing the Implied Volatility in Stochastic Volatility Models. *Communications on Pure and Applied Mathematics*, 57(10):1352–1373, 2004.

[216] Jan Obloj. Fine-tune your smile: Correction to Hagan et al. *Wilmott*, (May):1–4, 2008.

[217] Philippe Balland and Quan Tran. SABR goes normal. *Risk magazine*, (June):76–81, 2013.

[218] Álvaro Leitao, Lech A Grzelak, and Cornelis W Oosterlee. On an efficient multiple time step Monte Carlo simulation of the SABR model. *Quantitative Finance*, 17(10):1549–1565, 2017.

[219] Vladimir Piterbarg. Time to smile. *Risk magazine*, (May):71–75, 2005.

[220] Bruce Bartlett. Hedging under SABR Model. *Wilmott*, (February), 2006.

[221] F. A. Longstaff and Eduardo S. Schwartz. The Relative Valuation of Caps and Swaptions : Theory and Empirical Evidence. *Journal of Finance*, 56(6):2067–2109, 2001.

[222] Riccardo Rebonato and Andrey Pogudin. Is It Possible to Reconcile the Caplet and Swaption Markets? Evidence from the U.S.-Dollar Market. *The Journal of Derivatives*, 19(2):8–31, 2011.

[223] Nick Sawyer. A difference of opinion. *Risk magazine*, (October):1–8, 2005.

[224] Mourad Berrahoui. Pricing CMS Spread Options and Digital CMS Spread Options with Smile. *Wilmott*, (3):63–69, 2004.

[225] Paul Mccloud. The CMS triangle arbitrage. *Risk magazine*, (January):126–131, 2011.

[226] Leonard Tchuindjo. On Valuing Constant Maturity Swap Spread Derivatives. *Journal of Mathematical Finance*, 2(May):189–194, 2012.

[227] Jörg Kienitz. *Interest Rate Derivatives Explained: Volume 1: Products and Markets*. Palgrave Macmillan, 2014.

[228] Pierre Hanton and Marc Henrard. CMS spread options and simipar options in multi-factor HJM framework. *SSRN-id1604389*, (May):1–16, 2010.

[229] Ting-Pin Wu and Son-nan Chen. Valuation of CMS Spread Options with Nonzero Strike Rates in the LIBOR Market Model. *The Journal of Derivatives*, 19(1):41–55, 2011.

[230] Interest Rate Exotics. The gamma trap. *Risk magazine*, December:1–8, 2006.

[231] Peter Madigan. The rates escape. *Risk magazine*, August:1–8, 2008.

[232] Kris Devasabai. Remembering the range accrual bloodbath. *Risk magazine*, April:3–5, 2019.

[233] Vladimir V Piterbarg. Pricing and hedging callable Libor exotics in forward Libor models. *Journal of Computational Finance*, 8(2):65–117, 2004.

[234] Louis Bachelier. Théorie de la spéculation. *Annales scientifiques de l'É.N.S.*, 17(3):21–86, 1900.

[235] Dimitri Reiswich and Uwe Wystup. A Guide to FX Options Quoting Conventions. *Journal of Derivatives*, 18(2):58–69, 2010.

[236] Wystup Uwe Wystup. FX Greeks. *Wilmott*, January:16–19, 2019.

[237] Iain J. Clark. *Foreign Exchange Option Pricing: A Practitioner's Guide*. Wiley, 2011.

[238] Alexander Lipton and William McGhee. Universal barriers. *Risk magazine*, (May):81–85, 2002.

[239] Antonio Castagna and F. Mercurio. The vanna-volga method for implied volatilities. *Risk magazine*, 20(1):106, 2007.

[240] Uwe Wystup. How the Greeks would have hedged correlation risk of Foreign Exchange Options. In *Foreign Exchange Risk*, pages 143–146. Risk, 2002.

[241] Alvise De Col, Alessandro Gnoatto, and Martino Grasselli. Smiles all around : FX joint calibration in a multi-Heston model. *Journal of Banking and Finance*, 37(1973):3799–3818, 2013.

[242] Patrick Kuppinger and Alvise De Col. Pricing Multi-Dimensional FX Derivatives via Stochastic Local Correlations. *Wilmott*, September:72–77, 2014.

[243] Annika Alexius. Uncovered Interest Parity Revisited. *Review of International Economics*, 9(3):505–517, 2001.

[244] Michael Melvin and Duncan Shand. When carry goes bad: The magnitude, causes, and duration of currency carry unwinds. *Financial Analysts Journal*, 73(1):121–144, 2017.

[245] Jason Sippel and Shoichi Ohkoshi. All power to PRDC notes. *2Risk magazine*, (November), 2002.

[246] Vladimir Piterbarg. Smiling hybrids. *Risk magazine*, (May):66–71, 2006.

[247] Anthonie W Van Der Stoep, Lech A Grzelak, and Cornelis W Oosterlee. The Time-Dependent FX-SABR Model : Efficient Calibration based on Effective Parameters. *International Journal of Theoretical and Applied Finance*, 18(6), 2015.

[248] Richard Yamarone. *The Trader's Guide to Key Economic Indicators*. Bloomberg, 2004.

[249] Héylette Geman and Andrea Roncoroni. Understanding the Fine Structure of Electricity Prices. *The Journal of Business*, 79(3):1225–1261, 2006.

[250] Delphine Lautier. Convenience Yield and Commodity Markets. *Bankers, Markets & Investors*, 102:59–66, 2009.

[251] Svetlana Borovkova. Commodity Forward Curve Modeling. In *Encyclopedia of Quantitative Finance*, pages 1–7. Wiley, 2010.

[252] Svetlana Borovkova and Helyette Geman. Seasonal and stochastic effects in commodity forward curves. *Review of Derivatives Research*, 9(2):167–186, 2006.

[253] Christoph Jablonowski and Markus Schicks. A three-factor model on the natural gas forward curve including temperature forecasts. *The Journal of Energy Markets*, 10(3):87–105, 2017.

[254] Fred Espen Benth and Maren Diane Schmeck. Pricing and hedging options in energy markets using Black-76. *The Journal of Energy Markets*, 7(2):35–69, 2016.

[255] RAJNA GIBSON and Eduardo S Schwartz. Stochastic convenience yield and the pricing of oil conting.pdf. *The Journal of Finance*, XLV(3):959–976, 1990.

[256] Jacques Gabillon. The term structures of oil futures prices. *Oxford Institute for Energy Studies*, 1991.

[257] Qimou Su and Curt Randall. Putting Smiles Back to the Futures. *Wilmott*, 2012(61):38–47, 2012.

[258] Vinicius Albani, Uri M Ascher, and Jorge P Zubelli. Local volatility models in commodity markets and online calibration. *Journal of Computational Finance*, 21(5):63–95, 2018.

[259] Héylette Geman and A. Eydeland. Pricing power derivatives. *Risk magazine*, 10:71–73, 1998.

[260] Emanuele Nastasi, Andrea Pallavicini, and Giulio Sartorelli. Smile Modelling in Commodity Markets. *arXiv:1808.09685*, pages 1–26, 2018.

[261] Rene Carmona and Valdo Durrleman. Pricing and Hedging Spread Options. *SIAM REVIEW*, 45(4):627–685, 2003.

[262] W. Margrabe. The value of an option to exchange one asset for another. *The Journal of Finance*, 33(1):177–186, 1978.

[263] Aanand Venkatramanan and Carol Alexander. Closed Form Approximations for Spread Options. *Applied Mathematical Finance*, 18(5):1–26, 2011.

[264] C F Lo. A simple derivation of Kirk's approximation for spread options. *Applied Mathematics Letters*, 26:904–907, 2013.

[265] Ruggero Caldana and Gianluca Fusai. A general closed-form spread option pricing formula. *Journal of Banking & Finance*, 37:4893–4906, 2013.

[266] Carol Alexander and Andrew Scourse. Bivariate normal mixture spread option valuation. *Quantitative Finance*, 4(December):1–12, 2004.

[267] Rene Carmona and Valdo Durrleman. Pricing and hedging spread options in a log-normal model. Technical report, 2003.

[268] Nikunj Kapadia. Negative Vega? Understanding Options on Spreads. *The Journal of Alternative Investments*, (Spring):75–78, 1999.

[269] F. a. Longstaff. Valuing American options by simulation: a simple least-squares approach. *Review of Financial Studies*, 14(1):113–147, mar 2001.

[270] Rudiger Kiesel, Jochen Gernhard, and Sven-olaf Stoll. Valuation of commodity-based swing options. *The Journal of Energy Markets*, 3(3):91–112, 2010.

[271] Karl Larsson. Pricing Commodity Swaptions in Multifactor Models. *The Journal of Derivatives*, 19(2):32–44, 2011.

[272] Andreas Bluemke. *How to Invest in Structured Products: A Guide for Investors and Asset Managers*. Wiley, 2009.

[273] Thorsten Hens and Marc Oliver Rieger. Why do Investors Buy Structured Products ? In *EFA 2009 Bergen Meetings Paper*, pages 1–31, 2011.

[274] Marc Oliver Rieger and Thorsten Hens. Can utility optimization explain the demand for structured investment products ? *Quantitative Finance*, 14:673–681, 2014.

[275] By Laura Santini. Accumulators Are Collecting Fans Again. *The Wall Street Journal*, (August):7–9, 2009.

[276] Kin Lam, Philip L H Yu, and Ling Xin. Pricing an Accumulator with Continuous or Discrete Barrier. *Journal of Derivatives*, 24(4):93–107, 2017.

[277] Chris Davis. Trade war threatens Korea autocall losses. *Risk Magazine*, pages 1–6, 2018.

[278] Risk magazine. Deal of the year: Knock-out corridor variance swaps. *Risk magazine*, (August):1–15, 2016.

[279] Narayanan Somasundaram. Nervy Korean autocall investors lean on lizards. *Risk Magazine*, (April):5–8, 2018.

[280] Viren Vaghela. Korean crunch : How HSCEI fall hammered exotics desks. *Risk Magazine*, (November):1–10, 2015.

[281] Alvise De Col and Patrick Kuppinger. The interplay between stochastic volatility and correlations in equity autocallables. *Risk magazine*, February:1–6, 2019.

[282] Inc. Securities Litigation and Consulting Group. Structured Products In the Aftermath of Lehman Brothers. Technical report, 2009.

[283] George S Hills. Convertible Securities- Legal Aspects and Draftsmanship California Law Review. *Calif. L. Rev.*, 14(1), 1930.

[284] Jan De Spiegeleer, Wim Schoutens, and Cynthia Van Hulle. *The Handbook of Hybrid Securities: Convertible Bonds, CoCo Bonds, and Bail-In*. 2014.

[285] Jeff Brown. As Convertible-Bond Issuance Soars, Investors Should Be Cautious. *The Wall Street Journal*, (July):1–5, 2018.

[286] Stefan Avdjiev, Anastasia Kartasheva, and Bilyana Bogdanova. CoCos: a primer. *BIS Quarterly Review*, (September):43–56, 2013.

[287] Jan De Spiegeleer, Ine Marquet, and Wim Schoutens. *The Risk Management of Contingent Convertible (CoCo) Bonds*. Springer, 2018.

[288] Francesca Erica Di Girolamo, Francesca Campolongo, Jan De Spiegeleer, and Wim Schoutens. Contingent conversion convertible bond : New avenue to raise bank capital. *International Journal of Financial Engineering*, 4(1):1–31, 2017.

[289] Tracy Alloway. An explanatory CoCo death spiral. *FT Alphaville*, (March):2011, 2011.

[290] Stefan Avdjiev, Bilyana Bogdanova, and Patrick Bolton. CoCo issuance and bank fragility. *BIS Working Papers*, (678), 2017.

[291] Robert C. Merton. On the pricing of corporate debt: The risk structure of interest rates. *Journal of Finance*, 29:449–470.

[292] Terry Benzschawel, Julio DaGraca, and Cheng-Yen Lee. Pricing corporate loans under the risk-neutral measure. *The Journal of Credit Risk*, 8(1):29–62, 2016.

[293] I. Hart and M. Ross. Striking continuity. *Risk*, 7(6):46–51, 1994.

[294] Oldrich Alfons Vasicek, Stephen Kealhofer, and John McQuown. Credit Valuation. *KMV Corporation*, 1984.

[295] Boris Kollár and Barbora Gondžárová. Comparison of Current Credit Risk Models. *Procedia Economics and Finance*, 23(October 2014):341–347, 2015.

[296] Enron: Charting the legacy 10 years on. *Energy Risk*, (November), 2011.

[297] Antti Ilmanen. *Expected Returns: An Investor's Guide to Harvesting Market Rewards*. John Wiley & Sons, 2011.

[298] Kenneth Emery, Richard Cantor, David Keisman, and Sharon Ou. Moody's Ultimate Recovery Database Special Comment. Technical Report April, 2007.

[299] Lukas Becker. Traders shocked by $ 712m CVA loss at StanChart. *Risk magazine*, March:1–9, 2016.

[300] Jon Gregory. *Counterparty Credit Risk*. Number 1. John Wiley & Sons Ltd, 2010.

[301] Antulio N. Bomfim. *Understanding Credit Derivatives and Related Instruments*. Elsevier Academic Press, 2005.

[302] Wim Schoutens and K U Leuven. Credit Default Swaps: The Quest of the Hedge. *Wilmott Journal*, 1(5-6):245–253, 2009.

[303] Anne Duquerroy, Mathieu Gex, and Nicolas Gauthier. Credit default swaps and fi nancial stability: risks and regulatory issues. *Banque de France Financial Stability Review*, (13):75–88, 2009.

[304] Arthur M Berd. A Guide to Modeling Credit Term Structures. In *The Oxford Handbook of Credit Derivatives*. Oxford University Press, 2009.

[305] W Heynderickx, J Cariboni, W Schoutens, and B Smits. The relationship between risk-neutral and actual default probabilities: the credit risk premium. *Applied Economics*, 48(42):4066–4081, 2016.

[306] Jeromin Zettelmeyer, Christoph Trebesch, and Mitu Gulati. The Greek Debt Restructuring : An Autopsy. *Economic Policy*, 28(75):513–563, 2013.

[307] Franco Modigliani and Merton H. Miller. The Cost of Capital, Corporation Finance and the Theory of Investment. *The American Economic Review*, 48(3):261–297, 1958.

[308] J.P. Morgan. Bond-CDS Basis Handbook. Technical Report January, 2009.

[309] D.E. Shaw Group. The Basis Monster That Ate Wall Street. Technical Report 1, 2009.

[310] John C Cox and Fischer Black. Valuing Corporate Securities: Some Effects of Bond Indenture Provisions. *The Journal of Finance*, XXXI(2):351–367, 1976.

[311] George Pan. Equity to credit pricing. *Risk magazine*, (November):107–110, 2001.

[312] Tomáš Klieštik and Juraj Cúg. Comparison of Selected Models of Credit Risk. *Procedia Economics and Finance*, 23(November):356–361, 2015.

[313] Christopher C Finger and Robert Stamicar. Incorporating equity derivatives into the Credit-Grades model. *Journal of Credit Risk*, 2(1):35–64, 2006.

[314] Artur Sepp. Extended credit grades model with stochastic volatility and jumps. *Wilmott Magazine*, (2004):58–70, 2006.

[315] Stan Beckers. The Constant Elasticity of Variance Model and Its Implications For Option Pricing. *The Journal of Finance*, 35(3):661–673, 1980.

[316] John C. Cox. The Constant Elasticity of Variance Option Pricing Model. *The Journal of Portfolio Management*, 23(5):15–17, 1996.

[317] Marc Atlan and Boris Leblanc. Hybrid equity-credit modelling. *Risk magazine*, August:61–66, 2005.

[318] Y. L. Hsu, T. I. Lin, and C. F. Lee. Constant elasticity of variance (CEV) option pricing model: Integration and detailed derivation. *Mathematics and Computers in Simulation*, 79(1):60–71, 2008.

[319] Patrick S. Hagan and Diana E. Woodward. Equivalent Black Volatilities. *Applied Mathematical Finance*, 6(3):147–157, 1999.

[320] M. Schroder. Computing the constant elasticity of variance option pricing formula. *Journal of Finance*, 44:211–219, 1989.

[321] Dmitry Davydov and Vadim Linetsky. Pricing and Hedging Path-Dependent Options Under the CEV Process. *Management Science*, 47(7):949–965, 2001.

[322] Elie Ayache. Equity – Credit Problem. In *Encyclopedia of Quantitative Finance*, pages 1–4. Wiley, 2010.

[323] A. De Servigny and N. Jobst. An empirical analysis of equity default swaps (I): univariate insights. *Risk magazine*, 18(12):84, 2005.

[324] Claudio Albanese and Oliver Chen. Pricing equity default swaps. *Risk Magazine*, June:83–87, 2005.

[325] Norbert Jobst and Arnaud de Servigny. An Empirical Analysis of Equity Default Swaps II: Multivariate Insights. *Risk Magazine*, (January):97–103, 2006.

[326] Meredith Williams, Larry Cordell, and Yilin Huang. Collateral Damage: Sizing and Assessing the Subprime CDO Crisis. *Federal Reserve Bank of Philadelphia*, May(11-30):1–40, 2012.

[327] Jon Gregory. Why CDOs work. *Risk*, June:1–4, 2014.

[328] Lorenzo Ravagli. Isolating a risk premium on the volatility of volatility. *Risk magazine*, (December):1–6, 2015.

[329] J.L. Kelly. A New Interpretation of Information Rate. *Bell System Technical Journal*, 35(4):917–926, 1956.

[330] Patrick Augustin, Boris Valee, and Philippe Rich. Exotic Interest Rate Swaps : Snowballs in Portugal. *Harvard Business School Case Study*, 999-999:1–14, 2016.

[331] Mark Kantšukov and Darja Medvedskaja. *From Dishonesty to Disaster: The Reasons and Consequences of Rogue Traders' Fraudulent Behavior*, volume 10. Emerald Group Publishing Limited, 2016.

[332] Michael Jacobs Jr. The impact of asset price bubbles on liquidity risk measures from a financial institutions perspective. *Int. J. Bonds and Derivatives*, 2(2), 2016.

[333] Patrick Mcconnell. Dissecting the JPMorgan whale: a post-mortem. *Journal of Operational Risk*, 9(2):59–100, 2014.

[334] William F Sharpe. Capital Asset Prices : A Theory of Market Equilibrium under Conditions of Risk. *The Journal of Finance*, 19(3):425–442, 1964.

[335] John Lintner. The Valuation of Risk Assets and the Selection of Risky Investments in Stock Portfolios and Capital Budgets. *The Review ofEconomics and Statistics*, 47(1):13–37, 1965.

[336] Leonard MacLean and Bill Ziemba. Primer on Arbitrage and Asset Pricing. *Wilmott*, (March):26–29, 2014.

[337] Claudio Albanese, Simone Caenazzo, and Mark Syrkin. Optimising VAR and terminating Arnie-VAR. *Risk magazine*, (October), 2017.

[338] Didier Sornette, Peter Cauwels, and Georgi Smilyanov. Can We Use Volatility to Diagnose Financial Bubbles? Lessons from 40 Historical Bubbles. *Quantitative Finance and Economics*, 3(July 2017), 2017.

[339] Nassim Nicholas Taleb. *The black swan: The impact of the highly improbable*. Random House, 2007.

[340] Tilmann Gneiting. Making and evaluating point forecasts. *Journal of the American Statistical Association*, 106(494):746–762, 2011.

[341] Carlo Acerbi and Balazs Szekely. Back-testing expected shortfall. *Risk magazine*, December:1–6, 2014.

[342] Robert Löser, Dominik Wied, and Daniel Ziggel. New backtests for unconditional coverage of expected shortfall. *Journal of Risk*, 21(4):39–59, 2018.

[343] Philippe Artzner, Freddy Delbaen, Jean-Marc Eber, and David Heath. Coherent Measures of Risk. *Mathematical Finance*, 9:203–228, 1999.

[344] Bank for International Settlements. Fundamental review of the trading book: A revised market risk framework. Technical Report October 2013, BIS, 2013.

[345] Zari Rachev, Boryana Racheva-Iotova, and Stoyan Stoyanov. Capturing fat tails. *Risk magazine*, (May):76–80, 2010.

[346] Paul Embrechts, Sidney I Resnick, and Gennady Samorodnitsky. Extreme Value Theory as a Risk Management Tool. *North American Actuarial Journal*, 3(2), 1999.

[347] François Longin. *Extreme Events in Finance: A Handbook of Extreme Value Theory and its Applications*. John Wiley & Sons, Inc., 2016.

[348] Max Wong. Bubble VaR, a countercyclical value-at-risk approach. *FinRisk Young Professionals Journal*, 1:35–46, 2014.

[349] Thorsten Riedle. Using Market BuVaR as countercyclical Value at Risk approach to account for the risks of stock market crashes. *Quarterly Review of Economics and Finance*, 69(August):308–321, 2018.

[350] E.A. Cornish and R.A. Fisher. Moments and Cumulants in the specification of distributions. *Review of the International Statistical Institute*, 5(4):307–320, 1938.

[351] Didier Maillard. A User's Guide to the Cornish Fisher Expansion. *Ssrn*, (January):1–19, 2012.

[352] Ali Akansu. The Flash Crash: A Review. *Journal of Capital Markets Studies*, 1(1):89–100, 2017.

[353] Andrei Kirilenko, Albert S. Kyle, Mehrdad Samadi, and Tugkan Tuzun. The Flash Crash: High-Frequency Trading in an Electronic Market. *Journal of Finance*, 72(3):967–998, 2017.

[354] Bank for International Settlements. Markets Committee The sterling 'flash event' of 7 October 2016. Technical Report October 2016, 2017.

[355] Tobias Braun, Jonas A. Fiegen, Daniel C. Wagner, Sebastian M. Krause, and Thomas Guhr. Impact and recovery process of mini flash crashes: An empirical study. *PLoS ONE*, 13(5):1–11, 2018.

[356] Geir-Are Karvik, Joseph Noss, Jack Worlidge, and Daniel Beale. The Deeds of Speed: An Agent-Based Model of Market Liquidity and Flash Episodes. Technical report, 2018.

[357] Rob Mannix. Volatility scaling unravels as market patterns shift. *Risk magazine*, (May), 2019.

[358] Tom Osborn. Fundamental Review of the Trading Book (FRTB) 2017. *Risk magazine*, (April), 2017.

[359] Louie Woodall. FRTB : Basel guidance on backtesting frustrates dealers. *Risk magazine*, (February):1–5, 2017.

[360] Steve Marlin. Banks hope final FRTB rules will ease NMRF burden. *Risk magazine*, (February):1–8, 2019.

[361] Duncan Wood. One-way CSAs pile up funding risk for banks. *Risk magazine*, February:1–7, 2011.

[362] Matt Cameron. Goldman and the OIS gold rush : How fortunes were made from a discounting change. *Risk magazine*, (May):1–9, 2013.

[363] Michael Pykhtin. Counterparty risk capital and CVA. *Risk*, (August):74–79, 2011.

[364] Frederic Vriens and Jon Gregory. Getting CVA up and running. *Risk*, (November):76–79, 2011.

[365] David Kelly. How the Credit Crisis has Changed Counterparty Risk Management. *Risk Professional*, December:27–31, 2011.

[366] Nazneen Sherif. CVA desks suffer Brexit double whammy. *Risk magazine*, June:4–7, 2016.

[367] Louie Woodall. US CVA charges over seven times higher than EU. *Risk magazine*, (June):1–5, 2018.

[368] Philip Alexander. Staying alive: the EU's stubborn CVA exemption corporate hedging. *Risk magazine*, August:1–9, 2018.

[369] Alexander Lipton and Ioana Savescu. CDSs, CVA and DVA - a structural approach. *Risk magazine*, (April):60–65, 2013.

[370] Laurie Carver. DVA : a shameful scam. *Risk*, November:1–3, 2012.

[371] Nazneen Sherif. Traders see DVA adjustment as 'accounting fudge'. *Risk magazine*, October:1–3, 2015.

[372] Louie Woodall. XVA swings boost US bank trading revenues. *Risk magazine*, June:1–6, 2018.

[373] John Hull and Alan White. The FVA debate. *Risk magazine*, (October 2007):10–13, 2012.

[374] Matt Cameron. The black art of FVA : Banks spark double-counting fears. *Risk magazine*, March:1–7, 2013.

[375] Claudio Albanese, Leif Andersen, and In Albanese. FVA accounting, risk management and collateral trading. *Risk magazine*, February:64–69, 2015.

[376] Vladimir V Piterbarg. Landmarks in XVA. In Risk, editor, *Landmarks in XVA*, chapter Funding be, pages 1–22. Risk, 2016.

[377] John Hull and Alan White. XVAs: a gap between theory and practice. *Risk magazine*, (April):1–12, 2016.

[378] Nazneen Sherif. FVA sceptics lose ground in valuation debate. *Risk magazine*, (February):2–4, 2016.

[379] Leif Andersen, Darrell Duffie, and Yang Song. Funding Value Adjustments. *Journal of Finance*, LXXIV(1):145–192, 2019.

[380] Jon Gregory. *The xVA Challenge: Counterparty Credit Risk, Funding, Collateral and Capital.* Number 1. Wiley, 2015.

[381] T. Pang, W. Chen, and L. Li. On the correlation and parametric approaches to calculation of Credit value adjustment. *Journal of Risk Model Validation*, 11(3):49–67, 2017.

[382] Nazneen Sherif. JP Morgan turns to machine learning for options hedging It will be a real paradigm change in approach optimal. *Risk*, (May), 2019.

[383] Hans Buehler, Lukas Gonon, Josef Teichmann, and Ben Wood. Deep hedging. *Quantitative Finance*, 19(8):1271–1291, 2019.

[384] Blake Evans-Pritchard and Chris Davis. Global banks eye China's structured products surge. *Risk magazine*, (September):1–8, 2018.

Index